HOW THE EXPERTS HELP YOU PASS:

- **PROVEN TEACHING METHODOLOGY** Text based on thousands of hours of cl[...] gets people certified. (150,000 professionals can't be wrong!)

- **MORE PRACTICE TESTS** More practice exam questions than any other study guide/CD-ROM. Over 1,000! Includes hyperlinks from questions to answers in electronic book.

- **AUTHORITATIVE INFORMATION** Developed and reviewed by master MCSE and MCT professionals.

- **EXAM WATCH** Warnings based on post-exam research identifying troublesome exam questions.

MCSE Windows NT 4.0 Certification Track Candidates must pass 4 core and 2 elective exams	MCSE + Internet Windows NT 4.0 Certification Track Candidates must pass 7 core and 2 elective exams	
CHOOSE 4 CORE & 2 ELECTIVE	**CHOOSE 7 CORE & 2 ELECTIVE**	**CERTIFICATION PRESS STUDY GUIDES**
CORE	CORE	MCSE Windows NT Server 4.0 Study Guide (Exam 70-67) 0-07-882491-5
CORE	CORE	MCSE Windows NT Server 4.0 in the Enterprise Study Guide (Exam 70-68) 0-07-882490-7
CORE	CORE	MCSE Windows 95 Study Guide (Exam 70-64)
CORE	CORE	MCSE Windows NT Workstation 4.0 Study Guide (Exam 70-73) 0-07-882492-3
CORE	CORE	MCSE Windows 98 Study Guide (Exam 70-98) 0-07-882532-6
CORE	CORE	MCSE Networking Essentials Study Guide (Exam 70-58) 0-07-882493-1
ELECTIVE	CORE	MCSE Microsoft TCP/IP on Windows NT 4.0 Study Guide (Exam 70-59) 0-07-882489-3
ELECTIVE	CORE	MCSE Internet Information Server 4.0 with Proxy Server 2.0 and Internet Explorer Administration Kit 1.1 Study Guide (Exams 70-87, 70-79, 70-88) 0-07-882560-1
ELECTIVE	CORE	MCSE Internet Information Server 4.0 with Proxy Server 2.0 and Internet Explorer Administration Kit 1.1 Study Guide (Exams 70-87, 70-79, 70-88) 0-07-882560-1
ELECTIVE	ELECTIVE	
ELECTIVE		
ELECTIVE	ELECTIVE	
ELECTIVE	ELECTIVE	
ELECTIVE	ELECTIVE	
ELECTIVE	ELECTIVE	MCSE System Administration for SQL Server™ Study Guide (Exam 70-28)
ELECTIVE	ELECTIVE	MCSE Exchange Server 5.5 Study Guide (Exam 70-81) 0-07-882488-5
ELECTIVE	ELECTIVE	MCSE Internet Information Server 4.0 with Proxy Server 2.0 and Internet Explorer Administration Kit 1.1 Study Guide (Exams 70-87, 70-79, 70-88) 0-07-882560-1

MCSE Microsoft TCP/IP on Windows NT 4.0 Study Guide

(Exam 70-59)

Syngress Media, Inc.

Osborne McGraw-Hill

Berkeley New York St. Louis San Francisco Auckland Bogotá Hamburg London Madrid Mexico City
Milan Montreal New Delhi Panama City Paris São Paulo Singapore Sydney Tokyo Toronto

Osborne McGraw-Hill
2600 Tenth Street
Berkeley, California 94710
U.S.A.

For information on translations or book distributors outside the U.S.A.,
or to arrange bulk purchase discounts for sales promotions, premiums, or
fund-raisers, please contact Osborne/**McGraw-Hill** at the above address.

MCSE Microsoft TCP/IP on Windows NT 4.0 Study Guide (Exam 70-59)

1234567890 DOC DOC 901987654321098

ISBN 0-07-882489-3

Publisher	**Copy Editor**	**Illustrators**
Brandon A. Nordin	Eileen Kramer	Lance Ravella
		Brian Wells
Editor-in-Chief	**Indexer**	
Scott Rogers	Liz Cunningham	**Series Design**
		Roberta Steele
Acquisitions Editor	**Proofreader**	Arlette Crosland
Gareth Hancock	Pat Mannion	
		Cover Design
Project Editor	**Computer Designers**	Regan Honda
Cynthia Douglas	Ann Sellers	
	Mickey Galicia	**Editorial Management**
Technical Editor	Roberta Steele	Syngress Media, Inc.
D. Lynn White	Jean Butterfield	

From Global Knowledge Network

At Global Knowledge Network we strive to support the multiplicity of learning styles required by our students to achieve success as technical professionals. In this series of books, it is our intention to offer the reader a valuable tool for successful completion of the MCSE Certification Exam.

As the world's largest IT training company, Global Knowledge Network is uniquely positioned to offer these books. The expertise gained each year from providing instructor-led training to hundreds of thousands of students worldwide has been captured in book form to enhance your learning experience. We hope that the quality of these books demonstrates our commitment to your lifelong learning success. Whether you choose to learn through the written word, computer-based training, Web delivery, or instructor-led training, Global Knowledge Network is committed to providing you the very best in each of those categories. For those of you who know Global Knowledge Network, or those of you who have just found us for the first time, our goal is to be your lifelong competency partner.

Thank you for the opportunity to serve you. We look forward to serving your needs again in the future.

Warmest regards,

Duncan Anderson
Chief Operating Officer, Global Knowledge Network

January 12, 1998

Dear Osborne/McGraw-Hill Customer:

Microsoft is pleased to inform you that Osborne/McGraw-Hill is a participant in the Microsoft® Independent Courseware Vendor (ICV) program. Microsoft ICVs design, develop, and market self-paced courseware, books, and other products that support Microsoft software and the Microsoft Certified Professional (MCP) program.

To be accepted into the Microsoft ICV program, an ICV must meet set criteria. In addition, Microsoft reviews and approves each ICV training product before permission is granted to use the Microsoft Certified Professional Approved Study Guide logo on that product. This logo assures the consumer that the product has passed the following Microsoft standards:

- The course contains accurate product information.
- The course includes labs and activities during which the student can apply knowledge and skills learned from the course.
- The course teaches skills that help prepare the student to take corresponding MCP exams.

Microsoft ICVs continually develop and release new MCP Approved Study Guides. To prepare for a particular Microsoft certification exam, a student may choose one or more single, self-paced training courses or a series of training courses.

You will be pleased with the quality and effectiveness of the MCP Approved Study Guides available from Osborne/McGraw-Hill.

Sincerely,

Becky Kirsininkas

Becky Kirsininkas
ICV Program Manager
Microsoft Training & Certification

The Global Knowledge Network Advantage

Global Knowledge Network has a global delivery system for its products and services. The company has 28 subsidiaries, and offers its programs through a total of 60+ locations. No other vendor can provide consistent services across a geographic area this large. Global Knowledge Network is the largest independent information technology education company, offering programs on a variety of platforms. This enables our multi-platform and multi-national customers to obtain all of their programs from a single vendor. The company has developed the unique Competence Key™ software tool and methodology, which can quickly reconfigure courseware to the proficiency level of a student on an interactive basis. Combined with self-paced and on-line programs, this technology can reduce the time required for training by prescribing content in only the deficient skills areas. The company has fully automated every aspect of the education process, from registration and follow-up, to "just-in-time" production of courseware. Global Knowledge Network, through its Competus consultancy, can customize programs and products to suit the needs of an individual customer.

Global Knowledge Network Classroom Education Programs

The backbone of our delivery options is classroom-based education. Our modern, well-equipped facilities, staffed with the finest instructors, offer programs in a wide variety of information technology topics, many of which lead to professional certifications.

Custom Learning Solutions

This delivery option has been created for companies and governments that value customized learning solutions. For them, our consultancy-based approach of developing targeted education solutions is most effective at helping them meet specific objectives.

Self-Paced and Multimedia Products

This delivery option offers self-paced program titles in interactive CD-ROM, videotape and audio tape programs. In addition, we offer custom development of interactive multimedia courseware to customers and partners. Call us at 1-888-427-4228.

Electronic Delivery of Training

Our network-based training service delivers efficient competency-based, interactive training via the World Wide Web and organizational intranets. This leading-edge delivery option provides a custom learning path and "just-in-time" training for maximum convenience to students.

ARG

American Research Group (ARG), a wholly-owned subsidiary of Global Knowledge Network, one of the largest worldwide training partners of Cisco Systems, offers a wide range of internetworking, LAN/WAN, Bay Networks, FORE Systems, IBM, and UNIX courses. ARG offers hands on network training in both instructor-led classes and self-paced PC-based training.

Global Knowledge Network Courses Available

Networking Foundation

- Understanding Computer Networks
- Emerging Networking Technologies
- Telecommunications Fundamentals
- Computer Telephony Integration
- Understanding Networking Fundamentals
- Essentials of Wide Area Networking
- Implementing T1/T3 Services
- Introduction to LAN/WAN Protocols
- Internetworking with Bridges, Routers and Switches
- Cabling Voice and Data Networks
- Upgrading and Repairing PCs
- Introduction to Web Development Fundamentals
- Building a Web Site
- Web Security
- Building Electronic Storefronts
- Project Management for IT Professionals
- Advanced Project Management
- Communication Skills for IT Professionals

Internetworking

- Emerging Networking Technologies
- Understanding Network Fundamentals
- Essentials of Wide Area Networking
- Frame Relay Internetworking
- Introduction to LAN/WAN Protocols
- Internetworking with Bridges, Routers and Switches
- Migrating to High Performance Ethernet
- Network Troubleshooting
- Multi Layer Switching and Wire-Speed Routing
- Cabling Voice and Data Networks
- Internetworking with TCP/IP
- Troubleshooting TCP/IP Networks
- Network Management
- ATM Essentials
- ATM Internetworking
- Cisco Router Security and Performance Tuning
- OSPF Design and Configuration
- Border Gateway Protocol (BGP) Configuration
- Managing Switched Internetworks

Authorized vendor training

Cisco Systems

- Introduction to Cisco Router Configuration
- Advanced Cisco Router Configuration
- Installation and Maintenance of Cisco Routers
- Cisco Internetwork Troubleshooting
- Cisco Internetwork Design
- Catalyst 5000 Series Configuration
- Cisco LAN Switch Configuration
- Configuring, Monitoring and Troubleshooting Dial-Up Services
- Cisco AS5200 Installation and Configuration
- Cisco Campus ATM Solutions

Bay Networks

- Bay Networks Router Installation and Basic Configuration
- Bay Networks Router Configuration and Management
- Bay Networks Accelerated Router Configuration
- Bay Networks Advanced IP Routing
- Bay Networks Hub Connectivity
- Bay Networks Centillion Switching

FORE Systems

- Introduction to ATM
- ATM Enterprise Core Products
- ATM Enterprise Edge Products

IBM

- Authorized IBM NETeam Education

Operating systems & programming

Microsoft

- Windows NT 4.0 Workstation
- Windows NT 4.0 Server
- Windows NT Networking with TCP/IP
- Windows NT 4.0 Security
- Enterprise Internetworking with Windows NT 4.0
- Essentials of UNIX and NT Integration

UNIX

- UNIX Level I
- UNIX Level II
- Mastering UNIX Security
- Essentials UNIX & NT Integration

Programming

- Practical JavaScript for Web Development
- Java Programming
- PERL Programming
- Advanced PERL with CGI for the Web
- C++ Programming Featuring Microsoft's Visual C++

TCP/IP & network security

- Internetworking with TCP/IP
- Troubleshooting TCP/IP Networks
- Network Management
- Network Security Administration
- Mastering UNIX Security
- Cisco Router Security and Performance Tuning
- Windows NT Networking with TCP/IP
- Windows NT 4.0 Security

High speed networking

- Essentials of Wide Area Networking
- Implementing T1/T3 Services
- Frame Relay Internetworking
- Integrating ISDN
- Fiber Optic Network Design
- Fiber Optic Network Installation
- Migrating to High Performance Ethernet
- ATM Essentials
- ATM Internetworking

DIGITAL UNIX

- UNIX Utilities and Commands
- DIGITAL UNIX v4.0 System Administration
- DIGITAL UNIX v4.0 (TCP/ip) Network Management
- AdvFS, LSM, and RAID Configuration and Management
- DIGITAL UNIX TruCluster Software Configuration and Management
- UNIX Shell Programming Featuring Kornshell
- DIGITAL UNIX v4.0 Security Management
- DIGITAL UNIX v4.0 Performance Management
- DIGITAL UNIX v4.0 Intervals Overview

DIGITAL OpenVMS

- OpenVMS Skills for Users
- OpenVMS System and Network Node Management I
- OpenVMS System and Network Node Management II
- OpenVMS System and Network Node Management III
- OpenVMS System and Network Node Operations
- OpenVMS for Programmers
- OpenVMS System Troubleshooting for Systems Managers
- Configuring and Managing Complex VMScluster Systems
- Utilizing OpenVMS Features from C
- OpenVMS Performance Management
- Managing DEC TCP/IP Services for OpenVMS
- Programming in C

Hardware Courses

- AlphaServer 1000/1000A Installation, Configuration and Maintenance
- AlphaServer 2100 Server Maintenance
- AlphaServer 4100, Troubleshooting Techniques and Problem Solving

Alta Vista

- Installing and Configuring AltaVista Firewall 97 on Windows NT
- Installing and Configuring AltaVista Tunnel 97 on Windows NT
- Installing and Configuring AltaVista Firewall 97 on Digital UNIX
- Installing and Configuring AltaVista Tunnel 97 on Digital UNIX

Networking

- Digital MultiSwitch 900 Configuration and Installation
- Digital GIGAswitch/Ethernet Installation and Configuration
- Digital Gigaswitch/FDDI Installation and Management
- Digital ATM Solutions Installation and Configuration

ABOUT THE CONTRIBUTORS

Syngress Media creates books and software for Information Technology professionals seeking skill enhancement and career advancement. Its products are designed to comply with vendor and industry standard course curricula and are optimized for certification exam preperation. Contact them at www.syngress.com.

Stace Cunningham is a Systems Engineer with SDC Consulting located in Biloxi, Mississippi. SDC Consulting specializes in the design, engineering, and installation of networks. Stace received his MCSE in October 1996, and is also certified as an IBM Certified LAN Server Engineer, IBM Certified OS/2 Engineer, IBM Certified LAN Server Administrator, Microsoft Certified Product Specialist, IBM Certified LAN Server Instructor, and IBM Certified OS/2 Instructor.

Stace has participated as a Technical Contributor for the IIS 3.0 exam, SMS 1.2 exam, Proxy Server 1.0 exam, Exchange Server 5.0 exam, Exchange Server 5.5 exam, Proxy Server 2.0 exam, IIS 4.0 exam, IEAK exam, and the revised Windows 95 exam.

His wife Martha and daughter Marissa are very supportive of the time he spends on the computers located throughout his house. Without their love and support he would not be able to accomplish the goals he has set for himself.

Brian Frederick is an MCSE with more than five years of technical experience. Brian started his computer career at the ripe old age of seven with an Apple II+. Brian attended the University of Northern Iowa, and is married with two adorable children. Brian's hobbies include his kids primarily, as well as Little League baseball, and web page development. Brian also enjoys other sports, electronics, and multi-player gaming. Brian is involved with MCSE classroom training with a local ATEC.

Tim First began his computer experiences at the age of 10 with a Zenith Z-100. Since then he has gained the credentials of MCSE and MCP+Internet. He is currently preparing for the MCSE+Internet and Oracle DBA Certifications. Tim can be reached by e-mail at first@bus.msu.edu.

Dale Hackemeyer is an MCSE residing in Atlanta, Georgia. He has more than seven years experience in the IT field, the last several of which have been spent working with various Windows NT networks. When not shackled to a computer, he enjoys mountain biking and "Simpsons" reruns.

Tony Hinkle (MCSE, CNE) is from southern Indiana and holds a Bachelor's degree in Business Accounting from Oakland City University. His accounting career was quickly terminated by destiny, and he moved into the field of computer services. Although he started as a hardware technician, he knew that operating systems and networking would be his fields of excellence. With the assistance of his employer, Advanced Microelectronics, Inc., Tony completed the requirements to become a CNE, an A+ Certified Technician, and an MCSE.

Tony enjoys reading, Frisbee, Scrabble, computing, and participating in most non-contact sports. His claims to fame include being able to chirp like a cricket, knowing the alphabet backwards, not owning a television, and knowing how many bytes are in an ATM packet.

Nelson Minica currently lives in San Antonio, Texas with his wife and newborn son. He is an MCSE and has been working as a network administrator since 1994. He also enjoys object-oriented programming in C++ and Visual Basic. He holds a BS in Computer Science from Southwest Texas State University.

Michael Shaw (MCSE, MCP+Internet, MCP) achieved his B.S. from George Mason University with a degree in Management Information Systems and Decision Sciences. He works as a Systems Engineer with Compucom Systems, Inc. To his wife Claire ... happy anniversary!

Dave Dermon III has lived in Germantown, Tennessee for 14 years. He and his wife, Valerie, have two children. Dave graduated from Memphis State University, now the University of Memphis, in 1984 with a BBA. At that time he was programming on an Apple IIe with 16KB of memory. He installed and administered a small Arcnet network for Dave Dermon Insurance in 1985. By 1989 a XENIX system was added for the property management company. In 1993 he replaced the Arcnet system with a Novell 3.12 network. Dave left the company in 1997, after he began his MCSE Certification. Currently he is doing consulting work for both individuals and companies.

David W. Egan is an engineer and a Microsoft Certified Trainer. David has 20 years of programming and operating system experience. After receiving a BASc in Engineering in 1978 from the University of Toronto, David started his career working in the oilfield industry performing computerized, geological, downhole, formation.

After this David programmed in assembler and C for several years. Following this was a two-year lecturing position at a college in Southeast Asia. This led to four years as a VMS and UNIX instructor at Digital Equipment Corporation. For the past six years, David has since been writing course material and technical books, as well as consulting and teaching VMS, UNIX, and NT.

David lives with his wife and two children in the Vancouver, British Columbia area.

Technical Review and From the Classroom sidebars by:

D. Lynn White (MCPS, MCSE, MCT) is president of Independent Network Consultants, Inc. She is a technical author, editor, trainer, and consultant in the field of networking and computer-related technologies. She has been delivering mainframe, Microsoft-official curriculum and other networking courses across the country for more than 11 years.

ACKNOWLEDGMENTS

We would like to thank the following people:

- Richard Kristof of Global Knowledge Network for championing the series and providing us access to some great people and information. And to Patrick Von Schlag, Rhonda Harmon, Marian Turk, David Mantica, Stacey Cannon, and Kevin Murray for all their cooperation.

- To all the incredibly hard-working folks at Osborne/McGraw-Hill: Brandon Nordin, Scott Rogers, and Gareth Hancock for their help in launching a great series and being solid team players. In addition, Cynthia Douglas, Steve Emry, Anne Ellingsen, and Bernadette Jurich for their help in fine-tuning the book.

- Bruce Moran of BeachFrontQuizzer, Mary Anne Dane of Self Test Software, John Rose of Transcender Corporation, Parmol Soni of Microhard Technologies, and Michael Herrick of VFX Technologies.

- To Holly Heath at Microsoft, Corp. for being patient and diligent in answering all our questions.

CONTENTS

The Global Knowledge Network Advantage

Linking the Classroom to the Real World

Global Knowledge Network is the largest independent IT training company in the world, training more than 150,000 people every year in state-of-the-art network training centers or on location with major corporate customers. In addition, it is a Cisco Systems Training Partner, a Bay Networks Authorized Education Center, a FORE Systems Training Partner, and an Authorized IBM NETEAM Education provider. Now, for the first time, all of Global Knowledge Network's classroom expertise and real-world networking experience is available in the form of this Microsoft Certified Professional Approved Study Guide.

This book's primary objective is to help you prepare for and pass the required MCSE exam so you can begin to reap the career benefits of certification. We believe that the only way to do this is to help you increase your knowledge and build your skills. After completing this book, you should feel confident that you have thoroughly reviewed all of the objectives that Microsoft has established for the exam.

In This Book

This book is organized around the actual structure of the Microsoft exam administered at Sylvan Testing Centers. Most of the MCSE exams have six parts to them: Planning, Installation and Configuration, Managing Resources, Connectivity, Monitoring and Optimization, and Troubleshooting. Microsoft has let us know all the topics we need to cover for the exam. We've followed their list carefully, so you can be assured you're not missing anything.

In Every Chapter

We've created a set of chapter components that call your attention to important items, reinforce important points, and provide helpful exam-taking hints. Take a look at what you'll find in every chapter:

- Every chapter begins with the **Certification Objectives**—what you need to know in order to pass the section on the exam dealing with the chapter topic. The icon shown at left identifies the objectives within the chapter, so you'll always know an objective when you see it!

- **Exam Watch** notes call attention to information about, and potential pitfalls in, the exam. These helpful hints are written by MCSEs who have taken the exams and received their certification—who better to tell you what to worry about? They know what you're about to go through!

EXERCISE

- **Certification Exercises** are interspersed throughout the chapters. These are step-by-step exercises that mirror vendor-recommended labs. They help you master skills that are likely to be an area of focus on the exam. Don't just read through the exercises; they are hands-on practice that you should be comfortable completing. Learning by doing is an effective way to increase your competency with a product.

- **From the Classroom** sidebars describe the issues that come up most often in the training classroom setting. These sidebars give you a valuable perspective into certification- and product-related topics. They point out common mistakes and address questions that have arisen from classroom discussions.

- **Q & A** sections lay out problems and solutions in a quick-read format:

QUESTIONS AND ANSWERS

| I am installing NT and I have HPFS... | Convert it before you upgrade. NT 4 does not like HPFS. |

- The **Certification Summary** is a succinct review of the chapter and a re-statement of salient points regarding the exam.

■ The **Two-Minute Drill** at the end of every chapter is a checklist of the main points of the chapter. It can be used for last-minute review.

■ The **Self Test** offers questions similar to those found on the certification exams, including multiple choice, true/false questions, and fill-in-the-blank. The answers to these questions, as well as explanations of the answers, can be found in Appendix A. By taking the Self Test after completing each chapter, you'll reinforce what you've learned from that chapter, while becoming familiar with the structure of the exam questions.

Some Pointers

Once you've finished reading this book, set aside some time to do a thorough review. You might want to return to the book several times and make use of all the methods it offers for reviewing the material:

1. *Re-read all the Two-Minute Drills,* or have someone quiz you. You also can use the drills as a way to do a quick cram before the exam.

2. *Re-read all the Exam Watch notes.* Remember that these are written by MCSEs who have taken the exam and passed. They know what you should expect—and what you should be careful about.

3. *Review all the Q & A scenarios* for quick problem solving.

4. *Re-take the Self Tests.* Taking the tests right after you've read the chapter is a good idea, because it helps reinforce what you've just learned. However, it's an even better idea to go back later and do all the questions in the book in one sitting. Pretend you're taking the exam. (For this reason, you should mark your answers on a separate piece of paper when you go through the questions the first time.)

5. *Take the on-line tests.* Boot up the CD-ROM and take a look. We have more third-party tests on our CD than any other book out there, so you'll get quite a bit of practice.

6. *Complete the exercises.* Did you do the exercises when you read through each chapter? If not, do them! These exercises are designed to cover exam topics, and there's no better way to get to know this material than by practicing.

7. *Check out the web site.* Global Knowledge Network invites you to become an active member of the Access Global web site. This site is an online mall and an information repository that you'll find invaluable. You can access many types of products to assist you in your preparation for the exams, and you'll be able to participate in forums, on-line discussions, and threaded discussions. No other book brings you unlimited access to such a resource. You'll find more information about this site in Appendix C.

MCSE Certification

Although you've obviously picked up this book to study for a specific exam, we'd like to spend some time covering what you need to complete in order to attain MCSE status. Because this information can be found on the Microsoft web site, www.microsoft.com/train_cert, we've repeated only some of the more important information. You should review the train_cert site and check out Microsoft's information, along with their list of reasons to become an MCSE, including job advancement.

As you probably know, to attain MCSE status, you must pass a total of six exams —four requirements and two electives. One required exam is on networking basics, one on NT Server, one on NT Server in the Enterprise, and one on a client (either Windows NT Workstation or Windows 95 or 98). There are several electives from which to choose. The most popular electives now are on TCP/IP and Exchange Server 5. The following table lists the exam names, their corresponding course numbers, and whether they are required or elective. We're showing you the NT 4.0 track and not the NT 3.51 track (which is still offered).

Exam Number	Exam Name	Required or Elective
70-58	Networking Essentials	Required
70-63	Implementing and Supporting Microsoft Windows 95 or 98	Required (either 70-63/ 70-98 or 70-73)
70-67	Implementing and Supporting Microsoft Windows NT Server 4.0	Required

Exam Number	Exam Name	Required or Elective
70-68	Implementing and Supporting Microsoft Windows NT Server 4.0 in the Enterprise	Required
70-73	Implementing and Supporting Microsoft Windows NT Workstation 4.0	Required (either 70-73 or 70-63)
70-14	Supporting Microsoft System Management Server 1.2	Elective
70-59	Internetworking with Microsoft TCP/IP on Windows NT 4.0	Elective
70-81	Implementing and Supporting Microsoft Exchange Server 5.5	Elective
70-85	Implementing and Supporting Microsoft SNA Server 4.0	Elective
70-87	Implementing and Supporting Microsoft Internet Information Server 4.0	Elective
70-88	Implementing and Supporting Microsoft Proxy Server 2.0	Elective
TBA	System Administration for Microsoft SQL Server X	Elective
TBA	Implementing a Database Design on SQL Server X	Elective

The CD-ROM Resource

This book comes with a CD-ROM full of supplementary material you can use while preparing for the MCSE exams. We think you'll find our book/CD package one of the most useful on the market. It provides all the sample tests available from testing companies such as Transcender, Microhard, Self Test Software, BeachFront Quizzer, and VFX Technologies. In addition to all these third-party products, you'll find an electronic version of the book, where you can look up items easily and search on specific terms. The special self-study module contains another 300 sample questions, with links to the electronic book for further review. There's more about this resource in Appendix B.

How to Take a Microsoft Certification Examination

**by John C. Phillips, Vice President of Test Development,
Self Test Software
(Self Test's PEP is the official Microsoft practice test.)**

Good News and Bad News

If you are new to Microsoft certification, we have some good news and some bad news. The good news, of course, is that Microsoft certification is one of the most valuable credentials you can earn. It sets you apart from the crowd, and marks you as a valuable asset to your employer. You will gain the respect of your peers, and Microsoft certification can have a wonderful effect on your income.

The bad news is that Microsoft certification tests are not easy. You may think you will read through some study material, memorize a few facts, and pass the Microsoft examinations. After all, these certification exams are just computer-based, multiple-choice tests, so they must be easy. If you believe this, you are wrong. Unlike many "multiple guess" tests you have been exposed to in school, the questions on Microsoft certification examinations go beyond simple factual knowledge.

The purpose of this introduction is to teach you how to take a Microsoft certification examination. To be successful, you need to know something about the purpose and structure of these tests. We will also look at the latest innovations in Microsoft testing. Using *simulations* and *adaptive testing*, Microsoft is enhancing both the validity and security of the certification process. These factors have some important effects on how you should prepare for an exam, as well as your approach to each question during the test.

We will begin by looking at the purpose, focus, and structure of Microsoft certification tests, and examine the effect these factors have on the kinds of questions you will face on your certification exams. We will define the structure of examination questions and investigate some common formats. Next, we will present a strategy for answering these questions. Finally, we will give some specific guidelines on what you should do on the day of your test.

Why Vendor Certification?

The Microsoft Certified Professional program, like the certification programs from Lotus, Novell, Oracle, and other software vendors, is maintained for the ultimate purpose of increasing the corporation's profits. A successful vendor certification program accomplishes this goal by helping to create a pool of experts in a company's software, and by "branding" these experts so that companies using the software can identify them.

We know that vendor certification has become increasingly popular in the last few years because it helps employers find qualified workers, and because it helps software vendors like Microsoft sell their products. But why vendor certification rather than a more traditional approach like a college degree in computer science? A college education is a broadening and enriching experience, but a degree in computer science does not prepare students for most jobs in the IT industry.

A common truism in our business states, "If you are out of the IT industry for three years and want to return, you have to start over." The problem, of course, is *timeliness*; if a first-year student learns about a specific computer program, it probably will no longer be in wide use when he or she graduates. Although some colleges are trying to integrate Microsoft certification into their curriculum, the problem is not really a flaw in higher education, but a characteristic of the IT industry. Computer software is changing so rapidly that a four-year college just can't keep up.

A marked characteristic of the Microsoft certification program is an emphasis on performing specific job tasks rather than merely gathering knowledge. It may come as a shock, but most potential employers do not care how much you know about the theory of operating systems, networking, or database design. As one IT manager put it, "I don't really care what my employees know about the theory of our network. We don't need someone to sit at a desk and think about it. We need people who can actually do something to make it work better."

You should not think that this attitude is some kind of anti-intellectual revolt against "book learning." Knowledge is a necessary prerequisite, but it is not enough. More than one company has hired a computer science graduate as a network administrator, only to learn that the new employee has no idea how to add users, assign permissions, or perform the other day-to-day tasks necessary to maintain a network. This brings us to the second major characteristic of Microsoft certification that affects the questions you must be prepared to answer. In addition to timeliness, Microsoft certification is also job task oriented.

The timeliness of Microsoft's certification program is obvious, and is inherent in the fact that you will be tested on current versions of software in wide use today. The job task orientation of Microsoft certification is almost as obvious, but testing real-world job skills using a computer-based test is not easy.

Computerized Testing

Considering the popularity of Microsoft certification, and the fact that certification candidates are spread around the world, the only practical way to administer tests for the certification program is through Sylvan Prometric testing centers. Sylvan Prometric provides proctored testing services for Microsoft, Oracle, Novell, Lotus, and the A+ computer technician certification. Although the IT industry accounts for much of Sylvan's revenue, the company provides services for a number of other businesses and organizations, such as FAA pre-flight pilot tests. In fact, most companies that need secure test delivery over a wide geographic area use the services of Sylvan Prometric. In addition to delivery, Sylvan Prometric also scores the tests and provides statistical feedback on the performance of each test question to the companies and organizations that use their services.

Typically, several hundred questions are developed for a new Microsoft certification examination. The questions are first reviewed by a number of subject matter experts for technical accuracy, and then are presented in a beta test. The beta test may last for several hours, due to the large number of questions. After a few weeks, Microsoft Certification uses the statistical feedback from Sylvan to check the performance of the beta questions.

Questions are discarded if most test takers get them right (too easy) or wrong (too difficult), and a number of other statistical measures are taken of each question. Although the scope of our discussion precludes a rigorous treatment of question analysis, you should be aware that Microsoft and other vendors spend a great deal of time and effort making sure their examination questions are valid. In addition to the obvious desire for quality, the fairness of a vendor's certification program must be legally defensible.

The questions that survive statistical analysis form the pool of questions for the final certification examination.

Test Structure

The kind of test we are most familiar with is known as a *form* test. For Microsoft certification, a form usually consists of 50–70 questions and takes 60–90 minutes to complete. If there are 240 questions in the final pool for an examination, then four forms can be created. Thus, candidates who retake the test probably will not see the same questions.

Other variations are possible. From the same pool of 240 questions, *five* forms can be created, each containing 40 unique questions (200 questions) and 20 questions selected at random from the remaining 40.

The questions in a Microsoft form test are equally weighted. This means they all count the same when the test is scored. An interesting and useful characteristic of a form test is that you can mark a question you have doubts about as you take the test. Assuming you have time left when you finish all the questions, you can return and spend more time on the questions you have marked as doubtful.

Microsoft may soon implement *adaptive* testing. To use this interactive technique, a form test is first created and administered to several thousand certification candidates. The statistics generated are used to assign a weight, or difficulty level, for each question. For example, the questions in a form might be divided into levels one through five, with level one questions being the easiest and level five the hardest.

When an adaptive test begins, the candidate is first given a level three question. If it is answered correctly, a question from the next higher level is presented, and an incorrect response results in a question from the next lower level. When 15–20 questions have been answered in this manner, the scoring algorithm is able to predict, with a high degree of statistical certainty, whether the candidate would pass or fail if all the questions in the form were answered. When the required degree of certainty is attained, the test ends and the candidate receives a pass/fail grade.

Adaptive testing has some definite advantages for everyone involved in the certification process. Adaptive tests allow Sylvan Prometric to deliver more tests with the same resources, as certification candidates often are in and out in 30 minutes or less. For Microsoft, adaptive testing means that fewer test questions are exposed to each candidate, and this can enhance the security, and therefore the validity, of certification tests.

One possible problem you may have with adaptive testing is that you are not allowed to mark and revisit questions. Since the adaptive algorithm is interactive, and all questions but the first are selected on the basis of your response to the previous question, it is not possible to skip a particular question or change an answer.

Question Types

Computerized test questions can be presented in a number of ways. Some of the possible formats are used on Microsoft certification examinations, and some are not.

True/False

We are all familiar with True/False questions, but because of the inherent 50 percent chance of guessing the correct answer, you will not see questions of this type on Microsoft certification exams.

Multiple Choice

The majority of Microsoft certification questions are in the multiple-choice format, with either a single correct answer or multiple correct answers. One interesting variation on multiple-choice questions with multiple correct answers is whether or not the candidate is told how many answers are correct.

EXAMPLE:
Which two files can be altered to configure the MS-DOS environment? (Choose two.)
Or
Which files can be altered to configure the MS-DOS environment? (Choose all that apply.)

You may see both variations on Microsoft certification examinations, but the trend seems to be toward the first type, where candidates are told explicitly how many answers are correct. Questions of the "choose all that apply" variety are more difficult, and can be merely confusing.

Graphical Questions

One or more graphical elements are sometimes used as exhibits to help present or clarify an exam question. These elements may take the form of a network diagram, pictures of networking components, or screen shots from the software on which you are being tested. It is often easier to present the concepts required for a complex performance-based scenario with a graphic than with words.

Test questions known as *hotspots* actually incorporate graphics as part of the answer. These questions ask the certification candidate to click on a location or graphical element to answer the question. As an example, you might be shown the diagram of a network and asked to click on an appropriate location for a router. The answer is correct if the candidate clicks within the *hotspot* that defines the correct location.

Free Response Questions

Another kind of question you sometimes see on Microsoft certification examinations requires a *free response* or type-in answer. An example of this type of question might present a TCP/IP network scenario and ask the candidate to calculate and enter the correct subnet mask in dotted decimal notation.

Knowledge-Based and Performance-Based Questions

Microsoft Certification develops a blueprint for each Microsoft certification examination with input from subject matter experts. This blueprint defines the content areas and objectives for each test, and each test question is created to test a specific objective. The basic information from the examination blueprint can be found on Microsoft's web site in the Exam Prep Guide for each test.

Psychometricians (psychologists who specialize in designing and analyzing tests) categorize test questions as knowledge-based or performance-based. As the names imply, knowledge-based questions are designed to test knowledge, while performance-based questions are designed to test performance.

Some objectives demand a knowledge-based question. For example, objectives that use verbs like *list* and *identify* tend to test only what you know, not what you can do.

EXAMPLE:
Objective: Identify the MS-DOS configuration files.
Which two files can be altered to configure the MS-DOS environment? (Choose two.)

    A. COMMAND.COM

    B. AUTOEXEC.BAT

    C. IO.SYS

    D. CONFIG.SYS
    Correct answers: B,D

Other objectives use action verbs like *install, configure,* and *troubleshoot* to define job tasks. These objectives can often be tested with either a knowledge-based question or a performance-based question.

EXAMPLE:
Objective: Configure an MS-DOS installation appropriately using the PATH statement in AUTOEXEX.BAT.
Knowledge-based question:
What is the correct syntax to set a path to the D:\APP directory in AUTOEXEC.BAT?

    A. SET PATH EQUAL TO D:\APP

    B. PATH D:\APP

C. SETPATH D:\APP

D. D:\APP EQUALS PATH

Correct answer: B

Performance-based question:

Your company uses several DOS accounting applications that access a group of common utility programs. What is the best strategy for configuring the computers in the accounting department so that the accounting applications will always be able to access the utility programs?

A. Store all the utilities on a single floppy disk, and make a copy of the disk for each computer in the accounting department.

B. Copy all the utilities to a directory on the C: drive of each computer in the accounting department, and add a PATH statement pointing to this directory in the AUTOEXEC.BAT files.

C. Copy all the utilities to all application directories on each computer in the accounting department.

D. Place all the utilities in the C:\DOS directory on each computer, because the C:\DOS directory is automatically included in the PATH statement when AUTOEXEC.BAT is executed.

Correct answer: B

Even in this simple example, the superiority of the performance-based question is obvious. Whereas the knowledge-based question asks for a single fact, the performance-based question presents a real-life situation and requires that you make a decision based on this scenario. Thus, performance-based questions give more bang (validity) for the test author's buck (individual question).

Testing Job Performance

We have said that Microsoft certification focuses on timeliness and the ability to perform job tasks. We have also introduced the concept of performance-based questions, but even performance-based multiple-choice questions do not really measure performance. Another strategy is needed to test job skills.

Given unlimited resources, it is not difficult to test job skills. In an ideal world, Microsoft would fly MCP candidates to Redmond, place them in a controlled environment with a team of experts, and ask them to plan, install, maintain, and troubleshoot a Windows network. In a few days at most, the experts could reach a valid decision as to whether each candidate should or should not be granted MCSE status. Needless to say, this is not likely to happen.

Closer to reality, another way to test performance is by using the actual software, and creating a testing program to present tasks and automatically grade a candidate's performance when the tasks are completed. This *cooperative* approach would be practical in some testing situations, but the same test that is presented to MCP candidates in Boston must also be available in Bahrain and Botswana. Many Sylvan Prometric testing locations around the world cannot run 32-bit applications, much less provide the complex networked solutions required by cooperative testing applications.

The most workable solution for measuring performance in today's testing environment is a *simulation* program. When the program is launched during a test, the candidate sees a simulation of the actual software that looks, and behaves, just like the real thing. When the testing software presents a task, the simulation program is launched and the candidate performs the required task. The testing software then grades the candidate's performance on the required task and moves to the next question. In this way, a 16-bit simulation program can mimic the look and feel of 32-bit operating systems, a complicated network, or even the entire Internet.

Microsoft has introduced simulation questions on the certification examination for Internet Information Server 4.0. Simulation questions provide many advantages over other testing methodologies, and simulations are expected to become increasingly important in the Microsoft certification program. For example, studies have shown that there is a very high correlation between the ability to perform simulated tasks on a computer-based test and the ability to perform the actual job tasks. Thus, simulations enhance the validity of the certification process.

Another truly wonderful benefit of simulations is in the area of test security. It is just not possible to cheat on a simulation question. In fact, you will be told exactly what tasks you are expected to perform on the test. How can a certification candidate cheat? By learning to perform the tasks? What a concept!

Study Strategies

There are appropriate ways to study for the different types of questions you will see on a Microsoft certification examination.

Knowledge-Based Questions

Knowledge-based questions require that you memorize facts. There are hundreds of facts inherent in every content area of every Microsoft certification examination. There are several keys to memorizing facts:

■ **Repetition** The more times your brain is exposed to a fact, the more likely you are to remember it.

■ **Association** Connecting facts within a logical framework makes them easier to remember.

■ **Motor Association** It is often easier to remember something if you write it down or perform some other physical act, like clicking on a practice test answer.

We have said that the emphasis of Microsoft certification is job performance, and that there are very few knowledge-based questions on Microsoft certification exams. Why should you waste a lot of time learning file names, IP address formulas, and other minutiae? Read on.

Performance-Based Questions

Most of the questions you will face on a Microsoft certification exam are performance-based scenario questions. We have discussed the superiority of these questions over simple knowledge-based questions, but you should remember that the job task orientation of Microsoft certification extends the knowledge you need to pass the exams; it does not replace this knowledge. Therefore, the first step in preparing for scenario questions is to absorb as many facts relating to the exam content areas as you can. In other words, go back to the previous section and follow the steps to prepare for an exam composed of knowledge-based questions.

The second step is to familiarize yourself with the format of the questions you are likely to see on the exam. You can do this by answering the questions in this study guide, by using Microsoft assessment tests, or by using practice tests. The day of your test is not the time to be surprised by the convoluted construction of Microsoft exam questions.

For example, one of Microsoft Certification's favorite formats of late takes the following form:

Scenario: You have a network with...

Primary Objective: You want to...

Secondary Objective: You also want to...

Proposed Solution: Do this...

What does the proposed solution accomplish?

    A. satisfies the primary and the secondary objective

    B. satisfies the primary but not the secondary objective

    C. satisfies the secondary but not the primary objective

    D. satisfies neither the primary nor the secondary objective

This kind of question, with some variation, is seen on many Microsoft Certification examinations.

At best, these performance-based scenario questions really do test certification candidates at a higher cognitive level than knowledge-based questions. At worst, these questions can test your reading comprehension and test-taking ability rather than your ability to use Microsoft products. Be sure to get in the habit of reading the question carefully to determine what is being asked.

The third step in preparing for Microsoft scenario questions is to adopt the following attitude: Multiple-choice questions aren't really performance-based. It is all a cruel lie. These scenario questions are just knowledge-based questions with a little story wrapped around them.

To answer a scenario question, you have to sift through the story to the underlying facts of the situation, and apply your knowledge to determine the correct answer. This may sound silly at first, but the process we go through in solving real-life problems is quite similar. The key concept is that every scenario question (and every real-life problem) has a fact at its center, and if we can identify that fact, we can answer the question.

Simulations

Simulation questions really do measure your ability to perform job tasks. You must be able to perform the specified tasks. There are two ways to prepare for simulation questions:

1. Get experience with the actual software. If you have the resources, this is a great way to prepare for simulation questions.

2. Use official Microsoft practice tests. Practice tests are available that provide practice with the same simulation engine used on Microsoft certification exams. This approach has the added advantage of grading your efforts.

Signing Up

Signing up to take a Microsoft certification examination is easy. Sylvan operators in each country can schedule tests at any testing center. There are, however, a few things you should know:

1. If you call Sylvan during a busy time period, get a cup of coffee first, because you may be in for a long wait. Sylvan does an excellent job, but everyone in the world seems to want to sign up for a test on Monday morning.

2. You will need your social security number or some other unique identifier to sign up for a Sylvan test, so have it at hand.

3. Pay for your test by credit card if at all possible. This makes things easier, and you can even schedule tests for the same day you call, if space is available at your local testing center.

4. Know the number and title of the test you want to take before you call. This is not essential, and the Sylvan operators will help you if they can. Having this information in advance, however, speeds up the registration process.

Taking the Test

Teachers have always told you not to try to cram for examinations, because it does no good. Sometimes they lied. If you are faced with a knowledge-based test requiring only that you regurgitate facts, cramming can mean the difference between passing and failing. This is not the case, however, with Microsoft certification exams. If you don't know it the night before, don't bother to stay up and cram.

Instead, create a schedule and stick to it. Plan your study time carefully, and do not schedule your test until you think you are ready to succeed. Follow these guidelines on the day of your exam:

1. Get a good night's sleep. The scenario questions you will face on a Microsoft certification examination require a clear head.

2. Remember to take two forms of identification—at least one with a picture. A driver's license with your picture, and social security or credit cards are acceptable.

3. Leave home in time to arrive at your testing center a few minutes early. It is not a good idea to feel rushed as you begin your exam.

4. Do not spend too much time on any one question. If you are taking a form test, take your best guess and mark the question so you can come back to it if you have time. You cannot mark and revisit questions on an adaptive test, so you must do your best on each question as you go.

5. If you do not know the answer to a question, try to eliminate the obviously wrong answers and guess from the rest. If you can eliminate two out of four options, you have a 50 percent chance of guessing the correct answer.

6. For scenario questions, follow the steps we outlined earlier. Read the question carefully and try to identify the facts at the center of the story.

Finally, I would advise anyone attempting to earn Microsoft MCSE certification to adopt a philosophical attitude. Even if you are the kind of person who never fails a test, you are likely to fail at least one Microsoft certification test somewhere along the way. Do not get discouraged. If Microsoft certification were easy to obtain, more people would have it, and it would not be so respected and so valuable to your future in the IT industry.

1

Introduction to TCP/IP

This chapter covers the basics of how TCP/IP evolved and became the standard for the Internet and the worldwide networking industry. We discuss TCP/IP's early development and the governing agencies that control how the Internet is used. We also discuss the features of TCP/IP services that make it globally versatile and functional. Finally, we take a look at Microsoft's redesigned and rewritten 32-bit TCP/IP implementation.

TCP/IP History

Well, you've finally gotten around to picking up a book that will teach you about TCP/IP. You can expect to learn the fundamentals of TCP/IP and gain an excellent working knowledge of this versatile network protocol. Before we begin, let's take a look at the history of TCP/IP, the most popular networking protocol suite in the commercial and educational world!

TCP/IP was originally developed as a standard protocol to connect heterogeneous hardware and software operating systems in a network across cable or satellite, making it in effect a Wide Area Network (WAN). This network initially consisted of the University of Utah, the Stanford Research Institute, the University of California at Los Angeles, and the University of California at San Bernardino.

TCP/IP stands for *Transmission Control Protocol (TCP) / Internet Protocol (IP)*. Don't let its name fool you; TCP/IP is a *suite* of protocols, not just the two mentioned here. As we'll see in the next chapter, each protocol in the suite has a specific purpose and function. Before we go any further let's see how the world's largest network, the Internet, became a reality.

exam
Watch *Be sure you understand the TCP/IP acronym. You will be tested on it.*

Advanced Research Project Agency (ARPA)

Initially the Internet was known as the ARPANET. It started when the Department of Defense (DOD) needed to communicate across a Wide Area

Network, but the current networks weren't compatible or didn't have cross–platform communication features. In addition to building a network that communicated across platforms, numerous services and functions had to be addressed, as we'll see a little later in this chapter.

In the 1960s the U.S. Defense Advanced Research Projects Agency (DARPA) created and funded the development of a high-speed, packet switching network that would connect several research and government sites. ARPA was then renamed to DARPA. This network initially used the Xerox Networking System (XNS) protocol, but because of limitations XNS didn't pan out. Soon a new transport protocol and routing protocol were developed, which became known as the TCP/IP Suite.

exam
ⓦatch

TCP/IP was developed by the government to build a heterogeneous network across a wide area.

Funded by Department of Defense

The DARPA project was funded by the Department of Defense and was headed by Dr. J.C.R. Licklider. Dr. Licklider gathered a group of computer specialists, nicknamed the "Intergalactic Network." Their goal was to develop the architecture needed for the Internet, which included the protocols and services that eventually became known as TCP/IP.

This architecture had to be modular and independent of hardware or software. In addition, the information on how to implement this network had to be public. It's important to recognize that DARPA wasn't responsible for building the Internet, but for designing the Internet model. This model also included defining the structure for the network protocols, which later became the TCP/IP protocol suite.

In 1967 DARPA contracted with the Stanford Research Institute to develop the specification for this new communication system. In 1970 development began and by 1972 there were approximately 40 sites and support for TCP/IP utilities was begun. In 1973 the first international connection was established and 1974 released TCP/IP to the public.

The first implementation of this network consisted of government, military, and educational sites and it slowly grew to include commercial companies as well. This network has grown to enable communication throughout most of the countries in the world.

The Internet consists of many large networks that work together. If you have access from your PC to the Internet, you are using an *Internet Service Provider (ISP)*. Your ISP provides your access to the Internet, which may include Web services. We'll cover the Web in a later chapter.

Berkeley UNIX 4.3 Inclusion

In the late 1960s AT&T Bell Labs programmers Ken Thompson and Dennis Richards developed a new software operating system written entirely in C. This new operating system was called *UNIX*. In the early 70s AT&T gave the

---

FROM THE CLASSROOM

A Packet-Switching WAN

In 1969 the DOD created a packet-switching Wide Area Network (WAN) to transport data all over the world. This packet-switching WAN evolved into what we know today as the Internet.

Data is transported electronically by breaking it down into packets which are addressed, sequenced, and then sent. We'll use a snail mail example to explain what a packet is and how it transports data.

Suppose you write a very long letter and must use #10 envelopes to mail it. Due to the number of pages, you can't fold the entire letter and place it in a single #10 envelope so you decide to break it into smaller sections and put each section in a #10 envelope. You then number the envelopes sequentially so the

recipient can successfully reassemble your letter. The letter is equal to the data that is created within an application.

Switching refers to routing; that is, getting the packet to the destination address. Suppose in mailing the #10 envelopes, at the post office during the sorting process, the envelopes end up in different mail bags, placed on different mail trucks. The recipient will still get all the #10 envelopes and can reassemble them into the original letter. Just like the many #10 envelopes, each packet can go different physical routes to the destination address. Once there, the data that was generated by the application can be reassembled.

—*By D. Lynn White, MCT, MCSE*

operating system code to universities for further development. To encourage the use of these internetworking protocols, DARPA made a low-cost implementation available to UNIX developers and provided funds for its inclusion with the software distribution of UNIX. In 1980 the University of California at Berkeley integrated DARPA's TCP/IP protocol suite as the networking component of UNIX. Hence, the marriage of UNIX and TCP/IP.

UNIX has continued to use TCP/IP as its network protocol and development has continued by networking vendors to add additional services to the TCP/IP suite of protocols and services.

TCP/IP Features

The TCP/IP protocols were designed to meet the need for global communication. Let's take a look at the features that make TCP/IP the standard for Internet connectivity.

Modularity

Each layer in the TCP/IP protocol stack is modular, which means that it communicates with only the layer above or below it. So as long as network developers write their device drivers or applications based on public *Request for Comments* (RFCs), there is no need to rewrite the entire protocol stack. The developer has to write only the code for the layer that his/her software will be implementing.

Open Protocol Standards

Because TCP/IP is not tied to an operating system, any vendor developing a new operating system with a network component can reference the RFCs to build a TCP/IP component. So a UNIX system will be able to talk to a VMS system, and the VMS system will be able to talk to an IBM mainframe, and the beat goes on. Even those operating systems with proprietary networks are jumping on the bandwagon. For example, Digital Equipment Corporation, Inc. has implemented TCP/IP services for OpenVMS.

Universal Interconnection

TCP/IP allows any pair of processes running on different computers to communicate. This is most commonly used in a client/server environment. Here one process, typically the server, is residing on a central node and the client process will request certain tasks or information to be retrieved by the server.

32-bit Address

TCP/IP's unique addressing mechanism provides for over 4.2 billion addresses. Each host is referred to by its unique 32-bit address. These unique addresses are made up of network and host identification.

But with the growth of the Internet the *Network Information Center (NIC)* is already running out of addresses, and in fact since April 1995 has not assigned any new addresses. We will discuss a little later how to get an IP address and host name. The next implementation of TCP/IP and the Internet is in development now. IPV6 will use a 128-bit address, and hopefully this will last for a while!

Four-Octet Address

The 32-bit IP address is broken into four octets that can be represented in decimal or binary format:

```
11010100   00001111   10000100   01110101
Binaary Representation of Address

212.15.132.117
Dotted-Decimal Representation of the Address
```

Network ID

Using the IP address scheme we further fragment this address into the network ID and the host ID. The Internet is one large communication network that consists of multiple networks. Each machine uses part of the IP address to identify the network it belongs to and the rest of the address to identify its host or local computer address. In Chapter 3 you will learn how to distinguish the network ID from the host ID and all their different implications.

Remember that the IP address is a 32-bit decimal address, separated into four equal octets by a ".". This number is then converted to binary and used as a unique identifier.

Subnet Mask

A subnet mask is used to determine which part of the IP address is used for the network ID and which part for the host ID. There are two required parameters you must supply to initialize TCP/IP:

- **IP address**   4-octet address
- **Subnet mask**   4-octet value

Large-Sized Networks

As we just learned, the IP addressing scheme can build fairly large networks. Table 1-1 lists the three types of network addresses, called network classes, that are assigned to a company or an organization.

As you can see in Table 1-1, TCP/IP networks can become immense and still be able to transmit messages from one side of the world to another. In Chapter 3 we will examine all the possible combinations of addresses.

Routable

So how does a message move from one network to another?

We know that TCP/IP networks are made up of smaller networks either physically or logically segmented. To move between networks a *router* is used.

TABLE 1-1	Network Class	Number of Hosts
TCP/IP Network Classes and Number of Hosts	Class A	approximately 16,000,000
	Class B	approximately 64,000
	Class C	254

A router is a computer that is connected to two or more networks. This computer forwards messages from one network to the other. In some TCP/IP implementations a router is also known as a *gateway*. A gateway is a computer that does protocol translation as well as routing.

exam
Watch

Routing is the action of forwarding data between subnetworks.

For the large networks, network specialists use dedicated computers that perform nothing but routing operations. Bay Networks, Digital, 3Com, and Cisco are a few network vendors manufacturing large routers.

In small Microsoft networks, a Windows NT computer can hold two or more cards with different network addresses and act as a router. Each card can be assigned as many as five different addresses.

exam
Watch

The number of cards that can be placed into an NT server is dependent on whether the hardware has free resources and a free slot. The number of IP addresses assigned to a card is five.

Heterogeneous (Supports Multiple Platforms)

Microsoft's 32-bit version of TCP/IP can communicate with multiple hardware and software platforms. Communication works across vendors because both computers have a TCP/IP stack that is written to RFCs. Microsoft's TCP/IP has specifically been written to promote communication with multiple system types.

Internet Hosts

If you're on the Internet, then you're using TCP/IP. Internet hosts can be just about any system: Sun, IBM, VAX, ALPHA, and even Microsoft. As a user or even as a Network Specialist you don't need to know which operating system is being used on the other end; you just need to make sure you're using TCP/IP.

Apple Macintosh

In Windows NT Server 3.5x and 4.0 support has been built in for Macintosh coexistence. As long as the Apple Macintosh continues to support TCP/IP, any Macintosh user will be able to FTP and send e-mail to a TCP/IP host.

IBM Mainframes

IBM has implemented a TCP/IP stack. Therefore communication with IBM mainframes and Microsoft hosts works smoothly if both computers are using TCP/IP as a network protocol.

UNIX Systems

UNIX systems have been using TCP/IP since 1980. It's easy to connect to a UNIX system and download files as long as you are using TCP/IP services.

OpenVMS Systems

Digital has had a history of building proprietary systems, but with TCP/IP services for OpenVMS, Digital has stepped into the foray. The earlier name for TCP/IP on a Digital platform was UNIX Connection or UCX.

Printers with Network Adapters

Printers can also be connected to the Internet. Digital PrintServers and Hewlett-Packard Laser Jets are two examples of printers that can be adapted or come with Network Adapter cards. These cards can be assigned IP addresses and then used from any type of TCP/IP host that supports network printing.

CERTIFICATION OBJECTIVE 1.03

Internet Activities Board (IAB)

The coordinating committee for the Internet's design, engineering, and management is known as the *Internet Activities Board* (IAB). Formed in the early 1980s, the IAB has the following mission:

- Manage the existing Internet
- Maintain standards
- Manage technical issues
- Act as an internal liaison and representative for the Internet community
- Help evolve the Internet into a large-scale, high-speed Network of the Future

- Perform strategic planning for the Internet
- Identify long-range problems and opportunities

Know the responsibilities of the IAB.

Governing the Development of the Internet

The IAB manages two subcommittees focused on engineering and research. Each subcommittee is led by a chairperson and guided by a steering committee. The subcommittees report to the IAB via the chairperson.

Internet Research Task Force (IRTF)

The IRTF promotes research in networking and the development of future Internet technology. There will be some overlap of research between the IRTF and the IETF, but this overlap is considered crucial to the cross-fertilization and technology transfer.

Internet Engineering Task Force (IETF)

The IETF is responsible for the operation, management, and evolution of the Internet. The steering committee of the IETF is known as the *Internet Engineering Steering Group (IESG)*. The IAB has delegated to the IESG the general responsibility for making the Internet work and the resolution of all short- and mid-range protocol and architectural issues.

The Networking Community votes for the IAB and its two subcommittee members, who serve a two-year term. There is representation by major firms specializing in network design, hardware, and software development, as well as educational representatives from the most prestigious educational institutions in the world.

CERTIFICATION OBJECTIVE 1.04

Request for Comments (RFC)

The IAB informs the networking community of its decisions by publishing Requests for Comments. An RFC is an invitation to develop standards, recommendations, or requirements for TCP/IP and the Internet. It is a method of asking for multiple solutions and choosing the best one. The IAB uses its steering committees to evaluate the RFC responses. The RFC is then published under one of five classifications:

Required	Must be implemented
Recommended	Should be implemented and usually is
Elective	Optionally implemented and usually is not
Limited Use	Possible usage on some computer systems
Not Recommended	Not to be implemented

Recommendations, Standards, and Requirements

An RFC passes through several phases of development. First, it is assigned a number. Then it passes through three different stages: a Proposed Standard, a Draft Standard, and an Internet Standard. The RFC number is never used again. If another version or a more efficient method of implementing a service or protocol is developed, another number is assigned. You can get the latest RFCs from Microsoft's web site.

Network Locations of RFCs

The Stanford Research Institute (SRI) maintains an index of RFCs that provides the number, title, authors, issue date, and the total number of hardcopy pages. It also lists the online format for the RFC. The index also notes whether an RFC is obsolete or updated by another RFC. You can download this index from:

ftp.nisc.sri.com

and get the file FYI/FYI-index.txt.

E-Mail Request

You can also retrieve the RFC index by sending e-mail to:

mail-server@nisc.sri.com

In the body of the message place the following text:

RFCs	FYIs
send RFC-index	send FYI-index

IP Address
You can download RFCs from the following FTP sites:

- nis.nsf.net
- nisc.jvnc.net
- venera.isi.edu
- wuarchive.wustl.edu
- src.doc.ic.ac.uk
- ftp.concert.net
- ds.internic.net
- nic.ddn.mil

For specific help in retrieving RFCs from these sites, send an e-mail message to rfc-info@isi.edu with the following in the body of the message:

help: ways_to_get_rfcs

CERTIFICATION OBJECTIVE 1.05

Network Information Center (NIC)

The IAB is essentially responsible for assigning IP addresses to individuals, companies, organizations, and corporations on the Internet. The IAB has given the Network Information Center (NIC) the responsibility for assigning valid TCP/IP addresses. The only problem is that the NIC has been out of addresses since April 1995. You can obtain an IP address only through an ISP.

Assignment of Internet Addresses

Your ISP will assign you an IP address and domain name. You are then responsible for maintaining the connection to your ISP, which may include space for Web pages.

Registration of Domain Name

IP addresses are hard for humans to remember. The *Domain Name Service (DNS)* was created so that instead of having to type the IP address of a company's Web site, for example, you can access that site by a user-friendly name.

This service is based on a hierarchical structure that is read from right to left as you move down through the hosts. When the left-most name of an address is reached, the IP address of the host should be returned. You use domain names every time you search on the Web or send e-mail. Here are some DNS examples:

Type of Address	Example
Web-based address	www.syngress.com
E-mail address	RuddyM@globalknowledge.com

It's important to contact your ISP and verify that your host name, IP address, and domain name do not conflict with other hosts on their network.

CERTIFICATION OBJECTIVE 1.06

Management Services

Microsoft's TCP/IP services have definitely come of age. In the first version of NT some of these services needed just a little more work to even out the rough edges. With the release of Windows NT Server 4.0, it looks like they're finally there!

Dynamic Host Control Protocol (DHCP)

This service provides PCs with automatic configuration of the three necessary TCP/IP parameters: IP address, subnet mask, and default gateway.

The first step in a DHCP environment is to identify a server as a DHCP server. This server maintains a pool of addresses and maintains the assignment of these addresses to the requesting computers. During boot-up, requesting computers issue a request for IP parameters. The DHCP server then responds to the requesting computer with the appropriate parameters and maintains its assignment in the DHCP database.

The automatic assignment of IP parameters makes configuration of a large number of computers painless. DHCP also provides automation, reducing human error. (DHCP is discussed in Chapter 6.)

Windows Internet Name Service (WINS)

The second of many solutions to host name resolution is Microsoft's Windows Internet Name Service. This service provides a NetBIOS-computer-name to IP-address mapping in a database on a server. The main feature of WINS is that instead of having to maintain a separate LMHOSTS file for NetBIOS computer names on each separate computer, a large database can be maintained on a server that keeps track of IP to NetBIOS name mappings. The WINS server database is dynamic, unlike the LMHOSTS files that must be modified manually.

Whenever a NetBIOS computer needs to resolve a NetBIOS name to an IP address, the requesting computer contacts the WINS server for a name resolution. The server then responds with the latest known IP address of the requested client.

Dynamic Name Service (DNS)

Microsoft's implementation of DNS is finally ready to graduate. Windows NT version 3.5 did not fully support DNS, but in Windows NT 4.0 DNS is ready to roll. A Windows NT 4.0 server can be configured as a DNS server.

DNS provides a database and search algorithm for resolving the host name into an IP address. DNS is the service that takes a domain name and resolves it to an IP address for TCP/IP hosts. This is not the same as the WINS server, which resolves NetBIOS computer names. UNIX hosts do not use NetBIOS names; neither do OpenVMS hosts. The DNS server eliminates the need for HOSTS file but this database is not dynamic; therefore all changes must be made manually.

DNS provides a hierarchical naming structure. At the top of the hierarchy is the root domain where all the top-level domains reside. You have probably used a top-level domain name at one time or another, such as .org, .com, .net, or .edu.

You can tell immediately which domain type you're working with by the last domain specification, as shown in Table 1-2.

The word to the left of the domain name is usually the company or organization name; for example: microsoft.com, sri.net, unitedway.org, and stanford.edu. These intuitive names are much easier to remember than a series of numbers.

Simple Network Management Protocol (SNMP)

Microsoft provides an SNMP agent that will track specific TCP/IP events. The SNMP server identifies which events to track using a database structure called a Management Information Database (MIB). When started, the SNMP service collects and delivers these events to the SNMP server. As of this writing, Microsoft has provided the SNMP agent and service on Windows NT 4.0, but not an SNMP server bundled in as a part of the distribution.

TABLE 1-2	**Domain Name**	**Organization**
The Seven Domain Names	COM	Commercial organization
	EDU	Educational institution
	GOV	Government organization
	MIL	Military
	NET	Network support provider
	ORG	Non-profit or other than above
	INT	International organization

CERTIFICATION OBJECTIVE 1.07

Microsoft Implementation of TCP/IP

Microsoft's TCP/IP suite for Windows NT 4.0 was designed for enterprise environments of large government and corporate sites. In addition, it was designed and written to be Internet-ready. This means that when you install Microsoft's TCP/IP component, it is ready for connection to the Internet using Microsoft's Internet products and features.

There have also been some performance enhancements that have made TCP/IP for Windows NT 4.0 more effective than the stack used previously by Microsoft in LAN Manager or Windows for Workgroups. Specific features in this new TCP/IP protocol suite are:

- Standards compliant
- Interoperable
- Portable
- Scaleable
- High performance
- Versatile
- Self-tuning
- Easy to administer
- Adaptable

Redesigned and Rewritten Implementation of 32-Bit TCP/IP

This is a new TCP/IP stack that Microsoft is bundling in with NT 4.0.

Microsoft has taken the design specifications in RFCs and redesigned and rewritten their TCP/IP stack. They have included many services that were unavailable in earlier versions:

- DHCP server and client

- WINS server
- DNS
- PPP/SLIP dialup support
- Point-to-Point Tunneling Protocol (PPTP)
- TCP/IP network printing
- SNMP agent
- NetBIOS interface
- Windows socket interface
- Remote Procedure Call (RPC)
- Network Dynamic Data Exchange (NetDDE)
- Wide Area Network support
- Basic TCP/IP utilities
- Enhanced server software for simple network protocols
- TCP/IP management and diagnostic tools

TCP/IP Server

Microsoft has implemented TCP/IP server features in both the Windows NT and the LAN manager line of products.

Windows NT Server

Windows NT 4.0 contains the newly rewritten Microsoft TCP/IP protocol stack that implements all of the features we've discussed.

Microsoft LAN Manager

The Microsoft LAN manager was developed when the old TCP/IP protocol stack was used. It contained code that was not specifically implemented to support large enterprises.

However, all the newest Microsoft products (Windows NT, Windows 95 and 98, and TCP/IP-32) share the new TCP/IP protocol suite described in this book.

TCP/IP Clients

Microsoft products acting in the client role were also implemented with the rewritten, redesigned TCP/IP code.

Windows NT Workstation

The Windows NT workstation contains all the basic client services code. Windows NT Workstation 3.5x can be designated as a DHCP, WINS, or DNS client and can use basic utilities such as FTP, Telnet, and the majority of the TCP/IP client utilities.

Windows 95

Windows 95 has also implemented the new Microsoft TCP/IP protocol stack. This client has the capability to become a DHCP, WINS, or DNS client and can also use the basic utilities of TCP/IP.

TCP/IP-32 for Windows for Workgroups

The new Microsoft TCP/IP protocol stack was not released in time to be included with Windows for Workgroups. It is distributed as an add-on networking component and is available from the Microsoft Web site: www.microsoft.com.

Internet Information Server (IIS)

We've said that Microsoft's new TCP/IP protocol stack is Internet-ready. Let's discuss what that means to you as a Network Specialist.

Microsoft has created two new products that complement the TCP/IP protocol suite and provide specific features for an Internet or Intranet.

The Internet Information Server (IIS) is released as part of the Windows NT 4.0 distribution. It contains the ability to configure and maintain the following types of Internet services:

■ **FTP (File Transfer Protocol)**   Users connect to this service and copy files to and from the site. Files can be stored in a single directory or a group of directories.

■ **Gopher**   Gopher services can also be used for copying files. Although not widely in use today, support is still available.

■ **World Wide Web (WWW)**   This is the Internet service used to host Web pages written in HyperText Markup Language (HTML). Pages are viewed with a Web browser using HyperText Transfer Protocol (HTTP).

These repositories can then be secured using Microsoft's NTFS file system security. In addition, each Internet service can be maintained separatelyor or not at all. As an Administrator you can control the number of visits allowed at one time, or whether a user must log in to a valid NT account or use a guest account.

Internet Proxy Server

The second of Microsoft's Internet-ready products is the Internet Proxy Server, which is a firewall and Web cache server that installs on the Windows NT 4.0 Server platform. The Proxy Server acts as a gateway with firewall protection between your Intranet and the Internet. Proxy Server 2.0 includes the following features:

■ Dynamic packet filtering

■ Multilayered security

■ Altering and logging

■ Shielding of internal network addresses and Internet server applications

■ Virtual hosting

CERTIFICATION SUMMARY

We've taken a look at TCP/IP and its history, from its inception as part of the DARPA Project to its evolution as the protocol stack of choice for the Internet and Intranets.

TCP/IP's main feature is its modularity, which is defined as the ability to write device drivers or application for a specific portion of the protocol stack without having to write the other protocol layer components. Using the TCP/IP 32-bit addressing scheme, large enterprise-size networks can be built and are fully functional. In addition, TCP/IP allows you interconnection with any vendor software operating system as long as physical connectivity exists.

Requests for Comments are proposals for recommendations, standards, or requirements. RFCs are reviewed by the IAB and its two subcommittees. When an RFC is approved, it is assigned a number and then is classified as Required, Recommended, Elective, Limited Use, or Not Recommended. Copies of RFCs can be retrieved from several Internet locations.

The Network Information Center is responsible for the assignment of TCP/IP addresses, host names, and domain names on the Internet. The NIC has not given out any new addresses since April 1995 and you must contact an Internet Service Provider to connect to the Internet and be assigned an address.

TCP/IP management services such as DHCP, WINS, and DNS have been developed to make the configuration, maintenance, and management of TCP/IP easier.

Microsoft's redesigned, rewritten 32-bit TCP/IP protocol stack includes new features and services for Windows NT 4.0 Server and Workstation, Windows 95 and 98, as well as TCP/IP-32 for Windows for Workgroups.

 # TWO-MINUTE DRILL

- ❑ TCP/IP is the most popular networking protocol suite in the commercial and educational world.
- ❑ Be sure you understand the TCP/IP acronym. You will be tested on it.
- ❑ TCP/IP was developed by the government to build a heterogeneous network across a wide area.
- ❑ The TCP/IP protocols were designed to meet the need for global communication.
- ❑ Each layer in the TCP/IP protocol stack is modular, which means that it communicates with only the layer above or below it.
- ❑ Because TCP/IP is not tied to an operating system, any vendor developing a new operating system with a network component can reference the RFCs to build a TCP/IP component.

❑ TCP/IP's unique addressing mechanism provides for over 4.2 billion addresses. Each host is referred to by its unique 32-bit address.

❑ Remember that the IP address is a 32-bit decimal address, separated into four equal octets by a ".". This number is then converted to binary and used as a unique identifier.

❑ In some TCP/IP implementations a router is also known as a *gateway*.

❑ Routing is the action of forwarding data between subnetworks.

❑ The number of cards that can be placed into an NT server is dependent on whether the hardware has free resources and a free slot. The number of IP addresses assigned to a card is five.

❑ Microsoft's 32-bit version of TCP/IP can communicate with multiple hardware and software platforms.

❑ The coordinating committee for the Internet's design, engineering, and management is known as the *Internet Activities Board* (IAB).

❑ Know the responsibilities of the IAB.

❑ An RFC is an invitation to develop standards, recommendations, or requirements for TCP/IP and the Internet.

❑ The Stanford Research Institute (SRI) maintains an index of RFCs that provides the number, title, authors, issue date, and the total number of hardcopy pages.

❑ Your ISP will assign you an IP address and domain name.

❑ The *Domain Name Service (DNS)* was created so that instead of having to type the IP address of a company's Web site, you can access that site by a user-friendly name.

❑ The DHCP service provides PCs with automatic configuration of the three necessary TCP/IP parameters: IP address, subnet mask, and default gateway.

❑ Microsoft's Windows Internet Name Service provides a NetBIOS-computer-name to IP-address mapping in a database on a server.

❑ A Windows NT 4.0 server can be configured as a DNS server. DNS provides a database and search algorithm for resolving the host name into an IP address.

❏ Microsoft provides an SNMP agent that will track specific TCP/IP
     events. The SNMP server identifies which events to track using a
     database structure called a Management Information Database (MIB).

❏ When you install Microsoft's TCP/IP component, it is ready for
     connection to the Internet using Microsoft's Internet products and
     features.

❏ The Internet Information Server (IIS) is released as part of the
     Windows NT 4.0 distribution.

❏ The Internet Proxy Server is a firewall and Web cache server that
     installs on the Windows NT 4.0 Server platform.

SELF TEST

The following Self Test questions will help you measure your understanding of the material presented in this chapter. Read all the choices carefully, as there may be more than one correct answer. Choose all correct answers for each question.

1. TCP/IP software is available on which of the following:

   A. UNIX
   B. OpenVMS
   C. PC-DOS
   D. All of these

2. (True/False) The Internet is a collection of networks that communicate using the UDP/ARP protocol.

3. Internet protocol software is designed in:

   A. Modules
   B. Layers
   C. Sections
   D. Paragraphs

4. An IP address is:

   A. A 16-bit number written as a 4-decimal number with each 8 bits representing a byte.
   B. A 32-bit octal number separated into 4 bytes.

   C. A 32-bit number normally written as a 4-decimal number with each number representing 8 bits of the address.

5. A Windows NT machine with two network cards is known as a:

   A. Router
   B. Cisco router
   C. Translation gateway
   D. Multi-port repeater

6. The transmission of a message from one network to another through a router is known as:

   A. Redirection
   B. Routed daemon
   C. Routing

7. Which one of the following is not a valid TCP/IP network class:

   A. Class C
   B. Class B
   C. Class F
   D. Class A

8. A private or internal TCP/IP is known as:

   A. The Internet
   B. A private network
   C. A corporate network
   D. An Intranet

9. Which type of machine can a Windows NT Server 4.0 communicate with:

    A. UNIX host

    B. Print server

    C.   OpenVMS system

    D. All the above

10. RFC is an acronym for:

    A. Request Finalized Comments

    B. Recommended Finalized Comments

    C. Request For Consideration

    D. Request for Comments

11. The management service that automatically assigns IP parameters to clients is called:

    A. WINS

    B. DNS

    C. DHCP

    D. DEC

12. The new 32-bit TCP/IP protocol stack is available on which platforms:

    A. Windows 95

    B. Windows NT Workstation 3.5

    C. Windows 3.1

    D. Windows NT Server 4.0

2

TCP/IP
Architecture

L ike every network protocol, TCP/IP has an underlying specific architectural design that makes it function properly. In this chapter we focus on TCP/IP architecture and learn the details of how it works. In the first section, we will discuss the responsibilities of each layer in the Open System Interconnect (OSI) model and in the second section we discuss the TCP/IP model. Next, we will compare the TCP/IP protocol stack to the OSI model. Then we will examine which TCP/IP protocols operate at different levels within the TCP/IP model. Finally, we put it all together and examine how data flows through a network.

CERTIFICATION OBJECTIVE 2.01

OSI Model Layer Responsibilities

Back when networking was a new concept and only starting to be implemented in businesses, it was common to install equipment from different vendors only to find that the applications could not communicate with each other. This was because each vendor used their own method for communication, and it was highly unlikely that an application operating on equipment from one vendor would be able to communicate with equipment from other vendors. It didn't take long for vendors and users to see the need for a standard architecture so that network communication could take place between multiple vendors' equipment.

The members of the International Standards Organization (ISO) are from various companies, industries, and countries. Among other things, they are responsible for creating, maintaining, and implementing standards for hardware and software. ISO introduced a set of specifications in 1978 to standardize the architecture used to communicate on a network using devices from different vendors. In 1984, ISO revised the specifications and released them with the name Open Systems Interconnect (OSI) model. The OSI model is the best known and most widely used set of specifications used by vendors when they design equipment for networking environments.

OSI Layers

The OSI model consists of seven layers, as shown in Figure 2-1. A common mnemonic to help you remember the layers from top to bottom is, "**A**ll **P**eople **S**eem **T**o **N**eed **D**ata **P**rocessing." There are many more phrases, and you can always invent your own. Each of the seven layers of the OSI model exists as an independent module and performs a well-defined function as described later in this section. All the layers in the OSI model work in a hierarchy. If a computer is sending data, each layer receives the data from the layer above it, performs any applicable work on that data, and adds on its own information regarding that data. The layer then sends the data on down to the next layer. If a computer is receiving data, each layer receives data from the layer below it, strips away the applicable data, and passes it on to the next higher layer.

Each layer communicates and works with the functions of the layers that are immediately above and below it. For example, looking at Figure 2-1, you see that the Network layer sits between the Transport and Data Link layers. This means that the Network layer will communicate and work with both the Transport and Data Link layers. The Network layer cannot communicate directly with any other layer of the OSI model.

The layers are strategically organized. The higher the layer resides in the model, the more complex the task it performs. Each layer is separated from the

FIGURE 2-1

OSI model layer stack
showing the seven layers

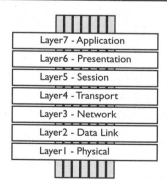

layers on each side of it by an *interface*, which defines which services are offered and how they will be accessed. Data passes from one layer, through the interface, to the next layer where additional processing is performed as necessary. The layers are organized so that it seems like each layer is communicating with the same layer on another computer using virtual communication as shown in Figure 2-2. However, communication is actually taking place between neighboring layers on only one computer.

As data passes from one layer to the next layer, additional formatting or addressing is added from the sending computer so that it can be transmitted successfully. When the data arrives at the receiving computer, the data passes through the layers in reverse order. Formatting and addressing information is stripped away at each layer as it is passed up the layers until it arrives at the seventh layer, the Application layer, where it is returned back to its original state that can be interpreted by the receiving computer.

FIGURE 2-2

OSI layer relationships

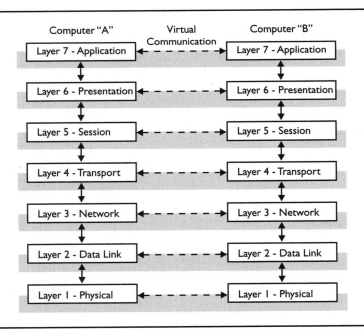

FROM THE CLASSROOM

Understanding Layers

We say that each layer is dedicated only to its own task and is unaware of the responsibilities of the layers above and below it.

To understand the layers model used by OSI and TCP/IP, let's look at an example from real life.

You and some friends start a company. You get together and think through the things that must be done. You answer questions such as:

■ What needs to be done?

■ In what order will they be done?

■ Who will do these things?

■ How do they relate or interact with each other?

After spending hours of brainstorming, you group these tasks into departments.

Each department has its own task list and you require that it focus only on that particular task. Each department will have to trust and rely on the other departments to do their designated tasks.

Similarly, OSI and TCP/IP layers are designed and implemented just like your hypothetical departments; that is, they are concerned only with their own specific tasks.

—*By D. Lynn White, MCT, MCSE*

The only OSI layer that can communicate directly with its equivalent on another computer system is Layer 1, the Physical layer. All other layers must communicate down the layers from the sending computer, across the media, and up the layers on the receiving computer. For example, if the Network layer had information for the Network layer of another computer system it would go from the Network layer to the Data Link and Physical layers of the sending computer, across the media, then up the Physical and Data Link layers to the Network layer of the receiving computer.

We will now discuss the purpose of each layer in the OSI model.

Application Layer

The Application layer is the top layer of the OSI model. It is used to allow applications to access network services. It handles general network access, flow control, and error recovery. Some of the functions it supports are:

- Accessing remote files
- Accessing remote printers
- Accessing remote databases
- Electronic mail

Presentation Layer

The next layer down is the Presentation layer which is located at layer 6. It is the translator for the network as it determines the format used to exchange data among the computers on the network. Some of its functions are:

- Protocol conversion
- Data translation
- Data encryption
- Data compression
- Conversion of the character set

Session Layer

Layer 5 is the Session layer, which establishes a communications connection between processes running on different computers. It performs name recognition and related functions—for example, user authentication and resource-access security that are needed to allow processes to communicate over the network. To ensure that all data gets sent, it uses checkpoints placed in the data stream to provide for synchronization. In the case of network failure the only data that needs to be sent again is the data after the last checkpoint. The Session layer is also responsible for controlling when and for how long each side transmits.

Transport Layer

Layer 4 is the Transport layer, which is responsible for ensuring that all the data is delivered in the correct sequence, error free, with no losses. It is the

Transport layer that breaks up large messages into smaller packets for delivery. Some of the other functions provided by the Transport layer are:

- Error handling
- Flow control, by notifying the transmitting computer to not transmit when the receiving computer has no available receive buffers

Network Layer

Layer 3, the Network layer, is responsible for determining the route that is taken from the transmitting computer to the receiving computer. It is also responsible for addressing messages and the translation of logical addresses into physical addresses. The Network layer determines what path the data should take based upon several factors, including the condition of the network and the priority of service.

Data Link Layer

Layer 2 is the Data Link layer, which is responsible for providing error-free transfer of frames from one computer to another using the Physical layer. A *frame* is a bundle of information sent as a single entity. Some of the other functions provided by the Data Link layer are:

- Transmitting and receiving frames sequentially
- Providing frame acknowledgment for frames it receives
- Retransmitting frames that are not acknowledged by the receiving computer

Physical Layer

The Physical layer is located at layer 1, the bottom of the OSI model. The Physical layer handles the unstructured, raw, bit-stream data that is transferred over a physical medium. It also defines how the physical medium, or cable, is attached to the Network Interface Card (NIC). It does that by determining how many pins are in the connector that is being used and also the function of each of the pins. The Physical layer sends out bits equaling 1s and 0s and determines how long each bit lasts and how it is translated into the suitable optical or electrical impulse for the network cable.

Remember the names and functions of each of the seven layers of the OSI model.

CERTIFICATION OBJECTIVE 2.02

TCP/IP Model Responsibilities

The TCP/IP model was not created by a standards developing committee but rather from research funded by the Department of Defense (DOD) Advanced Research Projects Agency (ARPA). ARPA begin working on TCP/IP technology in the mid 1970s with the protocols and architecture taking on their current structure in the 1977-1979 time frame.

TCP/IP Protocol Stack Layers

The TCP/IP protocol stack is organized into four layers as shown in Figure 2-3. Each of the four layers of the TCP/IP model exists as an independent module and performs a well-defined function as described later in this section. Each layer communicates and works with the functions of the layers that are immediately above and below it. For example, looking at Figure 2-3 you see that the Transport layer sits between the Application and Internet layers. This means that the Transport layer will communicate and work with both the Application and Internet layers. The Transport layer cannot communicate directly with any other layer of the TCP/IP model.

FIGURE 2-3

TCP/IP protocol stack

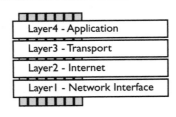

TCP/IP Application Layer

The Application layer is the highest layer in the TCP/IP model. It is used by applications to access services across a TCP/IP network. Some of the applications that operate at this layer are a Web browser, file transfer program (FTP), and a remote login program. The Application layer passes data to the next layer in the stack, the Transport layer.

TCP/IP Transport Layer

The Transport layer is located at layer 3 of the TCP/IP model. The main responsibility of the Transport layer is to provide communication from one application to another application. If several application programs are running on a computer then the Transport layer has to figure out how to control the data from each application so that it can be sent to the next lower layer correctly. The Transport layer adds the following additional information to each data packet:

- The identity of the application sending the data
- The identity of the application that should receive the data
- A checksum

The system that receives the data uses the checksum to verify that all of the data arrived. It also uses the identity of the receiving application so it can route the data appropriately.

TCP/IP Internet Layer

The Internet layer is located at layer two of the TCP/IP model. It is responsible for handling the communication from one computer to another computer. It accepts a request to send data from the Transport layer. It accepts the data, encapsulates it in a datagram, and then uses a routing algorithm to determine the best method for delivering it. After determining the best way to route the datagram, the Internet layer passes it to the Network Interface layer.

TCP/IP Network Interface Layer

The Network Interface layer is the lowest level in the TCP/IP model. It accepts the datagram from the Internet layer and transmits it over the network. To accomplish this task the Network Interface layer must be fully aware of the network hardware that it is using. The Network Interface layer is also responsible for translating an Internet address into a hardware address.

Remember the names and functions of each of the four layers of the TCP/IP model.

TCP/IP Protocol Stack Compared to OSI Layers

The TCP/IP model can be compared loosely to the OSI model as shown in Figure 2-4. The Application layer of the TCP/IP model performs the same functions as layers 5, 6, and 7 of the OSI model. The Transport layers in both models perform the same functions. The Internet layer of the TCP/IP model equates to the same functions as the Network layer of the OSI model. The Network Interface layer of the TCP/IP model compares to the functions of layers 1 and 2 of the OSI model.

Remember which layers of the TCP/IP model equate to the layers of the OSI model.

FIGURE 2-4

TCP/IP model compared to OSI model

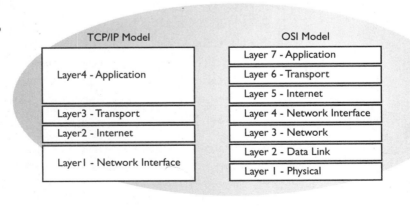

TCP/IP Model	OSI Model
Layer4 - Application	Layer 7 - Application
	Layer 6 - Transport
	Layer 5 - Internet
Layer3 - Transport	Layer 4 - Network Interface
Layer2 - Internet	Layer 3 - Network
Layer1 - Network Interface	Layer 2 - Data Link
	Layer 1 - Physical

TCP/IP Protocol Suite

Contained within the four layers of the TCP/IP model are several protocols that direct how computers connect and communicate using TCP/IP. Even though the protocol suite is called TCP/IP, many other protocols are available besides the TCP and IP protocols.

Identify Protocols by Layers

Each protocol can be identified with a layer of the TCP/IP model. We will examine several of the protocols available at each layer.

Application Layer

The Application layer supports both the NetBIOS interface and the Windows Sockets interface.

NETBIOS   NetBIOS over TCP/IP allows NetBIOS client and server applications to be run over the Wide Area Network (WAN). Some of the applications that are NetBIOS-over-TCP-compliant are the Windows NT browser service, netlogon service, messenger service, workstation service, and server service.

WINDOWS SOCKETS   Windows Sockets is a programming interface based on the "socket" interface that was originally developed at the University of California at Berkeley. Windows Sockets includes enhancements that take advantage of the message-driven characteristics of Windows. Windows NT 4.0 supports version 2.2.0, which was published in May 1996. Some of the common protocols that use Windows Sockets are telnet, ftp, and http.

Transport Layer

The Transport layer consists of two protocols, the Transmission Control Protocol (TCP) and the User Datagram Protocol (UDP). Both TCP and UDP support ports. When a program sends or receives data on a TCP/IP network, it has to connect to a port. Ports are identified in the header of both the TCP and UDP protocols. The header contains two 16-bit numbers that identify the source port and the destination port. The Transport layer examines the port numbers in the header and delivers the data to the correct port.

TCP   TCP is one of the protocols that the suite is named for. TCP provides a reliable, connection-based delivery service. Successful delivery of packets is guaranteed by the TCP protocol. It uses a checksum to ensure that data is sequenced correctly. If a TCP packet is lost or corrupted during transmission, TCP resends a good packet. The reliability of TCP is necessary for critical services, such as electronic mail. However, the reliability does not come cheaply as TCP headers have additional overhead added to them. The overhead is necessary to guarantee successful delivery of the data. Another factor to remember about TCP is that the protocol requires the recipient to acknowledge the successful receipt of data. Of course, all the acknowledgments, known as ACKs, generate additional traffic on the network, which causes a reduction in the amount of data that is passed for a given time frame.

The TCP header consists of six words of 32 bits each. The seventh word is the actual data. Figure 2-5 shows the format of a TCP header.

Table 2-1 describes each of the items that are contained in the TCP header.

UDP   UDP offers a connectionless datagram service that is an unreliable "best effort" delivery. The arrival of datagrams is not guaranteed by UDP nor does it promise that the delivered packets are in the correct sequence.

FIGURE 2-5

Transmission control protocol header

Word	Bit										
	0 1 2 3 4 5 6 7 8 9 10 11 12 13 14 15			16 17 18 19 20 21 22 23 24 25 26 27 28 29 30 31							
0	Source Port			Destination Port							
1	Sequence Number										
2	Acknowledgment Number										
3	Data Length	Reserved	URG ACK PSH RST SYN FIN	Window							
4	Checksum			Urgent Pointer							
5	Options									Padding	
6	Data										

Name	Bit Size	Purpose
TABLE 2-1 Description of the Contents in a TCP Header		
Source Port	16	The source port number.
Destination Port	16	The destination port number.
Sequence Number	32	The sequence number of the first data octet in this segment unless the SYN control bit is set. If the SYN control bit is set, then the sequence number is the initial sequence number (ISN) and the first data octet is ISN+1.
Acknowledgment Number	32	This portion of the header contains the value of the next sequence number that the sender of the segment is expecting to receive if the ACK control bit is set. Once a connection is established, this is always sent.
Data Length	4	The number of 32-bit words in the TCP header. This indicates where the data begins.
Reserved	6	Reserved for future use. It has to be zero.
Flags	6	The bits from left to right. URG: Urgent Pointer field significant ACK: Acknowledgment field significant PSH: Push function RST: Reset the connection SYN: Synchronize sequence numbers FIN: No more data from sender
Window	16	The number of data octets beginning with the one indicated in the acknowledgment field, which the sender of this segment is willing to accept.
Checksum	16	The checksum field is the 16-bit 1s complement of the 1s complement sum of all 16-bit words in the header and data.
Urgent Pointer	16	This field communicates the current value of the urgent pointer as a positive offset from the sequence number in this segment. The urgent pointer points to the sequence number of the octet following the urgent data. This field is interpreted only in segments that have the URG control bit set.

TABLE 2-1 Description of the Contents in a TCP Header (*continued*)

Name	Bit Size	Purpose
Options	variable	Options may occupy space at the end of the TCP header and are a multiple of 8 bits in length. All options are included in the checksum.
Padding	variable	The TCP header padding is used to ensure that the TCP header ends and data begins on a 32-bit boundary. The padding is composed of zeros.

Applications that don't require an acknowledgment of receipt of data use the User Datagram Protocol.

The UDP header consists of two words of 32 bits each. The third word is the actual data. Figure 2-6 shows the format of a UDP header.

Table 2-2 describes each of the items that are contained in the UDP header.

exam Watch

Keep in mind the key differences between the Transmission Control Protocol and User Datagram Protocol.

Internet Layer

The Internet layer consists of two protocols, the Internet Protocol (IP) and the Internet Control Message Protocol (ICMP).

IP IP is the other protocol that the suite is named for. It is a vital link in the suite as all information that is sent using the TCP/IP protocol suite must use it. IP provides packet delivery for all other protocols within the suite. It is a connectionless delivery system that makes a "best effort" attempt to deliver the packets to the correct destination. IP does not guarantee delivery nor does it promise that the IP packets will be received in the order they were sent. IP

FIGURE 2-6 User Datagram Protocol header

Word	Bit																														
	0	1	2	3	4	5	6	7	8	9	10	11	12	13	14	15	16	17	18	19	20	21	22	23	24	25	26	27	28	29	30	31
0	Source Port																Destination Port															
1	Length																Checksum															
2	Data																															

TABLE 2-2

Description of
the Contents in a
UDP Header

Name	Bit Size	Purpose
Source Port	16	The source port number.
Destination Port	16	The destination port number.
Length	16	The length in octets of this user datagram including the header and data.
Checksum	16	The checksum field is the 16-bit 1s complement of the 1s complement sum of all 16-bit words in the header and data. The checksum is an option in the UDP header and not always used.

does use a checksum but it confirms only the integrity of the IP header. Confirmation of the integrity of data contained within an IP packet can be accomplished only through higher level protocols.

The IP header consists of six words of 32 bits each. The seventh word is the actual data. Figure 2-7 shows the format of a IP header.

Table 2-3 describes each of the items that are contained in the IP header.

ICMP ICMP allows systems on a TCP/IP network to share status and error information. You can use the status information to detect network trouble. ICMP messages are encapsulated within IP datagrams, so they may be routed throughout an internetwork. Two of the most common usages of ICMP messages are *PING* and *TRACERT*.

You can use PING to send *ICMP Echo Requests* to an IP address and wait for ICMP Echo Responses. PING reports the time interval between sending the request and receiving the response. Using PING you can determine

FIGURE 2-7

Internet Protocol header

Word	Bit																															
	0	1	2	3	4	5	6	7	8	9	10	11	12	13	14	15	16	17	18	19	20	21	22	23	24	25	26	27	28	29	30	31
0	Version				IHL				Type of Service								Total Length															
1	Identification																Flags			Fragment Offset												
2	Time to Live								Protocol								Header Checksum															
3	Source Address																															
4	Destination Address																															
5	Options																								Padding							
6	Data																															

Name	Bit Size	Purpose
Version	4	The format of the Internet header.
IHL	4	Internet header length is the length of the Internet header in 32-bit words. The minimum value for a correct header is 5.
Type of Service	8	An indication of the abstract parameters of the quality of service desired.
Total Length	16	The length of the datagram, measured in octets, including Internet header and data.
Identification	16	An identifying value assigned by the sender to aid in assembling the fragments of a datagram.
Flags	3	Various control flags. Bit 0: reserved, must be zero Bit 1: (DF) 0 = may fragment, 1 = don't fragment. Bit 2: (MF) 0 = last fragment, 1 = more fragments.
Fragment Offset	13	Indicates where in the datagram this fragment belongs. The fragment offset is measured in units of 8 octets (64 bits). The first fragment has offset zero.
Time to Live	8	Indicates the maximum time the datagram is allowed to remain in the Internet system. If this field contains the value zero, then the datagram has to be destroyed.
Protocol	8	Indicates the next level protocol used in the data portion of the Internet datagram.
Header Checksum	16	A checksum on the header only. Since some header fields change, such as the time-to-live field, this is recomputed and verified at each point that the Internet header is processed.
Source Address	32	The source address.
Destination Address	32	The destination address.

TABLE 2-3

Description of
the Contents in an
IP Header (*continued*)

Name	Bit Size	Purpose
Options	variable	The options may or may not appear in datagrams. A couple of the available options are: Security: used to carry security, compartmentation, and handling restriction codes compatible with DOD requirements. Record Route: used to trace the route an Internet datagram takes.
Padding	variable	The Internet header padding is used to ensure that the Internet header ends on a 32-bit boundary. The padding is zero.

whether a particular IP system on your network is functioning correctly. There are many different options that can be used with the PING utility. These are covered in depth in Chapter 3.

TRACERT traces the path taken to a particular host. It can be very useful when troubleshooting internetworks. TRACERT sends ICMP echo requests to an IP address while it increments the time-to-live field in the IP header by a count of one after starting at one and then analyzing the ICMP errors that get returned. Each succeeding echo request should get one further into the network before the time-to-live field reaches 0 and an *ICMP Time Exceeded* error is returned by the router attempting to forward it.

Exercises 2-1 and 2-2 give you the opportunity to use both the PING and TRACERT utilities.

EXERCISE 2-1

PING — to Test Communication with a Distant Computer

1. Log on as Administrator to a system that has the TCP/IP Protocol installed and is connected to the Internet.

2. Click the Start button and select Programs | Command Prompt.

3. At the command prompt type **PING 207.159.134.58**. Was your PING successful?

4. Try to PING some of these other IP addresses: **206.66.12.43, 165.121.81, 206.151.75.79, 199.1.11.15, 199.227.250.70**. Did you PING them successfully?

TRACERT — to Trace the Route Taken to a Distant Computer

1. Log on as Administrator to a system that has the TCP/IP Protocol installed and is connected to the Internet.

2. Click the Start button and select Programs | Command Prompt.

3. At the command prompt type **TRACERT 207.159.134.58**. How many hops did it take to arrive at your destination?

4. Try running TRACERT on some of these other IP addresses: **206.66.12.43, 165.121.81, 206.151.75.79, 199.1.11.15, 199.227.250.70**.

Network Interface Layer

The Network Interface layer not only uses the Address Resolution Protocol (ARP) but it is also the location that the Network Driver Interface Specification (NDIS) 4.0 works from.

ARP   ARP is used to provide IP address-to-physical address resolution for IP packets. To accomplish this feat, ARP sends out a broadcast message with an *ARP request packet* in it that contains the IP address of the system it is trying to find. All systems on the local network detect the broadcast message and the system that owns the IP address ARP is looking for replies by sending its physical address to the originating system in an *ARP reply packet*. The physical/IP address combo is then stored in the ARP cache of the originating system for future use.

All systems maintain an ARP cache that includes their own IP address-to-physical address mapping. The ARP cache is always checked for an IP address-to-physical address mapping before initiating a broadcast.

You can see the contents of your ARP cache by using the ARP utility. There are many different options that can be used with the ARP utility. These are covered in depth in Chapter 3. Exercise 2-3 shows you how to check the contents of your ARP cache.

ARP — To view What Is in the Address Table

1. Log on as Administrator to a system that has the TCP/IP Protocol installed.

2. Click the Start button and select Programs | Command Prompt.

3. At the command prompt type **ARP -a**. The entries in your cache are displayed.

   Figure 2-8 shows entries in the ARP cache of my system.

NDIS 4.0   NDIS is a standard that allows multiple network adapters and multiple protocols to coexist on the same computer. By providing a standard interface, NDIS permits the high-level protocol components to be independent of the network interface card. All transport drivers call the NDIS interface to access network interface cards.

Figure 2-9 shows a sampling of the protocols available on the four TCP/IP layers.

FIGURE 2-8

The ARP cache for a system

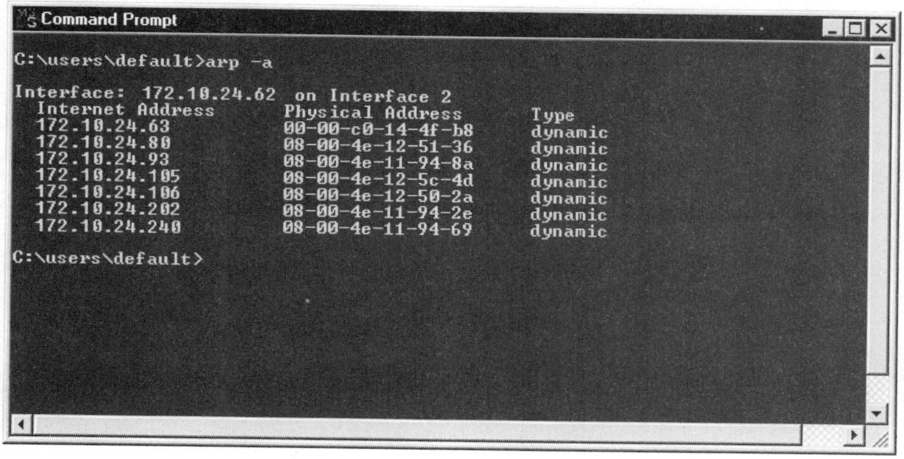

```
Command Prompt                                                    _ □ ×

C:\users\default>arp -a

Interface:  172.10.24.62  on Interface 2
  Internet Address      Physical Address      Type
  172.10.24.63          00-00-c0-14-4f-b8     dynamic
  172.10.24.80          08-00-4e-12-51-36     dynamic
  172.10.24.93          08-00-4e-11-94-8a     dynamic
  172.10.24.105         08-00-4e-12-5c-4d     dynamic
  172.10.24.106         08-00-4e-12-50-2a     dynamic
  172.10.24.202         08-00-4e-11-94-2e     dynamic
  172.10.24.240         08-00-4e-11-94-69     dynamic

C:\users\default>
```

FIGURE 2-9

Protocols by TCP/IP layers

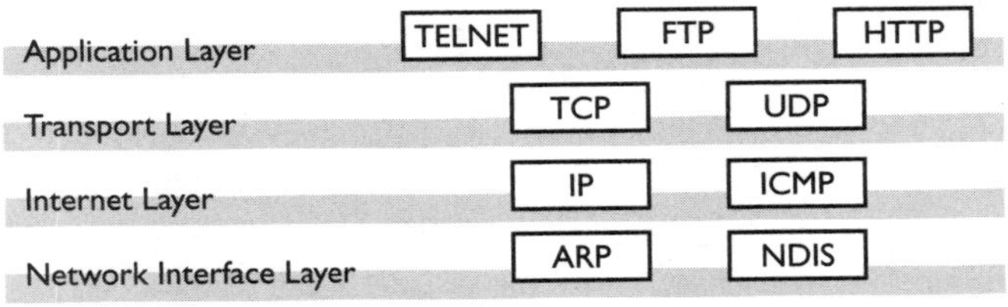

Application Layer	TELNET	FTP	HTTP
Transport Layer		TCP	UDP
Internet Layer		IP	ICMP
Network Interface Layer		ARP	NDIS

Now that you know about the different protocols used by the TCP/IP layers, here is a quick reference for possible scenario questions, and the appropriate answer:

QUESTIONS AND ANSWERS

Marissa says that it take her "forever" to reach a host in another city...	Use TRACERT to see the path her machine may be using to contact the other machine. You may be able to isolate a routing problem.
Martha is having a problem with inconsistent data she is receiving from a network application...	It is possible that the network application uses UDP instead of TCP. Since UDP provides unreliable "best effort" delivery, some data may be lost. You need to see if you can get her an equivalent network application that uses TCP to ensure that all data she needs arrives safely.
James from the sales department tells you that he cannot communicate with a machine in the accounting department...	You need to run the PING utility to see if the computer is operating correctly on the network.

CERTIFICATION OBJECTIVE 2.04

Network Data Flow

In the previous sections, we have seen the layers that make up the OSI and TCP/IP models and the purpose of each of those layers. Now it is time to see what happens as data begins to flow from one layer to the next.

How A Message Flows Through the TCP/IP Protocol Layers

The sending process passes data to the Application layer, which attaches an application header as shown in Figure 2-10.

The Application layer passes the packet to the Transport layer, which in turn adds its header to the packet as shown in Figure 2-11.

The Transport layer passes the packet to the Internet layer, which in turn adds its header to the packet as shown in Figure 2-12.

The Internet layer passes the packet to the Network Interface layer where it is actually transmitted to the receiving computer as shown in Figure 2-13.

On the receiving computer, the different headers are stripped off, one by one, as the packet goes up the layers until it finally reaches the receiving process.

FIGURE 2-10

Data passed to the
Application layer

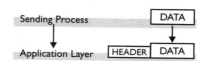

FIGURE 2-11

Application data passed to
the Transport layer

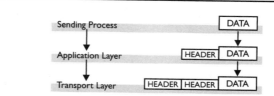

FIGURE 2-12

Transport data passed to
Internet layer

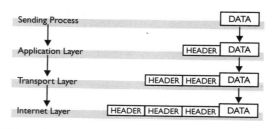

FIGURE 2-13

Data leaving the network interface layer, headed to the receiving computer

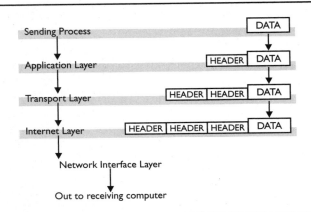

CERTIFICATION SUMMARY

The International Standards Organization developed the Open Systems Interconnect model. The OSI model consists of seven different layers that work as a hiearchy. Each layer can communicate only with the layer directly above or below it. The seven layers of the OSI model are Application, Presentation, Session, Transport, Network, Data Link, and Physical.

Development of the TCP/IP model was funded by the Advanced Research Projects Agency of the Department of Defense. It consists of four different layers that can be equated to the seven layers of the OSI model: Application, Transport, Internet, and Network Interface.

The TCP/IP protocol suite is actually made up of more protocols than just TCP and IP. Some of the other protocols are the Address Resolution Protocol, User Datagram Protocol, File Transfer Protocol, and the HyperText Transfer Protocol. These protocols, as well as others, operate on specific layers of the TCP/IP model.

As data flows from the sending process down the layers of the sending computer, each layer will add its own header prior to handing the packet to the next layer. When the packet starts flowing up the layers at the receiving computer, the headers will get stripped off at each layer until the packet arrives at the receiving process.

✓ TWO-MINUTE DRILL

- ❑ International Standards Organization (ISO) is responsible for creating, maintaining, and implementing standards for hardware and software.

- ❑ The OSI model consists of seven layers.

- ❑ A common mnemonic to help you remember the layers from top to bottom is, "**A**ll **P**eople **S**eem **T**o **N**eed **D**ata **P**rocessing."

- ❑ The Application layer is the top layer of the OSI model. It is used to allow applications to access network services. It handles general network access, flow control, and error recovery.

- ❑ The next layer down is the Presentation layer, which is located at layer 6. It is the translator for the network as it determines the format used to exchange data among the computers on the network.

- ❑ Layer 5 is the Session layer, which establishes a communications connection between processes running on different computers. It performs name recognition and related functions.

- ❑ Layer 4 is the Transport layer, which is responsible for ensuring that all the data is delivered in the correct sequence, error free, with no losses. It is the Transport layer that breaks up large messages into smaller packets for delivery.

- ❑ Layer 3, the Network layer, is responsible for determining the route that is taken from the transmitting computer to the receiving computer. It is also responsible for addressing messages and the translation of logical addresses into physical addresses.

- ❑ Layer 2 is the Data Link layer, which is responsible for providing error-free transfer of frames from one computer to another using the Physical layer.

- ❑ The Physical layer is located at layer 1, the bottom of the OSI model. The Physical layer handles the unstructured, raw, bit-stream data that is transferred over a physical medium. It also defines how the physical medium, or cable, is attached to the Network Interface Card.

- ❑ Remember the names and functions of each of the seven layers of the OSI model.

- ❑ The TCP/IP protocol stack is organized into four layers. Each of the four layers of the TCP/IP model exists as an independent module and performs a well-defined function.

❑ The Application layer supports both the NetBIOS interface and the Windows Sockets interface.

❑ NetBIOS over TCP/IP allows NetBIOS client and server applications to be run over the Wide Area Network (WAN).

❑ The Transport layer consists of two protocols, the Transmission Control Protocol (TCP) and the User Datagram Protocol (UDP).

❑ TCP provides a reliable, connection-based delivery service.

❑ UDP offers a connectionless datagram service that is an unreliable "best effort" delivery.

❑ Keep in mind the key differences between the Transmission Control Protocol and User Datagram Protocol.

❑ The Internet layer consists of two protocols, the Internet Protocol (IP) and the Internet Control Message Protocol (ICMP).

❑ IP provides packet delivery for all other protocols within the suite.

❑ ICMP allows systems on an TCP/IP network to share status and error information.

❑ Two of the most common usages of ICMP messages are *PING* and *TRACERT*.

❑ The Network Interface layer not only uses the Address Resolution Protocol (ARP) but it is also the location that the Network Driver Interface Specification (NDIS) 4.0 works from.

❑ ARP is used to provide IP address-to-physical address resolution for IP packets.

❑ NDIS is a standard that allows multiple network adapters and multiple protocols to coexist on the same computer.

❑ Remember the names and functions of each of the four layers of the TCP/IP model.

❑ Remember which layers of the TCP/IP model equate to the layers of the OSI model.

❑ Contained within the four layers of the TCP/IP model are several protocols that direct how computers connect and communicate using TCP/IP.

SELF TEST

The following Self Test questions will help you measure your understanding of the material presented in this chapter. Read all the choices carefully, as there may be more than one correct answer. Choose all correct answers for each question.

1. What layer of the OSI model does an electronic mail program use?

    A. Session

    B. Network

    C. Transport

    D. Application

2. How many layers are in the TCP/IP model?

    A. 2

    B. 4

    C. 7

    D. 9

3. What layer of the TCP/IP model does the User Datagram Protocol operate from?

    A. Transport

    B. Internet

    C. Network Interface

    D. Application

4. From the sending computer, what does each layer of the TCP/IP model add to the data when it receives it?

    A. A packet

    B. A frame

    C. A header

    D. A footer

5. The Application layer of the TCP/IP model equates to what layer(s) of the OSI model?

    A. Application

    B. Network

    C. Session

    D. Presentation

6. What protocol provides a reliable, connection-based delivery service?

    A. ARP

    B. TCP

    C. UDP

    D. IP

7. How many layers are in the OSI model?

    A. 2

    B. 4

    C. 7

    D. 9

8. What protocol(s) is available at the Internet layer of the TCP/IP model?

    A. TCP

    B. IP

    C. UDP

    D. ICMP

9. What protocol(s) provide(s) a connectionless datagram service that is an unreliable "best effort" delivery?

A. ARP

B. TCP

C. UDP

D. IP

10. What is the IP checksum used for?

   A. It checks the integrity of the IP header only.

   B. It checks the integrity of the IP header and data.

   C. It checks the integrity of the data only.

   D. IP does not use a checksum.

11. What layer of the TCP/IP model does the HyperText Transfer Protocol operate from?

   A. Session

   B. Physical

   C. Application

   D. Internet

12. What is the most common usage(s) of ICMP messages?

   A. ARP

   B. PING

   C. NDIS

   D. TRACERT

13. What layer of the OSI model performs data encryption?

   A. Application

   B. Physical

   C. Presentation

   D. Data Link

14. What makes up a TCP header?

A. 6 words of 32 bits each

B. 32 words of 6 bits each

C. 7 words of 16 bits each

D. 16 words of 7 bits each

15. What protocol provides IP address-to-physical address resolution for IP packets?

   A. ICMP

   B. IP

   C. NDIS

   D. ARP

16. What layer of the OSI model is responsible for providing error-free transfer of frames from one computer to another computer using the Physical layer?

   A. Transport

   B. Network

   C. Data Link

   D. Session

17. What is layer 4 of the TCP/IP model?

   A. Network

   B. Application

   C. Internet

   D. Transport

18. What is layer 5 of the OSI model?

   A. Session

   B. Presentation

   C. Physical

   D. Data Link

3

Internet Addressing

I n order for your computer to communicate using TCP/IP it must have a way of identifying itself as a unique entity on the network. It does this by using a 32-bit address. In the first sections of this chapter we will dissect the 32-bit address and see how IP addresses are broken down into different classes. In the third section we will investigate how an Internet Protocol address is resolved and converted into a hardware address. In the fourth section you will learn how to configure TCP/IP on your Windows NT Server. Finally, I will show you how to use a couple of different utilities to test your TCP/IP configuration.

CERTIFICATION OBJECTIVE 3.01

Understanding the Internet Protocol 32-Bit Address

The TCP/IP suite consists of several different protocols and the 32-bit address relates to the Internet Protocol (IP). In this section we will see how the 32-bit IP address is separated into a network portion and a host portion by using a subnet mask.

32-Bit Address

Just as a street address identifies a house located in your town, an IP address uniquely identifies a system located on your network. Figure 3-1 shows some examples of 32-bit IP addresses.

The Four Octets
As you see in Figure 3-1, each computer system is identified by a unique set of numbers, which are broken down into four separate octets. An *octet* is a unit of data that is 8 bits in length. It works like this: if you take the four octets and multiply them by 8 bits you will arrive at the 32-bit address. The two common methods of displaying the four octets are binary format and dotted-decimal notation.

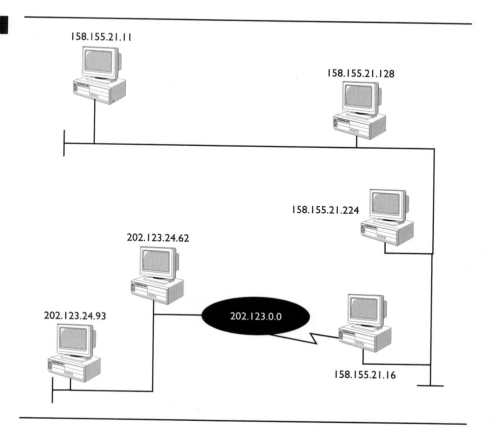

FIGURE 3-1

32-bit IP addresses

Binary Representation

The binary representation of a 32-bit address is broken down into four groups of binary digits as shown in Figure 3-2. Although your computer system operates on binary, it would be difficult for us humans to remember binary representations of IP addresses. Imagine if you asked a coworker what his IP address was and he said, in machine-gun speed, "00001010 00000001 11100000 01100000."

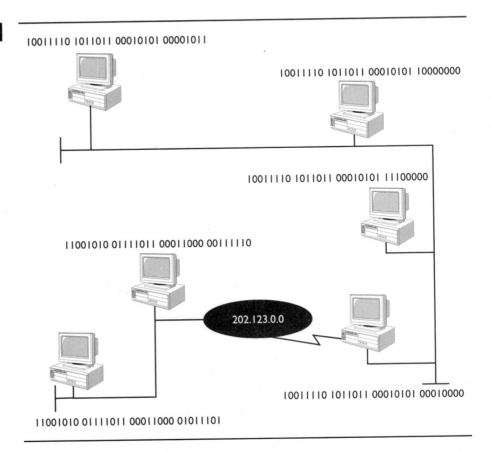

FIGURE 3-2

Binary address
representations

Dotted-Decimal Representation

Because it is too cumbersome for humans to communicate IP addresses
in a binary format, dotted-decimal representation is commonly used.
Dotted-decimal consists of four 8-bit fields written in base 10 with dots (periods)
separating the fields. Each 8-bit field is represented by a number ranging from 0
to 255. Figure 3-3 compares dotted-decimal representation to the equivalent
binary representation.

Converting an address from dotted-decimal to binary is actually a very easy
process. Each of the eight bits can be in either a 1 or 0 condition. The place

FIGURE 3-3

Dotted-decimal and binary representation

Dotted Decimal		Binary
197.18.42.78		11000101 00010010 00101010 01001110
223.18.75.34		11011111 00010010 01001011 00100010
29.18.124.61		00011101 00010010 01111100 00111101
130.1.201.12		10000010 00000001 11001001 00001100
158.157.21.14		10011110 10011101 00010101 00001110

occupied by the 1 in the 8 bits dictates its value. The Most Significant Bit (MSB) is at the far left of the octet while the Least Significant Bit (LSB) is at the far right of the octet. Figure 3-4 shows the values for the different placeholders starting with the MSB and also show examples of converting from binary to decimal and decimal to binary.

FIGURE 3-4

Binary to decimal and decimal to binary conversion

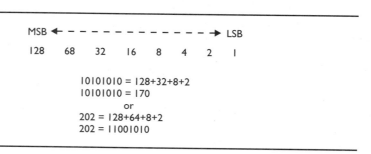

MSB ← – – – – – – – – – – → LSB

| 128 | 68 | 32 | 16 | 8 | 4 | 2 | 1 |

10101010 = 128+32+8+2
10101010 = 170
or
202 = 128+64+8+2
202 = 11001010

Network ID

The network ID is the portion of the 32-bit IP address that identifies which network a particular system is on. It is determined by performing an AND operation of the subnet mask and the IP address. The AND operation is a function of Boolean algebra. Subnet masks will be covered later in the chapter.

Internet Network IDs Assigned by InterNIC

The *Internet Network Information Center* (InterNIC) is the agency responsible for issuing all network IDs that will be used on the Internet. InterNIC operates under contract from the National Science Foundation (NSF) as the central authority for assigning the network ID portion of the IP address. This ensures that all addresses used on the Internet are unique and conflicts will not occur. The size of your organization dictates which network ID the InterNIC will issue to you. Later in this chapter you will see the different network IDs that are available.

Intranet Network IDs Assigned by Network Manager

The InterNIC assigns a network ID only for Internet IP addresses. An Intranet ID is assigned by your Network Manager. However, there are three address ranges set aside for systems not connected to the Internet (RFC 1597):

- 10.0.0.0 through 10.255.255.255
- 172.16.0.0 through 172.31.255.255
- 192.168.0.0 through 192.168.255.255

It is not wise to use an IP address from these reserved ranges because you may run into complications if you ever decide to put your network on the Internet. To connect your systems to the Internet, file the appropriate paperwork with the InterNIC and obtain your own unique network ID.

FROM THE CLASSROOM

Host IDs and Network IDs

Host IDs must be unique to the local network ID. When you assign valid host IDs, there are no rules in making the assignments. Many network administrators over the years have opted to use groups in handing out host IDs in order to easily identify the host.

The practice has been to assign host IDs in groups based on host type and give routers the lowest range; for example

w.x.y.1 through w.x.y.25	Routers
w.x.200.1 through w.x.200.254	NT servers
w.x.240.1 through w.x.240.254	UNIX hosts

Microsoft strongly recommends that you follow this practice in assigning host IDs.

—By D. Lynn White, MCT, MCSE

Host ID

The host ID is the portion of the 32-bit address that identifies any device that has an IP address on your network. This could be a computer system, a router, a bridge, a switch, or even the Simple Network Management Protocol (SNMP) module located in a 10BaseT hub. The host ID must be unique to the network ID. In other words you could not have two of the same host address on the same network. The host address cannot be set to all 1s as this will be interpreted as a broadcast rather than as a host address. It also cannot be set to all 0s because this is interpreted as "this network only."

Subnet Mask

The subnet mask is a 32-bit value that distinguishes the network ID portion of the IP address from the host ID. The bits corresponding to the network address are set to 1 and the bits corresponding to the host address are set to 0.

The subnet mask is applied to the IP address using Boolean algebra logic with the following AND statements:

- 1 AND 1 = 1
- 1 AND 0 = 0
- 0 AND 1 = 0
- 0 AND 0 = 0

A subnet mask is the same length as an IP address; in other words it is also a 32-bit address. Figure 3-5 shows the binary representation of an IP address with a subnet mask, and the masked address after applying the AND function.

Separates Network ID Portion from Host ID Portion

Each 32-bit address is a pair that consists of the network ID and the host ID. The subnet mask is used to separate the network ID from the host ID. Notice in Figure 3-5 that the subnet mask is made up of complete octets of 1s or 0s. The 1s are used to identify the network ID while the 0s identify the host ID. The mask used in Figure 3-5 is the default mask for the corresponding IP address. The default masks will be examined in more detail in the next section of this chapter. If a mask other than the default mask had been used, then 1s would have identified the network ID and also the subnetwork ID, while 0s would have identified the host ID.

FIGURE 3-5

IP address with subnet mask and resulting masked address

IP Address

11001010 00001100 01000101 00110101

+

Subnet Mask

11111111 11111111 11111111 00000000

=

Masked Address

11001010 00001100 01000101 00000000

Be careful when distinguishing the network ID and the host ID from the subnet mask.

CERTIFICATION OBJECTIVE 3.02

Classes of IP Addresses

Almost every IP address belongs to a distinct class. These classes were defined by the Internet community to accommodate networks of various sizes. The class that the IP address belongs to initially determines the network ID and host ID portions of the address. The classes range from Class A to Class E; however, Microsoft TCP/IP supports only Classes A, B, and C addresses assigned to hosts. In this section we will examine each class of addresses.

Class A

Class A addresses are assigned to networks with a very large number of hosts. A Class A IP address has a 0 in the Most Significant Bit location of the first octet. The network ID is the first octet as shown in Figure 3-6.

Class A Range

Class A addresses range from 0.1.0.0 to 126.0.0.0.

Number of Class A Networks

In the Class A range there is the possibility of having 126 networks with each network having the capability of 16,777,214 unique hosts when using the default subnet mask.

FIGURE 3-6

Class A network address breakdown

Default Subnet Mask

The default subnet mask for a Class A network is 255.0.0.0 or in binary representation 11111111 00000000 00000000 00000000.

Table 3-1 shows Class A IP addresses with various subnet masks.

Class B

Class B addresses are assigned to medium-sized networks. A Class B IP address has a 1 0 in the two Most Significant Bit locations of the first octet. The network ID is the first and second octet as shown in Figure 3-7.

Class B Range

Class B addresses range from 128.0.0.0 to 191.255.0.0.

Number of Class B Networks

In the Class B range there is the possibility of having 16,384 networks, with each network having the capability of 65,534 unique hosts when using the default subnet mask.

TABLE 3-1 Class A IP and Subnet Mask Examples	Class A Address	Subnet Mask	End Result
	114.x.x.x	255.0.0.0	16,777,214 hosts possible on the single network.
	114.x.x.x	255.255.0.0	254 possible subnets with 65,534 hosts for each subnet.
	108.x.x.x	255.255.240.0	4094 possible subnets with 4094 hosts for each subnet.
	29.x.x.x	255.255.255.128	131,070 possible subnets with 126 hosts for each subnet.
	58.x.x.x	255.248.0.0	30 possible subnets with 524,286 hosts for each subnet.

FIGURE 3-7

Class B network
address breakdown

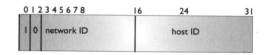

Default Subnet Mask

The default subnet mask for a Class B network is 255.255.0.0 or in binary
representation 11111111 11111111 00000000 00000000.

Table 3-2 shows Class B IP addresses with various subnet masks.

Class C

Class C addresses are usually assigned to small Local Area Networks (LANs).
A Class C IP address has a 1 1 0 in the three Most Significant Bit locations of
the first octet. The network ID is comprised of the first three octets as shown
in Figure 3-8.

Class C Ranges

Class C addresses range from 192.0.1.0 to 223.255.255.0.

TABLE 3-2

Class B IP and Subnet
Mask Examples

Class B Address	Subnet Mask	End Result
158.157.x.x	255.255.0.0	65,534 hosts possible on the single network.
142.13.x.x	255.255.192.0	2 possible subnets with 16,382 hosts per subnet.
183.214.x.x	255.255.255.0	254 possible subnets with 254 hosts per subnet.
191.222.x.x	255.255.255.252	16,382 possible subnets with 2 hosts per subnet.
130.12.x.x	255.255.248.0	30 possible subnets with 2046 hosts per subnet.

FIGURE 3-8

Class C network address
breakdown

Number of Class C Networks

In the Class C range there is the possibility of having 2,097,152 networks, with each network having the capability of 254 unique hosts when using the default subnet mask.

Default Subnet Mask

The default subnet mask for a Class C network is 255.255.255.0 or in binary representation 11111111 11111111 11111111 00000000.

Table 3-3 shows Class C IP addresses with various subnet masks.

Class D

Class D addresses are used for multicasting to a number of different hosts. Data is passed to one, two, three, or more users on a network. Only those hosts registered for the multicast address will receive the data. A Class D IP

TABLE 3-3

Class C IP and Subnet
Mask Examples

Class C Address	Subnet Mask	End Result
198.157.21.x	255.255.255.0	254 hosts possible on the single network.
202.14.18.x	255.255.255.248	30 possible subnets with 6 hosts per subnet.
223.211.1.x	255.255.255.192	2 possible subnets with 62 hosts per subnet.
194.19.62.x	255.255.255.252	62 possible subnets with 2 hosts per subnet.
220.19.93.x	255.255.255.224	6 possible subnets with 30 hosts per subnet.

address has a 1 1 1 0 in the four Most Significant Bit locations of the first octet. Figure 3-9 shows the layout of a Class D address.

Class D Ranges

Class D addresses range from 224.0.0.0 to 239.255.255.255. There is the potential for having 268,435,456 unique multicast groups.

Broadcast Examples

Currently Class D addresses are used mainly for experimentation. Membership in an IP multicast group is dynamic. A host can join or leave a group at any time they wish. You may see Class D addressing used for audio news multicasting, video presentations, or a music multicast.

Class E

Class E is an experimental address block that is reserved for future use. A Class E IP address has a 1 1 1 1 0 in the five Most Significant Bit locations of the first octet. Figure 3-10 shows the layout of a Class E address.

Class E Ranges

Class E addresses range from 240.0.0.0 to 247.255.255.255.

Special Internet Addresses

There are some special Internet addresses that we need to discsus next. You may wonder why a Class C address can have only 254 hosts and not 256 as it would seem, since an 8-bit number can have 256 different values. The reason for this is that two addresses are lost from the available host pool. The first is an address that has all 0s in the host ID, which signifies "this host" and is

---

FIGURE 3-9

Class D network
address breakdown

FIGURE 3-10

Class E network address
breakdown

normally used in a BOOTP process where a host doesn't yet know its IP
address. The second is an address that has all 1s in the host ID, which signifies
a broadcast address. So, for example, in the Class C network 200.158.157.x,
200.158.157.0, and 200.158.157.255 are not available to hosts, which reduces
the available number from 256 to 254.

If a network ID is all 1s, it will be used for limited broadcasts. If the network
ID is all 0s, it signifies "this network." The number of Class A networks is
reduced by one for this situation.

Loopback Addresses

Network IDs cannot start with 127 because this address is reserved for
loopback and is used mainly for testing TCP/IP and internal loopback
functions on the local system. If a program uses the loopback address as a
destination then the protocol software in the system returns the data without
sending traffic across the network. 127 is technically a Class A address due to
the high-order bit having a value of 0. But remember that 127 is reserved and
not in use for live networks.

exam
ⓦatch

*When calculating the number of networks or hosts that are available in
a particular class, remember to account for special IP addresses that
may be reserved for unique functions.*

Table 3-4 consolidates the information on networks and hosts of the
different classes we've discussed.

Class	Networks	Hosts
A	126	16,777,214
B	16,384	65,534
C	2,097,152	254
D	---	---
E	---	---

TABLE 3-4

Number of Networks and Hosts Per Class Address

CERTIFICATION OBJECTIVE 3.03

Address Resolution Overview

In the previous sections we have examined the 32-bit IP address that is used to identify hosts on an internet. Data packets are sent and received using the 32-bit address. Ultimately, however, two machines on a physical network can communicate only if they know each other's physical network address. In this section we will see how a host maps an IP address to the correct physical address.

IP Address to Hardware Address

If you are using a token ring network, resolution can be accomplished by direct mapping. With this type of network you have the capability of choosing both the IP and physical addresses that will be used. To make address resolution easy, you should select parts of both addresses that can be the same. For example, if you have a host with a Class C address of 204.121.27.62, then the network interface card (NIC) could be set for a physical address of 62 to match the host ID portion of the IP address.

Resolving IP Addresses to Ethernet Hardware Addresses

On an Ethernet network each host has an Ethernet NIC that is encoded with a 48-bit physical address when the NIC is manufactured. Since it is impossible to fit a 48-bit address into a 32-bit address space, some other method of resolution needs to occur. It is possible to manually maintain a table of mappings but this would be tedious and inefficient. A better method is to use a low-level protocol to dynamically bind addresses. In the next section we will examine this protocol.

ARP

In an Ethernet network the protocol used is appropriately named *Address Resolution Protocol* (ARP). ARP dynamically binds a high-level IP address to a low-level physical hardware address. ARP is used across a single physical network. For example, if host A needs to resolve the IP address for host B, then host A will broadcast a special packet to all hosts asking for host B to respond with its physical address. All the hosts will receive the special packet but they will disregard it, except for host B. Host B will recognize its IP address and send back a response to host A that contains its physical address. After host A receives the reply, it will use the physical address to send the packet directly to host B. ARP is defined in RFC 826.

ARP Utility

Windows NT comes with an ARP utility that can be used to view, add, or delete entries located in your ARP cache. The ARP cache is discussed in the next section of the chapter. Table 3-5 lists the commands available with the ARP utility. In conjunction with Table 3-5, here are definitions of a few of the common items you will see for each command:

- **inet_addr**   Specifies an IP address.
- **eth_addr**   Specifies a physical address.
- **if_addr**   If present, this specifies the IP address of the interface whose address translation table should be modified. If not present, the first applicable interface will be used.

| TABLE 3-5 | ARP Commands |

Command	Purpose
ARP -s inet_addr eth_addr [if_addr]	The -s adds the host and associates the inet_addr with the eth_addr. The eth_addr is given as six hexidecimal bytes separated by hyphens. The entry is permanent.
ARP -d inet_addr [if_addr]	Deletes the host specified by inet_addr.
ARP -a [inet_addr] [-N if_addr]	Displays current ARP entries by interrogating the current protocol data. If inet_addr is specified, the IP and Physical addresses for only the specified computer are displayed. If more than one network interface uses ARP, entries for each ARP table are displayed. If the -N if_addr option is specified, then it displays the ARP entries for the network interface specified by if_addr.
ARP -g [inet_addr] [-N if_addr]	Same as ARP -a.

ARP Cache

When the requesting host receives the physical address from an ARP request, it saves both the IP address and the physical address as an entry in the ARP cache. All hosts maintain an ARP cache that includes their own IP address to physical address mapping. The ARP cache is always checked for an IP address to physical address mapping before initiating a broadcast.

Windows NT Server automatically adjusts the size of the ARP cache. Entries are dropped out of the ARP cache if they are not used by any outgoing data packets for two minutes. Entries that are being referenced get dropped out of the ARP cache after ten minutes. This type of entry is shown as *dynamic* under the Type heading. Entries added manually are never dropped out of the cache and are shown as *static* under the Type heading.

Using Host Lookup Files

It is possible for computers located on remote subnets, where DNS and WINS are not used, to use the HOSTS and LMHOSTS files to provide mappings for names to IP addresses. This name-resolution method was used on internetworks long before DNS and WINS were developed. The HOSTS

FIGURE 3-11

ARP cache

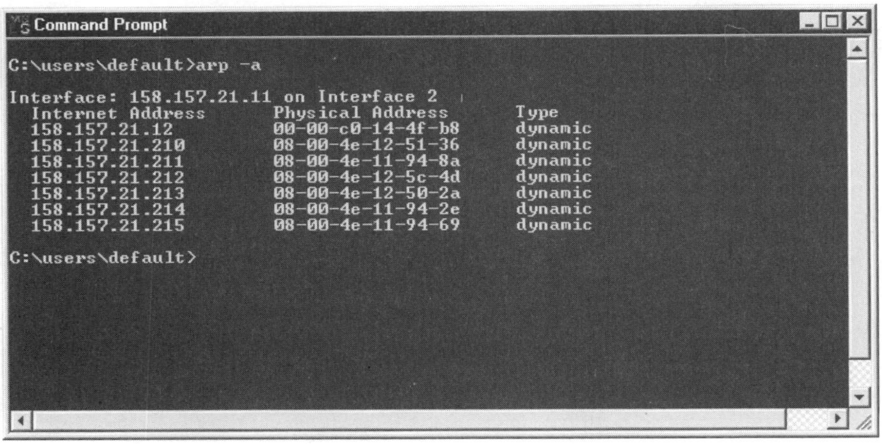

```
Command Prompt                                          _□×
C:\users\default>arp -a

Interface: 158.157.21.11 on Interface 2
  Internet Address      Physical Address      Type
  158.157.21.12         00-00-c0-14-4f-b8     dynamic
  158.157.21.210        08-00-4e-12-51-36     dynamic
  158.157.21.211        08-00-4e-11-94-8a     dynamic
  158.157.21.212        08-00-4e-12-5c-4d     dynamic
  158.157.21.213        08-00-4e-12-50-2a     dynamic
  158.157.21.214        08-00-4e-11-94-2e     dynamic
  158.157.21.215        08-00-4e-11-94-69     dynamic

C:\users\default>
```

file can be used as a local DNS replacement, and the LMHOSTS file can be used as a local WINS replacement.

Hosts

Windows NT Server can be configured to search the HOSTS file to obtain mappings of remote host names to IP addresses. The HOSTS file format is the same as the format used for host tables in version 4.3 of the Berkeley Software Distribution (BSD) UNIX /etc/hosts file.

The HOSTS file is an ASCII file that can be modified with any text editor. An example of the HOSTS format is provided in the file named HOSTS in the Windows NT %*systemroot*%\System32\Drivers\Etc directory. You should edit the sample HOSTS file to include remote host names and IP addresses for each computer you will communicate with. Figure 3-12 shows an example of a HOSTS file.

LMHOSTS

The LMHOSTS file is an ASCII file that maps IP addresses to NetBIOS computer names. It contains entries for Windows-networking computers located outside the local subnet. The LMHOSTS file is read when broadcast

FIGURE 3-12

HOSTS file

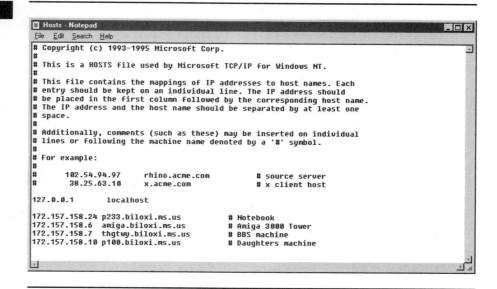

```
# Copyright (c) 1993-1995 Microsoft Corp.
#
# This is a HOSTS file used by Microsoft TCP/IP for Windows NT.
#
# This file contains the mappings of IP addresses to host names. Each
# entry should be kept on an individual line. The IP address should
# be placed in the first column followed by the corresponding host name.
# The IP address and the host name should be separated by at least one
# space.
#
# Additionally, comments (such as these) may be inserted on individual
# lines or following the machine name denoted by a '#' symbol.
#
# For example:
#
#      102.54.94.97        rhino.acme.com          # source server
#      38.25.63.10         x.acme.com              # x client host

127.0.0.1       localhost

172.157.158.24 p233.biloxi.ms.us        # Notebook
172.157.158.6  amiga.biloxi.ms.us       # Amiga 3000 Tower
172.157.158.7  thgtwy.biloxi.ms.us      # BBS machine
172.157.158.10 p100.biloxi.ms.us        # Daughters machine
```

name resolution or WINS fails. The resolved entries are stored in a local cache for later access.

Since LMHOSTS is an ASCII file, you can modify it using any text editor. An example of the LMHOSTS file is provided as a file named LMHOSTS.sam in the Windows NT %systemroot%\System32\Drivers\Etc directory.

Normally the LMHOSTS file is used for small-scale networks that do not have any servers available.

Figure 3-13 shows an example of the LMHOSTS file and Table 3-6 defines all the keywords that can be used with the LMHOSTS file.

exam
ⓦatch

Know how HOSTS and LMHOSTS files are organized and what keywords are available, as well as their functions.

Gateways

The term *gateway* can have different meanings. A gateway can be used to connect two LANs that use different transport protocols or data formats: for

FIGURE 3-13

LMHOSTS file

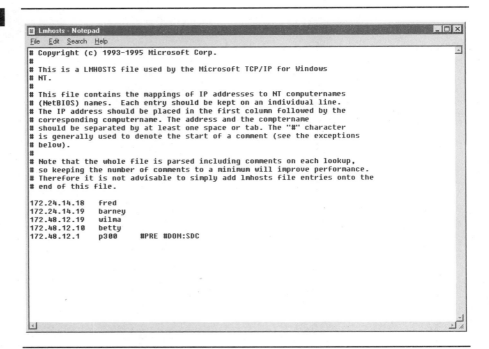

```
# Copyright (c) 1993-1995 Microsoft Corp.
#
# This is a LMHOSTS file used by the Microsoft TCP/IP for Windows
# NT.
#
# This file contains the mappings of IP addresses to NT computernames
# (NetBIOS) names.  Each entry should be kept on an individual line.
# The IP address should be placed in the first column followed by the
# corresponding computername. The address and the comptername
# should be separated by at least one space or tab. The "#" character
# is generally used to denote the start of a comment (see the exceptions
# below).
#
# Note that the whole file is parsed including comments on each lookup,
# so keeping the number of comments to a minimum will improve performance.
# Therefore it is not advisable to simply add lmhosts file entries onto the
# end of this file.

172.24.14.18    fred
172.24.14.19    barney
172.48.12.19    wilma
172.48.12.10    betty
172.48.12.1     p300       #PRE #DOM:SDC
```

TABLE 3-6

Keywords Available for
the LMHOSTS File

Keyword	Definition
#PRE	Defines which entries should initially be preloaded into the name cache. The entry is locked in the name cache and does not time out.
#DOM:<domain name>	Distinguishes a domain controller from non-domain controllers. This keyword is needed for all servers that validate logon requests.
#NOFNR	Avoid using Directed Name Queries (DNS). Some versions of LAN Manager cannot handle NetBIOS DNS requests and return an error. Specifying this flag on the same line will avoid using NetBIOS directed name queries.

TABLE 3-6

Keywords Available for
the LMHOSTS File
(*continued*)

#BEGIN_ALTERNATE #END_ALTERNATE	Defines a redundant list of alternate locations for LMHOSTS files. The recommended way to #INCLUDE remote files is to use a UNC path, to ensure access to the file. Be sure the UNC names exist in the LMHOSTS file with a proper IP address to NetBIOS name translation.
#MH	Associates a single, unique NetBIOS computer name to an IP address. You can create multiple entries for the same NetBIOS computer name for each NIC in the multihomed device, up to a maximum of 25 different IP addresses for the same name.
#SG	Defines a special group, such as printers or computers that belong to groups on the intranet for easy reference, browsing, or broadcasting. Special groups are limited to a total of 25 members.
#INCLUDE	Used with #BEGIN_ALTERNATE and #END_ALTERNATE to define other locations for the LMHOSTS file. For example: #INCLUDE <\\server_name\sharename\LMHOSTS>

example, connecting the IPX protocol to the IP protocol. In our discussion of TCP/IP, a gateway is simply a path for packets of data to be forwarded when there is no matching entry in the route table.

Default Gateway

The default gateway is needed only for systems that are part of an internetwork. Data packets with a destination IP address not on the local subnet nor elsewhere in the route table are automatically forwarded to the default gateway. The default gateway is normally a computer system or router connected to the local subnet and other networks that knows the network IDs for other networks in the internetwork and the best path to reach them. Since the default gateway knows the network IDs of the other networks in the internetwork, it can forward the data packet to other gateways until the packet is ultimately delivered to a gateway connected to the intended destination. However, if the default gateway becomes unavailable, the system cannot communicate outside its own subnet except for systems it had established connections with prior to the failure.

Multiple Gateways

If the default gateway becomes unavailable, data packets cannot reach their destination. Multiple gateways can be used to prevent this from happening. When a system is configured with multiple gateways, data transmission problems result in the system trying to use the other configured gateways, allowing internetworking communications capabilities to continue uninterrupted.

CERTIFICATION OBJECTIVE 3.04

Configuring TCP/IP on NT Server 4.0

With the arrival of Windows NT Server 4.0 the default protocol that is initially installed has changed to TCP/IP. We will now learn how to configure each of the options that is available with this protocol.

Single Adapter System

The majority of Windows NT Servers probably have only a single NIC in them configured for only a single IP address, as shown in Figure 3-14. Later in this section we will discuss each of the options available for configuration.

Multi-Homed System

When a computer is configured with more than one IP address, it is referred to as a *multi-homed* system. You can multi-home your system in three different ways:

- **Multiple IP addresses per NIC**   You can have several IP addresses bound to a single NIC. However, NetBIOS over TCP/IP (NetBT) binds only one IP address per NIC. When a NetBIOS name

FIGURE 3-14

TCP/IP Properties Sheet
of single adapter system

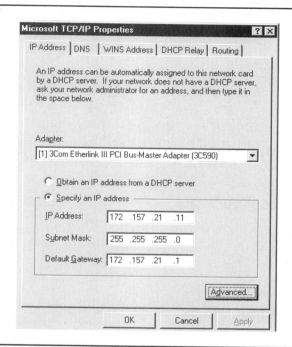

registration is sent out, only the first IP address listed in the network settings will be registered for each NIC.

- **Multiple NICs per physical network** You can have several NICS in your system that are on the same network and the only limitation is your hardware.

- **Multiple networks and media types** You can have several different networks supported by various media in your system. The main restrictions are hardware and media support. For example, you may have two different NICS in your system hooked to two separate networks. One may use fiber optics media and the other may use unshielded twisted pair cable.

When an IP packet is sent from a multi-homed host, it will be given to the NIC with the most obvious route to the destination. The IP packet may display the source IP address of one NIC in the multi-homed host, yet be sent out by a different NIC. If this happens, then the source physical address on the packet will be that of the NIC that actually transmitted the packet onto the media.

You may encounter routing problems when a computer is multi-homed with NICs attached to separate networks. To work around this dilemma you may need to set up static routes to the remote networks.

Figure 3-15 shows one way to multi-home a system. It has two separate network interface cards configured for the system. Figure 3-16 shows the TCP/IP Properties tab for the second NIC located in the system. As you can see, the IP address is different for each of the NICs.

TCP/IP Property Tabs

In this section we will examine each of the different tabs that is available for configuring TCP/IP on your system.

FIGURE 3-15

TCP/IP Properties
Sheet for NIC #1 of a
multi-homed system

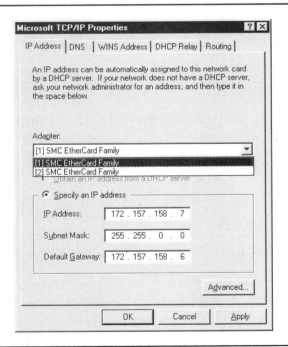

TCP/IP Properties
Sheet for NIC #2 of a
multi-homed system

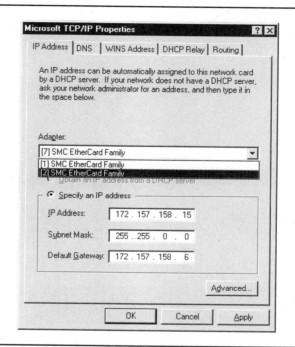

IP Address

The first tab is the IP Address tab shown in Figure 3-16. On this tab you can specify an IP address or have one issued from the DHCP Server. Since we are talking about configuring a Windows NT Server, I recommend that you give it a static IP address. Other selections on this tab are the subnet mask that is used on your network and the default gateway that will be used.

ADVANCED BUTTON   We mentioned earlier that there are several different ways to multi-home a system. If you select the Advanced button you will be presented with the option to add IP addresses to your NIC and also to specify additional gateways if necessary. Figure 3-17 shows the Advanced IP Addressing window in which two additional IP addresses have been bound to the NIC.

It is also possible to enable Security and Point to Point Tunneling Protocol (PPTP) filtering from this tab but they are optional and their use is dependent

FIGURE 3-17

Advanced IP Addressing
window with two additional
IP addresses

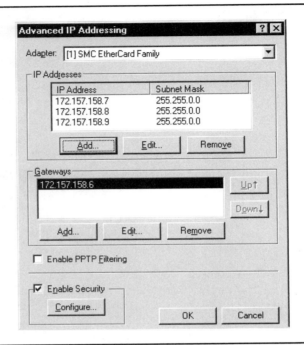

upon your particular situation. PPTP filtering is normally used only on a
server that is used as a PPTP Server. By using the Security feature it is possible
to restrict the ports and protocols that are permitted. Figure 3-18 shows the
TCP/IP Security window.

DNS

The second tab is where DNS settings are configured, as shown in Figure
3-19. Refer to Figure 3-19 as we discuss the options.

HOST NAME   By default, this value is the Windows NT computer name,
but it can be changed to another host name without affecting the computer
name. For example, the host name cannot include an underscore even though
the computer name may use an underscore in its name.

DOMAIN   The domain is usually an organization name followed by a
period and an extension that indicates the type of organization, such as

FIGURE 3-18

TCP/IP Security window

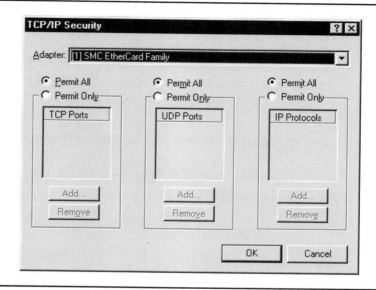

FIGURE 3-19

DNS tab of the TCP/IP
Properties

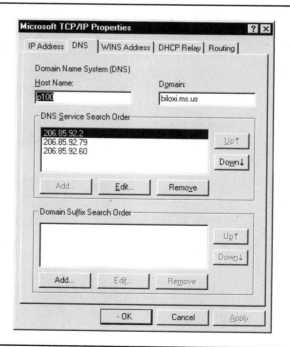

nasa.gov. The domain is used with the host name to create a fully qualified domain name (FQDN) for the computer. The FQDN is the host name followed by a period (.) followed by the domain. For example, in the FQDN of p100.biloxi.ms.us, p100 is the host name and biloxi.ms.us is the domain. It is important to not confuse a DNS domain with a Windows NT domain. They are definitely different animals!

DOMAIN SUFFIX SEARCH ORDER   The Domain Suffix Search Order specifies the domain suffixes to be appended to host names during name resolution. You can change the search order of the domain suffixes by selecting a domain name to move, and then using the up and down arrow buttons.

WINS Address

The third tab is where information pertaining to WINS is configured, as shown in Figure 3-20.

Refer to Figure 3-20 as we discuss the options.

WINS SERVER   It is possible to configure both a primary and a secondary WINS server for your system. If the primary WINS server cannot be reached for any function, then your system will request that function from its secondary WINS server. Periodically your system will attempt to switch back to its primary WINS server.

ENABLE DNS FOR WINDOWS RESOLUTION   Select this box if you want to ensure that DNS servers will also be used in conjunction with the WINS servers to resolve client requests.

ENABLE LMHOSTS LOOKUP   By default, the LMHOSTS lookup is enabled when TCP/IP is installed on your system. It is recommended that you do not disable LMHOSTS lookup because it provides a backup name service for WINS servers that are unavailable or off-line.

If you want to use an LMHOSTS file from a remote computer or different directory on your local system, click the Import LMHOSTS button and select the LMHOSTS file you want to use.

FIGURE 3-20

WINS Address tab of the
TCP/IP Properties

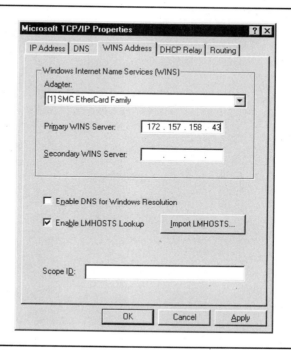

DHCP Relay

The fourth tab is where information for DHCP Relay is configured. This tab is used only if your system has had the DHCP Relay Agent service installed.

When a dynamic client system on the subnet where the DHCP Relay Agent resides requests an IP address, the request is forwarded to the subnet's DHCP Relay Agent. The DHCP Relay Agent forwards the request directly to the correct system running the DHCP server service. The computer running the DHCP server service returns an IP address directly to the requesting client.

Figure 3-21 shows the DHCP Relay tab. Refer to Figure 3-21 as we discuss the options available.

SECONDS THRESHOLD   This option will limit the clients discover broadcast to the local subnet until the seconds threshold is reached. It can reduce network traffic and increase the chance that a local server will service the request.

DHCP Relay tab of the
TCP/IP Properties

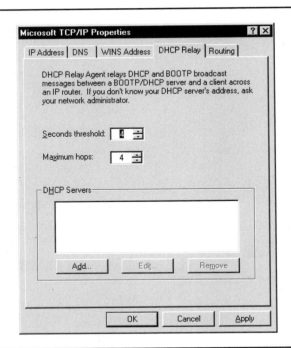

The Relay Agent will forward the packet only if the seconds field is higher
than the threshold set. RFC 1542 recommends the default to be 4 seconds.
The seconds field is defined as the number of seconds from the first packet
sent. For example, the first packet sent will have a value of 0. The next packet
sent would have a value of 5, if it was sent 5 seconds after the first packet.

MAXIMUM HOPS   The maximum hops is the number of hops the
DHCP Relay Agent will forward the request from the client.

DHCP SERVERS   This is where you type the IP address of the server that
will provide the IP addresses to the requesting clients.

Routing

The fifth tab is where information for routing is configured. Figure 3-22 shows this tab and the single option that is available.

ENABLE IP FORWARDING   Enable IP Forwarding is the only option available on the Routing tab. It is used to allow IP packets to be forwarded between two NICs on a multi-homed system or to allow packets to be forwarded between Remote Access Service (RAS) and a NIC.

Now that you have seen the options available for configuring TCP/IP, it is your turn to practice. Exercise 3-1 will let you configure a Windows NT Server with multiple IP addresses.

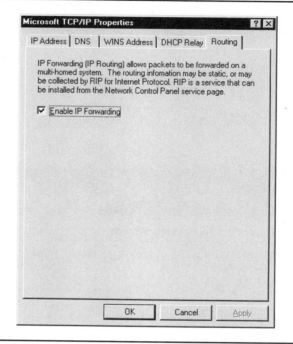

Configuring a Server with Multiple IP Addressesing

1. Log on as Administrator to a system that has the TCP/IP protocol installed.
2. Use the right mouse button to select Network Neighborhood and choose Properties from the drop-down menu.
3. Click the Protocols tab.
4. Double-click TCP/IP Protocol.
5. Click the Advanced button.
6. Click the Add button that is under IP addresses.
7. Type **172.110.1.1** in the IP Address: block.
8. Type **255.255.0.0** in the Subnet Mask: block.
9. Click the Add button.
10. Click the OK button. Your system is now configured for multiple IP addresses.

Now that you have seen the options available for configuring TCP/IP on Windows NT Server, here is a quick reference for possible scenario questions relating to the configuration, and the appropriate answer:

QUESTIONS AND ANSWERS

A multi-homed system has two network cards...	Select Enable IP Forwarding in the Routing tab.
The WINS servers are down and you cannot locate a machine on another network...	Make sure that Enable LMHOSTS Lookup is selected on the WINS Server tab.
You need to add several IP addresses to a single NIC...	Select the Advanced button on the IP Address tab and add them from there.

CERTIFICATION OBJECTIVE 3.05

Testing Configuration

Now that you have configured TCP/IP on your system, you want to be sure that it will function correctly. Luckily there are several utilities available to help you. In this section we will examine two of them, IPCONFIG and PING.

IPCONFIG Utility

If you are troubleshooting a system on a TCP/IP network, then you will need to know some basic information such as the IP address, subnet mask, and the default gateway. IPCONFIG is a command-line utility that can provide this information. Figure 3-23 shows the results after IPCONFIG has been executed on a system.

FIGURE 3-23

IPCONFIG utility running in DOS

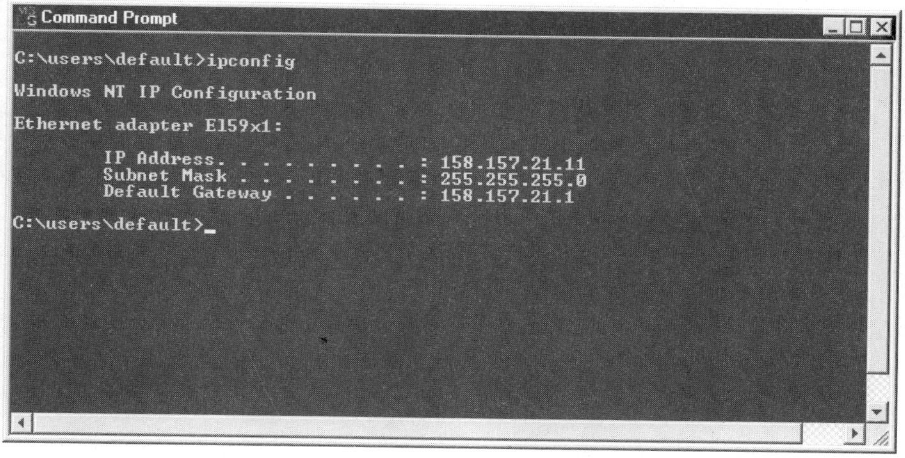
Command Prompt
C:\users\default>ipconfig
Windows NT IP Configuration
Ethernet adapter E159x1:
IP Address. . . . . : 158.157.21.11
Subnet Mask . . . . : 255.255.255.0
Default Gateway . . . . . . : 158.157.21.1
C:\users\default>_

It is always helpful to have as much information as possible. When IPCONFIG is used with the /all switch, it produces a very detailed configuration report for all interfaces in your system, including configured serial ports that are used for RAS. Figure 3-24 shows the results of using IPCONFIG /all on a system. Only the information for the first interface is displayed. The information for the second NIC and a serial port is not displayed. However, more information is displayed than when using the IPCONFIG command by itself.

Exercise 3-2 will give you the opportunity to try the IPCONFIG utility.

EXERCISE 3-2

Using IPCONFIG to Verify TCP/IP Configuration

1. Log on as Administrator to a system that has the TCP/IP protocol installed.

2. Click the Start button and select Programs | Command Prompt.

3. At the command prompt type **IPCONFIG /ALL**. Is the information displayed what you thought it would be?

FIGURE 3-24

IPCONFIG/ALL utility running in DOS

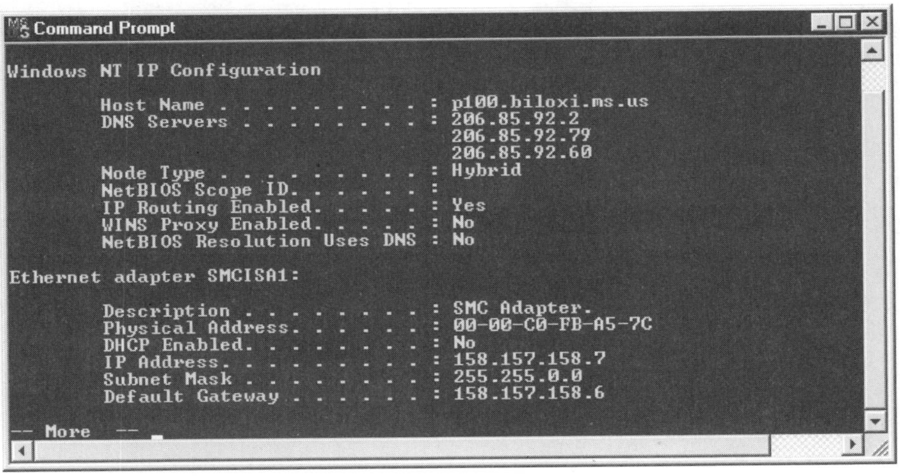

```
MS Command Prompt                                                    _ □ ✕

Windows NT IP Configuration

        Host Name . . . . . . . . . : p100.biloxi.ms.us
        DNS Servers . . . . . . . . : 206.85.92.2
                                      206.85.92.79
                                      206.85.92.60
        Node Type . . . . . . . . . : Hybrid
        NetBIOS Scope ID. . . . . . :
        IP Routing Enabled. . . . . : Yes
        WINS Proxy Enabled. . . . . : No
        NetBIOS Resolution Uses DNS : No

Ethernet adapter SMCISA1:

        Description . . . . . . . . : SMC Adapter.
        Physical Address. . . . . . : 00-00-C0-FB-A5-7C
        DHCP Enabled. . . . . . . . : No
        IP Address. . . . . . . . . : 158.157.158.7
        Subnet Mask . . . . . . . . : 255.255.0.0
        Default Gateway . . . . . . : 158.157.158.6

 -- More --
```

PING Utility

The PING (Packet InterNet Groper) utility helps you to confirm IP-level connectivity. When you troubleshoot a TCP/IP problem, use the PING command to send an Internet Control Message Protocol (ICMP) echo request to a host name or IP address. I usually try to PING the IP address of the host to see if it will respond. If I am successful, then I try to PING the host name. PING uses Windows Sockets name resolution to resolve the name to an address. If I can PING the IP address but not the host name, then I know the problem is with the name resolution and not with network connectivity.

Figure 3-25 shows the output of the PING command and Table 3-7 lists the options that can be used with PING.

Exercise 3-3 lets you use the PING utility to verify IP connectivity to other systems.

FIGURE 3-25

PING utility running in DOS

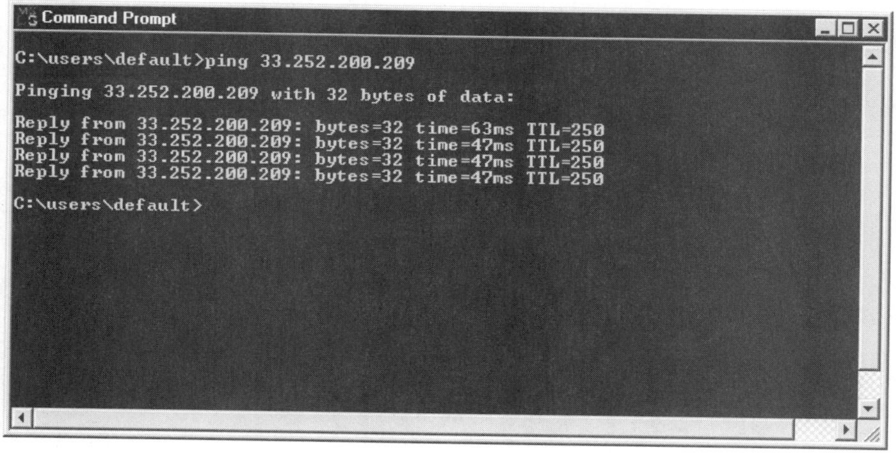

```
C:\users\default>ping 33.252.200.209

Pinging 33.252.200.209 with 32 bytes of data:

Reply from 33.252.200.209: bytes=32 time=63ms TTL=250
Reply from 33.252.200.209: bytes=32 time=47ms TTL=250
Reply from 33.252.200.209: bytes=32 time=47ms TTL=250
Reply from 33.252.200.209: bytes=32 time=47ms TTL=250

C:\users\default>
```

TABLE 3-7	Option	Purpose
Options for the PING Utility	-t	Ping the specified host until interrupted.
	-a	Resolve addresses to hostnames.
	-n count	Number of echo requests to send.
	-l size	Send buffer size.
	-f	Set Don't Fragment flag in packet.
	-i TTL	Time To Live.
	-v TOS	Type Of Service.
	-r count	Record route for count hops.
	-s count	Timestamp for count hops.
	-j host-list	Loose source route along host-list.
	-k host-list	Strict source route along host-list.
	-w timeout	Timeout in milliseconds to wait for each reply.

EXERCISE 3-3

Using PING to Connect to Other Servers

1. Log on as Administrator to a system that is connected to the Internet and has TCP/IP I installed.

2. Click the Start button and select Programs | Command Prompt.

3. At the command prompt type **PING 207.159.134.58**. Was your PING successful?

4. Try to PING some of these other IP addresses: 206.66.12.43, 165.121.81, 206.151.75.79, 199.1.11.15, and 199.227.250.70. Did you PING them successfully?

CERTIFICATION SUMMARY

In order for a computer system to communicate on a TCP/IP network it must have a unique 32-bit IP address to identify itself. The 32-bit address consists of four 8-bit octets. The 32-bit address can be represented in binary format or as dotted decimal. Dotted decimal is easier for humans to remember. The IP address consists of a network ID and a host ID. The InterNIC is responsible for initially issuing network IDs for the Internet. The subnet mask is used to separate the network ID from the host ID.

There are five available classes of IP addresses. Class A addresses are for networks that have a great number of hosts. Class B addresses are for medium-sized networks. Class C addresses are usually for small LANs. Class D addresses are used for multicasting to a number of different hosts. Class E addresses are reserved for future use. There are special IP addresses that are used for broadcasts and loopback functions.

Address resolution is used to map the IP address to the physical address of a host. It can be done with direct mapping on token ring networks or by using ARP to dynamically bind the IP address to the physical address on an ethernet network. The ARP utility can be used to examine, update, and delete entries in your ARP cache. Entries in your ARP cache can be dynamic or static. Dynamic entries are purged from the ARP cache if they are not used within a certain time frame. Other methods of address resolution are either to use a HOSTS or LMHOSTS file.

Configuring TCP/IP on a Windows NT Server can be done on a system that uses a single NIC and a single IP address as well as on a system that uses multiple NICs or multiple IP addresses. Several choices need to be made when configuring TCP/IP, including whether you will be using a dynamic or static IP address, the subnet mask, and the default gateway. If you plan to use DNS, then there are several options that need to be configured, including the host name and the domain. WINS servers can be configured for each NIC that is in your system. If you have multiple NICs on a single network, then you need to enable IP forwarding.

Two utilities available to help you test your TCP/IP configuration are IPCONFIG and PING. IPCONFIG can provide a great deal of information about a systems configuration when used with the /all parameter. PING can help to isolate a network problem by sending ICMP echo requests to a host.

TWO-MINUTE DRILL

❑ The TCP/IP suite consists of several different protocols and the 32-bit address relates to the Internet Protocol (IP).

❑ An IP address uniquely identifies a system located on your network.

❑ The network ID is the portion of the 32-bit IP address that identifies which network a particular system is on.

❑ The host ID is the portion of the 32-bit address that identifies any device that has an IP address on your network.

❑ The subnet mask is a 32-bit value that distinguishes the network ID portion of the IP address from the host ID.

❑ Be careful when distinguishing the network ID and the host ID from the subnet mask.

❑ The classes of IP addresses range from Class A to Class E; however, Microsoft TCP/IP supports only Classes A, B, and C addresses assigned to hosts.

❑ Class A addresses are assigned to networks with a very large number of hosts.

❑ Class B addresses are assigned to medium-sized networks.

❑ Class C addresses are usually assigned to small Local Area Networks (LANs).

❑ Class D addresses are used for multicasting to a number of different hosts.

❑ Class E is an experimental address block that is reserved for future use.

❑ When calculating the number of networks or hosts that are available in a particular class, remember to account for special IP addresses that may be reserved for unique functions.

❑ If you are using a token ring network, resolution can be accomplished by direct mapping.

❑ ARP dynamically binds a high-level IP address to a low-level physical hardware address.

❑ It is possible for computers located on remote subnets, where DNS and WINS are not used, to use the HOSTS and LMHOSTS files to provide mappings for names to IP addresses.

❑ Know how HOSTS and LMHOSTS files are organized and what keywords are available, as well as their functions.

❑ A gateway can be used to connect two LANs that use different transport protocols or data formats.

❑ A gateway can also be a path for packets of data to be forwarded when there is no matching entry in the route table.

❑ With the arrival of Windows NT Server 4.0 the default protocol that is initially installed has changed to TCP/IP.

❑ When a computer is configured with more than one IP address, it is referred to as a *multi-homed* system.

❑ If you are troubleshooting a system on a TCP/IP network, then you will need to know some basic information such as the IP address, subnet mask, and the default gateway. IPCONFIG is a command-line utility that can provide this information.

❑ The PING (Packet InterNet Groper) utility helps you to confirm IP-level connectivity. Use the PING command to send an Internet Control Message Protocol (ICMP) echo request to a host name or IP address.

SELF TEST

The following Self Test questions will help you measure your understanding of the material presented in this chapter. Read all the choices carefully, as there may be more than one correct answer. Choose all correct answers for each question.

1. Which address is valid for Class C?

    A. 33.114.17.24

    B. 199.45.283.24

    C. 202.67.13.87

    D. 155.23.94.2

2. What is the binary representation for 124.58.76.6?

    A. 01111100 00111010 01000010 00000111

    B. 01101100 01000111 01101101 00000110

    C. 01111010 01101101 01010110 00000101

    D. 01111100 00111010 01001100 00000110

3. What utility would you use to verify the internetwork connectivity of a system located in another state?

    A. IPCONFIG

    B. PING

    C. IP HELPER

    D. ARP

4. The IP address consists of _____ octets.

    A. 2

    B. 4

    C. 6

    D. 8

5. The purpose of using #PRE in the LMHOSTS file is _____

    A. to preload a name into the name cache.

    B. to show which is the preferred server.

    C. to get preliminary statistics for the domain.

    D. to prepare the system for use.

6. What is the default subnet mask for a Class C address?

    A. 255.0.0.0

    B. 255.255.0.0

    C. 255.255.255.0

    D. 255.255.255.255

7. How many hosts can a Class B network have if the default subnet mask is used?

    A. 65,435

    B. 16,384

    C. 16,483

    D. 65,534

8. A system has an IP address of 172.24.10.62. What is allowed to be done with this system?

    A. The system can be placed on the Internet.

B. The system can be placed on an Intranet.

C. The system cannot be placed on an Intranet.

D. The system cannot be used on any network.

9. What Class of addresses has a 0 as the Most Significant Bit in the first octet?

A. Class A

B. Class B

C. Class C

D. Class D

E. Class E

10. How do you add additional gateways to a Windows NT Server that is configured with TCP/IP?

A. Select the Import LMHOSTS button from the WINS tab of TCP/IP Properties.

B. Select the Advanced button from the IP Address tab of TCP/IP Properties.

C. Select the Add button on the DHCP Relay tab of TCP/IP Properties.

D. Select the Enable IP Forwarding box on the Routing tab of TCP/IP Properties.

11. What would you type at the command prompt to receive detailed IP information for a machine?

A. IPCONFIG /INFO

B. IPCONFIG

C. IPCONFIG /ALL

D. IPCONFIG /MORE

12. What file can be used as a replacement for local DNS?

A. LMHOSTS

B. HOST

C. LMHOST

D. HOSTS

13. What Class of addresses has 110 as the three Most Significant Bits in the first octet?

A. Class A

B. Class B

C. Class C

D. Class D

E. Class E

14. What is the purpose of the Class E addresses?

A. They are used for multicasting to a number of different hosts.

B. They are reserved for future use.

C. They are used for broadcasting to all other Classes of addresses.

D. They are used for loopback testing.

15. What is the network ID for the IP address 148.34.18.42 that has a subnet mask of 255.255.255.0?

A. 148

B. 148.34

C. 148.34.18

D. 148.34.18.42

4

Subnetting TCP/IP Networks

The current Internet Protocol, version IPv4, allocates 4,294,967,296 addresses for general Internet use. Sounds like a lot of addresses, but with the number of Internet users doubling in less than a year, these addresses are quickly used up. This has called for leading experts to devise what is known as IPv6 or IPng (next generation). Until the appropriate hardware is available to handle IPv6 we have to come up with a way to patch what is already in place and make it work a little longer.

Throughout this chapter we will discuss the various classes of IP addresses and the basis for subnetting within them. We will also cover in detail the available networks within each class.

CERTIFICATION OBJECTIVE 4.01

TCP/IP Review

With the Internet growing as large as it has, experts found that the two-level hierarchy of the addressing scheme was not meeting the demand for the number of networks.

As organizations grow in size, one network ID cannot meet the demand. The only answer is to implement a series of subnetworks. Subnetworks handle the limitation on the length a single medium can reach. If you have a large university campus that you must internetwork, you may not be able to cover the distance required with today's communication mediums. Creating individual subnetworks would be the right approach to this internetworking challenge.

Some organizations are large enough to experience network congestion. With a large number of hosts communicating all at once on one network, the network can become bogged down with transmissions. This is where subnetworks come into play; by having many smaller networks, congestion isn't an issue.

The two-level hierarchy basically helps with routing the information to the appropriate host on a particular network. To do this you have to have a network address and a host address. An IP address is a 32-bit number made up of 4 octets. The IP address is split into the network address and host address between octets. Figure 4-1 shows a network with three subnetworks.

Let's take two IP addresses, 210.168.10.12 and 210.168.11.15. Looking at these two IP addresses without knowing anything else, you could not tell whether they are on the same network. But if you know that the first 3 octets specify the network ID and the last octet specifies the host, then you know that these two IP addresses are on different networks. If the first 2 octets specify the network ID, then these two addresses would be on the same network. You determine which bits or octets are used for the network address and which are for the host address by what is called *masking*. Allocation of network IDs and host IDs takes careful planning. With the various needs and sizes of networks today, a system is needed to accommodate them.

One way that designers tried to accommodate the various size networks was *classful addressing*, which is based on the three distinct address classes: A, B, and C. The ranges for each class of IP address are determined by the first octet of the IP address (see Table 4-1).

FIGURE 4-1

A network with three subnetworks

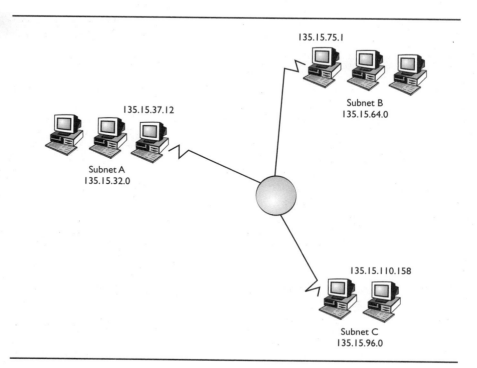

135.15.75.1

Subnet B
135.15.64.0

135.15.37.12

Subnet A
135.15.32.0

135.15.110.158

Subnet C
135.15.96.0

For example, if an IP address is 131.40.35.129, then this is considered a Class B address. From the following table you notice that 127 is not used. This particular octet was set aside for the loopback and diagnostic functions. Anything above 223 is not used in the first 3 classes. Classes D and E exist but are not relevant to Windows networking at this point in time.

Class	First Octet Range
Class A	1-126
Class B	128-191
Class C	192-223

As we mentioned earlier, there has to be something to tell us what kind of address it is and which octets are the network ID and which are the host ID. To do this we need a *subnet mask*. A subnet mask basically masks or denotes one portion of the IP as the network address and the other as the host address.

FROM THE CLASSROOM

Using Network ID to Determine Host Network

It is not always easy to determine whether two hosts are on the same network by comparing their network IDs.

Some cases are obvious:

151.173.28.160	Class B
217.63.143.230	Class C

Since these two addresses are in different classes, the hosts must be on different networks.

And some cases are not so obvious:

131.107.35.200	Class B
131.107.61.26	Class B

Since these two addresses are in the same class, the subnet mask must be used to determine if the hosts are on the same network.

If you use the default subnet mask of 255.255.0.0, then the hosts are on the same network. This can be proven with the ANDing process shown in Table 4-1.

FROM THE CLASSROOM

The ANDing results (a) and (b) in the same value; therefore the hosts are on the same network

Refer to Table 4-2 for the subnet mask of 255.255.240.0.

The ANDing results in a different value. Look at the third octets. Since the values are different, the hosts are on a different network.

Now try the subnet mask of 255.255.224.0 on your own.

This should result with the hosts being on the same network.

—*By D. Lynn White, MCT, MCSE*

exam
Ⓦatch

Don't accept the obvious; use the ANDing process to determine if the hosts are on the same network.

With classful addressing each class designates a certain series of bits for the network portion of the address and a certain series of bits for the host portion of the address. With Class A addresses the first eight bits, or first octet, determine the network ID and the last 24 bits, or 3 octets, determine the host ID. For example, if you have the following IP address:

```
10.123.45.16
```

10 is the network address. Any IP address beginning with 10 would be on the same network. Any IP address beginning with an octet other than 10

TABLE 4-1		
The ANDing Process	131.107.35.200	10000011 01101011 00100011 11001000
	255.255.0.0	11111111 11111111 00000000 00000000
	ANDing	10000011 01101011 00000000 00000000 (a)
	131.107.61.26	10000011 01101011 00111101 00011010
	255.255.0.0	11111111 11111111 00000000 00000000
	ANDing	10000011 01101011 00000000 00000000 (b)

TABLE 4-2	131.107.35.200	10000011 01101011 00100011 11001000
The Subnet Mask of 255.255.240.0	255.255.240.0	11111111 11111111 11110000 00000000
	ANDing	10000011 01101011 00100000 00000000 (a)
	131.107.61.26	10000011 01101011 00111101 00011010
	255.255.240.0	11111111 11111111 11110000 00000000
	ANDing	*10000011 01101011 00110000 00000000* (b)

would be on a different network. The remaining portion on the IP address denotes the host. This particular host has an address on 123.45.16.

With Class B addressing the first 16 bits, or first two octets, determine the network ID and the last 16 bits, or last two octets, determine the host ID. For the following IP address:

```
150.213.92.12
```

150.213 is the network address and the last two octets, 92.12, are the host address. All IP addresses beginning with 150.213 are on the same network.

With Class C addressing the first 24 bits, or first three octets, determine the network ID and the last 8 bits, or last octet, determine the host ID. For the following Class C address:

```
210.211.10.1
```

we know that all machines with IP addresses beginning with 210.211.10 are on the same network. The last two octets, 10.1, signify the host address.

As we learned in Chapter 3, there are default subnet masks within each class of addresses (see Table 4-3).

TABLE 4-3	Class	Default
Default Subnet Masks	Class A	255.0.0.0
	Class B	255.255.0.0
	Class C	255.255.255.0

Remember that the subnet mask designates which portion of the address is the network address and which portion is the host address. This is done by converting the address to binary. 255 in binary is 11111111. The number 0 in binary is 000000000. The decimal number 255 in binary is eight 1s and the decimal number 0 is eight 0s. With the default subnet mask anything with all 1s is considered part of the network address. Anything with all 0s is part of the host address.

Let's look at this again as a review. Take the IP address 10.123.45.16 and the subnet mask 255.0.0.0. We convert the subnet mask to binary and come up with:

```
1111111.00000000.00000000.00000000
```

If you draw a line where the 1s stop and 0s begin, you come up with:

```
11111111        |        00000000.00000000.00000000
```

If we draw a line at the same spot in the IP address, we have the following:

```
10              |        123.45.16
```

We can now see that 10 is the network address and the remaining octets are the host address.

RFC 950

In 1985 designers came up with RFC 950, which deals with the Internet Standard Subnetting Procedure. Within RFC 950 the designers discuss adding a third level to the hierarchy, the *subnetwork address*. Table 4-4 shows a comparison between the original two-level hierarchy and the new three-level hierarchy.

The three-level hierarchy adds a third component to the routing process, the subnet address, which takes a 4-octet IP address and divides it up three ways. This is known as *bit swiping*. It involves separating the IP address in the middle of an octet as shown in Figure 4-2.

TABLE 4-4			
NETWORK I.D.	HOST I.D.		
NETWORK I.D.	SUBNET I.D.		HOST I.D.

Two-Level Hierarchy Versus Three-Level Hieararchy

FIGURE 4-2

Bit swiping to create a
subnet address

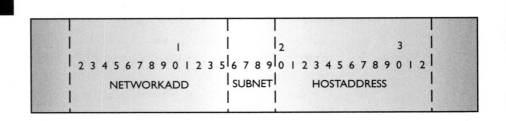

We will discuss bit swiping more later on. But a basic understanding of it
now will help in the following couple of sections.

CERTIFICATION OBJECTIVE 4.02

Subnetting Versus Supernetting

Supernetting came about when medium-sized organizations were having
difficulty with the standard addressing scheme.

Class A addresses were entirely too large for them and most Class A
addresses were taken by this point in time anyway. Medium-sized
organizations needed a Class B or C address. The only problem is that there
is a vast difference between these two classes in the number of hosts.

With Class C addresses you get 254 hosts out of every Class C network
address. For many organizations this was not enough host addresses. So
the first thought would be that any organization that cannot fit into the
boundaries of a Class C address would need either a series of Class C addresses
or a Class B address. With the limited number of Class C addresses available, a
medium-sized organization using multiple Class C addresses was not feasible.
Moving to a Class B address makes some sense, but then you have 65,534
host addresses available. Again, this is not really a good answer, as many host

addresses would potentially go to waste. This is where supernetting comes into the picture.

In 1992 RFC 1338 (An Address Assignment and Aggregation Strategy) proposed better use and allocation of IP addresses for medium-sized organizations.

The first proposal was to hierarchically allocate future IP address assignment, by delegating control of segments of the IP address space to Internet Service Providers.

This is why nowadays you can't simply contact InterNIC and apply for an IP address. IP addresses are controlled by your local ISP.

Supernetting Multiple Class C Licenses

Suppose you have an organization that needs no more than 2,048 host addresses (8 Class C networks), and another that needs just over 4,000 (but no more than 4,096, or 16 Class C networks). In this example neither a single Class C nor Class B range works. Since InterNIC designated ISPs as responsible for allocating IP addresses, we would contact our local service provider and they could assign the appropriate addressing scheme.

Supernetting involves dividing a Class B or Class C network into various other networks. Similar to subnetting, supernetting divides a single network address into various networks, but it splits the networks between different organizations. This makes for more efficient use of the IP address pool.

With the above two requirements let's say we have a service provider who has the Class C address range that begins with 217.152.0.0 and ends with 217.159.255.0 assigned to him. This range allows for 2,048 networks if supernetted. A "supernetted route" to this block of network numbers would be described as 217.152.0.0 with mask of 255.248.0.0. The service provider would allocate its available address space for these two clients in the following manner:

The first client needs no more than 2,048 (this allows for growth in the organization). Allocate 217.152.0.x through 217.152.7.x (eight Class C networks). The ranges of available IP addresses with this allocation are:

```
217.152.0.1-217.152.0.254 = 254 hosts
217.152.1.1-217.152.1.254 = 254 hosts
217.152.2.1-217.152.2.254 = 254 hosts
217.152.3.1-217.152.3.254 = 254 hosts
217.152.4.1-217.152.3.254 = 254 hosts
217.152.5.1-217.152.5.254 = 254 hosts
217.152.6.1-217.152.6.254 = 254 hosts
217.152.7.1-217.152.7.254 = 254 hosts
2,032 hosts
```

This block of networks is described by the "supernet route" 217.152.0.0 and mask 255.255.248.0. The supernet route allows for these eight Class C networks to be one "network."

The second client, needing no more than 4,096 addresses, would get a similar series of Class C address ranges that would include up to 16 different networks, as shown next:

```
217.152.8.1-217.152.8.254   = 254 hosts
217.152.9.1-217.152.9.254   = 254 hosts
217.152.10.1-217.152.10.254 = 254 hosts
217.152.11.1-217.152.11.254 = 254 hosts
217.152.12.1-217.152.12.254 = 254 hosts
217.152.13.1-217.152.13.254 = 254 hosts
217.152.14.1-217.152.14.254 = 254 hosts
217.152.15.1-217.152.15.254 = 254 hosts
217.152.16.1-217.152.16.254 = 254 hosts
217.152.17.1-217.152.17.254 = 254 hosts
217.152.18.1-217.152.18.254 = 254 hosts
217.152.19.1-217.152.19.254 = 254 hosts
217.152.20.1-217.152.20.254 = 254 hosts
217.152.21.1-217.152.21.254 = 254 hosts
217.152.22.1-217.152.22.254 = 254 hosts
217.152.23.1-217.152.23.254 = 254 hosts
4,064 hosts
```

exam
ⓦatch

The TCP/IP exam does not go into supernetting in depth. A good overview and understanding of its purpose and how it affects IP address assignments is needed, however.

Managing a Class A Network Address

When classful addressing first came about, companies that received a Class A address had over 16 million host addresses at their disposal. With only 126 allocated Class A networks there was a very large waste of prime host addresses.

This is where subnetting comes in. Breaking down one Class A network address into multiple subnetworks makes for better use of the available IP address pool.

Large Network of 16,000,000 Hosts

Managing large networks of over 16 million hosts is challenging and there are not many networks this big. These large networks require many administrators and very good documentation, tracking, and communication.

Managing Smaller Subnetworks

Most networks will be smaller, with from one hundred to a few thousand hosts. These smaller networks are more manageable and do not require as many administrators. Some networks of only a few hundred workstations require only one administrator.

CERTIFICATION OBJECTIVE 4.03

Decimal to Binary Address Representation

Computers can communicate only by a mix of 0s and 1s. Even though a TCP/IP address may look like 255.255.130.110, the computer understands this number only in binary form. Each number in 255.255.130.10 is considered an octet. An octet means it is made up of 8 bits, which are each a zero or a one. Having 4 octets means that an IP address is made up of 32 bits. Thus, an IP address is a 32-bit address.

Decimal View

The reason that IP addresses are shown in dotted-decimal form is so it is easier for humans to read. A number like 11111111111111111000001000001010 makes absolutely no sense to us. So to begin with we separate out a 32-bit address into 4 octets or four groups of 8 bits. Then our stream of 1s and 0s looks like this: 11111111.11111111.10000010.00001010. This is still hard to read so we convert the binary octets into a decimal number.

Each bit holds a specific value in each position. Figure 4-3 shows each bit position and the value if the bit is set to one.

The following illustration shows each decimal value. To make various decimal values you add the bit values together. If a bit is a 0, the decimal value is not counted. If the bit is a 1, then the decimal value is counted. The largest possible value for a decimal number in 8-bit form is 255. The smallest of course is zero.

1	1	1	1	1	1	1	1
128	64	32	16	8	4	2	1

Converting a Decimal Number to Binary

1. Take the decimal number 137

2. To make this number binary we draw out our eight positions:

128	64	32	16	8	4	2	1

3. We then have to put a 1 in the positions that would add up and give us 137. To do this we start at the left-most column and if the bit position value is less than or equal to our decimal number, we put a 1 in that column. Our number is 137, the first column's value is 128. So we put a 1 in that column:

137							
1							
128	64	32	16	8	4	2	1

4. After we put a 1 in a column, we have to subtract the bit value from the total number to see what our remaining number is. In this case it is 9.

5. We continue from left to right checking each bit position. Again, if the bit value is less than or equal to our number (now 9) we put a 1 in that column. We find that the next three bit values are too large. We get to the 5th bit position and can put a 1 since 8 is less than 9:

X	no	no	no	9			
1	0	0	0	1			
128	64	32	16	8	4	2	1

6. Since we put a 1 in the column, we again have to subtract the bit value from the number we have to see what our remaining number is. In this case we subtract 8 from 9 and now our number is 1.

7. We continue comparing the remaining bit positions to our number. Since the next two bit positions are not less than our number, we enter 0's in those positions. The last bit matches our value so we can put a 1 in that column.

X	X	X	X	X	no	no	1
1	0	0	0	1	0	0	1
128	64	32	16	8	4	2	1

8. We subtract 1 from 1 and end up with 0. We should always end up with a 0 value subtracting somewhere along the bit path. If we do not, we made a mistake and would have to start over.

9. We see that 137 represented in binary form is 10001001. This is how a computer and network would interpret an octet value.

Binary View

If you a picture a stream of 32 0s and 1s as an IP address, there would be no way to easily understand how the decimal representation looks. Since each octet is separated by a period, we look at the decimal view that way also. The IP address 255.255.130.10 would be represented as 11111111.11111111.10000010.00001010 in binary. Converting a binary number to decimal is not a complicated process.

EXERCISE 4-2

Converting a Binary Number to Decimal

1. Take the binary number: 01010010

2. Putting this into a table with each bit value we get:

0	1	0	1	0	0	1	0
128	64	32	16	8	4	2	1

3. We then add together any decimal values that have a 1 in their column.

4. In this case the values 64, 16, and 2 have a 1 in their column. If we add 64+16+2 we get an answer of 82.

5. So this means that the binary value of 01010010 in decimal form is 82.

If we put all 1s in the 8 available positions and add together all of the values, we come up with 255. This is the largest available 8-bit number. You will never see a 32-bit, 4-octet IP address with a number larger than 255. New versions of IP, however, may have numbers that are larger.

CERTIFICATION OBJECTIVE 4.04

Bit Swiping

There may be times when you need to get more subnetworks out of your network. Depending on your requirements you can subnet in various ways. The default method of masking either one, two, or three octets can serve your purpose in most cases. However, you may have to borrow bits from one of the first three octets.

When defining your subnet mask remember that any bit with a 1 as a value is part of the network address. Also, any bit with a 0 in the subnet mask is considered to be part of the host address.

Borrowing Bits from the Next Octet

When borrowing bits from an octet they have to be in a continuous block. That means there can be only certain values that fit into the subnet mask. Table 4-5 shows the representation of the contiguous values. The 1s will always be to the left and the 0s will always be to the right.

TABLE 4-5	Binary	Decimal
Borrowing Bits and Their Decimal Values	00000000	0
	10000000	128
	11000000	192
	11100000	224
	11110000	240
	11111000	248
	11111100	252
	11111110	254
	11111111	255

All 0s will make the subnet mask one of the defaults. With the default subnet masks you have either the value 255 or the value 0 in each of your octets. The value 255, remember, is all 1s in binary. So, again, if you have:

```
255.255.0.0
```

you then have:

```
11111111.11111111.00000000.00000000
```

in binary. This particular subnet mask means that the first two octets determine your network address and the last two octets determine your host address.

When borrowing bits from another octet you will have something like this:

```
255.255.224.0
```

which converts to:

```
11111111.11111111.11100000.00000000
```

in binary. What this means is that the first two octets, plus the first three bits in the third octet, determine your network address. So the last five bits in the third octet and the entire fourth octet determine your host address. Take your time, 'cause now it gets challenging.

Advantages to Stealing Bits

There are of course advantages and disadvantages to stealing bits in an octet. With this process you can create more subnetworks in your network, and it can be easier to manage in some instances.

More Networks

As you borrow bits, you increase the number of available subnetworks. This is great if you need to segment off certain divisions of your organization, or have remote offices spread out across the country or globe. The flip side to this is that the more networks you make available by stealing bits, the fewer hosts per subnetwork you have at your disposal. Keep this in mind when planning your subnetworks.

Be prepared to determine how many hosts vs. networks you need when doing the masking stages of your subnetworking plan.

More Manageable

As you segment your network and organize each subnet, you will find that your network can become easier to manage. Troubleshooting can be easier if you are able to isolate problems to one particular subnetwork.

The flip side again involves numbers. If you have a network that has too many subnets to manage, this can make things tougher administratively.

Disadvantages to Stealing Bits

There may be some disadvantages to subnetting if not properly planned and maintained. Proper planning and good documentation will help keep things manageable.

Restricted Number of Hosts per Subnet

As you steal bits from an octet to subnet your network, you find that the number of available networks grows. The other side to this, of course, is that as you add networks you lose hosts per network. With each bit swiped, you lose a certain number of hosts per subnet.

Administrative Nightmares

We just want to reemphasize that if careful planning of your network layout isn't done, then administering it can be a nightmare. Careful documentation of any changes and layouts is a must. As you administer the network, you will find that if too many subnetworks are implemented, you can cause yourself more work in the long run.

How to Define a Subnet Mask

When planning and maintaining your network you have to know how to determine the subnet mask if you add a new office or location. There is a three-step process that is followed by most administrators:

- Determine the number of segments on your network.

- Count the number of bits needed to represent the number of segments needed.

- Push this number of bits to the high-order end and pad the remaining bits with 0s.

Once you convert the information to high-order bits, you can convert it back to decimal and you will have the IP octet information you need.

Determine Number of Physical Segments

1. When designing your network it will help to diagram it so you can visualize the physical segments you need to have. Figure 4-3 shows a network that needs to have three segments.

2. Now that you know you need three segments for your network, you have to determine how the number 3 is represented in binary form:

X	X	X	X	X	X	3	I
0	0	0	0	0	0	I	I
128	64	32	16	8	4	2	I

3. Converting the number 3 to binary tells us how many bits we need to borrow. In this case it is two bits.

4. We convert these two bits to high order which gives us:

   11000000

5. The high-order version of our two required bits converts back into decimal as 192.

6. Our subnet ID then is 192. Possible subnet masks out of this could be

   - 255.255.255.192   -   Class C
   - 255.255.192.0   -   Class B
   - 255.192.0.0   -   Class A

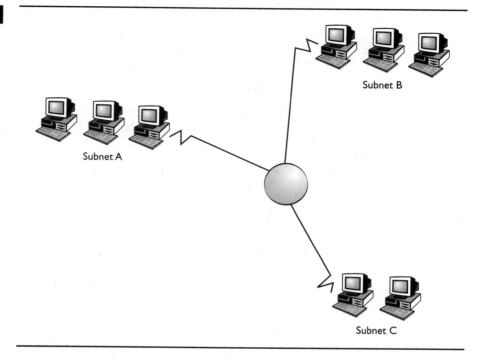

FIGURE 4-3

A three-subnet network

Subnet B

Subnet A

Subnet C

Determining Ranges and Masks

Determining the range of subnet addresses and the subnet mask itself is easier than you think. If you remember that the borrowed bits are contiguous, conversion is easy.

Table 4-6 shows an easy way to remember what the octet values are for various subnets. The values of course are dependent on how many bits are being swiped.

TABLE 4-6   Subnet Conversion Table

8	7	6	5	4	3	2	1	Bit position
128	64	32	16	8	4	2	1	Bit value
128	192	224	240	248	252	253	255	Value w/high-order consecutive bits added
1	2	3	4	5	6	7	8	Number of stolen bits

Looking at Table 4-6, you see the bit positions numbered with 8 as the left-most bit. The bit values again are shown in row 2. To determine the decimal value of your subnet ID, you simply add together all the bits that are stolen in high order. The fourth row shows how many bits are stolen, and just above that in row 3 is the decimal representation.

We will explain this another way to make it clearer. This isn't easy, so if you don't have it yet, don't worry, you will!

If you know the number of bits you want to swipe, there is a shortcut you can use to determine the number of networks and hosts.

EXERCISE 4-4

Planning Subnets Based on Configuration Needs

For this exercise it would be handy to use the Windows calculator since it is available on the exam.

1. Draw out your network and determine how many subnets you need.

2. Once you have the number of subnets, convert that number to binary.

3. Determine how many bits it took to form the number. This is how many bits you will have to steal.

4. Once you know how many bits you need, convert the number of bits to high order.

5. Once you have the high-order bits, convert the high-order value back to decimal.

6. This will give you the subnet mask value. If your network should be Class A, then use 255.x.0.0 (x being your value of course) for your subnet mask.

7. If your network should be a Class B, then use 255.255.x.0.

8. If your network should be a Class C, then use 255.255.255.x.

First Method is Formula $2^n - 2$ = Number of Networks

This method is known as the 2 to the power of bits - 2. You take the number of bits you want to swipe and take it to the power of two and then subtract 2. This will tell you how many networks you can get by swiping that number of bits.

NUMBER OF BITS SWIPED TO THE POWER OF 2   If you want
to swipe, say, 5 bits for your subnet, you would have the following:

2^5-2

This comes out to:

$2^5=32$
$32-2=30$

So in this instance you would be able to have 30 networks.

**SUBTRACT 2 (ALL BITS THROWN TO 0 AND ALL BITS
THROWN TO 1)**   We subtract 2 because of the first and last option,
which is all 0s, and the last option, which is all 1's. These two are thrown out
and this leaves us the possible number of networks.

NUMBER OF HOSTS   To determine the number of hosts available, you
take the binary value of the remaining host bits. The remaining host bits
include every bit that is involved in the host address. If you are planning a
Class A network and are stealing bits from the second octet, you would count
the remaining bits like this:

255.240.0.0 subnet mask

converts to

11111111.11110000.00000000.00000000 in binary

Any bit with a 0 is counted to determine the number of hosts. In this case
we have 20 bits. You can take the number of bits that are used for the host ID
and use them just like you did to determine the number of networks.

If you take 2 to the power of bits and subtract 2 you will get an answer
that is equal to the possible number of hosts. With 20 host bits it would look
like this:

$2^{20}-2$ =   1,048,574 possible hosts per subnet

We take the value and subtract 2 again because any values with all 0s or 1s are disqualified.

exam
Watch

Take advantage of the shortcut using the 2^n-2 formula. n, of course, is the number of bits. This will help save time on the TCP/IP exam.

Determining the number of subnets and hosts is an easy process once it is understood. The next challenge is to determine the subnet ranges. Planning and implementing your network requires a strong grasp on what your valid IP addresses are on each subnet and what their respective subnet address is.

EXERCISE 4-5

Determining the Number of Networks and Host Using 2^n-2

For this exercise you should complete and have a good grasp on how to determine the number of bits you will use. This exercise is a reverse approach to determine subnetworks and host from a decision based on bit swiping. It is also a good idea to use the Windows calculator since the exam allows you to use it.

1. Once you've determined how many bits will be swiped for your subnet address, plug the value into the n in the 2^n-2 formula. The answer you get will give you the number of networks that you can create by swiping that many bits.

2. Now count the total number of bits that will be used for the host address. Make sure to include all bits from all octets. Plug this number into the n in the 2^n-2 formula to get the number of hosts.

3. Try this with various n values and compare to the tables in this chapter to see if your values match up.

CERTIFICATION OBJECTIVE 4.05

Determining IP Addresses Within Subnets

The biggest challenge that students face in regards to TCP/IP is determining the subnet address and then determining the valid range of IP addresses within each subnet. This concept is not as difficult as it looks. Once you determine how many bits you have to swipe, the rest is easy.

When you know your subnet mask for your network, you can take the subnet address (the octet where bits are swiped) and then start determining the valid subnet ranges. Let's say that your subnet mask is:

255.255.224.0

You would take the octet that has the bits being split (or swiped as we've called it) and convert it to binary:

224   =   11100000

Since the swiped bits are always the bits with a 1 in their position you would take the right-most bit swiped and determine its value. In this example it is the third bit:

128	64	32	X	X	X	X	X
1	1	1	0	0	0	0	0
128	64	32	16	8	4	0	0

For this example the right-most bit is 32. This gives you your first subnet address. If your first two octets (in this example they would be the same throughout each subnet due to the subnet mask) are:

192.43

then your third octet would be:

32

for the first range of addresses. And your last octet for the subnet address is:

0

This gives you a subnet address of 192.43.32.0 for the first range of addresses. The first IP address would be 192.43.32.1. The last range is dependent on where the second range starts. To determine the second range we determine the next value by again using the first 3 bits (the swiped bits).

If you continue to move the bits to the next value you would find the following:

X	X	X	X	X	X	X	X	Row definition
1	1	1	0	0	0	0	0	Swiped bits
0	0	0						**INVALID**
0	0	1						Value is 32
0	1	0						Value is 64
0	1	1						Value is 96
1	0	0						Value is 128
1	0	1						Value is 160
1	1	0						Value is 192
1	1	1						**INVALID**
128	64	32	16	8	4	2	1	Bit value

Again the first and last values represented by all 0s or all 1s are thrown out. The values you end up with in this example for subnet addresses are:

- 192.43.32.0
- 192.43.64.0
- 192.43.96.0
- 192.43.128.0
- 192.43.160.0
- 192.43.192.0

This gives you six possible subnets when 3 bits are swiped. Going through our shortcut formula of 2^3-2 we find an answer of 6. This is a good way to double check our calculations.

We know that the IP addresses ending in zero on our network are the subnet addresses. The values ending in 255 are also thrown out due to our all

0s and all 1s rule. Knowing this we can determine the ranges within each subnet:

- 192.43.32.0   -   192.43.32.1-192.43.63.254
- 192.43.64.0   -   192.43.64.1-192.43.95.254
- 192.43.96.0   -   192.43.96.1-192.43.127.254
- 192.43.128.0   -   192.43.128.1-192.43.159.254
- 192.43.160.0   -   192.43.160.1-192.43.191.254
- 192.43.192.0   -   192.43.192.1-192.43.223.254

Reading through this you may have noticed a pattern developing. When we determine our first subnet address by using the right-most swiped bit, we can then make that the multiplier to determine our remaining subnets.

Again we borrow three bits so we take:

128	64	32	X	X	X	X	X
1	1	1	0	0	0	0	0
128	64	32	16	8	4	0	0

Since 32 is the right-most bit swiped, it is then our first subnet and our multiplier. You take the multiplier and add it to the last value until you reach the subnet mask octet value. In this case the subnet mask octet we are concerned with is the third, or 224. Let's look at this:

```
Starting value:    32
Add multiplier:    32+32=64
Add multiplier:    64+32=96
Add multiplier:    96+32=128
Add multiplier:    128+32=160
Add multiplier:    160+32=192
Add multiplier:    192+32=224 (not counted since it
                              matches our subnet mask value)
```

This gives us the different subnet addresses. We put the network octets in front:

and add the subnet address 32 and add a 0 at the end

We can do this for each of the above listed numbers.

Multiplying by Bit to Chart Subnet Ranges

Another way to look at this is to multiply by the right-most swiped bit. Take 32 and multiply by 1, then 2, then 3, and so on. Continue until you multiply the swiped bit by the value equal to the number of networks. You can again use the 2^n-2 shortcut to determine the number of networks. With 3 bits the value is 6 networks. You then multiply the right-most bit swiped by 1 and continue up to 6 like so:

```
32      X      1      =      32
32      X      2      =      64
32      X      3      =      96
32      X      4      =      128
32      X      5      =      160
32      X      6      =      192
```

We see the same values again for our various subnets.

exam
ⓦatch

Be sure to practice determining the subnet ranges. You will have to know how to do this on the exam for some of the scenario questions.

Now that we know how to determine the number of subnets based on the swiped bits and how to determine the various ranges within each subnet, we need to know what the basic values are within subnets. Each class has a certain number of networks and hosts available with each available subnet mask. If we memorize this information, it makes administration in the real world and the TCP/IP exam much easier.

EXERCISE 4-6

Troubleshooting Subnet Mask Errors

For this exercise you will need to have scratch paper or preferably a grease marker or something to erase and rewrite easily.

1. Draw yourself a diagram with 4 subnets each having 3 or 4 workstations on them.

2. Now assign the following subnet addresses to your 4 subnets:
   - Subnet 1:   210.210.128.0
   - Subnet 2:   210.210.96.0
   - Subnet 3:   210.210.64.0
   - Subnet 4:   210.210.32.0
   - Subnet Mask of: 255.255.224.0

3. Next assign a workstation in each subnet an IP address as follows:
   - Subnet 4:   210.210.43.12
   - Subnet 3:   210.210.100.192
   - Subnet 2:   210.210.110.210
   - Subnet 1:   210.210.126.4

4. Analyze your network configuration. What potential problems are there with this network setup and the subnet masks, and IPs that are assigned?

5. Fill in IP addresses and subnet mask values that will work. If you have access to the resource, setting this up would be super to see the real-world effects and what happens.

CERTIFICATION OBJECTIVE 4.06

How to Subnet a Class A Address

With Class A networks the valid network ranges are from 1.x.x.x to 126.x.x.x. When subnetting your network you will receive one or a series of network IDs from your local ISP. Once you receive this information, you can subnet your network. If you are using a firewall on your network, you could operate with one IP address for the Internet and then choose your addressing scheme for your network. The value of 127 is not used with standard IP addressing. This is reserved for loopback and diagnostic functions. This is a Class A octet, but not a valid IP octet.

Subnet Masks for Class A Addresses

The default subnet mask for a Class A network is 255.0.0.0. Again, this means that the first octet determines the network and the remaining octets determine the host address. Class A networks consist of only 126 available subnets in classful routing.

Using Bit Swiping

When using a Class A network subnet you will subnet with the second octet, and with one scenario you will use the third octet (see below). The octet values for subnets whether they are A, B, or C class networks are the same, just in different positions. Table 4-7 shows the breakdown of the various subnet masks, the available number of subnets and hosts, and how many bits are borrowed in each instance.

Using Class B Subnet Mask

As you look at Table 4-7 you notice that with Class A bit swiping we can potentially have a Class B subnet mask. In other words we may end up swiping all 8 bits of the second octet. With this option we get 254 available subnets. The most you could have originally was 126. This is good for large organizations that have too many locations to use a standard Class A subnet mask of 255.0.0.0. As long as they do not go over the 65,534 hosts

TABLE 4-7	Number of Subnets	Subnet Mask	Number of Borrowed Bits	Number of Hosts
	0	Invalid	1	Invalid
Range of Valid Class A Subnets Using Bit Swiping	2	255.192.x.x	2	4,194,302
	6	255.224.x.x	3	2,097,150
	14	255.240.x.x	4	1,048,574
	30	255.248.x.x	5	524,286
	62	255.252.x.x	6	262,142
	126	255.254.x.x	7	131,070
	254	255.255.x.x	8	65,534

within each subnet they can use a Class B subnet mask and achieve some unique results.

How to Subnet a Class B Address

With a Class B network the IP ranges are from 128.x.x.x to 191.x.x.x in classful routing. Again, the first octet of 127 (Class A) is not used, as it is for loopback and diagnostic testing.

Subnet Masks for Class B Addresses

The default subnet mask for a Class B network is 255.255.0.0. This means that the first two octets determine the network and the remaining two octets determine the host address. Class B networks consist of 16,384 available subnets in classful routing.

Using Bit Swiping

When using a Class B network subnet you will subnet with the third octet, and in one scenario you will use the fourth octet. Again, the octet values for subnets whether they are Class A, B, or C networks are the same, just in different positions. Table 4-8 shows the breakdown of the various subnet masks, the available number of subnets and hosts, and how many bits are borrowed in each instance.

EXERCISE 4-7

Entering Ranges of TCP/IP Addresses for A Subnet Masks

For this exercise paper and pen will be needed.

1. Given the following subnet mask, 255.255.192.0, determine the bit combinations for the octet where the bits have been split and fill in the proper column of the following chart.

255	255	192	0		
llllllll	llllllll	1100000	00000000		
		00			INVALID
		11			INVALID

2. Once you have the bit combinations, convert the numbers to decimal to determine your subnet address starter.

3. Draw out the subnet addresses and write the ranges next to them:

```
210.110.x.y              210.110.a.b-210.110.c.d
210.110.x.y              210.110.a.b-210.110.c.d
```

Using a Class C Subnet Mask

As with Class A addressing using Class B subnets, Class B addressing will take advantage of a Class C subnet mask if all eight bits are swiped. The nice thing about this option is that your hosts and subnets are equal. This is the way to get a balance between your hosts and subnets.

TABLE 4-8	Number of Subnets	Subnet Mask	Number of Borrowed Bits	Number of Hosts
Range of Valid Class B Subnets Using Bit Swiping	0	Invalid	1	Invalid
	2	255.255.192.x	2	16,382
	6	255.255.224.x	3	8,190
	14	255.255.240.x	4	4,094
	30	255.255.248.x	5	2,046
	62	255.255.252.x	6	1,022
	126	255.255.254.x	7	510
	254	255.255.255.x	8	254

CERTIFICATION OBJECTIVE 4.08

How to Subnet a Class C Address

With Class C networks the valid network ranges are from 192.x.x.x to 223.x.x.x. Anything beyond 223 is considered Class D and Class E, which currently aren't used in Windows networking.

Subnet Masks for Class C Addresses

The default subnet mask for a Class C network is 255.255.255.0. Again, this means that the first three octets determine the network and the fourth octet determines the host address. Class C networks consist of 2,097,152 available subnets in classful routing. This sounds great at first, but within each subnet you can have only 254 hosts. Organizations nowadays are likely to have a lot more than that, but not as many as 65,000 with a Class B address. This is where supernetting comes into play as we will see shortly.

Using Bit Swiping

When using a Class C network subnet you will subnet with the fourth octet. Again, the octet values for subnets whether they are Class A, B, or C networks are the same, just in different positions. Table 4-9 shows the breakdown of the various subnet masks, the available number of subnets and hosts, and how many bits are borrowed in each instance. With Class C bit swiping you can have a situation where you only have the ability to have 2 hosts per subnet. Planning and careful consideration are essential.

TABLE 4-9

Range of Valid Class C
Subnets Using Bit Swiping

Number of Subnets	Subnet Mask	Number of Borrowed Bits	Number of Hosts
Invalid	Invalid	1	Invalid
1-2	255.255.255.192	2	62
3-6	255.255.255.224	3	30
7-14	255.255.255.240	4	14
15-30	255.255.255.248	5	6
31-62	255.255.255.252	6	2
Invalid	Invalid	7	Invalid
Invalid	Invalid	8	Invalid

CERTIFICATION OBJECTIVE 4.09

Supernetting

If you have an organization that has a medium-sized number of hosts and Class C licenses will not fill your needs, then you may try supernetting. Some organizations will waste a vast amount of Class B IP addresses and supernetting was devised to help keep the IP address pool from being carelessly used up.

CERTIFICATION SUMMARY

You must understand subnetting in order to pass the TCP/IP exam. There are a few key items to remember when it comes to subnetting your TCP/IP network. Make sure you understand what the subnet mask does. It simply masks a series of bits to differentiate from the network portion of the address and the host portion of the address.

Once you are 100% sure on the basics of the subnet mask, then we get into bit swiping. Make sure to memorize the tables and have a good understanding of why there are a certain number of subnets for each mask and a certain number of hosts. Utilize the formula 2^n-2; this is the quickest way to determine the number of networks and hosts when you swipe a certain number of bits. Remember the n is equal to the number of bits that you swipe.

Being able to determine ranges within your subnet is a must for successful networking. The TCP/IP exam will test you on this knowledge as well. Being able to look at a network diagram and determine what is wrong with the picture is a common scenario question. Be sure to hone up your skills on determining the subnet address, the subnet mask, and the various ranges of IPs within each. You have to be able to do these things in about any order, as well.

A basic understanding of supernetting is good, but not really required for the exam.

TWO-MINUTE DRILL

- ❑ The two-level hierarchy basically helps with routing the information to the appropriate host on a particular network. To do this you have to have a network address and a host address.

- ❑ Subnetworks come into play by having many smaller networks, so congestion isn't an issue.

- ❑ You determine which bits or octets are used for the network address and which are for the host address by what is called *masking*.

- ❑ *Classful addressing* is based on the three distinct address classes: A, B, and C.

- ❑ A subnet mask basically masks or denotes one portion of the IP as the network address and the other as the host address.

- ❑ Don't accept the obvious; use the ANDing process to determine if the hosts are on the same network.

- ❑ The three-level hierarchy adds a third component to the routing process, the subnet address, which takes a 4-octet IP address and divides it up three ways.

- ❑ Supernetting came about when medium-sized organizations were having difficulty with the standard addressing scheme.

- ❑ IP addresses are controlled by your local ISP.

❑ Supernetting involves dividing a Class B or Class C network into various other networks.

❑ The TCP/IP exam does not go into supernetting in depth. However, you do need a basic understanding of its purpose and how it affects IP addresses.

❑ Breaking down one Class A network address into multiple subnetworks makes for better use of the available IP address pool.

❑ An octet means it is made up of 8 bits, which are each a 0 or a 1. Having 4 octets means that an IP address is made up of 32 bits.

❑ Converting a binary number to decimal is not a complicated process.

❑ When borrowing bits from an octet they have to be in a continuous block.

❑ By stealing bits in an octet you can create more subnetworks in your network, and it can be easier to manage in some instances.

❑ Be prepared to determine how many hosts vs. networks you need when doing the masking stages of your subnetworking plan.

❑ There may be some disadvantages to subnetting if not properly planned and maintained. Proper planning and good documentation will help keep things manageable.

❑ To define a Subnet Mask:

   ❑ Determine the number of segments on your network.

   ❑ Count the number of bits needed to represent the number of segments needed.

   ❑ Push this number of bits to the high-order end and pad the remaining bits with 0s.

❑ Take advantage of the shortcut using 2^n-2 formula. n is the number of bits. This will help save time on the TCP/IP exam.

❑ The biggest challenge that students face in regards to TCP/IP is determining the subnet address and then determining the valid range of IP addresses within each subnet.

❑ Be sure to practice determining the subnet ranges. You will have to know how to do this on the exam for some of the scenario questions.

❑ If you are using a firewall on your network, you could operate with one IP address for the Internet and then choose your addressing scheme for your network.

❑ With Class A networks the valid network ranges are from 1.x.x.x to 126.x.x.x.

❑ The default subnet mask for a Class A network is 255.0.0.0.

❑ With a Class B network the IP ranges are from 128.x.x.x to 191.x.x.x in classful routing.

❑ The default subnet mask for a Class B network is 255.255.0.0.

❑ With Class C networks the valid network ranges are from 192.x.x.x to 223.x.x.x.

❑ The default subnet mask for a Class C network is 255.255.255.0.

❑ Some organizations will waste a vast amount of Class B IP addresses and supernetting was devised to help keep the IP address pool from being carelessly used up.

SELF TEST

The following Self Test questions will help you measure your understanding of the material presented in this chapter. Read all the choices carefully, as there may be more than one correct answer. Choose all correct answers for each question.

1. Given Figure 4-4, answer the following scenario:
   The following network uses static IP addresses. The computer with IP address 210.116.204.12 on Subnet B is trying to communicate with a computer on Subnet A with IP address 210.116.135.17. The

machines are having trouble communicating. The computer on Subnet C with IP address 210.116.157.110 is able to communicate with the computer on Subnet B with no problems. Analyzing the information given, what is the problem?

A. The subnet address on Subnet A is incorrect.

B. The subnet address on Subnet B is incorrect.

C. The IP address of the workstation on Subnet B is incorrect.

FIGURE 4-4

Self Test question 1

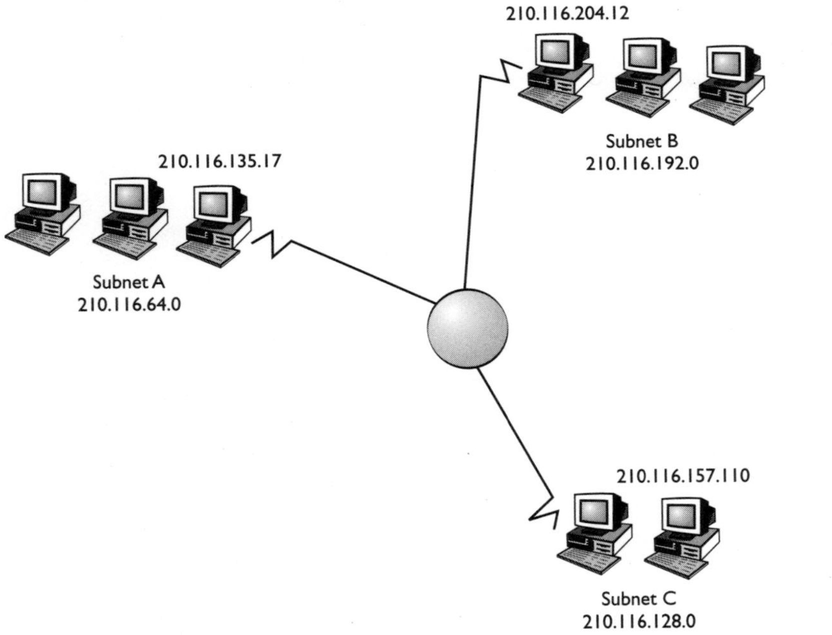

210.116.204.12

Subnet B
210.116.192.0

210.116.135.17

Subnet A
210.116.64.0

210.116.157.110

Subnet C
210.116.128.0

D. The IP address of the workstation on Subnet A is incorrect.

E. None of the above

2. Given Figure 4-5, answer the following: Considering the layout of IP addresses and subnet addresses, what would the value of the ? be in Figure 4-5?

A. 210.116.24.0

B. 210.116.17.0

C. 255.255.32.0

D. 255.255.255.0

E. none of the above

3. What is the following decimal value in 8-bit binary form: 179?

A. 10101010

B. 10110011

C. 01110110

D. 10110010

E. 10101111

4. What is the following 8 binary value in decimal form: 01111010?

A. 123

B. 120

C. 121

FIGURE 4-5

Self Test question 2

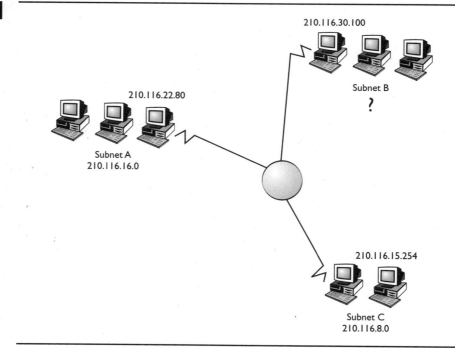

D.   122

E.   125

5.   Refer to Figure 4-6 for the following scenario:
     You have a network with six subnets. You know the following:

- You will never have more than 20 subnets.
- You will never need more than 2,048 hosts per subnet.
- You are running Windows 95 on your workstations.

- You use DHCP on your network.
- TCP/IP is your major protocol.
- Each subnet is a separate site connected via a router.
- All links are T1 connections between sites.

With a Class B network ID of 172.42.0.0 what would your subnet mask be?

A.   255.255.192.0

B.   255.255.224.0

C.   255.255.240.0

D.   255.255.248.0

FIGURE 4-6

Self Test question 5

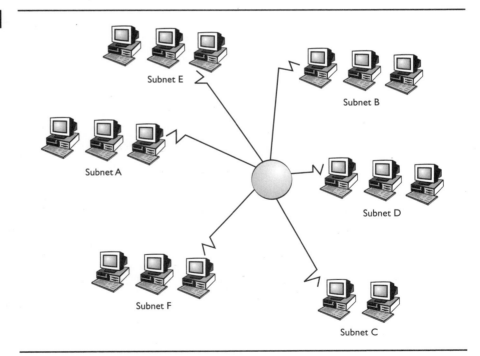

E. None of the above

6. Refer to Figure 4-7 for the following scenario:

   You have a large network divided up into subnets. You know the following:

   - You use TCP/IP and IPX/SPX as your protocols.
   - Each subnet is in a different city.
   - You will never have more than 15 subnets.

   - Your workstations are a mix of Windows NT Workstation and Windows 95.
   - You will never need more than 2,000 hosts per subnet.
   - You PDC is in your office with BDCs in each remote office.
   - You also have 3 BDCs at your location.

   Considering the list of known facts as well as Figure 4-7, which subnet mask would you use in this circumstance? You have a choice between a Class A, B, or C network.

FIGURE 4-7

Self Test question 6

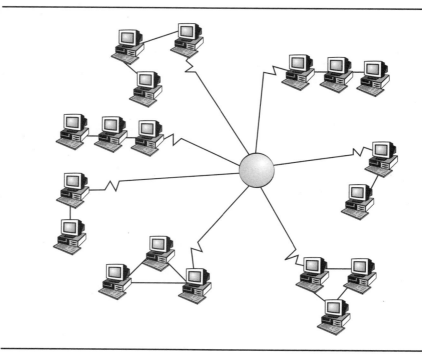

What do you choose and what subnet mask within the class do you use?

A. Class A with a subnet of 255.248.0.0

B. Class B with a subnet of 255.255.248.0

C. Class B with a subnet of 255.255.240.0

D. Class C with a subnet of 255.255.255.248

E. Class A with a subnet of 255.240.0.0

7. Refer to Figure 4-8 for the following scenario:

Using the box in the figure, convert the following decimal numbers to binary:

- 145
- 37
- 254
- 128
- 195

A. 145=10010111   37=00101111
   254=10000110   128=10001110
   195=11001011

B. 145=10010011   37=00100111
   254=01111110   128=10001110
   95=11001011

C. 145=10011001   37=00101101
   254=11111000   128=10110000
   195=11101011

D. 145=10010101   37=00110101
   254=11001110   128=10001000
   195=11001111

E. 145=10010001   37=00100101
   254=11111110   128=10000000
   195=11000011

8. Refer to Figure 4-9 for the following scenario:

The figure is missing some numbers. First fill in the missing decimal values for each bit. Next fill in either 0 or 1 to complete the binary equivalent of 166.

9. Take the following subnet mask and determine which of the following choices are valid subnet addresses for this mask: 255.240.0.0 (Choose all that apply.)

A. 210.16.0.0

B. 210.10.0.0

C. 210.48.0.0

D. 210.80.0.0

FIGURE 4-8

Self Test question 7

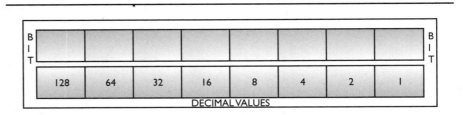

FIGURE 4-9

Self Test question 8

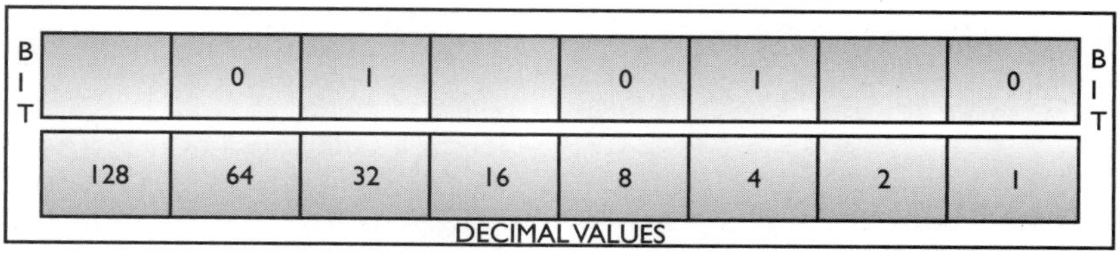

B I T		0	1		0	1		0	B I T
	128	64	32	16	8	4	2	1	

DECIMAL VALUES

E. 210.36.0.0

F. 210.40.0.0

10. You have a network with 4 subnets. The network addresses for your subnets are Network A: 192.1.16.0, Network B: 192.1.32.0, Network C: 192.1.48.0, and Network D: 192.1.64.0. With a subnet mask of 255.255.248.0 what will your ranges or addresses be?

A. Network A: 192.1.16.1-192.1.31.254, Network B: 192.1.32.1-192.1.47.254, Network C: 192.1.48.1-192.1.63.254, and Network D: 192.1.64.1-192.195.254

B. Network A: 192.1.16.1-192.1.23.254, Network B: 192.1.32.1-192.1.39.254, Network C: 192.1.48.1-192.1.55.254, and Network D: 192.1.64.1-192.71.254

C. Network A: 192.1.16.1-192.1.31.254, Network B: 192.1.32.1-192.1.48.254, Network C: 192.1.48.1-192.1.64.254, and Network D: 192.1.64.1-192.1.195.254.0

D. Network A: 192.216.1-192.2.31.254, Network B: 192.2.32.1-192.2.47.254, Network C: 192.2.48.1-192.2.63.254, and Network D: 192.1.64.1-192.195.254

5

Internet Routing

In this chapter we will discuss the concepts of multihomed hosts containing more than one network interface, IP packet forwarding (routing), and static and dynamic routing tables. Installation requirements to add dynamic routing to update routing tables automatically will be explained, as well as basic and advanced routing protocols: RIP, OSPF, and BGP. We will look at Microsoft's implementation of routing and also examine the ROUTE and TRACERT utilities supplied with the TCP/IP software.

CERTIFICATION OBJECTIVE 5.01

Using NT as a Router

In addition to the basic networking software services on your NT operating system there is a feature known as routing. Using a combination of software and hardware, routing gets a packet on one network to another network. An NT server with multiple network interface connections can act as a router between different networks of different protocols and media. The routing feature is provided for TCP/IP, AppleTalk, and IPX/SPX protocols. This section provides an overview of basic TCP/IP based routing: the terminology, features, required software components, and some benefits and drawbacks of these services.

If all machines could directly connect with every other machine, then each machine could simply keep a record of the IP address and intercommunication would be easy. Rarely can all machines be connected this way. More commonly, networks are broken up into related sets: by floor, building, office, corporate group, geographical region, or whatever you fancy. When the network is made up of many smaller networks, connections between them are handled by a host machine called a router, gateway, or bridge.

Gateway, Router, and Bridge

The term *router* is sometimes generically used to imply packet forwarding and protocol translation. Strictly speaking, this is a *gateway*, which is one step up from a pure router. A gateway provides router and protocol translation. Both a router and a gateway forward packets, also called *datagrams*, around a network;

this is true routing. A *bridge* provides selective connection between LANs where only packets destined for the other side cross the bridge.

Interior and Exterior Gateways

In the big picture of networks, there are small networks connected to large networks, which are in turn connected through backbone networks to each other. For instance, if the small networks are all the offices in each city, then the city is the large network. The backbone or core connections between the cities and other countries make up the entire network. The Internet was a major development ground for protocols to manage these networks.

Rather than having every router know about every other router, they are organized into interior and exterior, or small groups with borders, and these borders are connected by the *backbone*.

Interior Protocols

Router Internet Protocol (RIP) is a common Interior Gateway Protocol (IGP) used by neighboring networks to communicate with each other. RIP messages are sent frequently to all adjacent routers from every other router providing basic route and hop information.

Interior Gateway Routing Protocol (IGRP) is a proprietary router-to-router intra-domain protocol developed by Cisco for their routers. This protocol has five metrics instead of just the one used in RIP, the hop count. These five metrics provide speed, delay, packet size, loading, and reliability information about routes and can be used to find "best" routes.

Exterior Protocols

Gateway to Gateway Protocol (GGP) is used for traffic control between network cores. A *core* is a grouping of local subnets. The Exterior Gateway Protocol (EGP) is used between non-core machines. These protocols provide more detailed information about timing or vector distances. Each gateway needs to know about every other core gateway to compute the best route to a network, if there is more than one available.

Border Gateway Protocol (BGP) is an exterior gateway protocol that exchanges network reachability information only with other BGP routers, over a reliable transport layer connection, and does not require periodic updates.

Knowledge about interior and exterior protocols is provided just for your information and is not critical to know for basic routing. In the Internet world of hundreds of thousands of routers and the resultant array of paths to every destination, the improved traffic flow provided by these protocols is well worth knowing about.

NT 4.0 as a Router (Gateway)

Any multihomed (multiple Network Interface Cards) NT machine can be configured as a router, not only for the same protocol, such as TCP/IP, but for other protocols as well, like IPX/SPX using RIP for IPX/SPX, or between topologies like Ethernet and Token Ring.

With two or more network interfaces, NT can transfer, and translate for the protocol or topology if necessary, packets received at one interface but destined for some other network reachable by one or more of the other interfaces. This is called routing. The protocol that is used to send a packet must provide some routing information within it. A packet is considered routable by the protocol used. TCP/IP and IPX/SPX are routable protocols. NetBEUI is not considered a routing protocol although some specialized, high performance, dedicated routers can forward NetBEUI packets. This is not recommended because it floods both networks with broadcast messages.

CERTIFICATION OBJECTIVE 5.02

Understanding Routing

The postal system uses a similar concept to deliver letters. The address on an envelope or package (IP destination on a data packet) determines the letter's destination. If the letter's destination is local to the sender (same network, the Network Mask is used to determine this), then the sender can drop it off directly, in the same office, or locality (Local Area Network). If the address is not local, the letter is sent to the post office (the router), which then uses its internal forwarding system (routing table) to decide where next to send it (best or next route).

The postal code can be interpreted to represent whatever country, city, and street a letter is destined for. Similarly, the network number from an IP packet determines the remote area destination and whether to route or forward the packet to the destination.

FROM THE CLASSROOM

Routing a Packet on the Internet

Let's look at the packet information when the destination address is on a remote network and see how IP does routing. Workstation 160.45.100.1 wants to send a packet to the destination host at 160.20.10.105.

The workstation checks the destination address with the ANDing process and determines that the packet needs to be routed. The workstation ARPs to the default gateway and receives the IP address of the gateway. It then addresses the packet with the newly obtained address.

Packet information:

Source hardware address	11 (created the packet)
Source IP address	160.45.100.1
Destination hardware address	5
Destination IP address	160.20.0.3

IP on the gateway inspects the destination address and says, "This isn't for me." It then forwards the packet to network 160.20.

IP on network 160.20 uses ARP to obtain the hardware address for 160.20.10.105.

Receiving the hardware address, the packet is sent out with the newly obtained address.

Packet information:

Source hardware address	5 (created the packet)
Source IP address	160.45.100.1
Destination hardware address	13
Destination IP address	160.20.0.3

Once on the 160.20 network, the NIC recognizes itself and grabs the packet off the wire.

Looking at the packet information, you see that the hardware addresses are changing as the packet goes on its journey. The IP addresses are never changed.

—*By D. Lynn White, MCT, MCSE*

How Routing Works

For a network protocol to be routable, the protocol software design must provide a mechanism for determining whether a packet is local or not. If it is not local, it is sent on to the router or gateway. The router is programmed to forward the packet as the post office would forward a letter through the postal system to the final destination.

In Figure 5-1, the central host has two network cards, each with an address for their respective subnets. The left network is 223.4.5.0 and the right network is 223.4.6.0, based on the network mask of 255.255.255.0 used by both networks.

exam
ⓦatch

The central host in Figure 5-1 must have routing turned on and their respective gateway addresses must point to the other network card for routing to work.

If the two network cards use different topologies, like Ethernet and Token Ring, then this is called a gateway. A gateway will translate the packets between these topologies.

FIGURE 5-1

Subnetworks connected by router or gateways

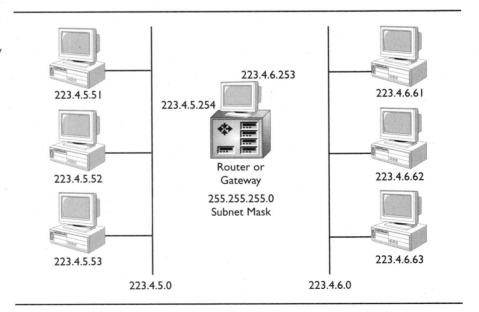

To turn on the routing software, in the Network Applet of Control Panel, navigate through the Protocol Panel to the TCP/IP Protocol Properties sheet's Routing Panel and click Enable Routing (see Figure 5-2):

START | Settings | Control Panel | Network | Protocols (Panel) | TCP/IP | Properties | Routing (Panel)

Router

For two small networks, as depicted in Figure 5-1, NT Routing can be efficient. For very large networks, where there are more than two networks being routed from the same point, dedicated routers are usually used, although you could use an NT host instead of a router. Each routing NT server would

FIGURE 5-2

Enable Routing panel in
TCP/IP Properties sheet

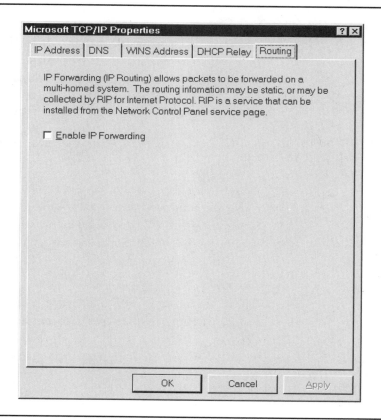

require multiple network interface cards properly configured within them. As long as this was the only service that each routing server was providing or it was a multi-CPU host with lots of horsepower to spare, you would not see much of a performance difference compared to a dedicated router.

DEDICATED COMPUTERS   Dedicated routers are machines that provide only routing and translation services between networks and topologies. Additional services may include security and routing path optimization software such as Border Gateway Protocol (BGP) or Open Shortest Path First (OSPF).

Most dedicated routers are not multiuser systems that provide file and print services as an NT server would; for example, there is usually no monitor or keyboard attached. Terminal access to dedicated routers is usually via a telnet session across the network or from a dial-in port on the router itself. Some routers do have terminal ports, not video ports like a PC, but just the dumb terminal ports that support terminals with a VT100 or better display emulation. Some of the well known brand names for routers include Bay Networks, Cisco, Digital, Fore Systems, IBM, and Cabletron Systems.

These routers have their own built-in language for managing their features. They are dedicated to routing functions only and can be programmed for many different features along with advanced routing features. NT 4.0 provides a few of the many possible features available on these dedicated routers.

Mixing routing vendors usually means losing some of the functionality that is proprietary in nature to each manufacturer, forcing you to use the lowest common denominator between them.

Gateway

The term gateway is used to identify the network interface that can transfer or route a packet from one network to another network interface on a different network.

In Figure 5-3, the central host has an interface on the 223.4.5.0 network with the IP address of 223.4.5.254. For each host on this network side to use the router, the TCP/IP setup would have to reflect this gateway address in its TCP/IP Protocol setup.

FIGURE 5-3

TCP/IP setup for 223.4.5.53
host to use Gateway

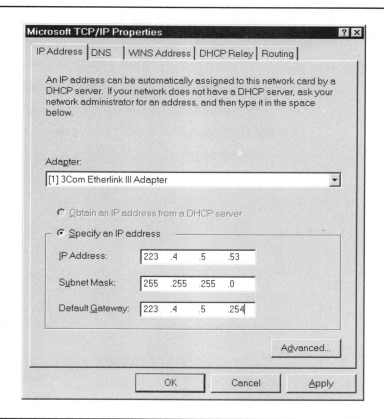

Each client machine on the left side of the network would be configured similarly, with the same Network Mask and Default Gateway IP address:

Left Network		
IP	**Network Mask**	**Default Gateway**
223.4.5.51	255.255.255.0	223.4.5.254
223.4.5.52	255.255.255.0	223.4.5.254
223.4.5.53	255.255.255.0	223.4.5.254

Each host on the right side network, 223.4.6.0, would have a similar setup except their Default Gateway would be 223.4.6.250, the interface on their network:

| Right Network | | |
IP	Network Mask	Default Gateway
223.4.6.61	255.255.255.0	223.4.6.253
223.4.6.62	255.255.255.0	223.4.6.253
223.4.6.63	255.255.255.0	223.4.6.253

The router ports would have a slightly different configuration; their default gateways would be each other.

exam
Watch

Gateways are routers that can also translate the packet format between topologies. For instance, a Token Ring NIC and an Ethernet NIC would require packet translation to the different formats. Pure routers simply use software to forward a packet between interfaces.

GATEWAY FORWARDS PACKETS When a packet from a left side host was destined for a right side host, then the network software on the host sending the packet would determine that it was a remote host and send it to the default gateway connection. This host would then route the packet onto the other network to the remote host. This action is also referred to as *forwarding* the packet.

exam
Watch

Enable IP Forwarding is the term used to enable routing in NT TCP/IP.

CERTIFICATION OBJECTIVE 5.03

Multihomed Hosts

Multihomed means there are two or more network interfaces on one machine. This is common on routers and switching equipment. Many Network

Operating Systems using TCP/IP (NT 4.0, Novell, Banyan, UNIX, and others) also provide this routing service between network interfaces.

Multhomed means multiple network interfaces.

Each network card or modem connection has a network interface number specific to the network it is attached to as in Figure 5-3 above. Routing is the transferring of a packet from one LAN to another via routing software.

Routing requires two or more network interface cards, including a modem acting as a network interface.

Multiple Cards with Two Different IP Addresses

Each network interface card gets an IP address specific to the network to which it is attached.

In Figure 5-3 above, the left side and the right side would be installed as follows:

IP	Network Mask	Default Gateway
Left Side		
223.4.5.254	255.255.255.0	223.4.6.253
Right Side		
223.4.6.253	255.255.255.0	223.4.5.254

Network setups are completely up to the individual administrators. Some administrators like to use the last few addresses for their router connections, as shown here, and some like to use the first few addresses for routers and possibly servers. It makes no difference technically. Microsoft course materials commonly uses low number assignments for their router IP addresses but there is no required standard.

The second network card acts as the default gateway for remote packets for the first network card and vice versa. The routing software then takes care of the actual packet transfer. In TPC/IP networks, the Network Mask is used to determine whether a packet should be routed. The packet is routed if the network number for the destination host does not match the network number of the local host.

Installing and Configuring a Two-NIC Server as a Router

The two networks are 222.123.1.0 and 222.123.2.0 and the server has two correctly installed network interface cards, NICs (proper IRQ, RAM, and PORT as required). You will use a default Class C Network Mask. The first NIC will be 222.123.1.10 and will use the second NIC as its gateway, 222.123.2.20. NIC 2 will be similarly set up with the IP numbers reversed.

Please note: You must be logged on with administrator privileges to correctly install all services in any of these exercises.

1. Go to the Network Icon in the Control Panel and Click to start the Network Control Screens.

2. Click the Protocols Panel. This will display all installed protocols. You should see TCP/IP Protocol listed in this display. If not, you need to add the protocol first.

3. Click the TCP/IP Protocol and then click Properties.

4. In the Network Card drop-down List there should be two Network Cards numbered [1] and [2]. For the first network card, enter the following
IP Address: **222.123.1.10**
Network Mask: **255.255.255.0**
Gateway: **222.123.2.20**

5. Click the drop-down box and click the second network card. Enter the following:
IP Address: **222.123.2.20**
Network Mask: **255.255.255.0**
Gateway: **222.123.1.10**

You should now see the following configuration changes:
222.123.1.0 → 222.123.1.10

Server: 10NT20
222.123.2.20 ← 222.123.2.0

6. Click the Routing tab at the top.

7. In the Routing Tab panel click the Enable IP Forwarding box.

8. Click the OK button at the bottom to accept all changes made to the TCP/IP properties. This will return you to the Network Control window.

You could click Close if you are finished now or move on to the exercise to install RIP for Internet Protocol and then click the Close button.

Single Adapter Systems

There is a special case of a single card acting as a router to two sets of networks that actually share the same local area cabling media.

In the case of the single network interface card you would have to have two distinct network IP addresses assigned to it, one for each network to be accessed. Static routes should be added to the interface so that packets from either network interface will use the other IP address on the same card as their default gateway. This is also known as a *logically multihomed network interface*.

Number of IP Addresses Assigned to an Interface

There is a limit of five IP addresses for any one network adapter, to make the sys admin's job manageable. Have you ever had to take two older machines with separate functions, like FTP and HTTP protocol servers, and integrate them onto one machine? The new machine can replace the two older machines and have both services appear as before, with independent IP addresses even though they are the same network card.

Number of IP Gateways Assigned to an Interface

Additionally, you can assign alternate gateways to use if there are multiple routers providing routing to other networks. This provides failover should the primary gateway fail to forward the packet.

Advanced IP Options: Multiple IP and Gateway Addresses

To add additional IP and/or gateway addresses to one network interface, click the Advanced option, lower right corner, on the IP Address panel of the TCP/IP Properties control window. Figure 5-4 shows the Advanced Options input control sheet.

Only if your network has multiple gateways to access the remote networks and only if you need to have multiple IP addresses responded to by this machine, would you ever need to add these extra addresses. Simple installations will not need this, such as in the example network in Figure 5-1.

FIGURE 5-4

Advanced IP Options -
Additional IP addresses and
Gateway addresses on one
network interface

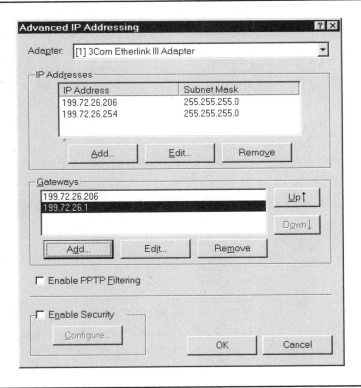

CERTIFICATION OBJECTIVE 5.04

Static Versus Dynamic Routing

Early routers had to be programmed with exactly which networks they could route between which interfaces, especially if there were many network interfaces. This configuration method is called *static routing*. Pre-set routing tables are loaded from a disk file or EPROM into the router software at boot time or after any reset or reboot.

Dynamic routing requires additional software that sends special route information packets between routers. One of the early versions that is still used extensively is called the Routing Internet Protocol (RIP). NT provides this as a service you can add. (See the section on RIP in this chapter for more details.)

There are some newer routing information services called Border Gateway Protocol (BGP) and Open Shortest Path First (OSPF). They require router software that understands the packets and can use the information to determine the best, shortest, least cost, or alternate route to a remote network based on information passed back to the local router. You would need to add the Steelhead Routing upgrade to NT 4.0 to get this additional service.

Features of Static Routing

Static routing refers to a specific table of routes input by you. This requires you as the router manager to manually configure the specific routing information for each interface. NT 4.0 is considered a static router until the addition of software to make it a dynamic router.

Each network card can be programmed with explicit routes to allow and or disallow specific routes. This gives the administrator explicit control over each interface. Additionally, you as the administrator can add the costs associated with routes as well as other related metrics to manage the flow of traffic between networks.

Advantages

You can be very specific about the routing, filtering, and settings on every routing interface.

It is very difficult to corrupt from external sources and can be more secure than dynamic routing.

Disadvantages

You must manually set up every interface and each interface will be different.

On large networks with many routers, gateways, and alternate routes, you also need to add information about metrics such as cost, which is a metric value you establish to compare route usage, to manage the flow of packets.

Features of Dynamic Routing

Dynamic routing protocols advertise the routes they are familiar with and pass on the metrics, number of other routers, or hops, required to get from their host to another network, either directly or indirectly through another router.

Advantages

No further set up is required for all the interfaces; they learn from the other routers over time.

Disadvantages

Dynamic routing generates continuous traffic from the routers with route update information.

They can be attacked from external sources with falsified RIP packets, which requires much more security and attention by a security officer, or you, for corruption and attacks.

They can create circle routes in complex networks with more than 16 hops.

Comparing Static and Dynamic Routing

With just two networks, the static routing setup is the most appropriate. In Figure 5-1, the routing interfaces have one static route and their default gateways are the other interface card. This is a basic static route. There are no other routes or options.

If your network has three or four parallel networks, as illustrated in Figure 5-5, then static routing may still be useful, although dynamic routing would be easier to set up.

However, the actual setup is far more complex. You cannot simply have the routers route to the other network by assigning the gateway addresses to the other network interface card. This simply moves the packet to the other side when in actual fact the router needs to send the packet on to the specific gateway from that network to the next network.

In Figure 5-5, the network 223.4.5.0, Net5, needs to route 223.4.6.0, Net6, packets to 223.4.6.253. But packets for Net7 and Net8 from Net5 need to be sent to the next gateway, 223.4.6.252, so they can be forwarded on their way. Same goes for every other router interface. You must program each interface as to where to send packets from every other network.

FIGURE 5-5

Four networks with routers

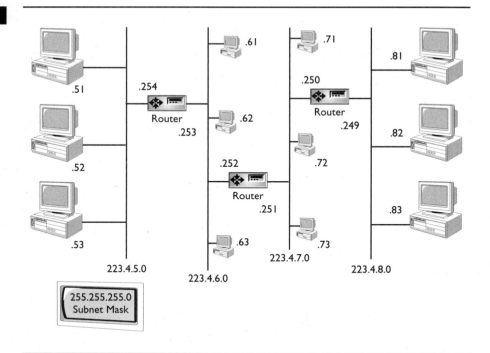

In Figure 5-5 the left-most network is numbered 223.4.5.0 and has hosts (223.4.5) .51, .52, and .53 plus the router interface .254 for a total of four interfaces. The right-most network also has four interfaces or nodes. The middle two networks have three hosts each and two router interfaces each.

Although the router is drawn as a single box, it may represent two servers with a dial-in connection using a modem from either side. The exact hardware is not important here, just the concepts.

For the outside networks, 223.4.5.0 and 223.4.8.0, all clients are configured with their gateway pointing to the only router on their networks, 223.4.5.254 and 223.4.8.249, respectively. For these two outside networks, the router is their only gateway to all the other networks. A packet destined for any network other than the next one over requires that you program the router interface for a network one or two more hops away.

The middle two networks have a more interesting setup. They both have two router ports or gateways. You can program your client host machines with only one IP gateway address, so which do you pick? Does it matter? Either and maybe are the answers. You can pick either gateway and then program each gateway with static routes for the other remote gateways or pick the one most likely to be used most often. Secondly, it does not matter once proper additional routes have been added, although if the most heavily used gateway is selected, this will reduce the number of routers that will handle the packet.

CERTIFICATION OBJECTIVE 5.05

Routing Tables

Each independent router port has a routing table. In Figure 5-1 with the two networks only, the routing table would be a simple one with one entry for each card pointing to the other network interface as the gateway. This is a simplified description, as there are other routes which are not discussed in detail, such as references to internal interfaces, network, and broadcast addresses. Some of these are seen in Table 5-1 which appears a bit later in this section.

In Figure 5-4, all three routers and their associated six ports would need to be programmed with the required static routes of the other networks if dynamic routing was not being used. You would want to make these permanent entries as well so that when the NT system is rebooted, the routes are re-established.

Entries

At the command prompt is a utility called ROUTE that is used to view and manage routes that are static and dynamic for an interface. You can delete and change dynamic routes but the next dynamic update may refresh the information.

At a command prompt if you have installed TCP/IP services, you can enter:

- ROUTE To get help on all the commands
- ROUTE PRINT To display the current routes configured

Default

The default routes set up initially define some standard network numbers used internally and locally for test and broadcast.

Even on a basic network card interface there are numerous routes. The following listing shows the output from a ROUTE PRINT command for a host with an IP address or 223.4.5.206.

```
C:\ > ROUTE PRINT

Active Routes:
  Network Address         Netmask       Gateway    Interface Metric
                                         Address
          0.0.0.0           0.0.0.0  223.4.5.206   223.4.5.206      1
        127.0.0.0         255.0.0.0    127.0.0.1     127.0.0.1      1
        223.4.5.0     255.255.255.0  223.4.5.206   223.4.5.206      1
      223.4.5.206   255.255.255.255    127.0.0.1     127.0.0.1      1
      223.4.5.255   255.255.255.255  223.4.5.206   223.4.5.206      1
  255.255.255.255   255.255.255.255  223.4.5.206   223.4.5.206      1

C: \ >
```

In the previous listing, the first route is for certain protocols like DHCP that use 0.0.0.0 as the host address initially. The third network is the local network. The last two routes are the broadcast address for the network and the general broadcast for the 0.0.0.0 network. All of these routes point to the local interface as their gateway.

The other network routes are internal routes that stop at the TCP/IP software itself. This is known as the *loopback address* and is usually 127.0.0.1 but it just has to start with 127; the rest of the numbers are not significant.

Subnet Broadcast

The broadcast address for every subnet is the network number combined with all the client bits being set to 1, or the last address in the network range. The broadcast address is used by many protocols to send a general query to all machines on the network so that one or more of them may respond. For example, the Address Resolution Protocol (ARP) uses a broadcast to the network to locate the IP address of a local host.

BRIEF OVERVIEW OF IP NUMBERING   IP (current version) addressing uses 32 bits conveniently broken into four octets, or four sets of 8 bits. A Network Number represents one combination of some of those 32 bits, from two minimum to 30 maximum. Generally, there are three well known groups called Class A, B, and C address ranges. The Class A addresses each have 24 bits that can be used for client numbers or over 16 million IP addresses; the network number in the first 8 bits does not change. The Class B network address is contained in the first 16 bits and the last 16 bits are used for client addresses, allowing for a total of 65,533 values. A Class C network address is in the first 24 bits and the last 8 bits are used for the client addresses.

Example of addresses in each basic class: (using default masks)

Class A 1-126 first octet value (127 reserved for Loopback)

12.33.234.23 255.0.0.0 12.0.0.0 Network 33.234.23 Client

58.38.94.123 255.0.0.0 58.0.0.0 Network 38.94.123 Client

Class B 128-191 first octet value

162.3.24.73 255.255.0.0   162.3.0.0 Network 24.73 Client

144.223.4.5 255.255.0.0 144.223.0.0 Network   4.5 Client

Class C 192- 223 first octet value

212.78.231.59 255.255.255.0 212.78.231.0 Network 59 Client

212.78.231.60 255.255.255.0 212.78.231.0 Network 60 Client

Classes D and E range from 224 to 254 in the first octet and are reserved for special uses.

BROADCAST ADDRESS   In a Class A network, the 24 bits for the clients represent all the numbers between 1 and 2**24-1. The zero address, like 12.0.0.0, is reserved as the network number. The last address, where all the client bits are set to the value 1 is the broadcast address, 12.255.255.255.

DEFAULT MASK   The *default mask* is a number that identifies all the bits that represent the network number part of the IP address. For a Class A address, 255.0.0.0 is the default mask. This implies that all of the first 8 bits represent the network number. For a Class B address, the first 16 bits indicate the network number; the mask is 255.255.0.0 by default. For a Class C network, the first 24 bits define the network number and the mask is 255.255.255.0 by default.

SUBNETTING   Subnetting allows you to further break up a standard Class A, B, or C network into smaller sections. By using some of what are normally considered the client bits as part of the network mask, then you can subdivide larger groups into smaller groups of IP addresses.

You can subnet using all but the first bit and last 2 bits of the client addresses. The Class A addresses allow 2 to 22 bits, Class B allow 2 to 14 bits, and Class C allow 2 to 6 bits of the client bits to be used in subnetting the network.

If you use the first 3 bits from any Class A, B, or C network address and include this as part of the subnet, your network masks become:

- 255.224.0.0 for Class A
- 255.255.224.0 for Class B
- 255.255.255.224 for Class C

The following section is a more complete example of subnetting various address classes using 2 bits. If you use the first 2 bits from any Class A, B, or C network address and include this as part of the subnet, your network masks become:

- 255.192.0.0 for Class A
- 255.255.192.0 for Class B
- 255.255.255.192 for Class C

This creates 4 blocks from the original set of addresses for any class since the 2 bits have 4 possible combinations: 00, 01, 10, and 11. Unfortunately, you should not use any block that uses all zeros or all ones. This excludes the 00 and 11 address blocks. You end up with the 01 and 10 blocks or 2 subnets. The formula for the number of groups created is 2**n-2 (2 to the power of n less 2) where n is the number of bits used to create the subnets. This is summarized in Table 5-1.

TABLE 5-1   Subnet Client Addresses, Network Number, and Broadcast Addresses for Each Network Class

Network	Using Netmask	First Client	Last Client	Broadcast Address
Basic Class A Network has 2**24-2 clients (~16 million)				
12.0.0.0	255.0.0.0	12.0.0.1	12.255.255.254	12.255.255.255
Class A Network With 2 subnets of 2**22-2 clients (~4 million) each				
12.64.0.0	255.192.0.0	12.64.0.1	12.127.255.254	12.127.255.255
12.128.0.0	255.192.0.0	12.128.0.1	12.191.255.254	12.191.255.255
Basic Class B Network has 2**16-2 clients (64K) clients				
162.2.0.0	255.255.0.0	162.2.0.1	162.2.255.254	162.2.255.255
Class B Network With 2 subnets of 2**14-2 clients (~16K) each				
162.2.64.0	255.255.192.0	162.2.64.1	162.2.127.254	162.2.127.255
162.2.128.0	255.255.192.0	162.2.128.1	162.2.191.254	162.2.191.255
Basic Class C Network has 2**8-2 = 254 clients				
212.3.6.0	255.255.255.0	212.3.6.1	212.3.6.254	212.3.6.255
Class C Network With 2 subnets of 2**6-2 clients (62) clients each				
212.3.6.64	255.255.255.192	212.3.6.65	212.3.6.126	212.3.6.127
212.3.6.192	255.255.255.192	212.3.6.129	212.3.6.190	212.3.6.191

Network Broadcasts

The network broadcast address is the last address available for a given network; all client bits are set to the value 1. This address is used to send general query packets to all hosts on the network. Broadcast packets are used extensively in all network protocols to establish information about zero or more hosts. The broadcast address for each network in Table 5-1 is the right-most column for each network. Any packet using this address as the destination address forces every host on the network to interpret the request and reply if the request pertains to that host. This is similar to requesting a show of hands from everyone in a theater lineup who has a ticket. This would be considered a broadcast message that everyone listens to, whether or not they respond. For example, a broadcast message might be to request the hardware address for a given host name.

Local Loopback

There is one specialized network address that is reserved on every machine to represent the "software." This is called the *local loopback address*. On every machine, the Class A network 127.0.0.0 is used to represent the TCP/IP software. You can ping the loopback to test if your software is running. Normally the loopback is numbered 127.0.0.1 but any numbers after the 127. are acceptable, for example, 127.23.45.67. Just remember the octet numbers vary between 0 and 255.

IP addresses use 8-bit numbers and can never exceed the value 255.

Local Network

Your local network is defined as all hosts using the same network number. In Table 5-1 the Class A network is 12.0.0.0 and all the local hosts are the IP addresses from 12.0.0.1 to 12.255.255.254. The broadcast address is the last address of this network, 12.255.255.255.

The assumption is that all host numbers for your local network are reachable directly; no gateway is needed. This defines a local area network. You could have 16 million connections on one Class A local area network but it would not be efficient. Nor would 64 thousand nodes on a Class B network be efficient, although you could try. You could not do this using one Ethernet segment as there is a limitation to number of nodes and overall wire length, but with enough bridges and repeaters, you might be able to do it.

Local Host

Each machine is known to itself as the *local host*. This is just another host name for your machine that may appear in a HOSTS file, for instance. Every other host is considered a *network host* (some are local and some are remote) reached via another specialized machine offering IP forwarding services, also called routing.

Add Static Entries

To add a static entry, you need to know the network number of the remote network, the gateway address to the next network that can pass it on, or the gateway to the network itself.

In Figure 5-4, the router between the 223.4.5.0 and 223.4.6.0 has two ports. When a packet for the network 223.4.7.0 or 223.4.8.0 arrives at either port, a static route should be added to forward the packet to the gateway address of the 223.4.7.0 network. The static routes to add would be for network 223.4.7.0 and network 223.4.8.0, both with network mask 255.255.255.0, to be sent to address 223.4.6.252. The port .252 would forward to its partner, 223.4.7.251, which would have a route to send packets bound for 223.4.8.0 to the router port 223.4.7.250. This router port, .250, would forward to port 223.4.8.249, which is on the correct network.

TCP/IP Diagnostic Utilities

Part of the software provided with the NT TCP/IP package includes standard utilities like TELNET (client), FTP (client), PING, ARP, NETSTAT, NBTSTAT (Microsoft network specific), TRACERT (may be called traceroute on UNIX systems), and ROUTE.

The PING command is used to test connectivity and to provide timing information over a specific route. By default, the NT version of PING sends only four packets to the remote host and then quits. You can change this to continuous with the -T, continuous until CTRL-C, or '-N integer-value' options.

ARP is used to display the current ARP table, hardware MAC addresses where packets are to be sent for a given IP address. Note in Figure 5-6 that the MAC address for the remote site remains as the gateway address since this is where all local packets are sent to be forwarded. This is a good test to see if the packets are going to the right location.

CERTIFICATION OBJECTIVE 5.06

ROUTE Command

The ROUTE command can be used to add, modify, delete, and display route information for one or all interfaces. Enter the ROUTE command with no arguments to provide basic help instructions (see Figure 5-7). Figures 5-8 and 5-9 show the Print, Add Route, and Print Updated Table commands, all done at the DOS command-line.

FIGURE 5-6

ARP and PING commands

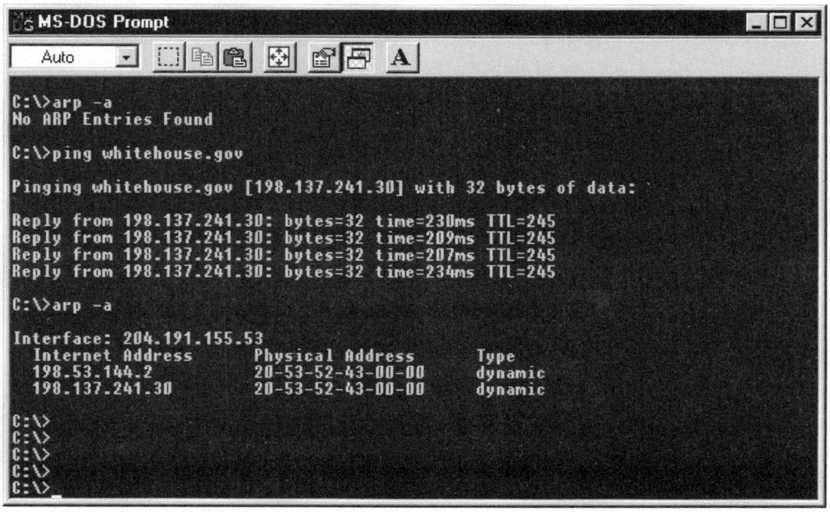

FIGURE 5-7

Entering the ROUTE command at the DOS prompt

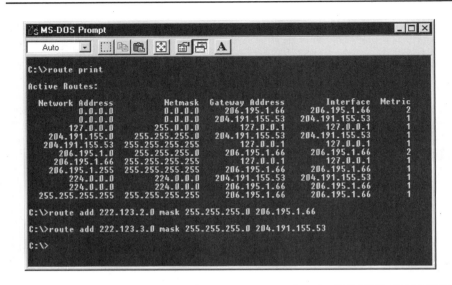

FIGURE 5-8

Print and add route

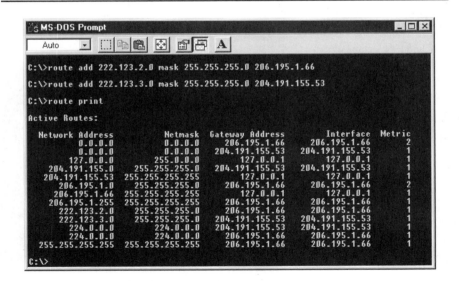

FIGURE 5-9

Print updated table

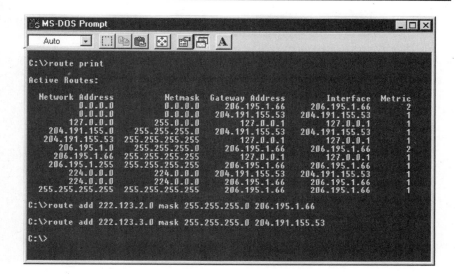

```
C:\>route print

Active Routes:

  Network Address          Netmask  Gateway Address        Interface  Metric
        0.0.0.0          0.0.0.0      206.195.1.66       206.195.1.66       2
        0.0.0.0          0.0.0.0    204.191.155.53     204.191.155.53       1
      127.0.0.0        255.0.0.0         127.0.0.1          127.0.0.1       1
  204.191.155.0    255.255.255.0    204.191.155.53     204.191.155.53       1
 204.191.155.53  255.255.255.255         127.0.0.1          127.0.0.1       1
    206.195.1.0    255.255.255.0      206.195.1.66       206.195.1.66       2
   206.195.1.66  255.255.255.255         127.0.0.1          127.0.0.1       1
  206.195.1.255  255.255.255.255      206.195.1.66       206.195.1.66       1
      224.0.0.0        224.0.0.0    204.191.155.53     204.191.155.53       1
      224.0.0.0        224.0.0.0      206.195.1.66       206.195.1.66       1
255.255.255.255  255.255.255.255      206.195.1.66       206.195.1.66       1

C:\>route add 222.123.2.0 mask 255.255.255.0 206.195.1.66

C:\>route add 222.123.3.0 mask 255.255.255.0 204.191.155.53

C:\>
```

Normally, you would pipe the output from any command to MORE for page control (any key to see one more page or the end). But the help screen is actually written to error output. To save this information to a file and then view it:

C:\> ROUTE 2> ROUTE.TXT

C:\> TYPE ROUTE.TXT | MORE

Using the ROUTE Command

You need to be at a command prompt to run the ROUTE command; there is no GUI based application (see the following listing for a summary of ROUTE command arguments):

```
C:\ > ROUTE

Manipulates network routing tables.
```

```
ROUTE [-f] [command [destination] [MASK netmask] [gateway]
[METRIC metric]]
```

    -f   Clears the routing tables of all gateway entries. if this is used in conjunction with one of the commands, the tables are cleared prior to running the command.

    -p   When used with the ADD command, makes a route persistent across boots of the system. By default,routes are not preserved when the system is restarted. When used with the PRINT command, displays the list of registered persistent routes. Ignored for all other commands, which always affect the appropriate persistent routes.

    command   Specifies one of four commands
                        PRINT   Prints a route
                        ADD   Adds a route
                        DELETE   Deletes a route
                        CHANGE   Modifies an existing route

    destination Specifies the host.

    MASK   If the MASK keyword is present, the next parameter is interpreted as the netmask parameter.

    netmask   If provided, specifies a sub-net mask value to be associated with this route entry. If not specified, it defaults to 255.255.255.255.

    gateway   Specifies gateway.

    METRIC   specifies the metric/cost for the destination

                    All symbolic names used for destination are looked up in the network database file NETWORKS. The symbolic names for gateway are looked up in the host name database file HOSTS.

If the command is print or delete, wildcards may be used for the destination and gateway, or the gateway argument may be omitted.

Using ROUTE to View Routing Tables

In this exercise you will be adding a third network, 222.123.3.0, to the two networks used in the last exercise. The third network will be accessible via another port on your 222.123.2.0 network with IP address 222.123.2.254. You will add this route to the second network card.

$$222.123.1.0 \rightarrow 222.123.1.10$$
$$\text{Server: 10NT20}$$
$$222.123.2.20 \leftarrow 222.123.2.0 \rightarrow 222.123.2.252$$
$$\text{Server: 20NT30}$$
$$222.123.3.0 \leftarrow 222.123.3.0$$
$$222.123.4.0$$

1. Start a command prompt by clicking Start, then Programs, and finally MS DOS Prompt.

2. To display all current routes, enter at the prompt:
   C:\> **ROUTE PRINT**

3. To add the route to the second network card (if you get an error of any type, check your syntax):
   C:\> **ROUTE ADD 222.123.3.0 MASK 255.255.255.0 222.123.2.252**
   C:\>

4. Display all current routes including the route just added:
   C:\> **ROUTE PRINT**

Where To Add Static Routes

The route commands needed at each interface are similar but all different. At each interface, you must program a route via a known gateway for all reachable networks.

Shown next are some example usages of the ROUTE command:

- ROUTE PRINT   Show all routes
- ROUTE -P ADD 223.4.7.0 223.4.6.252   Add a permanent (stored in registry) route to a network via a gateway on the local net

- **ROUTE CHANGE 223.4.7.0 MASK 255.255.255.0 223.4.6.252** Change some parameter about a route.

- **ROUTE DELETE 223.4.7.0** Delete a permanent or not single route from the routing table.

- **ROUTE -F ADD 223.4.7.0 223.4.6.252 METRIC 2** Delete all other routes and add one route to a gateway on the local net 2 hops away.

These are basic commands that must be entered at each interface. As you add networks to your intranet, you need to program each additional network at each interface. This is easy for two or three networks, but it can become very confusing as the network grows.

For a network of any size, there are easier methods. One of the most common is to use the dynamic routing protocol that has each router updating other routers about known paths so that you do not have to manually add each network route to every interface.

EXERCISE 5-3

Configuring Static Routing Entries

In this exercise, you will be adding a route from the first network for a fourth network beyond the third. In this case, the local gateway remains 222.123.2.252 for network 222.123.4.0.

222.123.1.0 → 222.123.1.10
        Server: NT10RTR20
        222.123.2.20 ← 222.123.2.0 → 222.123.2.252
                                  Server: NT20RTR30
        222.123.3.253 ← 222.123.3.0 → 222.123.3.30
        Server: NT30RTR40
        222.123.4.40 ← 222.123.4.0

1. Start a command prompt by clicking Start, then Programs, and finally MS DOS Prompt.

2. To add the route to the third network card (if you get an error of any type, check your syntax):
   C:\> **ROUTE ADD 222.123.4.0 MASK 255.255.255.0 222.123.2.252**

3. Display all current routes including the route just added:
   C:\> **ROUTE PRINT**

This route says that packets received at this address from any host on network 1 or 2 and destined for network 4 will be forwarded to the gateway address 222.123.2.252, which will then forward the packets on. This will require additional routing information at the port leading to network 3 and onward to network 4.

CERTIFICATION OBJECTIVE 5.07

Routing Protocols

There are a several routing protocols, such as BGP and OSPF, but the original protocol is called Routing Internet Protocol (RIP) and is supported by NT 4.0 and most current dedicated routers.

RIP functions at two levels:

- **Passive** listens for route information and stores it.
- **Active** listens, stores, and sends its routing information on all subnets served by it.

RIP provides the hop count, number of routers, or a cost value, assigned to provide more of a distance/speed vector than a pure hop count, to go through to get to a network. There is no real indication of speed or reliability.

A hop count of 1 indicates a direct connection; any other number indicates indirect paths. If a new route arrives with a similar hop count, it is ignored. A hop count of 16 means the network is unreachable.

Steelhead: Multi-Protocol Routing

Microsoft has put out an upgrade called Multi-Protocol Routing, also known as Steelhead. This provides DHCP Relay Agent, OSPF by Bay Networks, and RIP Version 2 for Internet Protocol.

By installing the Multi-Protocol Router free upgrade from Microsoft, you can include the newer Version 2 of RIP as well as OSPF functionality if your network is large and could be improved with the additional functionality of groupings and backbones.

Routing Internet Protocol (RIP)

The RIP service, for each interface card, broadcasts the routes it can access as a general broadcast message type that RIP-enabled routers listen for and record in dynamic route tables.

Features
It is a very well known standard packet protocol that provides single vector based hop/cost metric.

It is dynamic and no further configuration is needed.

RIP works on most other protocols and can pass information between them.

It provides basic information about known networks and a single metric about them.

ADVANTAGES   RIP's main advantages are that it is a very well known protocol that is supported by all known router manufacturers. Furthermore, it is easy to install and is self-configuring.

DISADVANTAGES   RIP's disadvantages include the fact that it does not provide any information about flow, quality, speed, or congestion. Also no security information is given and it is not secure by nature.

RIP routes stalls when a critical member fails, and a slow convergence on the failed router can occur.

Open Shortest Path First (OSPF)

The Open Shortest Path First (OSPF) protocol is a link state protocol better suited for large complex networks with many routers. OSPF is an interior gateway protocol that distributes routing information between routers in a grouping called a single autonomous system (AS). OSPF chooses the least-cost path and can be programmed to send to more than one interface simultaneously.

Features

Each router maintains a database describing the entire AS topology. OSPF datagrams are sent from all members, by flooding to all other members, to build this database.

Each multiaccess network with two or more attached routers has a designated router and backup routers. The designated router floods a link-state advertisement for the multiaccess network and has other specialized duties as well.

OSPF uses a multicast advertisement meant for other OSPF routers.

OSPF can also include authentication and can route onto multiple paths.

OSPF allows networks to be grouped into AS areas. Routes are then categorized into four groups, in order of precedence:

- **Intra-area**   Destinations within the same AS
- **Inter-area**   Routes between AS areas

- **ASE Type 1 external**   Non-OSPF Routes with similar metrics to OSPF
- **ASE Type 2 external**   Non-OSPF Routes with non-similar metrics

Autonomous System External are routes to external destinations non-OSPF.

OSPF uses the HELLO protocol to pass state information between gateways.

ADVANTAGES   Each route provides local metric values about speed, traffic, and reliability as well as other information.

Its dynamic nature reduces administrative management required in large networks.

External route information can be determined from OSPF or EGP protocol information.

Large local area networks can be divided into smaller areas with their own gateway (border router) and routing algorithms separate from the backbone routing servers.

DISADVANTAGES   OSPF uses similar area and backbone terminology to the Internet but not exactly the same, which can cause confusion for administrators.

Another disadvantage is that it is not available on all routers.

To use it, you must establish SA borders and gateways.

OSPF requires significantly more memory for various tables at each router.

The route calculation is a more optimum path than the shortest path, based on known topology metrics.

Comparison of RIP and OSPF

RIP provides hop information, the number of machines between source and destination networks. This does not provide any physical or distance characteristics of the routes.

OSPF provides more advanced routing information to the routers themselves and can better manage large area network traffic patterns by breaking the networks into smaller groups with borders between them. OSPF can segment your network into larger groups that act as one AS, and then set up border machines that act much like a bridge between each of the AS areas. Table 5-2 summarizes the features of RIP and OSPF.

Rip and OSPF Used Together

You can use RIP within a small segment of your network and then use OSPF for the larger network structure. They do not share any data and keep separate information at each router. This requires some maintenance but saves having to set up each of the smaller areas. The backbone and area border routers could be managed using OSPF and could thus be more reliable and secure, especially if connected to the Internet.

CERTIFICATION OBJECTIVE 5.08

Microsoft's Implementation of Routing

Microsoft TCP/IP services provide a very basic routing service that is static in nature; all additional routes must be manually added. During the year after the release of NT 4.0, Microsoft continued to improve the routing capability by

TABLE 5-2	RIP	OSPF
Features of RIP and OSPF	Vector Distance (Hops)	Link state - reliability, speed, etc.
	No security	Authentication from a known source
	Basic Masking	Variable masking - each area can use separate mask
	Hop Count Routing	Type of Service Routing - selective based on state
	Single Path - database per port	Multiple Paths - central database with many ports
	No Choice other than hops	Load sharing based on link state values
	Broadcast to all hosts	Multicast to OSPF hosts only

updating to RIP Version 2 and adding OSPF. This was called the Steelhead project and was released in late 1997 as Multi-Protocol Routing (MPR).

Supports Routing Protocols

The base installation of TCP/IP and the subsequent selection of Enable IP Routing on the Routing panel of the TCP/IP properties sheet provides static routing only. This means additional routing information must be entered manually.

If you want dynamic RIP routing to be enabled, you must also install the additional RIP for Internet Protocol service. Only RIP Version 1 service is provided with the standard NT 4.0 installation files. If you want to upgrade to RIP Version 2 and or OSPF, you will need to download the Multi-Protocol Router software from Microsoft's Web site: http://www.microsoft.com.

RIP

The Routing Internet Protocol advertises known local routes with a hop count of 1 and adjacent routes obtained from other routers with a hop count incremented by 1 to the other gateways.

INSTALLING AND CONFIGURING RIP   You must add the RIP for Internet Protocol service to your network services if you want dynamic RIP services.

Installing the RIP for Internet Protocol Service

1. Double-click the Network Icon in Control Panel to display the Network control window.
2. Click the Services tab to list the currently installed services.
3. Click the Add button; the Select Network Service dialog box will appear, as shown in Figure 5-10.
4. Click OK. You will be asked to verify the location of the installation files. Unless this location has changed, click OK. If it has changed put the new path in this input box.
5. Click Close when the installation has completed. The system will now need to be rebooted.

FIGURE 5-10

Routing Property Page

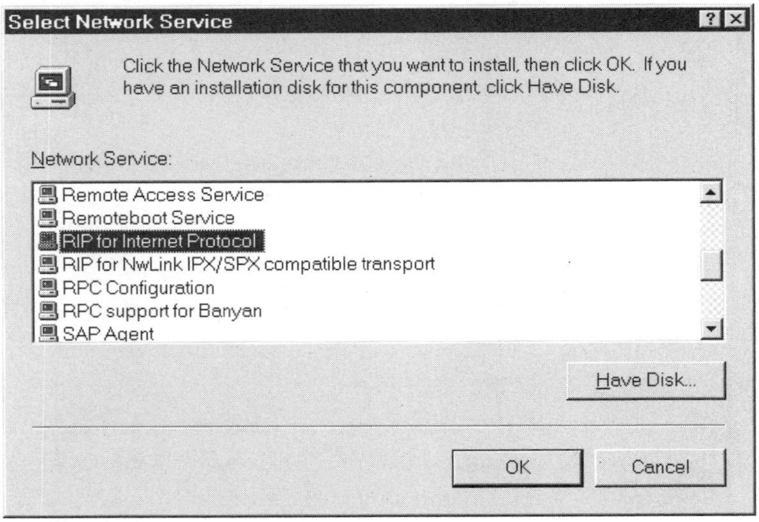

Multihomed System

To configure basic static routing on a multihomed NT computer, you need to have two or more network interface cards, NIC's, installed and configured correctly along with the TCP/IP protocol. Each NIC will then get a unique address on the attached network, the proper network mask for the network, and the gateway address will point to the address of the other NIC in the machine in both cases. You must then Enable IP Forwarding on the Routing panel of TCP/IP Properties. This will provide static routing.

To upgrade to full dynamic routing, install the RIP for Internet Protocol service as we did in Exercise 5-4. No further configuration is required.

CERTIFICATION OBJECTIVE 5.09

TRACERT Command

Another useful utility supplied with the TCP/IP software is the TRACERT utility used to trace a route from origin to destination. Each router interface encountered is echoed to the screen along with some statistical information about the path timing.

TRACERT Explained

The actual mechanism used by TRACERT is to send a series of sequentially marked packets destined for the remote location with the Time-To-Live (TTL) setting started off at 1 and incremented by 1 after each interface returns an Internet Communication Message Protocol, ICMP (in other words, a reply). A known control for network floods was the TTL value. Every interface that handles a packet decrements the TTL value by 1. This ensures the packet does not continue on forever in some unknown loop. The receiving host returns an error message, via ICMP, because the TTL value is zero at this interface. The following listing shows the TRACERT commands available.

```
Usage: tracert [-d] [-h maximum_hops] [-j host-list] [-w
timeout] target_name
```

```
Options:

    -d                 Do not resolve addresses to hostnames.

    -h maximum_hops    Maximum number of hops to search for target.

    -j host-list       Loose source route along host-list.

    -w timeout         Wait timeout milliseconds for each reply.
```

The TRACERT command can be very useful in determining serviceability of a route since the output includes three average timing values. The comparison of these values from time to time can indicate the congestion, reliability, and if alternate routes are ever used.

Sometimes a route becomes congested or unreachable and the TRACERT command can show this, as well as retry the request a number of times, just in case, as seen in Figure 5-11. Figure 5-12 shows a successful (completed) connection to a host.

TRACERT: Unreachable routes are retried multiple times before failure

```
MS-DOS Prompt                                                    _ □ ×
 Auto       ▾   ☐ ▣ ▣ 🔲 🗗 🖨 A
C:\WIN95>cd ..

C:\>tracert www.microsoft.com

Tracing route to www.microsoft.com [207.68.137.59]
over a maximum of 30 hops:

  1    142 ms    144 ms    143 ms  ts12.vcr.istar.ca [204.191.152.21]
  2    141 ms    144 ms    145 ms  204.191.152.1
  3    141 ms    145 ms    143 ms  core2.Vancouver.iSTAR.net [198.53.245.1]
  4    146 ms    148 ms    147 ms  border3-hssi1-0.Seattle.mci.net [204.70.54.5]
  5    328 ms    268 ms    266 ms  core1-fddi-0.Seattle.mci.net [204.70.2.145]
  6    148 ms    175 ms    143 ms  bordercore2.Seattle.mci.net [166.48.208.1]
  7    148 ms    151 ms    150 ms  microsoft.Seattle.mci.net [166.48.209.250]
  8    264 ms    352 ms    358 ms  207.68.145.46
  9      *         *         *     Request timed out.
 10      *         *         *     Request timed out.
 11      *         *         *     Request timed out.
 12      *         *         *     Request timed out.
 13      *         *         *     Request timed out.
 14      *         *         *     Request timed out.
 15      *         *         *     Request timed out.
 16      *         *         *     Request timed out.
 17
C:\>
```

FIGURE 5-12

TRACERT: Completed
connection to
whitehouse.gov Host

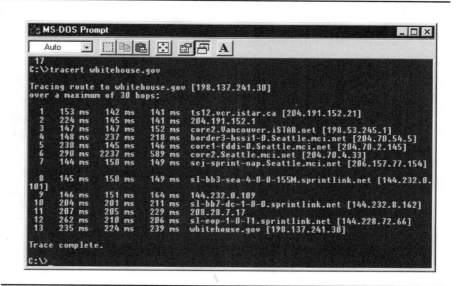

```
 MS-DOS Prompt                                                    _ □ ×
 Auto        ▼   [ ]  🔲 🔳 🔲  🗗 🖨 A
 17
C:\>tracert whitehouse.gov

Tracing route to whitehouse.gov [198.137.241.30]
over a maximum of 30 hops:

  1   153 ms    142 ms    141 ms  ts12.vcr.istar.ca [204.191.152.21]
  2   224 ms    145 ms    141 ms  204.191.152.1
  3   147 ms    147 ms    152 ms  core2.Vancouver.iSTAR.net [198.53.245.1]
  4   148 ms    237 ms    218 ms  border3-hssi1-0.Seattle.mci.net [204.70.54.5]
  5   230 ms    145 ms    146 ms  core1-fddi-0.Seattle.mci.net [204.70.2.145]
  6   290 ms   2237 ms    589 ms  core2.Seattle.mci.net [204.70.4.33]
  7   144 ms    150 ms    149 ms  sej-sprint-nap.Seattle.mci.net [206.157.77.154]

  8   145 ms    150 ms    149 ms  sl-bb3-sea-4-0-0-155M.sprintlink.net [144.232.0.
101]
  9   146 ms    151 ms    164 ms  144.232.0.109
 10   204 ms    201 ms    211 ms  sl-bb7-dc-1-0-0.sprintlink.net [144.232.8.162]
 11   207 ms    205 ms    229 ms  208.28.7.17
 12   262 ms    210 ms    206 ms  sl-eop-1-0-T1.sprintlink.net [144.228.72.66]
 13   235 ms    224 ms    239 ms  whitehouse.gov [198.137.241.30]

Trace complete.

C:\>
```

EXERCISE 5-5

Using TRACERT to Follow a Message Through Its Route

In this exercise you will trace the route taken to get to the third network
from the first. You should do this from a client and not the routing server.
Select a client in the first network like 222.123.1.15. You can ping the gateway
port on the third network, 222.123.3.30.

1. Start a command prompt on a client on the first network.

2. At the prompt, trace the route to the gateway port on the third
network, 222.123.3.30:
C:\> **TRACERT 222.123.3.30**

EXERCISE 5-6

Configuring 3 Routers Between 4 Networks

In this exercise you will complete the routing requirements for all gateways to
support all other networks. Each gateway interface must know to which next
gateway interface a packet must go if it is not local to that interface.

1. On the first router, named NT1RTR2 in this exercise, configure the
first port to route to port 222.123.2.20 for all 3 other networks.

2. Configure the second port 222.123.2.20 to route 222.123.1.0 packets to port 222.123.1.10 and networks 3 and 4 to the gateway to network 3, 222.123.2.252.

3. On the second router, named NT2RTR3 in this exercise, configure the first port 222.123.3.30 to route network 1 to port 222.123.2.252 and networks 3 and 4 to port 222.123.3.30.

4. On the second router, network 3 port, configure 222.123.3.30 to send networks 1 and 2 to 222.123.2.252 and network 4 to 222.123.3.253.

5. On the third router, named NT3RTR4 in this exercise, configure the first port 222.123.30.253 to route networks 1 and 2 to 222.123.3.30.

6. On the second port of third router, configure port 222.123.4.40 to route all other 3 networks to the first port, 222.123.3.253.

The end result looks something like this:

Network   →   Gateway IP

222.123.1.0 → 222.123.1.10

route Add	222.123.2.0 MASK 255.255.255.0 222.123.2.20	
route Add	222.123:3.0 MASK 255.255.255.0 222.123.2.20	
route Add	222.123.4.0 MASK 255.255.255.0 222.123.2.20 metric 2	

        222.123.1.10

        Server: NT10RTR20

        222.123.2.20

route Add	222.123.1.0 MASK 255.255.255.0 222.123.1.10
route Add	222.123.3.0 MASK 255.255.255.0 222.123.2.252
route Add	222.123.4.0 MASK 255.255.255.0 222.123.2.252

        Gateway IP ←   Network → Gateway IP

        222.123.2.20 ← 222.123.2.0 → 222.123.2.252

route Add	222.123.1.0 MASK 255.255.255.0 222.123.2.20
route Add	222.123.3.0 MASK 255.255.255.0 222.123.3.30
route Add	222.123.4.0 MASK 255.255.255.0 222.123.3.30

        222.123.2.252

        Server: NT20RTR30

222.123.3.30

route Add	222.123.1.0	MASK	255.255.255.0	222.123.2.252
route Add	222.123.2.0	MASK	255.255.255.0	222.123.2.252
route Add	222.123.4.0	MASK	255.255.255.0	222.123.3.253

Gateway IP ← Network → Gateway IP

222.123.3.253 ← **222.123.3.0** → **222.123.3.30**

route Add	222.123.1.0	MASK	255.255.255.0	222.123.3.30 metric 2
route Add	222.123.2.0	MASK	255.255.255.0	222.123.3.30
route Add	222.123.4.0	MASK	255.255.255.0	222.123.4.40

222.123.3.253

Server: NT30RTR40

222.123.4.40

route Add	222.123.1.0	MASK	255.255.255.0	222.123.3.253 metric 3
route Add	222.123.2.0	MASK	255.255.255.0	222.123.3.253
route Add	222.123.3.0	MASK	255.255.255.0	222.123.3.253

Network → Gateway IP

222.123.4.0 ← **222.123.4.40**

CERTIFICATION SUMMARY

This chapter has introduced you to the concepts of multihomed hosts containing more than one network interface, either network cards or modem connections; the concept of IP packet forwarding, also known as routing, explained for simple and complex networks; and static and dynamic routing tables. We learned the installation requirements to add dynamic routing to update routing tables automatically. We discussed basic and advanced routing protocols: RIP, OSPF, and BGP. Finally, we looked at Microsoft's implementation of routing, which is static by default. We learned how to add RIP for Internet service to provide dynamic routing, or multiprotocol routing, Steelhead. We examined the ROUTE and TRACERT utilities supplied with the TCP/IP software for management and information.

✓ TWO-MINUTE DRILL

❏ Using a combination of software and hardware, routing gets a packet on one network to another network.

❏ The term *router* is sometimes generically used to imply packet forwarding and protocol translation.

❏ A gateway provides router and protocol translation.

❏ Both a router and a gateway forward packets, also called *datagrams*, around a network; this is true routing.

❏ A *bridge* provides selective connection between LANs where only packets destined for the other side cross the bridge.

❏ Router Internet Protocol (RIP) is a common Interior Gateway Protocol (IGP) used by neighboring networks to communicate with each other.

❏ Gateway to Gateway Protocol (GGP) is used for traffic control between network cores.

❏ A *core* is a grouping of local subnets.

❏ Any multihomed (multiple Network Interface Cards) NT machine can be configured as a router, not only for the same protocol, such as TCP/IP, but for other protocols as well, like IPX/SPX using RIP for IPX/SPX, or between topologies like Ethernet and Token Ring.

❏ The central host in Figure 5-1 must have routing turned on and their respective gateway addresses must point to the other network card for routing to work.

❏ Gateways are routers that can also translate the packet format between topologies. For instance, a Token Ring NIC and an Ethernet NIC would require packet translation to the different formats. Pure routers simply use software to forward a packet between interfaces.

❏ Enable IP Forwarding is the term used to enable routing in NT TCP/IP.

❏ Multihomed means multiple network interfaces.

❏ Routing requires two or more network interface cards, including a modem acting as a network interface.

❑ Network setups are completely up to the individual administrators. Some administrators like to use the last few addresses for their router connections and some like to use the first few addresses for routers and possibly servers. It makes no difference technically. Microsoft course materials commonly use low number assignments for their router IP addresses but there is no required standard.

❑ Early routers had to be programmed with exactly which networks they could route between which interfaces, especially if there were many network interfaces. This configuration method is called *static routing*.

❑ *Dynamic routing* requires additional software that sends special route information packets between routers.

❑ Each independent router port has a routing table.

❑ IP addresses use 8-bit numbers and can never exceed the value 255.

❑ The ROUTE command can be used to add, modify, delete, and display route information for one or all interfaces.

❑ There are a several routing protocols, such as BGP and OSPF, but the original protocol is called Routing Internet Protocol (RIP) and is supported by NT 4.0 and most current dedicated routers.

❑ Another useful utility supplied with the TCP/IP software is the TRACERT utility used to trace a route from origin to destination.

SELF TEST

The Self Test questions will help you measure your understanding of the material presented in this chapter. Read all the choices carefully, as there may be more than one correct answer. Choose all correct answers for each question.

1. What are the two characteristics of a gateway?

   A. Protocol Translation

   B. Security Provider

   C. Packet Scheduler

   D. IP Forwarding

2. How do you print the current routing table?

   A. ROUTE

   B. ROUTE -P

   C. ROUTE DISPLAY

   D. ROUTE PRINT

3. How do you add a route to 221.2.3.0 via port 221.2.2.20 requiring two hops to the routing table?

   A. route Add 221.2.3.0 MASK 255.255.255.0 222.123.3.30 metric 2

   B. route Add 221.2.3.0 255.255.0.0 222.123.3.30

   C. route Add 221.2.3.0 MASK 255.255.255.0 222.2.2.20 metric 2

   D. route Add 221.2.3.0 222.2.2.20

4. What must you configure for static routing?

   A. RIP for Internet Protocol

   B. Enable IP Forwarding

   C. RIP for IPX/SPX

   D. Enable ROUTE service

5. What does OSPF stand for?

   A. Operating System Protocol Forwarder

   B. Offer and Selection Permanent Frame

   C. Open Shortest Path First

   D. Open Secure Path Frame

6. How do you delete the 221.2.3.0 route from the current routing table?

   A. route delete 221.2.3.0 MASK 255.255.255.0 222.2.2.20 metric 2

   B. route delete 221.2.3.0 MASK 255.255.255.0 222.2.2.20

   C. route delete 221.2.3.0 MASK 255.255.255.0

   D. route delete 221.2.3.0

7. What does RIP provide?

   A. Static Routing

   B. Dynamic Routing

   C. Static Routing Information Display

   D. Dynamic Routing Information Display

8. What utility will display the gateways between two hosts?

   A. RIP

   B. OSPF

   C. ROUTE

   D. TRACERT

9. How many IP addresses can be maintained for one network interface?

   A. 1

   B. 2

   C. 5

   D. 255

10. How would you add additional gateway IP addresses to any client?

   A. TCP/IP Properties - IP Address → Advanced option

   B. TCP/IP Properties → Advanced option

   C. RIP Properties - IP Address → Advanced option

   D. IP Gateway Properties → Advanced option

11. What is the default Network Mask for a Class B network?

   A. 255.255.255.255

   B. 255.255.255.0

   C. 255.255.0.0

   D. 255.0.0.0

12. What is the default Network Mask for six subnets in a Class B network? (Hint: Subnets is 2**n-2 where n is the number of bits.)

   A. 255.255.255.248

   B. 255.255.255.240

   C. 255.255.224.0

   D. 255.192.0.0

MCSE
MICROSOFT CERTIFIED SYSTEMS ENGINEER

6

Dynamic Host Configuration Protocol

CERTIFICATION OBJECTIVES

Configuring IP addressing on a large TCP/IP-based network can be a nightmare, especially if users move machines from one subnet to another without consulting you. The Dynamic Host Configuration Protocol (DHCP) can help with configuration problems in these, as well as other situations.

In the first section of this chapter we examine the differences between manual and automatic address assignment. In the second section we discuss the requirements necessary for servers and clients to use DHCP and in the third section we learn how to install and configure a server for DHCP. In the next two sections we learn how to create scopes and how to use a DHCP Relay Agent. In the final two sections, we discuss the purpose of using IPCONFIG and maintaining the DHCP database.

CERTIFICATION OBJECTIVE 6.01

Manual or Automatic Address Assignment

There are two methods of assigning an IP address to a client computer. It can be configured manually by an individual, or automatically by a server computer.

Assigning Multiple Addresses

Suppose your boss tells you that 240 computers on your TCP/IP-based network were recently moved from one building to another and that you must reconfigure them all to work properly on the new subnet. This is a tedious process if you are using manual IP addressing. You will have to go to each machine and enter the correct IP address, subnet mask, and default gateway, along with the WINS and DNS addresses if you are using those services on your network.

Errors in Manual Entry

Not only is this time consuming, it is also vulnerable to human error. If the same IP address is configured for two or more computer systems, then network problems will occur and they can be difficult to trace. Also, an error in entering any of the numbers for the IP address, subnet mask, or default gateway can lead to problems communicating through TCP/IP.

How DHCP Works Magic for You

Looking back at the situation with the 240 computers, I imagine that you are groaning, thinking of how long it will take you to accomplish this task manually. Fortunately, there is a better way to handle this situation, by using DHCP. DHCP, as described in RFC 1541, provides a dependable, flexible option to manual TCP/IP configuration.

Server Assigns IP Addresses

All items normally configured manually can be assigned to the client system by the DHCP server. At a minimum, a DHCP server provides the DHCP client with the IP address, subnet mask, and usually a default gateway.

IP ADDRESS   The DHCP server issues an IP address to each DHCP client system on the network. Each system connected to a TCP/IP-based network is identified by a unique IP address. As we learned in Chapter 3, the IP address consists of four 8-bit octets separated by periods. The IP address is normally shown in dotted-decimal notation, for example, 127.10.24.62.

SUBNET MASK   The IP address actually consists of two parts, the network ID and the host ID. The subnet mask is used to identify the part of the IP address that is the network ID and the part that is the host ID. Subnet masks assign 1s to the network ID bits and 0s to the host ID bits of the IP address.

DEFAULT GATEWAY   A default gateway is required when the client system needs to communicate outside its own subnet. Normally, the default gateway is a router connected to the local subnet, which allows IP packets to be passed to other network segments. If the default gateway is not configured in the DHCP server, then it defaults to 0.0.0.0.

SCOPE OPTIONS A DHCP *scope* is a managerial arrangement that identifies the configuration parameters for all of the DHCP clients on a physical subnet. As previously mentioned, the IP address and subnet mask are required items that the DHCP scope must include. Another requirement in the scope is the *lease duration*. It specifies how long a DHCP client can use an IP address before it must renew it with the DHCP server. It can be set for an unlimited time period or for a predetermined time period. An available option that can be configured within a scope is that a specific IP address can be reserved for a DHCP client or even a system on the network that is not DHCP-enabled.

In addition, there are about sixty DHCP options that can be configured by an administrator. We will examine DHCP options in more detail later in this chapter.

Server Responds to Client Request

A DHCP client goes through a number of different states during the process of receiving an IP address from the DHCP server as shown in Figure 6-1.

The first state is the *initializing state*. During the initializing state a DHCP client boots with a null IP address since it does not have an assigned IP address. After booting, the DHCP client broadcasts a *DHCPDISCOVER* message to its local subnet. The DHCP client's media access control (MAC) address and computer name are contained in the DHCPDISCOVER message. The DHCPDISCOVER message has a source IP address of 0.0.0.0 and the destination is 255.255.255:255.

The second state is the *selecting state*. During the selecting state any DHCP server that receives the DHCPDISCOVER message and has a valid configuration for the DHCP client will answer with a *DHCPOFFER* message. The DHCP server sends the DHCPOFFER message through a broadcast since the DHCP client does not have an IP address. The DHCPOFFER message contains the DHCP client's MAC address, an offered IP address, the correct subnet mask, the IP address of the DHCP server, and the length of the lease. But what happens if the client does not receive an DHCPOFFER from any DHCP server? In that case, it will retry four times every five minutes. If the DHCP client does not receive a DHCPOFFER after its four attempts, it will wait and retry again in another five minutes.

The third state is the *requesting state*. During the requesting state the DHCP client sends a *DHCPREQUEST* message to the DHCP server accepting the offered IP address. The DHCPREQUEST message includes the server identifier from the accepted DHCPOFFER and is sent by broadcast so all other DHCP servers can remove their offers.

The fourth state is the *bound state*. During the bound state the DHCP server responds to the DHCPREQUEST message with a DHCPACK (ack is short for acknowledgment) message that contains a lease for the IP address as well as any necessary configuration parameters. The DHCPACK message is sent by the DHCP server through a broadcast. When the DHCP client receives the DHCPACK message, it completes initialization of TCP/IP and is now considered a bound DHCP client. The client can now use TCP/IP and the IP address it was given to communicate on the network.

BOOTP Extension

DHCP was designed as an extension to the pre-existing bootstrap protocol (BOOTP). BOOTP is used to boot and configure diskless workstations across the network. Originally BOOTP was defined in RFC 951; however, the

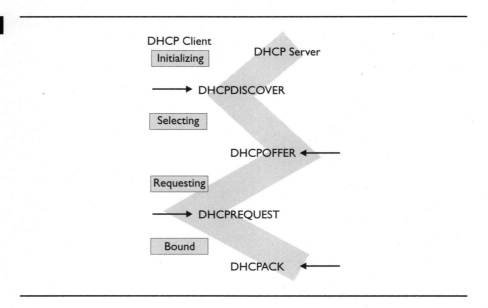

FIGURE 6-1

DHCP client states when requesting an IP address from a DHCP server newest BOOTP RFC, which includes support for DHCP, is RFC 1542. The DHCP message format is almost identical to the BOOTP format. The main difference between the two is that the DHCP message includes new fields not present in the BOOTP message. DHCP also uses some of the existing fields for different purposes. DHCP uses the same User Datagram Protocol (UDP) ports that BOOTP uses, ports 67 and 68.

DHCP Relay Agent

Since DHCP uses broadcasts to send the DHCP messages it is logical to conclude that each subnet must have its own DHCP server. While this is feasible, it is not necessary. Since the DHCP message is an extension of the BOOTP message, then routers that can act as an RFC 1542 (BOOTP) relay agent can be used to relay DHCP messages between multiple subnets. So it is possible to have a single DHCP server providing IP addresses and configuration information for systems on multiple subnets.

It is also possible to turn a Windows NT workstation or server into a DHCP relay agent. The DHCP client sends the request for an IP address and the Windows NT workstation (or server that is acting as a DHCP relay agent) receives the request and forwards the request directly to the correct DHCP server. The DHCP server returns an IP address directly to the requesting client. Later in this chapter you will have the opportunity to configure a DHCP relay agent.

Requirements When Requests Are Across Networks

If your network is designed to use only one or two DHCP servers, then you can use a relay agent. It can be a Windows NT system or a router that complies with RFC 1542. The relay agent on the router forwards requests from local DHCP clients to the remote DHCP server and also relays the DHCP server responses back to the DHCP clients.

Renewal Process

A DHCP client cannot use an IP address after the lease has expired. This is why a DHCP client must renew its lease on the IP address, preferably before the lease has expired or is about to expire. During the process of renewing its lease, a DHCP client goes through a number of different states as shown in Figure 6-2.

50% of Lease Time Expired

The first state encountered while renewing a lease is called the *renewing state.* During the renewing state a DHCP client, by default, tries to renew their lease when 50% of the lease time has expired. For example, if the lease time is 4 days, then the renewal will first occur on day 2 of the lease. To renew its lease, the DHCP client sends a directed DHCPREQUEST message to the DHCP server from which it obtained the lease. The DHCP server will automatically renew the lease by responding with a DHCPACK message. This DHCPACK message contains the new lease and any configuration parameters so that the DHCP client can update its settings in case any have changed on the scope of the DHCP server. Once the DHCP client has renewed its lease, it returns to the bound state.

FIGURE 6-2

DHCP client states when renewing a lease from a DHCP server

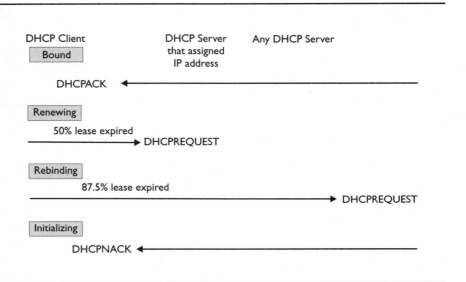

87.5% of Lease Time Expired

It's possible that the DHCP client will not be able to reach the DHCP server to renew the lease. After 87.5% of the lease time has expired, the DHCP client will attempt to contact any available DHCP server by broadcasting DHCPREQUEST messages so that any DHCP server can renew its lease. Any DHCP server can respond with a DHCPACK message, thereby renewing the lease.

Lease Expires

The DHCP client immediately ceases using an IP address if the lease expires or a *DHCPNACK* (nack is short for no acknowledgment) message is received from any DHCP server. If the lease expires or a DHCPNACK is received, then the DHCP client can return to the initializing state and attempt to obtain another IP address lease.

Make sure that you fully understand which message is sent during each of the four states: initializing, selecting, requesting, and bound.

DHCP Server and Client Requirements

To successfully use DHCP on your network, your servers and clients must be able to support the protocol. In this section, our discussion centers on Microsoft products. To see if another product supports DHCP, refer to the documentation that comes with the product.

Server

Several versions of Windows NT Server can act as a DHCP server on your network, including versions 3.5, 3.51, and 4.0. But is it necessary to set up each of the servers on your network to support DHCP? Actually, the answer depends on the layout and the needs of your network.

Single Server

If your network is small, then a single DHCP server may be adequate. The main item to consider if you have multiple subnets is that your routers must comply with RFC 1542 so that the broadcast for an IP address from the DHCP client can be received by the single DHCP server. It is wise to keep in mind that if your single DHCP server goes down and your DHCP clients cannot renew their lease, then your network will cease to function! Of course, this is assuming that TCP/IP is the only protocol used on your network.

Multiple Servers

One of the benefits from using multiple DHCP servers is redundancy. Redundancy can prevent your network from going down. If you decide to use multiple DHCP servers, you should place them on different subnets to achieve a higher degree of fault tolerance in case one of the subnets becomes unavailable. You can manage multiple servers on different subnets with the DHCP Manager, which we will discuss in more detail in the section on installing the DHCP service.

When using multiple DHCP servers, make sure that address pools do not overlap. If the address pools of the DHCP servers overlap, then it is possible that two DHCP clients can be assigned the same IP address.

Remember that scopes must never overlap when implementing multiple DHCP servers.

Supported Clients

The following Microsoft operating systems can perform as DHCP clients on your network:

- Windows NT Server versions 3.5, 3.51, and 4.0
- Windows NT Workstation versions 3.5, 3.51, and 4.0
- Windows 95
- Windows for Workgroups versions 3.11, 3.11a, and 3.11b when using TCP/IP-32

- Microsoft Network Client version 3.0 for MS-DOS
- Microsoft LAN Manager Client version 2.2c for MS-DOS

Of course, DHCP clients are not limited to only Microsoft operating systems. Any system that conforms to RFC 1541 can be a DHCP client.

CERTIFICATION OBJECTIVE 6.03

Installing a DHCP Server

In order to successfully implement DHCP on your network you have to set up at least one of your servers as a DHCP server. In this section, we cover all the steps necessary to install and configure a DHCP server on your network.

Before a DHCP client can successfully communicate on the network, it has to receive an IP address from a DHCP server, which is a Windows NT server that has the DHCP service installed.

Requirements

A Windows NT server that is going to be a DHCP server must have a static IP address. A static IP address is one that never changes. If your network does not already use DHCP, then all systems on the network use static IP addresses. DHCP clients depend on being able to locate the DHCP server responsible for leasing it an IP address, so the address for the DHCP server must stay the same.

Installing

Installing the DHCP service on your Windows NT server is the same as installing any other service. Figure 6-3 shows the Network Service window with the Microsoft DHCP Server option highlighted. Exercise 6-1 gives you the opportunity to install the DHCP service on your system.

Choosing the Microsoft
DHCP server from the
Select Network Service
window

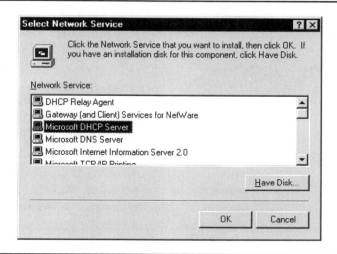

Installing the Microsoft DHCP Server Service

1. Log on as an Administrator.

2. Click the Start button and choose Settings | Control Panel.

3. Double-click the Network icon.

4. Select the Services tab.

5. Click the Add... button.

6. Scroll down the list until Microsoft DHCP Server is highlighted.

7. Click the OK button.

8. Type the full path to the location of your Windows NT CD so that the appropriate files can be copied to your system.

9. After the files are successfully copied, a dialog box pops up telling you that the server must use a static IP address. Click the OK button.

10. Click the Close button.

11. After the bindings are configured, the system notifies you to shut down and restart so the new settings can take effect. Click the Yes button to restart your system.

CERTIFICATION OBJECTIVE 6.04

Creating Scopes

Now that the DHCP service is successfully installed, it is time to create a scope so that it can start being used as a DHCP server on the network. Installing the DHCP service also adds the DHCP Manager to the Administrative Tools menu. The DHCP Manager is used to create scopes and also to manage other DHCP servers on the network. Figure 6-4 shows the DHCP Manager being started for the first time. Local Machine is the DHCP server that the DHCP Manager has been started on. No scopes have been installed on the Local Machine yet.

Scope Parameters

The parameters that are required for you to input into a scope are the starting IP address, the ending IP address, and the subnet mask. Figure 6-5 shows the

---

FIGURE 6-4

DHCP Manager started for the first time

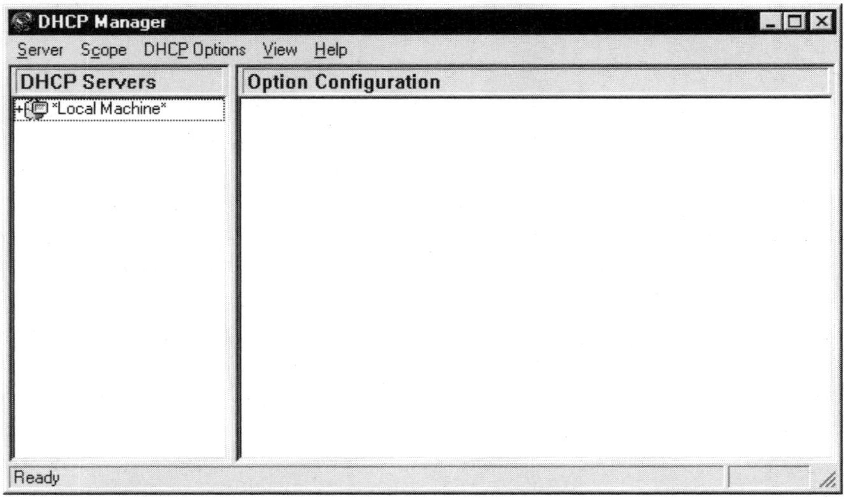

Create Scope window
from the DHCP Manager

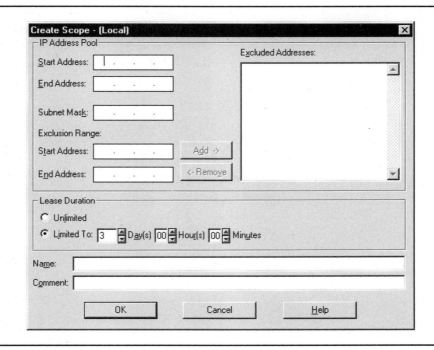

Create Scope window. Notice that the IP address and subnet mask fall into the
IP Address Pool section of the window.

Scope Exclusions

Also within the IP Address Pool is the Exclusion Range. The exclusion range
should include all IP addresses that are assigned manually to other DHCP
servers, diskless workstations, client systems that do not use DHCP, and
Remote Access Service (RAS) clients. Once a range of IP addresses has been
excluded, they will be displayed in the Excluded Addresses window in the right
side of the Create Scope window as shown in Figure 6-6.

Exercise 6-2 shows you how to create a scope. The scope you create is for
educational purposes only and not designed to be used in a production network.

FIGURE 6-6

Scope properties showing a
list of excluded addresses

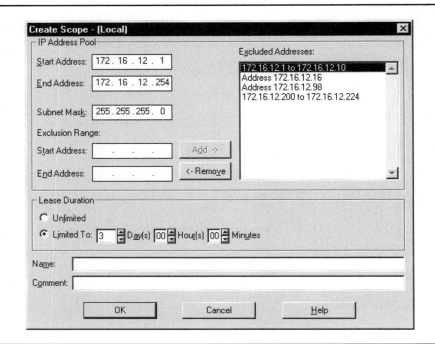

EXERCISE 6-2

Creating a Scope

1. Log on as an Administrator.

2. Click the Start button and choose Programs | Administrative Tools | DHCP Manager.

3. Select the Scope menu and choose Create....

4. Type **172.16.12.10** in the IP Address Pool Start Address: dialog box.

5. Type **172.16.12.254** in the IP Address Pool End Address: dialog box.

6. Type **255.255.255.0** in the IP Address Pool Subnet Mask: dialog box.

7. Type **172.16.12.16** in the Exclusion Range: Start Address: and End Address: dialog boxes. Click the Add -> button.

8. Type **172.16.12.98** in the Exclusion Range: Start Address: and End Address: dialog boxes. Click the Add -> button.

9. Type **172.16.12.200** in the Exclusion Range: Start Address: dialog box.
10. Type **172.16.12.224** in the Exclusion Range: End Address: dialog box. Click the Add -> button.
11. Click the OK button. A scope for the 172.16.12.0 subnet is now displayed under Local Machine in the DHCP Manager.

Adding Reservations

After a scope has been successfully created, it is possible to add reservations. A *reservation* is an IP address that is reserved for a specific DHCP client. The Add Reserved Clients window has four dialog boxes to input data. The first dialog box is for the IP Address that will be reserved for a client. The second dialog box is used to input a Unique Identifier to identify the correct client that will receive the IP address. The data that goes in the Unique Identifier is the Media Access Control (MAC) address of the client's network interface card (NIC). The third and fourth dialog boxes are for the Client Name and Client Comment, respectively. The Client Name is used for identification purposes only and does not affect the real computer name of the client. Figure 6-7 shows a reservation for the IP address of 172.16.12.50. Exercise 6-3 shows you how to add a reservation for an IP address.

EXERCISE 6-3

Adding a Reservation for an IP Address

1. Log on as an Administrator.
2. Click the Start button and choose Programs | Administrative Tools | DHCP Manager.
3. Select the Scope menu and choose Add Reservations....
4. Type **50** in the last octet of the IP Address: dialog box so it shows 172.16.12.50.
5. Type **000000FBA53C** in the Unique Identifier: dialog box.
6. Type **Exercise 3** in the Client Name: dialog box.
7. Click the Add button.
8. Click the Close button.

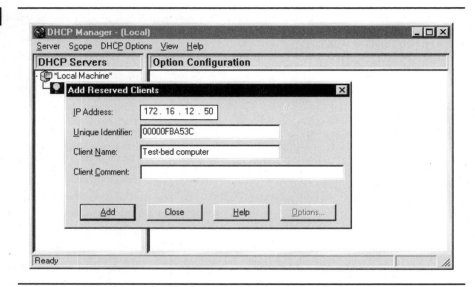

FIGURE 6-7

Reserving the IP address
172.16.12.50 for a client
computer

Scope Options

As we discussed earlier in the chapter, a DHCP server must provide the DHCP client with a minimum amount of information so the client can successfully use TCP/IP. The minimum requirements are:

- A valid IP address to lease. The address will come from the IP address pool, which is configured when the scope is created.

- A valid subnet mask, which is also configured when the scope is created.

- A default gateway. If the default gateway is not configured, then it defaults to an IP address of 0.0.0.0.

The key word is *minimum.* The three minimum requirements are not the only parameters that can be configured on a DHCP server. There are almost 60 other DHCP options that can be configured using the DHCP Manager. Table 6-1 shows the DHCP options that are available for Windows- and Windows NT-based clients.

TABLE 6-1

DHCP Options for
Windows- and Windows
NT-Based Operating
Systems

Option	Definition
003 Router	Specifies one or more IP addresses for routers on the DHCP client's subnet.
006 DNS servers	Specifies one or more IP addresses for DNS servers available to the client. Multihomed computers have only one set for each computer, not one for each NIC.
015 Domain name	Specifies the DNS domain name that the client uses for DNS host name resolution.
044 WINS/NBNS servers	Specifies one or more IP addresses for NetBIOS name servers (NBNS).
046 WINS/NBT node type	Allows configurable NetBIOS over TCP/IP (NetBT) clients to be configured as described in RFC 1001/1002. A 1 signifies b-node, a 2 signifies p-node, a 4 signifies m-node, and an 8 signifies h-node. On multihomed computers, the node type is assigned to the entire computer, not to each NIC.
Lease time	Specifies the time in seconds from address assignment until the client's lease on the address expires. The Create Scope or Scope Properties dialog box in DHCP Manager is used to specify lease time. It cannot be set directly from the DHCP Options menu.
Renewal (T1) time value	Specifies the time in seconds from address assignment until the client enters the renewing state. Renewal time is a function of the lease time option, which is specified in the Create Scope or Scope Properties dialog box of DHCP Manager. It cannot be set directly from the DHCP Options menu.
Rebinding (T2) time value	Specifies the time in seconds from address assignment until the client enters the rebinding state. Rebinding time is a function of the lease time option, which is specified in the Create Scope or Scope Properties dialog box of DHCP Manager. It cannot be set directly from the DHCP Options menu.

FROM THE CLASSROOM

Configuring Registry Values

As you configure the DHCP server, most of the information can be provided by using the DHCP Manager. This information is written to the NT Registry. However, some registry values cannot be configured with the DHCP Manager. You must use the registry editor to modify these configuration values:

- **BackupDatabasePath**   Specifies location of the backup copy of the DHCP database.

- **DatabaseName**   Specifies the database filename to be used by the DHCP Server Service
Default=DHCP.MDB

- **DatabasePath**   Specifies the location of the DHCP database files
Default = winnt_root\system32\DHCP

- **RestoreFlag**   Specifies whether the DHCP Server should restore from its backup copy
Default = 0   Set to 1 to force a restore.

- **BackupInterval**   Specifies the default backup interval in minutes
Default = 60

- **DatabaseCleanupInterval**   Specifies the interval in minutes for the time to remove expired client records from the database
Default = 864000 (24 hours)

- **DatabaseLoggingFlag**   Specifies whether to record the database changes in the Jet.log file
Default:= 1 (Logging enabled)

These values are located at:

HKEY_LOCAL_MACHINE\Systems\ CurrentControlSet\Services\ DHCPServer\Parameters

—By D. Lynn White, MCT, MCSE

There are four methods available to set DHCP options:

- **Global**   If you need a DHCP option to affect all the DHCP scopes on the selected DHCP server, then use a global DHCP option. Any option appearing in the DHCP Manager with a globe icon indicates that it is a global DHCP option.

■ **Scope**   If you need a DHCP option to affect only a specific scope, then use a scope DHCP option. Any option appearing in the DHCP Manager as a series of computer icons indicates that it is a scope DHCP option.

■ **Default**   You can change the default value for DHCP options. After changing a default value, it will be the one set during administration rather than the DHCP default that was set during installation of DHCP. This probably sounds confusing but will become clear when you change the default for a DHCP option in a later exercise.

■ **Client**   It is possible to set DHCP options for a specific DHCP client. This works only if the DHCP client has a reserved IP address.

exam

ⓦatch

It is important to remember that client options override scope options, which override global options.

Exercises 6-4 and 6-5 show you how to add global and scope DHCP options using the DHCP Manager.

Adding a Global Option

1. Log on as an Administrator.

2. Click the Start button and choose Programs | Administrative Tools | DHCP Manager.

3. The first DHCP option you are going to set is the DNS server address for all DHCP scopes. Select the DHCP Options menu and choose Global....

4. Highlight DNS Servers in the Unused Options: box and click the Add -> button.

5. Click the Value >>> button.

6. Click the Edit Array... button.

7. Type **172.16.12.5** in the New IP Address: dialog box.

8. Type **Global DNS Server** in the Server Name: dialog box.

9. Click the Add -> button and then the OK button.

10. Click the OK button. A globe icon is displayed to the left of DNS Servers within the Option Configuration window. Leave the DHCP Manager open for the next exercise.

| EXERCISE 6-5 | **Adding a Scope Option** |

1. Highlight the 172.16.12.0 scope that was created in Exercise 6-2.

2. Select the DHCP Options menu and choose Scope....

3. Highlight Router in the Unused Options: box and click the Add -> button.

4. Click the Value >>> button.

5. Click the Edit Array... button.

6. Type **172.16.12.1** in the New IP Address: dialog box.

7. Type Router for the .12 subnet in the Server Name: dialog box.

8. Click the Add -> button and then the OK button.

9. Click the OK button. You should see a series of computers on an icon to the left of Router within the Option Configuration window. If the Local Machine had more than one scope, you would see that the router is displayed only for the .12 subnet.

Now that you know how to create scopes in DHCP Manager, here is a quick reference for possible scenario questions, and the appropriate answer:

QUESTIONS AND ANSWERS

All the DHCP clients on a subnet cannot communicate with anyone outside...	The gateway is not configured correctly in the scope options.
You have 3 subnets, each with its own scope. None of the DHCP clients can resolve domain names...	The DNS Server is not correctly configured in the global options.
You try to set a reservation for an IP address and receive the message 'The specified address is not available'....	The address is one that was excluded when the scope was created.

CERTIFICATION OBJECTIVE 6.05

Manipulating Client Leases

It is not difficult to configure a DHCP server to lease IP addresses to DHCP clients. But a situation may occur in which you need to see what IP addresses are leased, especially if you need to track down a client that has a certain IP address.

Viewing Active Leases

You can view the active leases for a scope by choosing Active Leases... from the Scope menu in DHCP Manager. The Active Leases dialog box not only shows you information about active leases for the scope you currently have selected but also several other statistics. The other statistics shown include the total number of addresses in the scope, the number and percentage of addresses that are unavailable because they are active or excluded, and the number and percentage of addresses that are currently available, as shown in Figure 6-8.

The count of active leases and excluded addresses shown in Active/Excluded is an aggregate so it does not just give you statistics about the active leases. However, when you deactivate a scope, the Active/Excluded count reflects only excluded addresses. If you need to know the number of active leases, then you can compare the Active/Excluded count when the scope is deactivated and activated.

Even though a lease is set for a certain period of time, it does not disappear automatically when the lease expires. The DHCP server database retains the lease for approximately one day after it expires. The expired lease is maintained in the DHCP server database to provide a grace period for the client. You're probably wondering why the client needs a grace period. A few of the reasons are to protect a client's lease in case the client and server are located in different time zones; it also compensates for a time difference in case the DHCP client's

FIGURE 6-8

Active leases for the
172.16.12.0 subnet

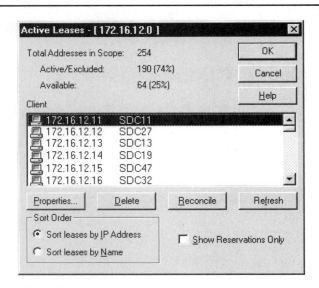

and DHCP server's clocks are not synchronized, or in case the client computer
was not on the network when the lease expired. Expired leases are identified by
a dimmed icon and are included in the list of active clients in the Active Leases
dialog box as well as the aggregate Active/Excluded count.

To view when a lease will expire, highlight the client and click the
Properties… button. The lease expiration is shown at the bottom of the
window as shown in Figure 6-9.

By highlighting an IP address in the Client window and clicking the Delete
button, you can delete the lease for a DHCP client listed in the scope. A lease
is normally deleted because it conflicts with an IP address exclusion or a client
reservation that you want to add. Deleting a lease causes the same result as if
the client's lease expired. The client has to start the process from the beginning
of the initialization state and obtain a new IP address and configuration
information from a DHCP server. Be careful when you delete a lease. Make
sure that you delete only entries for clients that are no longer using the lease.
Deleting a client that is actively using a lease could result in duplicate IP
addresses on the network because deleted addresses can be assigned to new
clients immediately.

FIGURE 6-9

Client Properties window
showing when the lease
expires

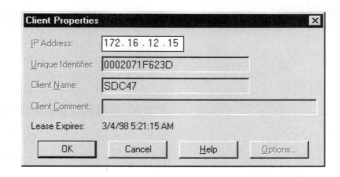

Viewing Client Reservations

Viewing client reservations is very similar to the method used for viewing
active leases. Using DHCP Manager, choose Active Leases… from the Scope
menu. Client Reservations are shown in the Client window along with all the
active leases for the scope. You can scroll down the list or, if you want to
isolate only client reservations, you may choose the checkbox located to the left
of Show Reservations Only. Figure 6-10 shows the client reservations for the
172.16.12.0 subnet by filtering out the active leases, using Show Reservations
Only. The only reservation is the one you created in Exercise 6-3.

As mentioned earlier, it is possible to set DHCP options for a client that has
a reservation. Exercise 6-6 shows you how to add a client option using the
DHCP Manager.

EXERCISE 6-6

Adding a Client Option

1. Log on as an Administrator.

2. Click the Start button and choose Programs | Administrative Tools |
   DHCP Manager.

3. Highlight the 172.16.12.0 scope and choose Active Leases… from the
   Scope menu.

4. Highlight 172.16.12.50 and choose Properties….

5. Click the Options… button in the Client Properties window.

FIGURE 6-10

Client reservations for only the 172.16.12.0 subnet

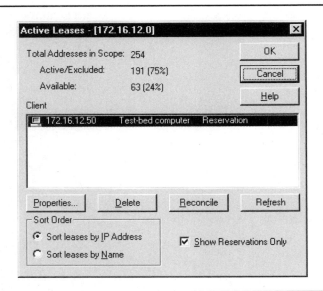

6. Scroll down the Unused Options: list and highlight Domain Name.

7. Click the Add - > button.

8. Click the Value >>> button.

9. Type **exercise6.com** in the String dialog box and click the OK button.

10. Click the OK button.

11. Click the OK button.

The DHCP client that is assigned the IP address of 172.16.12.50 will use exercise6.com as its domain name for client resolutions.

For purposes of the exercise, there was a reserved client already visible when you opened the Active Leases window. On a scope that is used in a production environment you may want to click the check box located to the left of Show Reservations Only so that only the clients with a reservation are displayed.

Manipulating an IP Address with IPCONFIG

IPCONFIG is a command-line utility that displays current TCP/IP configuration information for each NIC in a Windows NT system.

IPCONFIG is very useful when you need to know the IP address assigned to a Windows NT DHCP client, especially since the client could receive a different IP address every time it boots.

Typing IPCONFIG without any switches will display the IP address, subnet mask, and default gateway for all NICs that are bound to TCP/IP as shown in Figure 6-11.

Using IPCONFIG without any switches may tell you all the information that you want to know. However, there are many other items of information that you can glean from IPCONFIG if you use the /all switch. Using IPCONFIG /all displays all of the TCP/IP configuration information for each NIC, including DHCP information. Figure 6-12 shows the output of using IPCONFIG /all for the same system shown in Figure 6-11.

There are two other switches that are very useful when using IPCONFIG in a DHCP environment.

Renew Address

The first switch is IPCONFIG /renew. IPCONFIG /renew actually serves two purposes. It can renew an existing lease for an IP address and it can also obtain a new IP address if you have released the address using another switch. If your system has multiple NICs, then you need to specify which NIC to renew the

---

FIGURE 6-11

IPCONFIG showing IP address information for a single NIC system

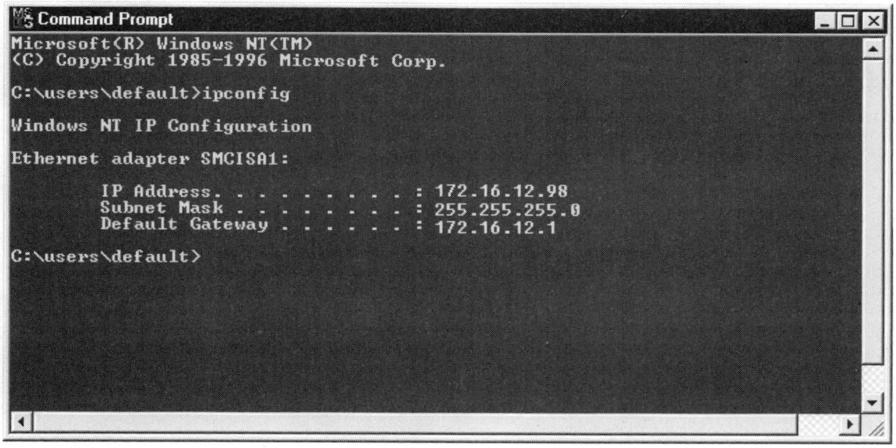

```
Command Prompt                                                    _ □ ×
Microsoft(R) Windows NT(TM)
(C) Copyright 1985-1996 Microsoft Corp.

C:\users\default>ipconfig

Windows NT IP Configuration

Ethernet adapter SMCISA1:

        IP Address. . . . . . . . . : 172.16.12.98
        Subnet Mask . . . . . . . . : 255.255.255.0
        Default Gateway . . . . . . : 172.16.12.1

C:\users\default>
```

```
Command Prompt                                                    _ □ ✕
Microsoft(R) Windows NT(TM)
(C) Copyright 1985-1996 Microsoft Corp.

C:\users\default>ipconfig /all

Windows NT IP Configuration

        Host Name . . . . . . . . . : chapter6.tcpip.com
        DNS Servers . . . . . . . . : 172.16.12.5
                                      172.16.12.7
        Node Type . . . . . . . . . : Hybrid
        NetBIOS Scope ID. . . . . . :
        IP Routing Enabled. . . . . : No
        WINS Proxy Enabled. . . . . : No
        NetBIOS Resolution Uses DNS : No

Ethernet adapter SMCISA1:

        Description . . . . . . . . : SMC Adapter.
        Physical Address. . . . . . : 00-00-C0-8E-F3-B9
        DHCP Enabled. . . . . . . . : Yes
        IP Address. . . . . . . . . : 172.16.12.98
        Subnet Mask . . . . . . . . : 255.255.255.0
        Default Gateway . . . . . . : 172.16.12.1
        DHCP Server . . . . . . . . : 172.16.12.8
        Primary WINS Server . . . . : 172.16.12.4
        Secondary WINS Server . . . : 172.16.12.6
        Lease Obtained. . . . . . . : Tuesday, February 24, 1998 1:12:15 PM
        Lease Expires . . . . . . . : Wednesday, March 04, 1998 1:12:15 PM

C:\users\default>
◄                                                                ►
```

address for by typing **IPCONFIG /renew [adapter]**. Replace [adapter] with
the name of your NIC. Figure 6-13 shows a lease being renewed for a
Windows NT DHCP client. Does the output on the screen look familiar? It

```
Command Prompt                                                    _ □ ✕
Microsoft(R) Windows NT(TM)
(C) Copyright 1985-1996 Microsoft Corp.

C:\users\default>ipconfig /renew

Windows NT IP Configuration

Ethernet adapter SMCISA1:

        IP Address. . . . . . . . . : 172.16.12.98
        Subnet Mask . . . . . . . . : 255.255.255.0
        Default Gateway . . . . . . : 172.16.12.1

C:\users\default>_
◄                                                                ►
```

IPCONFIG /renewal for
a Windows NT DHCP
client

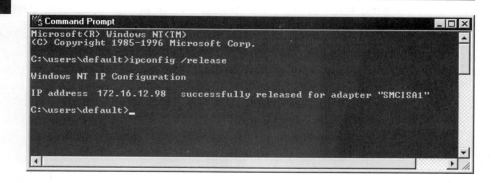

should, because it is the same as what you see using an IPCONFIG with no
switches, however your lease is renewed.

Release Address

The second switch is IPCONFIG /release. The /release switch can be used to
release the IP address obtained from a DHCP server, so that the NIC no
longer has an IP address. If your system has multiple NICs, then you need to
specify which NIC to release the address for by typing **IPCONFIG /release
[adapter]**. Replace [adapter] with the name of your NIC. Figure 6-14 shows
the IP address being released from a system.

CERTIFICATION OBJECTIVE 6.06

Creating a DHCP Relay Agent

As discussed earlier in this chapter, any computer running a Windows NT
workstation or server can be a DHCP Relay Agent. Successful configuration of
a DHCP Relay Agent is a two-step process. The first step is the installation of
the DHCP Relay Agent service. After installation of the DHCP Relay Agent
service, you can move to the second step, which is configuring the parameters
for the service. Use the Network applet in the Control Panel to install the
service and configure the agent.

Installing and Configuring the DHCP Relay Agent Service

The procedure for installing the DHCP Relay Agent is the same as for any other service. Figure 6-15 shows the window for installing network services. Exercise 6-7 shows you how to install the DHCP Relay Agent service for use on your system.

EXERCISE 6-7

Installing the DHCP Relay Agent Service

1. Log on as an Administrator.
2. Click the Start button and select Settings | Control Panel.
3. Double-click the Network applet.
4. Select the Services tab.
5. Click the Add... button.

FIGURE 6-15

Selecting DHCP Relay Agent service from the Select Network Service window

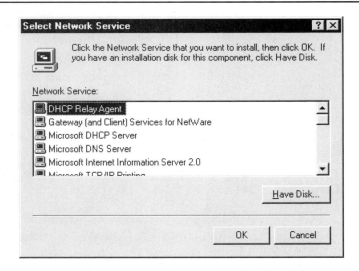

6. Highlight DHCP Relay Agent from the Select Network Service window and click the OK button.

7. Click the Close button.

8. After the bindings are reviewed, the system notifies you to shut down and restart so the new settings can take effect. Click the Yes button to restart your system.

Now that the DHCP Relay Agent is installed on your system, it is time to configure it for use on your network. Exercise 6-8 shows you how to configure the DHCP Relay Agent so that it can act as a router for the DHCP broadcast message sent from the clients on the subnet.

EXERCISE 6-8

Configuring the DHCP Relay Agent

1. Log on as an Administrator.

2. Click the Start button and select Settings | Control Panel.

3. Double-click the Network applet.

4. Select the Protocols tab.

5. Highlight TCP/IP Protocol and click the Properties... button.

6. Select the DHCP Relay tab.

7. Ensure that the Seconds threshold: and Maximum hops: boxes are set to 4.

8. Click the Add... button.

9. Type **172.16.12.8** in the DHCP Server: dialog box. The address appears in the DHCP Servers window.

10. Click the OK button.

11. Click the Close button.

12. The system notifies you to shut down and restart so the new settings can take effect. Click the Yes button to restart your system.

Figure 6-16 shows the DHCP Relay tab with a server identified where all DHCP requests from clients are forwarded.

FIGURE 6-16

DHCP Relay tab showing the IP address for a DHCP server

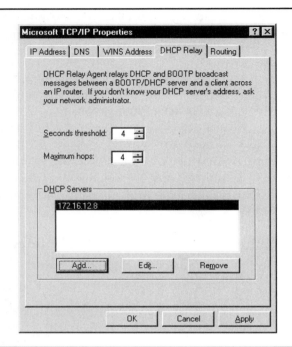

CERTIFICATION OBJECTIVE 6.07

Maintaining a DHCP Database

DHCP data, such as active IP address leases and excluded addresses, are stored by the DHCP server service in a database. The following files are located in the %systemroot%\system32\dhcp folder:

- **Dhcp.mdb** The DHCP database.

- **J50.log and J50#####.log** All log files that track transactions that have occurred in the DHCP database are prefixed with J50. In case of failure, the DHCP server service uses the J50.log and J50#####.log files to recover the dhcp.mdb. The ##### is replaced with numbers; for example, you may have a file named J5000036.log.

- **J50.chk**   A checkpoint file.
- **Dhcp.tmp**   A temporary file used by the DHCP server service to store database information.
- **dhcpsrv.log**   A file showing the event ID, date, time, description, IP address, host name, and MAC address for all DHCP server activity.

Don't try to open the DHCP database file using Microsoft Access. Even though the file ends with an .mdb extension, Access does not recognize the format.

Database Maintenance

The DHCP database is automatically backed up to the %systemroot%\ system32\dhcp\backup\jet folder every 60 minutes. The default backup interval can be changed by modifying the following registry key:

```
\HKEY_LOCAL_MACHINE\SYSTEM\CurrentControlSet\Services\
DHCPServer\Parameters\BackupInterval
```

JETPACK Utility

Microsoft recommends that you compact the DHCP database when it reaches 30MB. The DHCP database is automatically compacted by Windows NT Server 4.0 so you should not have to run the following procedure very often.

JETPACK is the command-line utility that compacts the DHCP database. The syntax for JETPACK is: JETPACK <DHCP database name> <temp database name>. For example:

```
c:\>cd %systemroot%\system32\dhcp
c:\>JETPACK dhcp.mdb tmp.mdb
```

Before you can use JETPACK, the DHCP server service must be stopped.

CERTIFICATION SUMMARY

There are two methods to assign an IP address to a system on your network. The first method is to assign the address by manually entering the correct information for each machine. The second method is to configure a DHCP server and let it automatically issue the IP address to each client connected to the network. Allowing the DHCP server to issue the IP addresses eliminates the possibility of errors that could occur from manual entry.

A DHCP client goes through a number of different states during the process of receiving an IP address from the DHCP server. During each state, messages are exchanged between the DHCP client and the DHCP server until the DHCP client is fully bound with an IP address.

If you decide to use a single DHCP server across subnets, then the routers must support RFC 1542. This is required so that the broadcasts from the DHCP clients can reach the single DHCP server. Using multiple DHCP servers on different subnets increases redundancy. The multiple DHCP servers can be managed from a central location using the DHCP Manager.

The system that you are using for a DHCP server must have a static IP address. The static IP address is required so that DHCP clients are able to find the DHCP server when renewing their IP address.

A scope is required for each subnet that has DHCP clients. It contains a pool of IP addresses to be issued, as well as other configuration parameters such as a subnet mask and default gateway. Scopes are created using the DHCP Manager and each scope can have different options. Besides scope options, there are also global options, default options, and client options. Client options can be applied only to a DHCP client that has a reserved IP address.

Client leases for a scope can be viewed from the Active Leases window. You can also delete a lease by highlighting the IP address and clicking the delete button while in the Active Leases window.

The IPCONFIG command-line utility can be used to determine the IP address for a DHCP client, as well as other TCP/IP configuration information. You can also renew or release an IP address by using the correct switch with IPCONFIG.

If your routers do not comply with RFC 1542, then it is possible for you to set up a Windows NT workstation or server as a DHCP Relay Agent. Once configured, the DHCP Relay Agent will forward requests for IP addresses from DHCP clients to the correct DHCP server.

The DHCP database is named dhcp.mdb and is located in the %systemroot%\system32\dhcp folder. It is automatically backed up into the %systemroot%\system32\dhcp\backup folder every 15 minutes. If your DHCP database is larger than 30MB then you may want to run the JETPACK command-line utility to compact it. Prior to using JETPACK, the DHCP server service must be stopped.

 # TWO-MINUTE DRILL

❑ There are two methods of assigning an IP address to a client computer.

❑ Manual Entry is not only time consuming, it is also vulnerable to human error.

❑ DHCP provides a dependable, flexible option to manual TCP/IP configuration.

❑ DHCP server provides the DHCP client with the IP address, subnet mask, and usually a default gateway.

❑ A DHCP *scope* is a managerial arrangement that identifies the configuration parameters for all of the DHCP clients on a physical subnet.

❑ During the initializing state a DHCP client boots with a null IP address since it does not have an assigned IP address.

❑ After booting, the DHCP client broadcasts a *DHCPDISCOVER* message to its local subnet.

❑ During the selecting state any DHCP server that receives the DHCPDISCOVER message and has a valid configuration for the DHCP client will answer with a *DHCPOFFER* message.

❑ During the requesting state the DHCP client sends a *DHCPREQUEST* message to the DHCP server accepting the offered IP address.

❑ During the bound state the DHCP server responds to the DHCPREQUEST message with a DHCPACK (ack is short for acknowledgment) message that contains a lease for the IP address as well as any necessary configuration parameters.

❑ BOOTP is used to boot and configure diskless workstations across the network.

❑ Since the DHCP message is an extension of the BOOTP message, the routers that can act as an RFC 1542 (BOOTP) relay agent can be used to relay DHCP messages between multiple subnets.

❑ A DHCP client cannot use an IP address after the lease has expired.

❑ Make sure that you fully understand which message is sent during each of the four states: initializing, selecting, requesting, and bound.

❑ To successfully use DHCP on your network, your servers and clients must be able to support the protocol.

❑ Several versions of Windows NT Server can act as a DHCP server on your network.

❑ Remember that scopes must never overlap when implementing multiple DHCP servers.

❑ In order to successfully implement DHCP on your network you have to set up at least one of your servers as a DHCP server.

❑ The DHCP Manager is used to create scopes and also to manage other DHCP servers on the network.

❑ A *reservation* is an IP address that is reserved for a specific DHCP client.

❑ There are almost 60 other DHCP options that can be configured using the DHCP Manager.

❑ It is important to remember that client options override scope options, which override global options.

❑ The Active Leases dialog box not only shows you information about active leases for the scope you currently have selected but also several other statistics.

❑ Client Reservations are shown in the Client window along with all the active leases for the scope.

❑ IPCONFIG is a command-line utility that displays current TCP/IP configuration information for each NIC in a Windows NT system.

❑ The procedure for installing the DHCP Relay Agent is the same as for any other service.

❑   DHCP data, such as active IP address leases and excluded addresses, are stored by the DHCP server service in a database.

❑   The DHCP database is automatically backed up to the %systemroot%\system32\dhcp\backup\jet folder every 60 minutes.

❑   JETPACK is the command-line utility that compacts the DHCP database.

SELF TEST

The following Self Test questions will help you measure your understanding of the material presented in this chapter. Read all the choices carefully, as there may be more than one correct answer. Choose all correct answers for each question.

1. What type of option is used in a scope if you want it to affect all DHCP clients?

   A. Default
   B. Client
   C. Scope
   D. Global

2. What is required if you are using a single DHCP server to support DHCP clients on remote subnets?

   A. A single scope for all subnets
   B. A router that conforms to RFC 1542
   C. Client options for each DHCP client
   D. A DHCP Relay Agent

3. What message is sent from the DHCP server during the *requesting* state?

   A. DHCPOFFER
   B. DHCPREQUEST
   C. Both A and B
   D. Neither A or B

4. Your network uses multiple DHCP servers located on separate subnets. What is a benefit that can be realized from this configuration?

   A. A high degree of fault tolerance
   B. All DHCP servers use the same router
   C. Overlapping of IP address pools between DHCP servers
   D. One DHCP server automatically backing up all the other DHCP servers

5. When does a DHCP client first attempt to renew its lease?

   A. After 37.5% of the lease time has expired
   B. After 50% of the lease time has expired
   C. After 73.5% of the lease time has expired
   D. After 87.5% of the lease time has expired

6. What command do you use to return an IP address to the DHCP server?

   A. IPCONFIG
   B. IPCONFIG /all
   C. IPCONFIG /release
   D. IPCONFIG /renew

7. What is the purpose of the JETPACK utility?

   A. It is used to compact the IP address pool.
   B. It is used to compact the DHCP log file.
   C. It is used to compact the scopes on a DHCP server.
   D. It is used to compact the DHCP database.

8. What option would you use if you wanted to set the default gateway for a subnet?

   A. Global
   B. Scope

C. Default

D. Client

9. During what state is the DHCPACK message sent from the DHCP server?

   A. Initializing state

   B. Selecting state

   C. Requesting state

   D. Bound state

10. A DHCP client tried to renew its lease with the DHCP server that originally issued the IP address. What happens when 87.5% of the lease time has expired?

    A. The DHCP client will once again attempt to contact only the original DHCP server.

    B. The DHCP client will attempt to contact any DHCP server using a DHCPDISCOVER message.

    C. The DHCP client will automatically renew its lease if it cannot reach the original DHCP server.

    D. The DHCP client will attempt to contact any DHCP server.

11. What information is required in the Unique Identifier dialog box when adding a reservation for a client?

    A. The serial number for the client system

    B. The MAC address for the client system

    C. The computer name for the client system

    D. The building number for the location of the client system

12. What file is used if DHCP needs to recover the database from a failure?

    A. dhcp.tmp

    B. J50.chk

    C. J50.log

    D. dhcpsrv.log

13. What can be configured to be a DHCP Relay Agent?

    A. A Windows for Workgroups system

    B. A Windows NT Server system

    C. A Windows 95 system

    D. A Windows NT Workstation system

14. What information is contained in the DHCPOFFER message?

    A. The DHCP client's MAC address, an offered IP address, the correct subnet mask, the IP address of the DHCP server, and the length of the lease.

    B. The DHCP server's MAC address, an offered IP address, the correct subnet mask, the IP address of the DHCP server, and the length of the lease.

    C. The DHCP client's MAC address, an offered IP address, the correct subnet mask, the IP address of the DHCP server, the length of the lease, and the DNS server address.

    D. The DHCP server's MAC address, an offered IP address, the correct subnet mask, the IP address of the DHCP server, the length of the lease, and the DNS server address.

15. Which default gateway is used if one is not specified?

    A. 127.0.0.1

    B. 172.16.12.1

    C. 0.0.0.0

    D. 255.255.255.255

7

NetBIOS Host Name Resolution

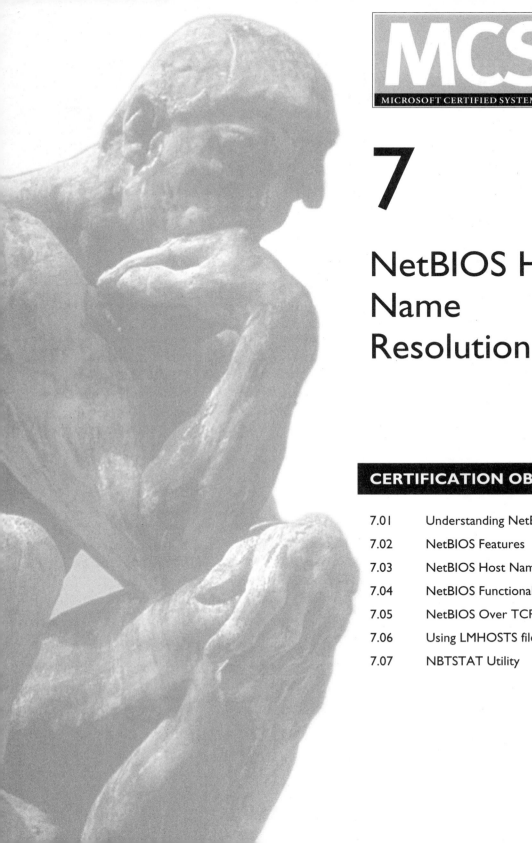

CERTIFICATION OBJECTIVES

Y ou may have heard that NetBIOS is the same thing as NetBEUI, which it is not, as you will discover as you read this chapter. You may wonder what a chapter on NetBIOS is doing in a book about TCP/IP. When you install TCP/IP on Windows NT, you automatically get NetBIOS; there is no separating the two.

For the purposes of this chapter and the Internetworking with Microsoft TCP/IP section of the exam, you should refer to this connectivity as NetBIOS over TCP/IP, or NBT for short. NetBIOS name resolution refers to the process of converting NetBIOS names to TCP/IP addresses. As a Microsoft Certified Systems Engineer you will most assuredly be called on to plan, install, configure, manage, monitor, optimize, and troubleshoot NetBIOS host name resolution in various Microsoft networking situations.

In the working world you will hear a lot of myths and rumors about what NetBIOS actually is and what it does for networking. The first section of this chapter contains some definitions, background material, and concepts about NetBIOS that you need to know. The next section explains how NetBIOS runs over TCP/IP using the TCP and UDP protocols. Next you will learn that NetBIOS host names are composed of 15 characters plus a special byte. The fourth section covers the three NetBIOS functional processes: Name Registration, Name Discovery, and Name Release. The next section explains the name resolution methods. Finally, the last two sections detail how to use the LMHOSTS file and NBTSTAT command.

CERTIFICATION OBJECTIVE 7.01

Understanding NetBIOS

NetBIOS is not a protocol or protocol stack. It is an interface that software can use and is commonly called an application programming interface (API). NetBIOS is the acronym for *Network Basic Input/Output System.* Host names are used to connect two NetBIOS computers together. Since NetBIOS is not a transport protocol, it does not directly support routing but depends on one of three transport protocols it can run on Windows NT: TCP/IP, NWLink

IPX/SPX, or NetBEUI. Since TCP/IP and NWLink IPX/SPX are both routable protocols, NetBIOS information can be sent across routers when it is running on one or both of these protocols. NetBEUI is not a routable protocol; therefore any NetBIOS packets sent over NetBEUI cannot be sent past routers.

Implemented for IBM in 1983

NetBIOS was first implemented for IBM in 1983 for its early PC network. It has since been adopted by Microsoft and used in DOS, Windows for Workgroups, Windows 95, and Windows NT operating systems for file and printer sharing. It has been used for network communications by IBM, DEC, Samba, and so many other situations that it has become a de facto industry standard. (A *de facto* standard is usually initially developed or owned by one entity but so widely used in the industry that it becomes a standard.) TCP/IP has become an industry standard protocol because of its widespread use on the Internet, but it is a *de jure* standard because it was developed openly by many different groups and entities.

No "official" standard exists for NetBIOS services. The IBM PC-network version is usually used as a reference point for new implementations of NetBIOS. This version is described in the IBM document 6322916, "Technical Reference PC Network.". There are, however, official standards for using NetBIOS over TCP/IP. They can be found under the following RFCs in many places on the Internet:

- **RFC 1001** Protocol Standard for a NetBIOS Service on a TCP/UDP TransportT: Concepts and Methods
- **RFC 1002** Protocol Standard for a NetBIOS Service on a TCP/UDP Transport: Detailed Specifications
- **RFC 1088** A Standard for the Transmission of IP Datagrams over NetBIOS Networks

Session Level Interface

The first thing to understand about NetBIOS is that it is not a "complete" networking protocol suite like TCP/IP, IPX/SPX, or NetBEUI. Before you continue, be sure to review the OSI Model Layers and the TCP/IP Protocol Stack in Chapter 2, TCP/IP Architecture. NetBIOS is only an API that programmers use to connect two computers using names like MYCOMPUTER or SERVER1. This programming interface is what places NetBIOS at the session level according to the OSI model.

Microsoft has implemented NetBIOS so that the TCP/IP, IPX/SPX, and NetBEUI protocol stacks can all carry NetBIOS information. On Windows NT and other Microsoft networking platforms, NetBIOS can run over TCP/IP, IPX/SPX, and NetBEUI separately or even simultaneously. Using NetBIOS to communicate between two computers requires at least one of the three protocols. The NetBIOS interface is automatically included whenever you install one of the three protocols and cannot be separated or removed.

Session Management Transport Protocol

NetBIOS operates at the session and transport levels of the OSI Model. Remember that the seven layers of the OSI model are: Application, Presentation, Session, Transport, Network, Data Link, and Physical. NetBIOS operates at the session level since it manages communication between two computers by establishing, administering, and terminating connections. It operates at the Transport Layer by providing datagram and session services to applications. Datagram services provide connectionless communication for information that does not need the guarantee of reliable delivery. Session services are connection-oriented communication for information that needs reliable transport and guaranteed delivery.

For the TCP/IP protocol stack the NetBIOS interface operates at the Application and Transport Layers. Remember that the four layers of the TCP/IP protocol stack are: Application, Transport, Internet, and Network Interface. Windows Sockets, another popular API many programmers use for connection-oriented and connectionless communication, also resides in the Application Layer of the TCP/IP protocol stack. NetBIOS is in the Application Layer because it provides an interface for software and other applications. It is in the Transport Layer also since it provides for different levels of reliability in the datagram and session services offered.

CERTIFICATION OBJECTIVE 7.02

NetBIOS Features

In this chapter we focus on running NetBIOS session services over TCP/IP. The NetBIOS interface to the TCP/IP stack provides the following three services: a name service, a datagram service, and a session service.

Uses TCP/UDP

In Chapter 2 you learned about the TCP/IP transport protocols, TCP and UDP. Remember that TCP is a connection-oriented service that guarantees proper data delivery. UDP is a connectionless service that does not guarantee proper data delivery. The application that uses UDP will be responsible for making sure the information sent is correctly received. Follow the instructions in Exercise 7-1 to see how the three NetBIOS services hook into the TCP and UDP transport level protocols.

EXERCISE 7-1

Viewing TCP and UDP Port Numbers Used by NetBIOS

1. First click Start | Programs | Windows NT Explorer so we can take a look at the file system.

2. Navigate to %SystemRoot%\system32\drivers\etc. %SystemRoot% is an environment variable that contains the drive letter and name of your Windows NT System directory, C:\WINNT.

3. This is the directory that holds the *HOSTS*, *LMHOSTS*, *networks*, *protocol*, and *services* files. These files hold important information about Windows NT networking. On Windows 95 and Windows for Workgroups they are usually in the C:\Windows directory. For this example, run notepad and open the file named *services*.

4. Scroll down in Notepad and you will see three services from port numbers 137 to 139 that are named nbname, nbdatagram, and nbsession.

5. Note the port number used for each service and more importantly whether they use the TCP or UDP protocols.

Figure 7-1 contains a portion of the services file for Exercise 7-1. Be sure to come back and navigate through the exercise later since it will help you remember the location of the important %SystemRoot%\system32\drivers\etc directory. After all, your memory and your experiences are all you can take with you to the exam!

Port Numbers for NetBIOS Support

There are three TCP/IP port numbers that support NetBIOS functionality: Port 137 supports the NetBIOS name service; Port 138 supports the NetBIOS datagram service; and Port 139 supports the NetBIOS session service.

Port 137, NetBIOS Name Service

If you followed Exercise 7-1 you discovered that the nbname service, which is an abbreviation for NetBIOS name service, accepts information from and sends information to port 137 of the UDP protocol. It is important to note that a port numbered 137 can exist for the TCP protocol too, as you will see for other ports that accept both UDP and TCP packets. We already know that UDP is a connectionless protocol that does not guarantee delivery of information. Why does the NetBIOS name service use UDP and not TCP?

FIGURE 7-1

Viewing the services file

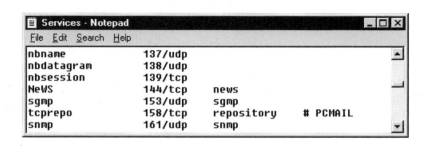

To answer this question you need to know specifically what the NetBIOS name server does.

The first thing NetBIOS does when Windows NT boots up is announce the computer's names to other computers on the network through the NetBIOS Name Service. If the computer is configured to use a NetBIOS name server (such as WINS), the computer gives its NetBIOS names (such as the computer name, domain name, or named services offered) to the name server. If the name server can identify that the names are already in use on the network, then it sends a *negative name registration response* back to the computer, and NetBIOS fails to initialize. Only the NetBIOS names in conflict will not be registered.

If there is not a name server then the computer broadcasts its NetBIOS names to all computers on the network. Now we will see why the NetBIOS name service uses UDP. The information is broadcast to all computers but it is not known whether any computers will receive the information or not. Computers that are currently turned on will receive the information, but computers that are turned off will not. Any computer that receives the name announcement broadcast with conflicting names that it has already successfully registered with the network will also generate a negative name registration response that informs the announcing computer that it cannot use those names.

Besides name registration the NetBIOS name service also handles and responds to name query requests. Before two computers can communicate over NBT, they need to know each other's IP address. TCP/IP will then take the IP address and use the address resolution protocol (ARP) to find out the hardware address encoded on the network interface card (NIC). The NetBIOS name service either sends a broadcast to all computers on the network or queries the name server for the IP address of the computer associated with the name.

In the working world, broadcasting can be a significant detriment to performance of Microsoft networks. Network degradation will increase exponentially if NetBIOS is also running over protocols other than TCP/IP. Suppose COMP1 wants to talk to COMP2 and there is no name server. COMP1 broadcasts a question, "Who is COMP2?" Every computer that uses NetBIOS receives the question on port 137 and passes it to the NetBIOS name service. The computer decides whether it is COMP2 or not. If the computer is COMP2, it responds by telling COMP1 its IP address.

NetBIOS will send three broadcasts trying to find out who COMP2 is. Each broadcast uses some processing power on every computer on the network. If TCP/IP, NWLink IPX/SPX, and NetBEUI are all installed, the broadcast happens one to three times for each protocol for each name query. Multiple protocols greatly increase broadcasting and can be the bane of an uninformed network administrator. The ideal situation is to use TCP/IP and LMHOSTS or WINS to reduce name query broadcasts.

Port 138, Datagram Service

The NetBIOS datagram service exists on port 138 and as you saw in Exercise 7-1, it uses UDP for communication. Since the datagram service is a connectionless service without guaranteed delivery, we can understand why it uses UDP. The datagram service can send information to one computer name or a group of computers, such as a domain. The most important thing to remember about the datagram service is that the source computer cannot be sure that the destination computer received the message, unless the application program itself checks for delivery.

Port 139, Session Service

The NetBIOS session service exists on port 139. From Exercise 7-1 we know that the session service uses TCP for inter-computer communication. The session service is connection-oriented, which means that two-way communication can occur that is guaranteed to have arrived or else an error message is returned. The net use command is an example of an application that uses the session service. This command connects a local drive letter to another computer's shared network drive.

CERTIFICATION OBJECTIVE 7.03

NetBIOS Host Names

Applications use NetBIOS host names to tell the NetBIOS interface which computer they want to connect to. NetBIOS host names must be unique within an organization. This is a big irritation for many systems administrators who are used to the hierarchical DNS name space. For example, a NetBIOS name could be SERVER1 but a DNS name could be www.companyname.com. NetBIOS will be fully supported in Windows NT 5.0 for legacy systems, but the good news is that Windows NT 5.0 will no longer be dependent on NetBIOS naming. Coming from many generations of NetBIOS-dependent operating systems, this is a huge change in direction for Microsoft and it is being cheered by many systems administrators who had problems with the NetBIOS flat name space.

Please don't think that NetBIOS names will be gone soon though. There are countless installations of Windows for Workgroups, Windows 95, and Windows NT that still depend on NetBIOS names for file and printer sharing and other domain level activities. Being able to accurately and correctly identify problems with NetBIOS host name resolution is an important skill for systems administrators.

16-Byte Address

NetBIOS names are always 16 bytes. They consist of 15 bytes followed by a special byte that is simply a control character in hexadecimal. For example, when you enter a 10-character computer name, the NetBIOS name registered will be the 10-character computer name suffixed with 5 spaces and the hexadecimal control character. Windows NT will not allow you to enter a computer name that is longer than 15 characters.

15 Characters

The limit for a computer name, domain name, or any other NetBIOS name is 15 characters. What happens to the extra byte in the 16-byte address? The 16th character is part of the NetBIOS host name and is used by Microsoft to identify which service or application the name belongs to.

1 Hexadecimal Control Character

The 16th character is actually a one-digit hexadecimal control character. The values can range from <00> to <FF> so the characters are indeed not printable. Exercise 7-2 will give you a detailed look at NetBIOS names that your own computer has registered.

Viewing a Remote NetBIOS Name Table Using NBTSTAT

1. First click Start | Programs | Command Prompt.

2. Run NBTSTAT -a *IP address*, where the IP address is assigned to the machine you are working on or some other Windows NT machine on the network. You can use NBTSTAT -n to view the local names of the machine you are working at.

3. Note the 15 characters of each NetBIOS host name in printable text and the 16th character in a hexadecimal format, <00> to <FF>. Also note the type of name registration for each name.

4. You will also see a status entry for each name. If you received no errors during startup, all the names' status should be registered.

5. The last entry you will see is the MAC or hardware address of your network interface card. This is what TCP/IP uses to communicate with hardware on the local subnet. The hardware address information can also be found with the ipconfig /all command.

Be sure to complete the exercise and feel free to NBTSTAT -a as many different computers as you can. You can't hurt anything with this command. The following is sample output from running an NBSTAT -a command:

```
C:\>nbtstat -a 123.145.27.10

        NetBIOS Remote Machine Name Table

    Name                    Type        Status
    ---------------------------------------------
    NTSERVER        <00>    UNIQUE      Registered
    SERVER_DOMAIN   <00>    GROUP       Registered
    SERVER_DOMAIN   <1C>    GROUP       Registered
    NTSERVER        <03>    UNIQUE      Registered
    __SQLANYWHERE   <20>    UNIQUE      Registered
    NTSERVER        <20>    UNIQUE      Registered
    SERVER_DOMAIN   <1B>    UNIQUE      Registered
    SERVER_DOMAIN   <1E>    GROUP       Registered
    SERVER_DOMAIN   <1D>    UNIQUE      Registered
    .._MSBROWSE__.<01>      GROUP       Registered
    INet~Services   <1C>    GROUP       Registered
    IS~DMHRSTST....<00>     UNIQUE      Registered
    TESTUSERNAME    <03>    UNIQUE      Registered
    MYALIAS1        <03>    UNIQUE      Registered

    MAC Address = 00-80-5F-B4-A6-2C
```

You should at least recognize your computer name, user name, and domain name (if you belong to a domain). Your computer name will probably be associated with at least three NetBIOS names depending on what you have installed with Windows NT. If you are running the Workstation service, you will see a <00> UNIQUE entry beside your computer name and a <00> GROUP by your domain name. GROUP names can be used by many computers but registered UNIQUE names will exist only on your computer within the scope of your network. If you are running the server service, you will see a <20> UNIQUE beside your computer name. If the Messenger service is running, you should see a <03> UNIQUE entry for your computer name and a <03> UNIQUE entry for your username. The net send command appends the hexadecimal character <03> to user and computer names that you are sending messages to.

Another common hexadecimal character is <1C> GROUP, which is appended to the name of the domain or workgroup you belong to, and is used for Master Browser Elections. If you are running the NBTSTAT -a command in a domain, you will probably see the _MSBROWSE_ <01> GROUP name on a Windows NT Server machine indicating that the server is a master browser. Many of the most common NetBIOS names have to do with browsing. If you have other applications running that use NetBIOS, you will also see other entries in the name table. Table 7-1 lists all the common NetBIOS names used by Windows NT.

Used by Net Commands

NetBIOS host names are used by all the net commands to carry information from one computer to another. The commands use the Universal Naming Convention (UNC) syntax to specify which computer and resource to access. The syntax for UNC names is *Servername\Sharename* where *Servername* is the computer name of the server to connect to and *Sharename* is the name assigned to the shared resource on the server. UNC names can also include directories and file paths in the following format: *Servername\Sharename\Directoryname\Filename.* The *Servername* used is a NetBIOS host name to which the net commands append the appropriate hex character, in this case <20>, to connect to the Server service. For a list of Net commands, enter NET HELP at a command prompt. For further help on any command enter NET COMMAND HELP at a command prompt where

TABLE 7-1   Common NetBIOS Names

Name	Hex	Associated NT Service, Application, or Functionality
COMPUTER NAME DOMAIN NAME	<00>	Workstation Service
MSBROWSE	<01>	Domain Announcement
COMPUTER NAME	<06>	RAS Server
COMPUTER NAME USER NAME	<03>	Messenger Service
DOMAIN NAME	<1B>	Domain Master Browser
DOMAIN NAME	<1C>	Named Domain Groups
DOMAIN NAME	<1D>	Subnet Master Browser
DOMAIN NAME	<1E>	Master Browser Election
COMPUTER NAME	<1F>	NetDDE
COMPUTER NAME	<20>	Server Service
COMPUTER NAME	<21>	RAS Client
COMPUTER NAME	<BE>	Network Monitor Agent
COMPUTER NAME	<BF>	Network Monitor Utility

COMMAND is the name of the command you want more information on. Figure 7-2 shows part of the indexed lst available on Windows NT commands. It can be found in Start | Help | Contents | Windows NT Commands | Windows NT Commands.

NET USE   Net Use is by far the most useful net command, pun intended. You can use it to connect drive letters and printer ports to remote shares and printers. You can even use it to establish permission in the same way you use the Connect As textbox when using My Computer | Map Network Drive.

Indexed list of Windows
NT commands

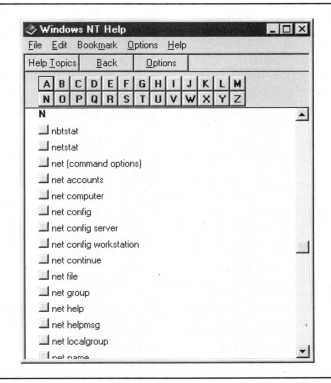

When you want to write a login script, you can employ net use to delete some
or all of your clients' manual drive mappings and replace them with standard
drive mappings for your organization. No more getting confused as to whose S
drive is someone else's N drive.

Sample output from a net use command follows this paragraph. Notice that
drive J: is connected to a file share and LPT3 is connected to a shared printer.
A disconnected status simply means that the connection has not been used
recently and is in a disconnected state. Windows NT will automatically
reconnect the remote share whenever the share is accessed. The IPC$ is one of
the Windows NT default shares. This one in particular is for interprocess

communication. You can map to it using the net use command with a username and password to establish a Connect As connection.

```
C:\>net use
New connections will not be remembered.

Status          Local     Remote                    Network
-------------------------------------------------------------------
                J:    \\NTSERVER\DFS        Microsoft Windows Network
Disconnected    LPT3  \\NTSERVER\plotter    Microsoft Windows Network
Disconnected          \\USER1\IPC$          Microsoft Windows Network
OK                    \\USER2\IPC           Microsoft Windows Network
The command completed successfully.
```

NET   The other net commands are listed in Table 7-2. They all use UNC to access remote computer resources. The server name in the UNC syntax is always a NetBIOS name, so the net commands that work remotely all use the 16-byte NetBIOS host name to communicate with other computers.

Used by NetBIOS Commands
The 16-byte NetBIOS host names are used by any application that uses NetBIOS communication. Whether the application is a database, game, or chat, they all have to use 16-byte NetBIOS host names to communicate.

CERTIFICATION OBJECTIVE 7.04

NetBIOS Functional Processes

In this section we discuss the three NetBIOS functional processes: Name Registration, Name Discovery, and Name Release. These functional processes are run for NetBIOS no matter which transport protocol it is running over. However, we will focus only on the functional processes from a NetBIOS over TCP/IP standpoint because that's what is on the exam.

TABLE 7-2   Windows NT Net Commands

Command	Functionality
NET ACCOUNTS	View or set account policy.
NET COMPUTER	Add or remove computers to the domain.
NET CONFIG	View configuration for server and workstation services.
NET CONFIG SERVER	Set automatic client disconnection on the server.
NET CONFIG WORKSTATION	Set communication rates.
NET CONTINUE	Continue a paused service.
NET FILE	List of files currently opened by remote users.
NET GROUP	Manage domain global groups.
NET HELP	Lists net commands available, in case you don't carry this book everywhere.
NET HELP Command	Detailed help on every net command available.
NET HELPMSG	Information on numerical error codes.
NET LOCALGROUP	Manage local groups.
NET NAME	Add or remove messaging name receiving messages. Creates name as *Alias*<03> in NBTSTAT -a.
NET PAUSE	Pauses service.
NET PRINT	Print job and print queue information.
NET SEND	Sends messages to a user or users in the domain. The messages are received only by computers that have the Messenger service on.
NET SESSION	List computers and users that currently have remote resources or sessions connected to the server.
NET SHARE	Add, remove, or view shared resources.
NET START	Start a service.
NET STATISTICS	View statistics for server and workstation services.
NET STOP	Stop a service.
NET TIME	Manually set or automatically synchronize time with another computer.
NET USE	Connect devices to remote shared resources.

TABLE 7-2	Windows NT Net Commands (*continued*)
Command	**Functionality**
NET USER	Add, remove, or view user accounts.
NET VIEW	View shared resources remotely or list computers on the network.

Name Registration

When you first boot up a Windows NT computer from a powered-off state, you see the familiar message, "Press Ctrl + Alt + Delete to log on," which means the network services are still starting in the background. The first functional process NetBIOS runs is Name Registration. To accomplish this process the computer sends a message, called a NetBIOS name registration request, to the network. If the computer is set up to register with a NetBIOS name server (NBNS), the message is sent directly to the name server. This is called a directed packet; it is not a broadcast, and therefore only one receiving computer, the name server, needs to process the information. All other computers discard the message as soon as it hits the network card and they recognize that the hardware address does not belong to them. If the computer is not set up to register with a name server then it broadcasts the message to all computers on the local subnet using the UDP protocol.

For group names, like a domain or workgroup name that multiple computers belong to, the NetBIOS name registration request is never challenged. NetBIOS name registration requests will be challenged if requested unique names, like a computer name, are already being used somewhere on the network.

If the name registration request is broadcast to the network and another computer is already using the NetBIOS name, then a negative name registration response message will be returned to the source computer informing it that it cannot register those NetBIOS names. Depending on which names are unusable, the computer may not initialize NetBIOS, start the Messenger service, or some other functionality or application may be inhibited. Always check Start | Programs | Administrative Tools | Event Viewer to check out any error messages you receive during logon. Positive name registration responses are not returned to the source computer during broadcast registration requests since no one computer is acting as a keeper of all the addresses.

If the name registration request is sent to a WINS server that already has the NetBIOS name in its database, the WINS server will not automatically send back a negative response. First, the WINS server will check to see if the IP address registered in the database is the same as the one in the request. If the IP addresses are the same, then it is just the same computer having been powered off without shutting down. If the IP addresses are not the same then the WINS server must check to see whether the computer associated with the conflicting names is still on. The WINS server challenges the registered host to defend its right to keep the conflicting names. If the registered host responds, it wins the challenge and WINS sends a negative name registration response back to the requesting computer. If the registered host does not respond, then WINS sends back a positive name registration response and the original computer will keep on trucking.

Broadcast or WINS

If you leave Windows NT set at its defaults, it will choose WINS over broadcasting if you have WINS enabled. If WINS is unable to register an address, NT will use broadcast registration. As far as performance for the Name Registration functional process goes, there is not a big difference, although it is generally better to use WINS, especially on larger networks. Once all the computers have registered their names on the network for the day, the broadcast traffic is over. During rush hours, like morning or after lunch, you may see some network degradation from broadcasts but it will be slight. The same applies to a WINS server trying to handle name registrations. You need to make sure that the server has enough horsepower during the rush hours, but once the rush hours are over name registration traffic should be minimal. If I had to pick one method, I would favor WINS for performance since broadcasts steal processing power from every computer on the network. Chapter 8 covers WINS in more detail.

Name Discovery

Name Discovery is actually very similar to Name Registration. NetBIOS host name resolution for NetBIOS over TCP/IP simply means translating a given name into an IP address. Name Discovery is really only part of the puzzle since everything will fall apart if Name Registration or Name Release goes haywire.

First, NetBIOS will consult the NetBIOS name cache to see if the name has been resolved recently. This saves the network from a whole lot of useless broadcasts. If the name needed is not in the name cache, the computer, if registered with WINS, will send a directed packet to the WINS server trying to resolve the name. If the name is not found in the WINS server database, the computer will broadcast to the local network up to three times trying to get the destination computer to respond. If the broadcasts fail, it will scan the LMHOSTS database text file line by line looking for a match. If the LMHOSTS file does not contain the name, it will try the HOSTS file and finally a DNS query. You can easily configure the computer to query or not query WINS, LMHOSTS, HOSTS, and DNS through the Network Control Panel applet. Go to Start | Settings | Control Panel | Network | Protocols | TCP/IP Protocol | Properties | WINS Address and you should see a dialog box like the one shown in Figure 7-3.

Figure 7-3 shows the dialog box to register a client computer with WINS. If the primary WINS server does not respond during name registration, the computer will try using the secondary WINS server. If the secondary WINS server also fails to respond, the computer will then broadcast name registration.

If you enable DNS for Windows Resolution, the Name Discovery functional process will also try to look in the HOSTS file and DNS server to find the NetBIOS name. I suggest not enabling DNS for Windows Resolution because it will slow down the Name Discovery process and NetBIOS names should not be stored in the HOSTS file or DNS anyway. If you enter a name like www.server.com, NT automatically recognizes the Fully Qualified Domain Name (FQDN) syntax and runs a DNS and host file query first.

If you enable LMHOSTS Lookup, the Name Registration will first scan the LMHOSTS files for entries to preload into the NetBIOS name cache. During

FIGURE 7-3

FIGURE 7-3

Enabling LMHOSTS Lookup

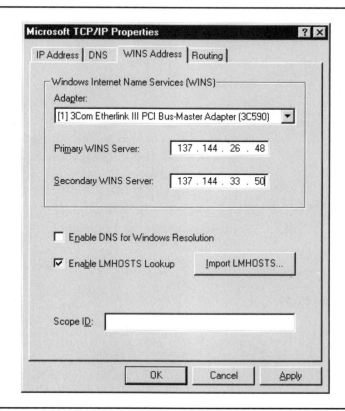

the Name Discovery phase, the LMHOSTS file will be scanned after everything else has failed but before any HOST file or DNS lookup. The Enable LMHOSTS Lookup box needs to be checked even if all you have in your LMHOSTS file are name mappings to be loaded into the NetBIOS name cache.

The Scope ID box should always remain blank. Only computers that have the same word for their Scope ID can communicate with each other. It is one way to establish weak security and also cause yourself a lot of connectivity problems. If you need security, it's better to use username, passwords, and NTFS.

Broadcast or WINS

Broadcasting for Name Discovery is good only if you have a small computer network. NetBIOS was originally designed for small networks. Networks of 25 or fewer users would not want the hassles of setting up and maintaining a name server since broadcasting is automatic. For larger networks, broadcasting will multiply the network and processing load with each computer that is added to the network. Take some good advice and use WINS if at all possible. If your computers are also using DHCP for dynamic configuration, you can set the scope options to automatically point every DHCP client to your WINS server.

Name Release

The last NetBIOS functional process is Name Release, and it really is very simple. If the computer is registered with WINS, it informs WINS while shutting down that it will no longer need the names it registered. If the computer it not registered with WINS, it sends a broadcast to inform the network of the released names.

Broadcast or WINS

One of the challenges WINS faces is maintaining the database when users turn off the power switch instead of properly shutting down. If the power switch is hit, then the Name Release process does not happen and the names are still registered with WINS. This is why WINS has to challenge the registered name owner when a name request turns up conflicting names in the database. If this challenge did not occur, the WINS database would fill up with names and names could never be reused. This is not a problem since Name Release plays such a small part in the overall network load generated by NetBIOS. For large networks WINS is still far better than broadcasting even in the Name Release process simply because it involves only a few computers communicating. You have to use WINS if your network spans different subnets because broadcasts will not be forwarded by routers.

NetBIOS Over TCP/IP

We've talked a lot about NetBIOS over TCP/IP (NBT) and hopefully you now have a good idea of what it is all about. This section will cover even more technical details and specifications about NBT.

NetBIOS and IP Mapping

To define NetBIOS over TCP/IP, you could say that it is a network component that performs computer name to IP mapping. Or you could say it is the quarterback that takes a NetBIOS name, turns it into an IP address, and hands it off to TCP/IP to run with it. That is the primary function of NBT. NetBIOS is the interface to the applications; TCP/IP is the transport protocol that carries the information from one computer to another; and NBT is the glue in between. NetBIOS uses 16-byte names; TCP/IP uses 32-bit addresses; and NBT is the translator.

Node Types

RFC1001 and RFC1002 define three ways NBT can work: b-node, p-node, and m-node. It took me a while to figure out that node was not actually mode, so I'll just give you that little piece of information. A node is basically a computer, and b-node, p-node, and m-node describe how the NBT functional processes work for that computer (node). Microsoft has added a few more methods into the list, namely, enhanced b-node and h-node. A Windows NT computer will use enhanced b-node by default unless it is configured to register with a WINS server, in which case it uses h-node. All these methods determine whether the computer uses, and in which order, the NetBIOS name cache, WINS, broadcasts, LMHOSTS, HOSTS, and DNS for NetBIOS host name resolution.

b-Node (The Broadcast Method)

The b-node method uses NetBIOS name registration request broadcasts for Name Registration and NetBIOS name query broadcasts for Name Discovery. To enable this method starting from a Microsoft default installation that is not WINS enabled, simply disable LMHOSTS Lookup.

BROADCAST   The NetBIOS name cache helps reduce repetitious broadcasting by caching resolved names and their associated IP addresses for a certain small length of time. A name is by default placed on the NetBIOS name cache for ten minutes if it is used again within two minutes after being placed in cache. If not used a second time within two minutes it is removed at the end of two minutes.

Of course by now you know that this method is not recommended for large networks. Relying solely on broadcasts for name resolution and registration on networks with a large amount of nodes (computers) can cause significant network traffic congestion for all computers. The b-node method also limits name resolution and registration to one subnet unless you have special routers that are configured to pass along the b-node NetBIOS broadcasts to the next subnet.

Microsoft Modified b-Node

If Windows NT is not configured to register with WINS, then the modified b-node method is the default configuration when networking is set up. This method is similar to the b-node method except it uses the LMHOSTS file to preload name to IP address mappings into the NetBIOS name cache and also as a database for looking up names that could not be resolved by broadcasting.

NETBIOS NAME CACHE   You will see the LMHOSTS file syntax in the next section. What you need to know about the modified b-node method is that it searches the LMHOSTS file when the computer starts up for entries marked with #PRE. These entries are then loaded into the NetBIOS name cache and will never expire. The NetBIOS name cache is the first place NBT will look when resolving names. Putting commonly used computer names (like the servers) into the NetBIOS name cache can speed up network responsiveness. You can force NBT to reload the name cache with the NBTSTAT -R command. The -R command switch is case sensitive.

BROADCASTING   Like the b-node method, the primary method for resolving names is to do a NetBIOS name query broadcast and hope the computer responds. The enhanced b-node method is no more efficient than b-node if you do not use name cache preloading.

LMHOSTS FILE   The LMHOSTS database file is found in the %SystemRoot%\system32\drivers\etc directory. You should not just add lines to the sample file Microsoft provides; instead start with a blank file since NT scans the file line by line each time resolving a name by broadcasting fails. Maintaining the LMHOSTS file can become an administrative chore because the static entries need to be changed with every new computer added or removed from the network. Also, it is a lot of trouble distributing and maintaining the files on every machine on the network.

EXERCISE 7-3

Pinging NetBIOS Hosts with an LMHOSTS File

1. On a Windows NT computer start notepad by going to Start | Programs | Accessories | Notepad.
2. Type the following line. Feel free to change the IP address or server name.

   122.133.44.6   SERVER1
3. Now save the file in %SystemRoot\system32\drivers\etc as LMHOSTS.
4. Now start a command prompt by going to Start | Programs | Command Prompt.

5. Enter the command **ping SERVER1**.

6. You should see NT trying to ping the IP address you entered in the LMHOSTS file for SERVER1. For the purposes of this exercise it does not matter whether the ping is successful or not. Once you see NT trying to ping, you know that NetBIOS successfully resolved the name into an IP address.

p-Node (The Peer to Peer Method)

The p-node method can be enabled only by editing the registry or setting the scope option dynamically from DHCP enabled computers. When Microsoft makes you edit the registry, it's a big hint that it is usually not preferable to use this method. In the p-node method broadcasts are never sent. Only a NetBIOS name server is used, or in other words, a WINS server. This works fine until there is a problem with the name server, then no names can be resolved. The h-node method has a better level of fault tolerance since it falls back on broadcasts if WINS resolution fails.

NAME SERVER REGISTRATION ONLY   This method could potentially speed up an h-node network somewhat, especially for Name Resolution failures. Since broadcasts are never sent, the error message would return quicker. If we expected more failures than success we would want to use this method, but of course we expect most name queries to succeed one way or another. That is why the h-node method is better because names can also be resolved by trying broadcasts (which adds some fault tolerance) instead of just quickly returning the error message.

m-Node (The Mixed Node Method)

The m-node method first tries to use broadcasts for name resolution; then once the broadcasts time out, it will send the query directly to the NetBIOS name server (WINS). You would think the RFC documents would have defined this method to reduce broadcasts but unfortunately they did not.

MIXED NODE   The m-node method really stands for mixed node method. This is because it combines both the b-node and p-node methods into one. What is important here is the order in which the RFC documents define which method happens first.

USES B-NODE, THEN P-NODE   The m-node method is called the mixed node method because it first tries to use the b-node method (broadcasts), then uses the p-node method (directed name server query) for name resolution. This is exactly opposite of the way it should be for reducing broadcasts for performance reasons. That is why Microsoft invented the h-node method, which is really just the exact opposite of the m-node method.

h-Node (The Hybrid Node Method)

The h-node method is a combination of the p-node and b-node methods. The h-node method specifies that the p-node method (directed name server query) be used first and if that fails the b-node method (broadcasts) will be tried. If every computer on your network registers with the WINS name server, then this method will never produce a single NetBIOS broadcast (wow!). It is better than the p-node method because it will try broadcasts as a backup pending the failure of the name server to resolve the name.

HYBRID NODE   The h-node method is called the hybrid node method but I might have named it something like "Name Server, then Broadcast method" since that is the most important point to remember. Broadcast is used only if the name server query fails.

Name Resolution Methods

Well, now that you have made it past nodes, modes, and methods, you can get into what is really important: what you need to know for the exam and also for the real world. In the next two sections, we discuss the standard name resolution method used by other NetBIOS equipped operating systems and applications and the default Microsoft name resolution method. Some of the Microsoft specific steps may be enabled or disabled by configuring TCP/IP with the Network Control Panel applet.

For the exam I would focus on the Microsoft-specific methods discussed next. The exam is about TCP/IP on Windows NT 4.0 and will focus on Windows NT and not the way the rest of the world does it. The other standard methods may be useful in troubleshooting inter-system connectivity in the working world.

Standard Methods

There are three standard methods used by most NetBIOS implementations (besides Microsoft). They may vary from implementation to implementation.

NETBIOS NAME CACHE   Generally all NetBIOS over TCP/IP implementations will have a NetBIOS name cache. This is mentioned in the RFC documents but is not required of all NetBIOS over TCP/IP implementations. Generally all implementations will use a name cache since it can greatly reduce network broadcasts and speed up repetitious name resolution requests.

LOCAL BROADCAST   If the name desired is not in the name cache, then most implementations will try to resolve the name using local broadcasts. This works fine for installations with a small client base.

NETBIOS NAME SERVER   If the name is not found in the name cache or by local broadcasts, then most implementations will try to resolve the name using a NetBIOS name server. You should notice that this sequence of steps is just a repeat of the m-node description given in the previous section.

Microsoft-Specific Methods

Finally, you get to what you really need to know for the exam. Commit this sequence to memory because it is not only easy test material but it is invaluable knowledge to carry with you when troubleshooting network connectivity. Table 7-3 lists the six name resolution sources in sequence that Microsoft NBT will use. The table is followed by a description of each source.

Be sure to commit Table 7-3 to memory. A question that involves several mixed-up situations of name resolution sources will be easy to answer if you know the sequence in which the sources are tried.

Sequence	Name Resolution Source
1st	NetBIOS Name Cache
2nd	NetBIOS Name Server (WINS for example)
3rd	B-Node Broadcasts
4th	LMHOSTS File
5th	HOSTS File
6th	DNS Server

TABLE 7-3

NetBIOS Name Resolution Sources in Sequence

NETBIOS NAME CACHE   The first thing any name resolution query method will do is check the NetBIOS name cache. Whenever a name is resolved, it is automatically placed in the name cache whether it is resolved from WINS, broadcasts, LMHOSTS, HOSTS, or DNS. Each entry when placed in the cache is given a time-to-live value in seconds and when this time expires the name is removed from the cache. You can view entries in the NetBIOS name cache with the NBTSTAT -c command. NBTSTAT is covered in further detail in the last section of this chapter.

NAME SERVER   After checking the name cache the next place a Microsoft NetBIOS implementation will look for a name is at the WINS NetBIOS name server (NBNS) if TCP/IP is configured with a primary or secondary WINS address. The query goes directly to the name server using directed packets, so WINS does not need to be on the same subnet as your clients.

   On an Ethernet bus type network where every computer "sees" every packet on the wire the network interface card (NIC) only looks as far as the ethernet hardware address before it discards a directed packet. Another way of saying this is that directed packets don't get processed by any layers except the physical layer of the OSI model. Using a name server saves the network from "NetBIOS broadcast indigestion" where every computer must process the broadcast to the session layer of the OSI model where NetBIOS resides.

B-NODE BROADCASTS   If the name is not found in the name cache or WINS, then Microsoft NBT will send up to three broadcasts trying to resolve the name. The local broadcast IP address is normally 255.255.255.255, as you learned earlier in this book. On an Ethernet this IP address is usually turned into a hardware address of FF-FF-FF-FF-FF-FF. Routers by default should block all broadcasts and will not forward NetBIOS broadcasts unless you specifically enable UDP ports 137 and 138 on the router. We saw these ports in Exercise 7-1.

Routers will not block the NetBIOS session service since it uses TCP port 139, and TCP means it is using directed packets. But to establish a session you need a name mapped to an IP address, and if the router is blocking your name resolution broadcasts, then you are out of luck. A quick way around this problem of routers blocking name resolution broadcasts is to make an entry into the LMHOSTS file. Once the name resolution occurs, the session can be established no matter where in the world the IP address points to.

LMHOSTS FILE   The next place Microsoft NBT will check is the LMHOSTS file. This file is really just a database of IP addresses and NetBIOS host names along with some special switch information. We look at this in more detail in the next section.

HOSTS FILE   The HOSTS file will be scanned for NetBIOS names only if the "Enable DNS for Windows Resolution" checkbox is checked in the TCP/IP protocol setup. This is not the default at installation and must be manually enabled. This file is very similar to LMHOSTS but it just contains IP addresses and host names (without any special switches). You should not enable this unless you have a special need since it will slow down returning error messages to the user.

DNS SERVER   Like the HOSTS file the DNS server will be queried for NetBIOS names only if the Enable DNS for Windows Resolution checkbox is selected in the TCP/IP protocol setup. When you check this box, you get both hosts lookup and DNS; there is no way to separate the two. Again, enable this only if you have a very special need.

CERTIFICATION OBJECTIVE 7.06

Using **LMHOSTS** File

This section covers the specifics of creating an LMHOSTS file. The "lm" stands for LAN Manager, an early predecessor of Windows NT. To use the LMHOSTS file you need to make sure you have LMHOSTS Lookup enabled by going to Start | Settings | Control Panel | Network | Protocol | TCP/IP Protocol | WINS Address and checking the Enable LMHOSTS Lookup checkbox.

Default Location

Don't forget that the LMHOSTS file location for Windows NT is in a different place than the rest of Microsoft's operating systems.

NT is %SystemRoot%\system32\drivers\etc

The default location for the LMHOSTS file is %SystemRoot%\system32\ drivers\etc. Don't ever forget this location (at least not until Microsoft changes it again). An example of the default %SystemRoot% in Windows NT is C:\WINNT.

Windows for Workgroups and Windows 95 is %SystemRoot%

The default location for Windows 95 and Windows for Workgroups is the %SystemRoot% directory. An example of the default %SystemRoot% would be C:\WINDOWS. Don't expect that Windows 95 will have the %SystemRoot% environment variable defined either.

Sample Available as LMHOSTS.SAM

Microsoft has created a sample LMHOSTS file with instructions and examples in it. It is available in the default location for the LMHOSTS file and is named

LMHOSTS.SAM. I would not suggest editing this file and then deploying it. Rather, start from scratch with an empty file and add entries one by one. NBT scans the file line by line and will quit when there is a successful match, so you can speed up name resolution if NBT does not have to read a bunch of useless lines each time it scans the file. You should also put #PRE statements at the end of the file since they will always be resolved from the NetBIOS cache and never the LMHOSTS file. The following Microsoft sample LMHOSTS.SAM file has been included for your reading pleasure:

```
# Copyright (c) 1993-1995 Microsoft Corp.
#
# This is a sample LMHOSTS file used by the Microsoft TCP/IP
# for Windows NT.
#
# This file contains the mappings of IP addresses to NT
# computernames(NetBIOS) names. Each entry should be kept on
# an individual line. The IP address should be placed in the
# first column followed by the corresponding computername.
# The address and the comptername should be separated by at
# least one space or tab. The "#" character is generally
# used to denote the start of a comment (see the exceptions
# below).
#
# This file is compatible with Microsoft LAN Manager 2.x
# TCP/IP lmhosts files and offers the following extensions:
#
#      #PRE
#      #DOM:<domain>
#      #INCLUDE <filename>
#      #BEGIN_ALTERNATE
#      #END_ALTERNATE
#      \0xnn (non-printing character support)
#
# Following any entry in the file with the characters "#PRE"
# will cause the entry to be preloaded into the name cache.
# By default, entries are not preloaded, but are parsed only
# after dynamic name resolution fails.
#
# Following an entry with the "#DOM:<domain>" tag will
# associate the entry with the domain specified by <domain>.
# This affects how the browser and logon services behave in
# TCP/IP environments. To preload the host name associated
# with #DOM entry, it is necessary to also add a PRE to the
```

```
# line. The <domain> is always preloaded although it will
# not be shown when the name cache is viewed.
#
# Specifying "#INCLUDE <filename>" will force the RFC
# NetBIOS (NBT)software to seek the specified <filename> and
# parse it as if it were local. <filename> is generally a
# UNC-based name, allowing a centralized lmhosts file to be
# maintained on a server. It is ALWAYS necessary to provide
# a mapping for the IP address of the server prior to the
# #INCLUDE. This mapping must use the #PRE directive. In
# addtion the share "public" in the example below must be in
# the LanManServer list of "NullSessionShares" in order for
# client machines to be able to read the lmhosts file
# successfully. This key is under
#
# \machine\system\currentcontrolset\services\lanmanserver\
# parameters\nullsessionshares in the registry. Simply add
# "public" to the list found there.
#
# The #BEGIN_ and #END_ALTERNATE keywords allow multiple
# #INCLUDE statements to be grouped together. Any single
# successful include will cause the group to succeed.
#
# Finally, non-printing characters can be embedded in
# mappings by first surrounding the NetBIOS name in
# quotations, then using the \0xnn notation to specify a hex
# value for a non-printing character.
#
# The following example illustrates all of these extensions:
#
# 102.54.94.97  rhino #PRE #DOM:networking #net group's DC
# 102.54.94.102 "appname  \0x14"             #special app server
# 102.54.94.123 popular   #PRE               #source server
# 102.54.94.117 localsrv  #PRE               #needed for the include
#
# #BEGIN_ALTERNATE
# #INCLUDE \\localsrv\public\lmhosts
# #INCLUDE \\rhino\public\lmhosts
# #END_ALTERNATE
#
# In the above example, the "appname" server contains a
# special character in its name, the "popular" and
# "localsrv" server names are preloaded, and the "rhino"
# server name is specified so it can be used to later
# #INCLUDE a centrally maintained lmhosts file if the
```

```
# "localsrv" system is unavailable.
#
# Note that the whole file is parsed including comments on
# each lookup, so keeping the number of comments to a
# minimum will improve performance. Therefore it is not
# advisable to simply add lmhosts file entries onto the
# end of this file.
```

Keywords

The format of the LMHOSTS file is an IP address, followed by a NetBIOS host name, followed by keywords with each entry on a separate line. There are seven keywords that you can use in your LMHOSTS file.

EXERCISE 7-4

Entering LMHOSTS Keywords

1. On a Windows NT computer start notepad by going to Start | Programs | Accessories | Notepad.

2. Type the following lines. Feel free to change the IP address or server names.

   122.133.44.5 SERVER1   #PRE
   122.133.44.6 SERVER2

3. Now save the file in %SystemRoot%\system32\drivers\etc as LMHOSTS.

4. Now start a command prompt by going to Start | Programs | Command Prompt.

5. Enter the NBTSTAT -R command to flush and reload the NetBIOS name cache.

6. Enter the NBTSTAT -c command to view the NetBIOS name cache.

7. Since it was preloaded, the name entries for SERVER1 have a life of -1, meaning they will never expire from the name cache.

8. Enter the ping SERVER1 command.

9. Enter the ping SERVER2 command.

10. View the name cache again with NBTSTAT -c.

Notice that now the name entries for SERVER2 are in the name cache. The entries should have a life of 660 seconds, meaning they will expire and be removed from the name cache in 11 minutes.

Table 7-4 lists the LMHOSTS keywords and a short description for each command.

#PRE

The #PRE keyword is the one you will use most often. #PRE designates that the name to IP address mapping will be placed into the NetBIOS name cache whenever the machine starts. The name cache in main memory is the first place NT will look for name resolutions. If you are able to distribute an LMHOSTS file to all your clients, I suggest placing the names and addresses of your primary servers in #PRE statements. Since most everyone accesses servers most of the time, this should greatly speed up network access and will decrease network traffic, even if you are using WINS and especially if you are using broadcasts.

After you add #PRE entries to your LMHOSTS file, you do not have to reboot to get those entries loaded into the NetBIOS name cache. Use the

TABLE 7-4   LMHOSTS Keywords

Keyword	Description
#PRE	Preloads the entry into the NetBIOS name cache.
#DOM:domain	Marks a computer as a domain controller. Names of domain controllers are stored in a special list.
#NOFNR	Bypasses directed name verification query to the machine.
#INCLUDE <filename>	Includes a remote LMHOSTS file when parsing the local one.
#BEGIN_ALTERNATE	Marks the start of a block of #INCLUDE statements.
#END_ALTERNATE	Marks the end of a block of #INCLUDE statements.
#MH	Marks entries for multihomed computers.

NBTSTAT -R command to flush the old name cache and reload it. The NBTSTAT command-line switches are case sensitive so the -R must be uppercase.

#DOM:domain

You can use the #DOM keyword to specific that a machine is a backup or primary domain controller. This can be useful for functionality like browsing which normally doesn't work across subnets since it uses broadcasts to communicate among computers and domains. Since each domain has a master browser and domains are likely to be separated by subnets, this can get the master browser in one domain talking to the master browser in the remote domain. Note that this should create a group entry for the specified domain into the name cache and not a unique entry. Therefore you should use this keyword for all domain controllers in a domain. The #PRE keyword must be placed on the line before #DOM. NBT places entries into a special domain name list so you will not see anything different when looking at the NetBIOS name cache with the NBTSTAT -c command. If you have a choice though, it is much easier to use a WINS server and save yourself a lot of hassle and confusion.

#NOFNR

The #NOFNR keyword was added to the LMHOSTS file because some of the older LAN managers for UNIX and DEC Pathworks servers do not respond to directed name verification queries sent by Windows NT. NBT usually asks a machine if it is on and if it is the right name before trying to send any information to it. This keyword tells Windows NT to bypass the directed name query for the specified machine. For more information you can look up article Q103765 in the Microsoft Knowledge Base.

#INCLUDE <filename>

Whenever NBT is parsing the LMHOSTS file line by line and it encounters the #INCLUDE statement, it parses the new file as if it were actually in the LMHOSTS file. The filename can be given in the UNC syntax so files from other servers can be included. When using UNC names the server name still needs to be resolved so it must be inserted before the #INCLUDE keyword. You must put a #PRE statement for the server before the #INCLUDE or the #INCLUDE will be ignored. Following is an example:

```
123.144.11.1    SERVER1       #PRE      #necessary for include
statement #INCLUDE \\SERVER1\ETC$\lmhosts
```

The #INCLUDE statement needs to know where SERVER1 is so that is why we must put the IP address for SERVER1 in a preloaded line prior to the #INCLUDE. This is a very inefficient way of having a centralized LMHOSTS file since the remote LMHOSTS file must be downloaded and parsed every single time the local LMHOSTS file is downloaded and parsed for names. It might be an okay solution if all the statements in each LMHOSTS were preloaded into the NetBIOS name cache, which would mean the files would be parsed only on name query failures. This solution still causes unnecessary network traffic that can be detrimental in large LAN installations.

Also, before SERVER1 will let the remote client have its LMHOSTS file, its share must be listed as a Null Session Share in its Windows NT Registry. To accomplish this you need to add the directory (C:\WINNT\system32\ drivers\etc) for the share to the list in HKEY_LOCAL_MACHINE\System\ CurrentControlSet\Services\LanManServer\Parameters.

One solution for distributing a centralized LMHOSTS files would be to put an XCOPY /d into the user's login script followed by an NBTSTAT -R. The XCOPY command switch /d checks the dates on the files and copies the master LMHOSTS file only if it is newer. The NBTSTAT -R purges and updates the NetBIOS name cache if the LMHOSTS file has changed. You need to make sure that every user has permissions to the directory where the LMHOSTS file is stored on their machine.

#BEGIN_ALTERNATE

#BEGIN_ALTERNATE marks the start of a block of #INCLUDE statements. NBT will process each #INCLUDE statement until one is successful. It will include one and only one of the master LMHOSTS files. This allows you some fault tolerance since the master LMHOSTS file will be stored on several servers.

#END_ALTERNATE

#END_ALTERNATE marks the end of a block of #INCLUDE statements.
Remember that each server in an #INCLUDE statement needs to already have
its IP address previously defined in the LMHOSTS file. Following is an
example of #BEGIN_ALTERNATE and #END_ALTERNATE:

```
123.144.11.1   SERVER1    #PRE   #necessary for include statement
123.144.11.2   SERVER2    #PRE   #necessary for include statement
#BEGIN_ALTERNATE
#INCLUDE  \\SERVER1\ETC$\lmhosts
#INCLUDE  \\SERVER2\ETC$\lmhosts
#END_ALTERNATE
```

Once one of the included files is found, the other include statements in the
block will be bypassed. You need to make sure all the LMHOSTS files in the
block statement are the same to avoid confusion and failed name queries. This
is still a crude way to distribute LMHOSTS files and will be an administrative
burden on large networks.

#MH

The #MH keyword is used to mark multihomed servers. Multihomed servers
have two network interface cards with two IP address being viable for one
NetBIOS name. Following is an example:

```
110.155.22.1   MYPDC    #MH    #entry for NIC 1 of MYPDC machine
110.155.22.2   MYPDC    #MH    #entry for NIC 2 of MYPDC machine
```

Notice that the server name MYPDC has two entries with two
corresponding IP addresses. The #MH keyword must be included on both
entries so as to mark the entries as multihomed. Note that WINS accomplishes
the same functionality automatically.

EXERCISE 7-5

Using an LMHOSTS File

1. Using your computer at home, log on to the Internet.

2. Make an entry in your LMHOSTS file for the IP address and name of a
   computer you have access to somewhere on the Internet.

3. Using My Computer | Map Network Drive type the UNC name of a share on the remote computer, i.e., \\SERVERNAME\SHARENAME.

4. If necessary, enter the username that you want to Connect As and the password when prompted.

5. Though it will probably be very slow, you have just connected to a drive share on your computer over the Internet. This is one of the best uses for LMHOSTS files.

CERTIFICATION OBJECTIVE 7.07

NBTSTAT Utility

The NBTSTAT is the most useful utility related to NetBIOS over TCP/IP. Remember the NBT in NBTSTAT stands for NetBIOS over TCP/IP and the STAT stands for statistics. The NBTSTAT command-line switches are listed in Table 7-5 along with a short description of what each command does. For your convenience the command-line help for NBTSTAT is included after the table.

TABLE 7-5   NBTSTAT Commands

Command	Function
NBTSTAT -a or -A	Lists NetBIOS names for a remote computer.
NBTSTAT -c	Lists entries in the NetBIOS name cache.
NBTSTAT -n	Lists NetBIOS names for the local computer.
NBTSTAT -r	Lists counters for names resolved by broadcasts and WINS. Also gives list of names resolved by broadcast.
NBTSTAT -R	Purges and reloads the NetBIOS name cache.
NBTSTAT -S or -s	Lists sessions for the local computer.

```
C:\>nbtstat /?

Displays protocol statistics and current TCP/IP connections using NBT
(NetBIOS over TCP/IP).

NBTSTAT [-a RemoteName] [-A IP address] [-c] [-n]
        [-r] [-R] [-s] [-S] [interval] ]

  -a   (adapter status) Lists the remote machine's name
       table given its name
  -A   (Adapter status) Lists the remote machine's name
       table given its
                         IP address.
  -c   (cache)          Lists the remote name cache
                        including the IP addresses
  -n   (names)          Lists local NetBIOS names.
  -r   (resolved)       Lists names resolved by broadcast
                        and via WINS
  -R   (Reload)         Purges and reloads the remote cache
                        name table
  -S   (Sessions)       Lists sessions table with the
                        destination IP addresses
  -s   (sessions)       Lists sessions table converting
                        destination IP
                        addresses to host names via the hosts file.


  RemoteName   Remote host machine name.
  IP address   Dotted decimal representation of the IP
               address.
  interval     Redisplays selected statistics, pausing
               interval seconds
               between each display. Press Ctrl+C to stop
               redisplaying statistics.
```

The NBTSTAT -a command lists the names used by a remote computer. It is a good way to easily see what names a computer thinks it owns if you are having naming conflicts. You can also see which names failed to register by examining the status column. The following is sample output from running an NBTSTAT -a command:

```
C:\>nbtstat -a 123.44.155.6

         NetBIOS Remote Machine Name Table
```

```
       Name               Type       Status
       ------------------------------------------------
       MYSERVER      <00>  UNIQUE     Registered
       MY_DOMAIN     <00>  GROUP      Registered
       MY_DOMAIN     <1C>  GROUP      Registered
       MYSERVER      <03>  UNIQUE     Registered
       __SQLANYWHERE <20>  UNIQUE     Registered
       MYSERVER      <20>  UNIQUE     Registered
       MY_DOMAIN     <1B>  UNIQUE     Registered
       MY_DOMAIN     <1E>  GROUP      Registered
       MY_DOMAIN     <1D>  UNIQUE     Registered
       ..__MSBROWSE__.<01> GROUP      Registered
       MYSERVER      <01>  UNIQUE     Registered

       MAC Address = 00-80-5F-A4-B6-CA
```

The NBTSTAT -c command is very helpful when troubleshooting name resolution problems. It lists the NetBIOS name cache for the local machine. When you are having trouble connecting computers, this is the first place to look to see if the names are being resolved correctly. You can also check here to make sure the NetBIOS Scope ID is blank. The following is sample output from running an NBTSTAT -c command:

```
C:\>nbtstat -c

Node IpAddress: [123.44.166.7] Scope Id: []

             NetBIOS Remote Cache Name Table

       Name             Type      Host Address     Life [sec]
       -------------------------------------------------------
       GATEWAY    <03>  UNIQUE    123.44.166.7        -1
       GATEWAY    <00>  UNIQUE    123.44.166.7        -1
       GATEWAY    <20>  UNIQUE    123.44.166.7        -1
       TESTBDC    <00>  UNIQUE    123.44.166.88       600
       NTSERVER   <03>  UNIQUE    123.44.166.55       -1
       NTSERVER   <00>  UNIQUE    123.44.166.55       -1
       NTSERVER   <20>  UNIQUE    123.44.166.55       -1
```

The NBTSTAT -n command is exactly the same as the NBTSTAT -a command except that it lists name information for the local machine (not including the MAC hardware address). The following is sample output from running an NBTSTAT -n command:

```
C:\>nbtstat -n

Node IpAddress: [123.44.166.55] Scope Id: []

            NetBIOS Local Name Table

    Name                Type            Status
    ---------------------------------------------
    MYPC        <00>    UNIQUE      Registered
    MY_DOMAIN   <00>    GROUP       Registered
    MYPC        <03>    UNIQUE      Registered
    USERNAME1   <03>    UNIQUE      Registered
    MYPC        <20>    UNIQUE      Registered
```

The NBTSTAT -r command tells you how many broadcasts a machine has
made since NetBIOS over TCP/IP was started. This command is also useful
once you have installed WINS for tracking down those machines that are still
using broadcasting. The following is sample output from running an
NBTSTAT -r command:

```
C:\WINNT\system32>nbtstat -r

NetBIOS Names Resolution and Registration Statistics
----------------------------------------------------

Resolved By Broadcast    = 7
Resolved By Name Server  = 146
Registered By Broadcast  = 0
Registered By Name Server = 8

    NetBIOS Names Resolved By Broadcast
----------------------------------------------
    BROADCASTER1    <00>
    BROADCASTER1    <00>
    BROADCASTER1    <00>
    MYSERVER        <00>
    MYPC            <00>
    SERVER1         <00>
    BROADCASTER2    <00>
```

The NBTSTAT -S command determines what machines you have
NetBIOS connection to or what machines have NetBIOS connection to you.
This might help you track who exactly is using a server and how much

bandwidth they are using. The following is sample output from running an NBTSTAT -S command:

```
C:\>nbtstat -S

                NetBIOS Connection Table

Local Name          State    In/Out  Remote Host     Input Output
--------------------------------------------------------------------
MYPC          <00> Connected  Out    111.23.45.56    3MB   231KB
MYPC          <00> Connected  Out    111.23.45.101   2KB     3KB
MYPC          <03> Listening
MYPC          <03> Listening
MYUSERNAME    <03> Listening
MYUSERNAME    <03> Listening
```

CERTIFICATION SUMMARY

This chapter covered everything you need to know about NetBIOS host name resolution for the Internetworking with Microsoft TCP/IP on Microsoft Windows NT 4.0 exam. You should now have some properly grounded definitions, background material, and concepts about NetBIOS. You know how NetBIOS runs over TCP/IP using the TCP and UDP protocols and that NetBIOS host names are composed of 15 characters plus a special byte. We discussed the three NetBIOS functional processes: Name Registration, Name Discovery, and Name Release. You should know what you need to about nodes, modes, and name resolution methods. Finally, you should know how to use the LMHOSTS file and NBTSTAT command with practiced flair and grace. Armed with all this information you will not only be able to pass the exam, but you will be able to impress all your peers when they just can't seem to get two machines to talk to each other.

TWO-MINUTE DRILL

- ❑ NetBIOS is an interface that software can use and is commonly called an application programming interface (API).
- ❑ There are official standards for using NetBIOS over TCP/IP.

❑ The first thing to understand about NetBIOS is that it is not a "complete" networking protocol suite like TCP/IP, IPX/SPX, or NetBEUI.

❑ NetBIOS is only an API that programmers use to connect two computers using names like MYCOMPUTER or SERVER1.

❑ On Windows NT and other Microsoft networking platforms, NetBIOS can run over TCP/IP, IPX/SPX, and NetBEUI separately or even simultaneously.

❑ NetBIOS operates at the session and transport levels of the OSI Model.

❑ The NetBIOS interface to the TCP/IP stack provides the following three services: a name service, a datagram service, and a session service.

❑ Remember that TCP is a connection-oriented service that guarantees proper data delivery.

❑ UDP is a connectionless service that does not guarantee proper data delivery.

❑ Figure 7-1 contains a portion of the services file for Exercise 7-1. Be sure to go back and navigate through the exercise later since it will help you remember the location of the important %SystemRoot%\system32\drivers\etc directory. After all, your memory and your experiences are all you can take with you to the exam!

❑ There are three TCP/IP port numbers that support NetBIOS functionality:

   ❑ Port 137 supports the NetBIOS name service.
   ❑ Port 138 supports the NetBIOS datagram service.
   ❑ Port 139 supports the NetBIOS session service.

❑ Applications use NetBIOS host names to tell the NetBIOS interface which computer they want to connect to.

❑ NetBIOS names are always 16 bytes. They consist of 15 bytes followed by a special byte that is simply a control character in hexadecimal.

❑ The three NetBIOS functional processes are: Name Registration, Name Discovery, and Name Release.

❏ NetBIOS host name resolution for NetBIOS over TCP/IP simply means translating a given name into an IP address.

❏ NetBIOS is the interface to the applications; TCP/IP is the transport protocol that carries the information from one computer to another; and NBT is the glue in between.

❏ RFC1001 and RFC1002 define three ways NBT can work: b-node, p-node, and m-node.

❏ For the exam focus on the Microsoft-specific methods discussed in this chapter. The exam is about TCP/IP on Windows NT 4.0 and will focus on Windows NT and not the way the rest of the world does it. The other standard methods may be useful in troubleshooting inter-system connectivity in the working world.

❏ Be sure to commit Table 7-3 to memory. A question that involves several mixed-up situations of name resolution sources will be easy to answer if you know the sequence in which the sources are tried.

❏ To use the LMHOSTS file you need to make sure you have LMHOSTS Lookup enabled.

❏ Don't forget that the LMHOSTS file location for Windows NT is in a different place than the rest of Microsoft's operating systems.

❏ The format of the LMHOSTS file is an IP address, followed by a NetBIOS host name, followed by keywords with each entry on a separate line.

❏ The NBTSTAT is the most useful utility related to NetBIOS over TCP/IP.

SELF TEST

The following Self Test questions will help you measure your understanding of the material presented in this chapter. Read all the choices carefully, as there may be more than one correct answer. Choose all correct answers for each question.

1. NetBIOS is a _____.

    A. Application

    B. Protocol

    C. API

    D. Mail Transport

2. NetBIOS uses _____ to connect remote computers.

    A. MAC Addresses

    B. Names

    C. IP Addresses

    D. Home Addresses

3. NBT provides which of the following services?

    A. Session Service

    B. Name Service

    C. Datagram Service

    D. All the above

4. How many bytes are used in a NetBIOS Host Name?

    A. 8 bytes

    B. 15 bytes

    C. 16 bytes

    D. 32 bytes

5. An example of an NT command that uses NetBIOS is _____.

    A. netstat

    B. nslookup

    C. net use

    D. tracert

6. One of the three NetBIOS Functional Processes is _____.

    A. Name Release

    B. Session Service

    C. LMHOSTS Lookup

    D. Name Caching

7. Which of the following methods are used in Windows NT by default?

    A. b-node

    B. p-node

    C. m-node

    D. h-node

8. Which name resolution source does NT use just before looking in the LMHOSTS file when configured to use the h-node method?

    A. Broadcasts

    B. Name Cache

    C. HOSTS

    D. WINS

9. On NT the default location for the LMHOSTS file is _____.

   A. C:\WINNT

   B. C:\WINNT\system32

   C. C:\WINNT\system32\drivers\etc

   D. C:\WINNT\system32\devices\etc

10. The command to list the NetBIOS Name Cache is _____.

   A. NETSTAT -n

   B. NBTSTAT -a

   C. NBTSTAT -n

   D. NBTSTAT -c

8

Windows Internet Name Service (WINS)

The Windows Internet Name Service (WINS), provides tools that enhance Windows NT to manage the names of servers and workstations in a TCP/IP networking environment. In order to understand WINS, it is necessary to understand the precursor to it, NetBIOS. NetBIOS names are 16 characters in length. The NetBIOS name space is flat, meaning that names may be used only once within a network. These names are registered dynamically when computers boot, services start, or users log on. NetBIOS names can be registered as unique or as group names. All Windows NT network commands, such as Explorer, use NetBIOS names to access services.

Unique names have one address associated with a name. Group names have more than one address mapped to a name. NetBIOS is responsible for establishing logical names on the network, establishing sessions between two logical names on the network, and supporting reliable data transfer between computers that have established a session.

Before WINS, the LMHOSTS file was used to assist with remote NetBIOS name resolution. The LMHOSTS file is a static file that maps NetBIOS names to IP addresses. This is similar to the HOSTS file in functionality; the only difference is that the HOSTS file is used for mapping host names to IP addresses.

Microsoft has developed a system for NetBIOS name resolution for Windows NT (see Figure 8-1). The first place checked is the local NetBIOS name cache. The command nbtstat –c, when issued at the command prompt, will show all resolutions in the NetBIOS name cache. This cache will contain resolutions for the most recently mapped names. After the cache is checked, the WINS Server, if present, will be queried. If WINS fails, a broadcast message will be sent. If the name is outside the subnet, the broadcast will fail at the router.

If no name is found, the local machine's LMHOSTS file is read. The LMHOSTS file can be bypassed by unchecking the "Enable LMHOSTS Lookup" box on the WIN Address Tab, under TCP/IP Protocol. By checking the Enable DNS for Windows Resolution check box on this same dialog box, NT will continue and use the HOSTS file, and finally, the DNS Server, if present, to resolve the NetBIOS name.

FIGURE 8-1	Microsoft's name resolution methods

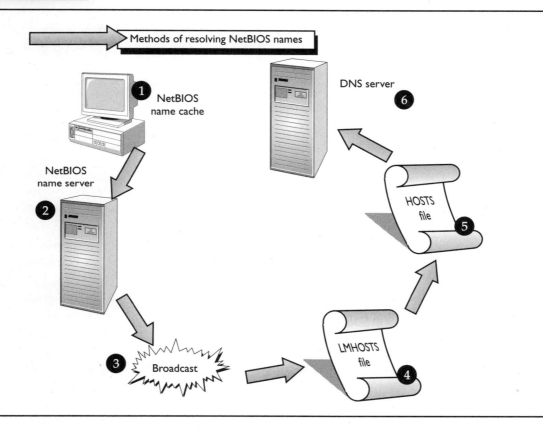

CERTIFICATION OBJECTIVE 8.01

WINS Features

WINS includes many features that allow simpler networking. By allowing computers to register NetBIOS names in one location, the maintenance and management become easier. A WINS Server eliminates the need for many network broadcasts, and therefore reduces network usage. This is accomplished by using directed, or point to point transmissions for name resolution. WINS is dynamic, and is updated when machines are started or stopped, or by replication with other WINS Servers. When a name is registered, it will be reserved for that one computer, further simplifying naming schemes. Each computer will always have its own unique name.

Requirements for WINS

The WINS Server is any Windows NT Server on a TCP/IP network. This server should also have a static IP address, not one obtained dynamically from a Dynamic Host Configuration Protocol (DHCP) server. The WINS Server maintains a database of mappings for IP addresses to NetBIOS names. When a WINS Client requests an IP address, the WINS Server will check its database and return the address to the client. It is not required, but a secondary WINS Server can be implemented for larger networks.

A WINS Client is the machine that requests a NetBIOS mapping. This computer can use one of several operating systems. In addition to an acceptable operating system, a WINS Client must also be configured with the address of the WINS Server. For computers running Windows NT or 95, enter this under Network | Properties, select TCP/IP Protocol, and then the WINS address tab. The address of the WINS Server may be obtained dynamically from a DHCP server.

LMHOSTS Disadvantages

The LMHOSTS file contains mappings of IP addresses to NetBIOS names. Its greatest limitation is that it is a static file. As this file grows in size, it will take longer and longer to resolve names, because the file is always parsed from top to bottom sequentially. The LMHOSTS file resides in the *\systemroot*\system32\drivers\etc directory. Each computer on the network has its own file that must be maintained manually. This can rapidly become a nightmare for network administrators.

Manual Update of Files

Because the LMHOSTS file is static, entries have to be updated if the name or the IP address of the computer changes. An IP address might change for several reasons. Physically moving the computer between subnets would require a new IP address, as would a remote user dialing in via the Remote Access Server (RAS). A new address might also be acquired from a DHCP Server after lease expiration. In addition to modifying the LMHOSTS file when such changes occur, these changes must be sent to all the computers needing access to the resource whose name to IP address mapping has been modified. A centrally maintained LMHOSTS file can reduce the manual administration effort involved in propagating these mappings to the required computers. Even for a central file, entering and changing the mappings is still a manual, labor intensive process.

Sequential Search of LMHOSTS

The LMHOSTS file is searched sequentially, from top to bottom, each time it is read. The more mappings the file contains, the longer it takes to resolve the name. To speed up name resolution, the most commonly used names should be placed at the top of the LMHOSTS, or even the HOSTS, file. A typical LMHOSTS entry looks like this:

```
122.107.9.10        Accounting      #Accounting Server
```

Each line contains an IP address, a NetBIOS name mapping, and possibly a # sign followed by a remark.

It is entirely possibly that an LMHOSTS file may contain duplicate IP mappings. In this case, the first mapping read is used, and all others are ignored. This not only increases the file size, but also may result in improper mappings. Spelling is extremely important in this file. Names must match exactly in order for the mapping to be successful.

In addition to supplying static mappings, an LMHOSTS file can be used to pre-load the NetBIOS name cache. The #PRE keyword defines which entries are pre-loaded in the cache when the machine is started:

```
122.107.9.10        Accounting   #PRE   #Accounting Server
```

Since the cache is read first to resolve names, this method will actually speed up name resolution. Remember, this is a static mapping, and will not be updated automatically.

Multiple LMHOSTS Files to Search For

Windows NT is not limited to a single LMHOSTS file. Virtually any number of files may be chained together to enable name resolution. The #INCLUDE keyword placed in the LMHOSTS file forces the inclusion of an additional file to the name resolution search. Another means of searching through other mappings files is to use the #BEGIN_ALTERNATE keyword. This marks the beginning of a list of other files to search, usually LMHOSTS files on other computers. The end of the list is marked #END_ALTERNATE.

exam
ⓦatch

Remember that an LMHOSTS file is used for NetBIOS name mappings and a HOSTS file is for host name mappings. These roughly correspond to a WINS Server and a DNS Server. You need to know which file corresponds to which server.

Broadcasts

Broadcast messages can be used for NetBIOS name resolution. The biggest drawback to broadcasts is the inability to cross routers. Only machines on the local subnet will respond to a broadcast. Another problem with broadcast messages is increased network traffic. All computers will receive and process the broadcast. This may not be a problem for small networks, but several computers performing several broadcasts, combined with other network traffic, can certainly lead to bottlenecks.

EXERCISE 8-1

Using nbtstat and ping to View and Test Name Resolution

In this exercise you will open an NT Command Prompt and use nbtstat to view the entries in the NetBIOS Name Cache.

1. Click Start, point to Programs, and then click Command Prompt. The Windows NT Command Prompt box appears.

2. Type **ping 127.0.0.1** to ping the local machine. A ping verifies the connection to a remote computer. You should receive a response, repeated four times, similar to:

"reply from 127.0.0.1: bytes=32 time<ms TTL=128"

3. Type **nbtstat –c** to view the NetBIOS Name Cache. This shows all names resolved via WINS, broadcast, or LMHOSTS that have been active within the Default Cache Time of 10 minutes. Make a note of at least one of the resolved remote host names.

4. Type **ping *another computer name*** to ping the remote machine. Again, you should receive a series of successful ping replies.

5. Type **nbtstat –R** to purge the Cache. This also reloads any #PRE entries from the LMHOSTS file.

6. Type **nbtstat –c** to view the purged and reloaded Cache.

7. Type **ping *another computer name***, but use a name that is no longer in the cache (remembered from Step 2). WINS should resolve this name, and you should again receive a ping reply. If this ping fails, then WINS may not be running or not be configured properly.

8. Type **nbtstat –c** to view the Cache. The pinged computer from Step 6 should appear in the Cache now.

Dynamic Registration

WINS provides a distributed database for registering and querying dynamic NetBIOS names to IP address mappings in a routed network environment. When a computer in a WINS-enabled network is started, it will automatically register all its NetBIOS names with the WINS Server. If the computer's IP address has changed, the WINS Server will know immediately. This is WINS' strength, its ability to keep an accurate IP mapping database in an ever-changing network environment. It is the best choice for NetBIOS name resolution in a routed network because it is designed to solve the problems that occur with name resolution.

Simple Unicast to WINS Server

The LMHOSTS file addressed only one disadvantage of broadcast-based systems by allowing resolution of names across routers. Since the system itself was still broadcast based, the problems of broadcast traffic and load on local nodes were not solved. A protocol was defined that allows name registration and resolution through unicast datagrams to a NetBIOS Name Server. Since unicast datagrams are used, the system inherently works across routers. The only address needed for resolution is for the name server. This eliminates the need for an LMHOSTS file, restoring the dynamic nature of NetBIOS name resolution. This, in turn, allows the system to work seamlessly with DHCP. For example, when dynamic addressing through DHCP results in new IP addresses for computers that move between subnets, the changes are automatically updated in the WINS database. Network administrators and users no longer need to make manual changes for name resolution.

Point-to-Point Name Resolution

WINS provides for Point-to-Point name resolution, in that a computer requests an IP address mapping directly from the WINS Server. A broadcast, from point-to-all, is not generated. This reduces network traffic, and quickens response time. The WINS Server is always up to date since all computers register their NetBIOS names at startup. The WINS Server IP address may be obtained from DHCP, or be manually input. Obviously, if the WINS Server address changes, WINS Clients must be updated. By utilizing DHCP, this update occurs only on the DHCP server, and not on each local machine.

CERTIFICATION OBJECTIVE 8.02

WINS Processes

The WINS process is relatively simple, and, when implemented properly, will not significantly affect network utilization (see Figure 8-2). Typically, WINS accounts for no more than 1% of all network traffic. Again, on startup, each computer will register its name and IP address. These machines are the WINS Clients, and will be referred to as a Client. When a Client initiates a Windows NT command to communicate with another host, the name query is sent directly to the WINS Server. The WINS Server will then reply directly to the Client with the appropriate mapping. The Client will then store this mapping in its NetBIOS name cache for the appropriate time, 10 minutes by default. Remember, this cache is checked first for NetBIOS name resolution, so frequently requested addresses may not actually come from the WINS Server after an initial check.

Name Registration

The first step in the WINS process is the Name Registration Request. A Name cannot be registered until a machine requests it from the designated WINS Server. This occurs each time a Client is started, and registers its NetBIOS names with the designated WINS Server. Each Client may register more than one name, one for the machine, and then others for different services or applications on that machine. For example, both the Workstation and Server Services will register their names with a WINS Server. Network Monitor also registers as an application with the WINS Server. These requests may be for unique names, or for shared (group) names. Most clients will register three or four names.

FIGURE 8-2   The WINS process

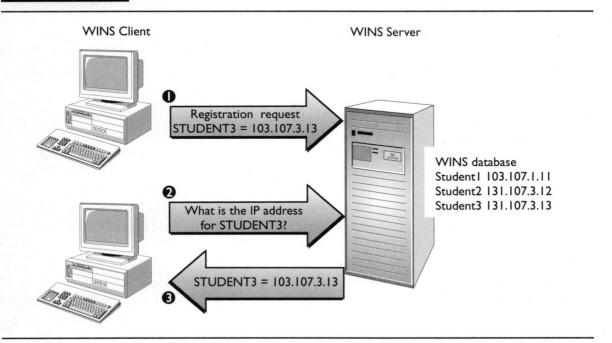

Defined Process

Each registration begins with the Client sending a Name Registration Request packet to the WINS Server. This frame is 110 bytes in size and includes the Client's address, WINS Server's address, and the name requested. An example frame summary would look like this:

Frame	Time	Source	Destination	Protocol and Description
10	10.135	CLIENT	SERVER	NBT_NS: Registration Req. for NAME <03>

This is a request from Client at address "CLIENT" to the WINS Server at address "SERVER" to register the NetBIOS Name of "NAME <03>." The <03> is one of several identifiers that tell WINS the use of the name; in this case it is for the messenger service so that the user may receive messages.

After receiving a registration request there are several possible scenarios for the WINS Server. The simplest is when the requested name is not in the database. This is a new name registration so the WINS Server will send a Positive Name Registration Response to the Client, and enter the mapping with a new version ID, a Time Stamp of Current Time + Renewal Interval, and the WINS Server's owner ID. Time Stamps will be discussed later with Name Renewal.

The next resolution scenario occurs when the name is already in the database with the same IP address as the Client. If this is an active entry, owned by this WINS Server, the Server will update the Time Stamp and send a Positive Name Registration Response back. If the entry is in the released state, or if another WINS Server owns the entry, the registration is treated as new. Time stamp, version ID, and ownership are all updated and a Positive Name Registration Response is sent.

If the name already exists in the database, but has a different IP address, WINS must not assign duplicate names. In this case, the status is checked first. If the name has been released, the WINS Server will treat the request as a new registration. However, if the name is active, the WINS Server will query the holder of the name. A Wait for Acknowledgment Response is first sent to the requesting Client, specifying a time to wait. The WINS Server then issues a Name Query Response to the IP address registered in the database. If this IP address is still valid, it will return a Positive Name Query Response to the WINS Server, which will then issue a Negative Name Registration Response to the Client. If no Positive Name Query Response comes back, the WINS Server will try two more times at 500 millisecond intervals. After the third attempt, if no Positive Name Query Response is returned, the WINS Server will treat this registration as a new name registration.

In any scenario, a name is not registered until the WINS Server replies with a Positive Name Registration Response. After determining success or failure, the WINS Server then sends the response. The response frame is 104 bytes in size, regardless of indicating success or failure:

Frame	Time	Source	Destination	Protocol and Description
11	10.185	SERVER	CLIENT	NBT_NS: Registration (node status) resp. for NAME <03>, Success

At this point, since this frame indicates success, the name is successfully registered with the WINS Server. The name is entered into the database with a version ID, a Time Stamp of Current Time + Renewal Interval, and the WINS Server's owner ID. The Renewal Interval reflects the Time To Live (TTL) of the name. This entire transaction uses only 214 bytes of network traffic, and generally takes less than 100 milliseconds. Failures should be unusual, because each computer will be given a unique name for its network ID.

A Client will attempt to register with the primary WINS Server three times. If the WINS Server fails to respond, the Client will attempt to locate the secondary WINS Server. Both of these addresses can be obtained through DHCP, or input manually under Network - Properties, Protocols, TCP/IP - Properties, WINS Address. If no WINS Server responds, the Client will initiate a broadcast to attempt name registration. See Table 8-1 for a list of commonly registered names and their descriptions.

Name Renewal

The owner must renew a name in order to continue to use the same NetBIOS name. It is the Client's responsibility to renew its names. A Name Renewal Request will stop the WINS Server from reassigning a registered name by

TABLE 8-1		
Commonly Registered Names	**Name Registered**	**Description**
	Unique Names	
	\\computer_name[00h]	Registered by the Workstation Service on the WINS Client.
	\\computer_name[03h]	Registered by the Messenger Service on the WINS Client.
	\\computer_name[06h]	Registered by the Remote Access Service (RAS).
	\\computer_name[1Fh]	Registered by the Network Dynamic Data Exchange.
	\\computer_name[20h]	Registered by the Server Service on the WINS Client.
	\\computer_name[21h]	Registered by the RAS Client Service.
	\\computer_name[BEh]	Registered by the Network Monitoring Agent Service.
	\\computer_name[BFh]	Registered by the Network Monitoring Utility.
	\\username[03h]	User names for the currently logged on users are registered in the WINS database. The username is registered by the Server component so that the user can receive any "net send" commands sent to their username. If more than one user is logged on with the same username, only the first computer at which a user logged on with the username will register the name.
	\\domain_name[1Bh]	Registered by the Windows NT Server primary domain controller (PDC) that is running as the Domain Master Browser and is used to allow remote browsing of domains.
	\\domain_name[1Dh]	Registered only by the Master Browser, of which there can be only one for each subnet. This name is used by the Backup Browsers to communicate with the Master Browser to retrieve the list of available servers from the Master Browser. WINS Servers always return a positive registration response for domain_name[1D], even though the WINS Server does not "register" this name in its database. Therefore, when a WINS Server is queried for the domain_name[1D], the WINS Server returns a negative response, which will cause the client to broadcast to resolve the name.

TABLE 8-1

Commonly
Registered Names
(*continued*)

Group Names	
\\domain_name[00h]	Registered by the Workstation Service so that it can receive browser broadcasts from LAN Manager-based computers.
\\domain_name[1Ch]	Registered for use by the domain controllers within the domain. Can contain up to 25 IP addresses. One IP address will be that of the primary domain controller (PDC) and the other 24 will be the IP addresses of backup domain controllers (BDCs).
\\domain_name[1Eh]	Registered for browsing purposes and is used by the browsers to elect a Master Browser (this is how a statically mapped group name will register itself). When a WINS Server receives a name query for a name ending with [1E], the WINS Server will always return the network broadcast address for the requesting client's local network.
\\--__MSBROWSE__[01h]	Registered by the Master Browser for each subnet. When a WINS Server receives a name query for this name, the WINS Server will always return the network broadcast address for the requesting client's local network.

keeping it in an active state in the database. Once the renewal occurs, the WINS Server will not assign the name to another Client.

Defined Process

When a name is registered, it is assigned a Time To Live (TTL). For WINS, the default TTL is 144 hours, so the WINS Server assigns a TTL of 518,400 seconds. This is the Renewal Interval, and, when used in conjunction with the Time Stamp, determines when Name Renewal occurs. There are two different procedures for Name Renewal.

The first procedure is used only the first time a name is renewed. After 1/8 of the TTL has expired, by default 18 hours, the Client will send a Name Refresh Request to its primary WINS Server. If the Client does not a get a response, it will continue sending a Refresh Request every 2 minutes until 1/2 TTL has expired. At this point, the Client will wait again until 1/8 TTL has expired, and then send a Name Refresh Request to the secondary WINS Server. After four tries, 1/2 TTL, the Client will again attempt to locate the primary WINS Server.

After successfully renewing a name the first time, a Client will attempt to renew at only 1/2 TTL, or 3 days by default. Again, if the primary WINS Server is not found, the Client will attempt to contact the secondary WINS Server. After a successful renewal the WINS Server will update the database with a new TTL and Time Stamp.

In either case, the Name Refresh Request and Name Refresh Response frames contain the same information as a Name Registration Request and Response frames. Again, these frames generate a total of 214 bytes of network traffic, 110 for the request and 104 for the response:

Frame	Time	Source	Destination	Protocol and Description
12	12.135	CLIENT	SERVER	NBT_NS: Registration Req. for NAME <03>
13	12.185	SERVER	CLIENT	NBT_NS: Registration (node status) resp. for NAME <03>, Success

Name Lookup

The real function of WINS is the Name Lookup or Name Query (see Figure 8-3). It is for this purpose that WINS was defined. By using names instead of IP addresses, computers become much easier to use. It is much easier to remember www.microsoft.com than 207.68.156.52, although this is actually a DNS resolution. As IP addresses change from their current 4-octet form to 8 octets, the need for name resolution becomes even greater. The process involves a series of packets, or frames, sent between the Client and WINS Server. The first is a Client request, followed by a WINS Server response. If resolution fails, a broadcast will be sent.

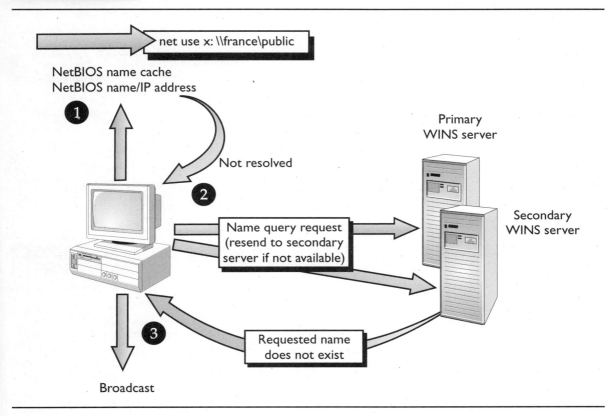

FIGURE 8-3   Name resolution sequence

Defined Process

The place checked for name resolution is the local NetBIOS name cache. All these entries are the most recently resolved names, or ones placed there upon startup. The default TTL for names in the cache is 10 minutes. This default is changed by entering a value in the Registry key:

HKEY_LOCAL_MACHINE\SYSTEM\CurrentControlSet\Services\NetBT\

Parameters\CacheTimeout

If a name is not resolved from the cache, a WINS Client will then issue a Name Query Request to its primary WINS Server. This request is only 92 bytes long:

Frame	Time	Source	Destination	Protocol and Description
14	24.548	CLIENT	SERVER	NBT_NS: Query req. for NAME

When this frame is received, the WINS Server checks its database for the requested name. If the primary WINS Server does not respond at all, the Client will attempt to locate it two more times. Should all three attempts fail, the secondary WINS Server is queried. When the name is found, a Name Query Response is generated and returned to the Client. This response has the IP mapping for the requested name, and will be 104 bytes in size:

Frame	Time	Source	Destination	Protocol and Description
15	24.551	SERVER	CLIENT	NBT_NS: Query (node status) resp. for NAME, Success

For names not found, a "Requested name does not exist" message is sent. The Client will then perform a broadcast over the local subnet to find the proper computer. After the broadcast, the LMHOSTS file, the HOSTS file, and the DNS server can be checked to resolve the name.

Because larger networks will have more then one subnet, WINS Servers can, and should, be configured to share their databases. This provides for the maximum in name resolution and flexibility. This process is known as Database Replication, and will be discussed later in this chapter. If the name is not found, the databases could be out of sync with a replication partner.

Name resolution traffic is the largest part of WINS network traffic. A completed query results in 196 bytes of traffic. Remember, name resolution occurs during logon validation, resource browsing, server connections, and print job notifications.

Name Release

Once a computer registers a name, the host owns the name until it releases it. Only after a name has been released can a different computer register it. When a Client stops a service, or is shut down, it releases the names that it holds. The WINS Server is then free to reassign these names to different machines.

Defined Process

Whenever a computer is shut down, or a service is stopped, a Name Release Request will be sent to the WINS Server. The Client will send this request to its primary WINS Server. The WINS Server will check its own database for the name. The entry is then changed from active to inactive, and the TTL is changed to zero. A Name Release Response frame is then sent to the Client. Once again, these two exchanges are 110 and 104 bytes in size, and look similar to these examples:

Frame	Time	Source	Destination	Protocol and Description
16	32.883	CLIENT	SERVER	NBT_NS: Release Req. for NAME <03>
17	32.936	SERVER	CLIENT s	NBT_NS: Release (node status) resp. for NAME <03>, Succes

Only if there is some sort of database error, or incorrect IP mapping, will the WINS Server return a failure message on a Release request. Since WINS is dynamic, an error here is extremely rare. Since most registered names are unique, the next time the Client is started the Registration process cleans up errors.

Optimizing WINS

Very little optimization is needed for WINS as it typically accounts for less than 1% of all network traffic. Unnecessary services should be disabled for several reasons, one of which is to reduce WINS traffic. If a service is not needed and not allowed to register its name, network traffic is reduced, and the WINS database is smaller. Disabling services may also speed up the local machine where the service is turned off.

As mentioned earlier, the NetBIOS name cache is the first place checked for name resolution. The default TTL of 10 minutes (600,000 milliseconds) can be changed to a larger number, which may also reduce WINS traffic by keeping the most frequently used names in the cache. The downside is that updates to the cache will not be made as frequently. This change is made by increasing the value of the registry key:

HKEY_LOCAL_MACHINE\SYSTEM\CurrentControlSet\Services\NetBT\

Parameters\CacheTimeout

Using LMHOSTS to pre-load the cache with commonly used addresses can also reduce network traffic. This is done by using the #PRE key in the file. For efficiency, entries marked with the #PRE key should be placed at the end of the LMHOSTS file. Since these entries will be in the NetBIOS Name Cache, they should be read last if the file is checked for name resolution. Be careful, because the LMHOSTS file is not dynamic, and will need to be manually updated if changes occur.

The default renewal rate (TTL) can also be changed, but it is not recommended. It can be changed through WINS Manager, but the default of 72 hours is fine in all but the rarest of circumstances. Since renewals occur only every 3 days, there is not a lot of network traffic generated.

A relatively drastic means to make your WINS Server faster is to tell it to stop logging all changes to its database. Open the WINS Manager, highlight a server, and click Server/Configuration. Click Advanced, and clear Logging enabled. This procedure tells WINS to stop creating a transaction log. Not having a transaction log will make rebuilding your WINS system's names database harder if a WINS Server crashes, but preventing logging also will roughly double the number of resolutions the WINS Server can handle per minute. WINS gets its information from computers doing name registrations whenever they boot, probably once a day for most machines. Rebooting the PCs in a network would let WINS restore its database in minutes.

For logging to be effective, fill in the text field Database Backup Path in Server/Configuration/Advanced to tell WINS to back up its database every three hours. If you don't fill in that field, your WINS Server won't back up its entire database, so logging changes to the database would not be useful.

Another way to speed up WINS a bit is to modify its runtime priority. Just go to the Registry at HKEY_LOCAL_MACHINE\SYSTEM\CurrentControlSet\Services\WINS\ Parameters and create an entry called PriorityClassHigh. Its type is REG_DWORD, and its value is either 1 or 0. Zero, the default, says to keep the priority at normal. Set it to 1, and you increase the WINS Server priority to high, and ensure that it is not preempted by other processes. Before you set the priority, look at the Performance Monitor to see whether the machine is usually busy. If it isn't, changing the priority of the WINS Server isn't going to matter much. A high priority setting won't make a WINS Server running alone on a slow machine run more quickly. The priority will help the WINS Server grab more CPU cycles from file and print services.

A final way to get faster name resolution is to add a CPU to a WINS Server. A second CPU improves performance about 25%. A third, fourth, or additional CPUs don't improve performance further.

Keep each of the optimization tips in mind when determining proper placement and configuration of WINS. Know which methods work best in both large and small networks.

CERTIFICATION OBJECTIVE 8.03

Installing and Configuring WINS Server

Using WINS on a TCP/IP network is a relatively simple process. As with all Network services, WINS is installed through the Network Properties, Services tab. Most configuration can be done through the TCP/IP protocol for Clients, and by using the WINS Manager for WINS Servers. There are several considerations before implementing WINS.

For WINS to work, there must be at least one WINS Server. To provide for fault tolerance, and load sharing, two or more WINS Servers may be ideal. There is no built-in limit to the number of requests that a WINS Server can handle, although a typical WINS Server can handle 1,500 name registrations and 4,500 name queries per minute. Based on these numbers, there should be one WINS Server and Backup for every 10,000 Clients; however, if the WINS Server has multiple processors, these numbers can be increased by about 25%.

WINS Servers can use logging, which is turned on and off through the WINS Manager, but this will impede performance. The advantage to logging is that it reduces the risk of losing the last few updates to the database before replication occurs.

Installing WINS Service

To install the WINS Server service, log on with Administrator privileges and open Network Properties either through the Control Panel or Network Neighborhood icon. On the Services tab, choose install Windows Internet Name Service. Windows will require access to the Windows NT installation files, either from the CD or from a hard disk location, to complete the installation. After the necessary files are copied, the WINS Server will need to be restarted for the changes to take effect.

Static mappings should be given to all non-WINS Clients to enable WINS Clients on remote network access to them. A WINS Proxy Agent can be configured to extend the name resolution capabilities to non-WINS Clients. DHCP Servers should also be enabled to support WINS, so IP addressing can be done automatically, and the WINS Server address given to Clients.

EXERCISE 8-2

Installing a WINS Server

In this exercise, you will install a WINS Server to automatically resolve NetBIOS names to IP addresses for WINS Clients.
To install the WINS Server service:

   1. Click Start, point to Settings, and then click Control Panel.

2. From Control Panel, double-click Network, click the Services tab, and then click Add. The Select Network Service dialog box appears.

3. Select Windows Internet Name Service, and then click OK. The Windows NT Setup box appears, prompting for the full path of the Windows NT distribution files.

4. Type the appropriate path and then click Continue. The appropriate files are copied to your computer, and then the Network dialog box appears.

5. Click Close. A Network Settings Change dialog box appears, indicating that the computer needs to be restarted to initialize the new configuration.

6. Click Yes.

If desired, and if they exist, delete the HOSTS and LMHOSTS files from the %systemroot%\system32\drivers\etc folder to prevent them from interfering with WINS.

EXERCISE 8-3

Configuring Clients to Use WINS Server

In this exercise, you will install a WINS Client to use your WINS Server.
To install the WINS Client:

1. Click Start, point to Settings, and then click Control Panel.

2. From Control Panel, double-click Network, and click the Protocols tab. Select TCP/IP and click Properties.

3. Choose the appropriate Adapter.

4. If NOT using DHCP, skip to #7 .

5. Select, Obtain an IP address from a DHCP server. This will complete WINS Client configuration, assuming that the DHCP Server will furnish the WINS Server addresses.

6. Go to step #11.

7. Fill in the IP Address, Subnet Mask, and Default Gateway.

8. Click on the WINS Address tab.

9. Choose the appropriate Adapter.

10. Fill in the IP addresses for both Primary and Secondary WINS Server.

11. Click OK.

12. Click Close. You will be prompted to restart the computer.

13. Click Yes. The computer will restart.

Your computer is now configured as a WINS Client, and can be tested by browsing the network for a remote resource. You can use either Network Neighborhood or NT Explorer as a test. You should see all remotely registered names.

Starting WINS Configuration Manager

The WINS Configuration Manager is automatically installed and added to the Administrative Tools (Common) group when WINS is installed on an NT Server. Once the installation is complete on the computer running Windows NT Server, use WINS Manager to complete the configuration of WINS. Before you can administer and manage WINS Servers, you must add the WINS Servers to the Server List using WINS Manager. All computers running the WINS service can be added to the WINS Server List. Until the WINS Servers are added to the list, no WINS features are available. Once the servers are added to the list, administration of any computer running Windows WINS Service can take place from any other computer running the WINS Manager.

To Add a WINS Server to the Server List, open the WINS Manager Server menu (see Figure 8-4), click Add to see the Add WINS Server to Server List dialog box. In WINS Server, type the IP address of the WINS Server to be added to the list, and then click OK.

Once a WINS Server is added to the list (see Figure 8-5), configuration of the server can take place. You must be a member of the administrators group of the WINS Server in order to perform the configuration. To configure a WINS Server, start WINS Manager and choose the WINS Server to be configured. From the Server menu, click configuration, and the WINS Server Configuration box opens (see Figure 8-6).

Select the configuration options you want:

- To specify how often a WINS Client will renew its name registration with the WINS Server, type a value in Renewal Interval. The default is 144 hours or 6 days.

WINS Manager

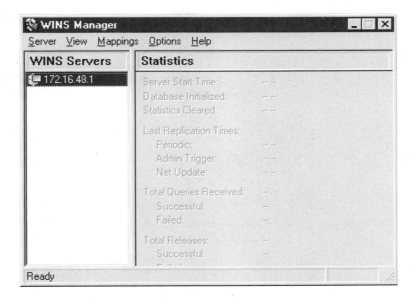

- To specify the interval between when an entry in the WINS database is marked as released (no longer registered) and when it is marked as extinct, type a value in Extinction Interval.

- To specify the interval between when an entry is marked extinct and when the entry is removed from the WINS database, type a value in Extinction Timeout.

Add WINS Server

WINS Server Configuration

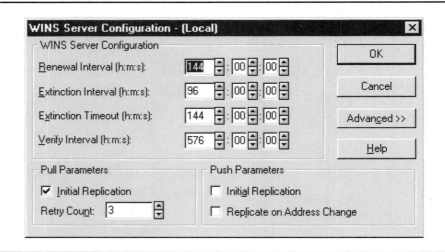

■ To specify when the WINS Server will verify that old names it does not own (those replicated from other WINS Servers) are still active, type a value in Verify Interval.

■ To specify pull parameters, select the Initial Replication check box under Pull.

■ To specify the number of times that the WINS Server will attempt to contact a replication partner for pulling new WINS database entries, type a value in Retry Count.

■ To have the WINS Server notify its replication partners of the status of its WINS database when the system is initialized, select the Initial Replication check box under Push Parameters.

■ To notify the replication partners of the WINS Server when a name registration changes the WINS database status, select the Replicate on Address Change check box.

Click Advanced to configure these other options:

■ To specify logging of database changes to Jet.log, select the Logging Enabled check box.

- To log events in detail, select the Log Detailed Events check box.

- To replicate only with WINS push or pull partners, select the Replicate Only With Partners check box.

- To automatically back up the database when WINS Manager stops, select the Backup On Termination check box. The database backup path must have a directory specified.

- To treat static unique and static multihomed records in the database as dynamic when they conflict with a new registration or replica, select the Migrate On/Off check box. This means that if they are no longer valid, the new registration or replica will overwrite them. By default, this option is not checked.

- To set the highest version ID number for the database, enter that number in Starting Version Count.

- To specify the directory where the WINS database backups will be stored, type the path in Database Backup Path. The database will not be backed up until this path is set.

Some important notes and considerations when configuring a WINS Server:

- Logging events in detail requires considerable system resources and should be turned off if you are tuning for performance.

- If the Replicate Only With Partners check box is not selected, an administrator can ask a WINS Server to pull or push from or to a non-listed WINS Server partner. By default, this option is checked.

- Usually, you will not need to change the value in Starting Version Count unless the database becomes corrupted and needs to start fresh. In such a case, set this value to a number higher than appears as the version number counter for this WINS Server on all the remote partners that earlier replicated the local WINS Server's records. WINS may adjust the value you specify to a higher one to ensure that database records are quickly replicated to other WINS Servers.

■ If you specify a backup path, WINS automatically performs a full backup of its database to this directory every 24 hours. WINS uses this directory to perform an automatic restoration of the database in the event that the database is found to be corrupted when WINS is started. Use only a local directory, not a directory on the network.

Static Mappings

Static mappings are permanent lists of computer name-to-IP address mappings. In a static mapping table, the administrator indicates the computer name and matches the IP address with the computer. When a network client sends a name request to the WINS Server, it will always respond with the name entered by the administrator. In most cases, all DNS Servers, DHCP Servers, and other WINS Servers will be mapped statically. If DHCP is also used on the network, a static IP address will override any WINS Server settings. Static mappings should not be assigned to WINS Clients.

Static mappings may be added to the WINS database either by typing static mappings in a dialog box, or importing files that contain static mappings.

QUESTIONS AND ANSWERS

How can I administer a remote WINS Server?	Use the Add WINS Server dialog box to add the WINS Server.
How can I register names for two weeks?	Change the default Renewal Interval from 144 hours to 336 hours.
How can I keep all the databases as updated as possible?	Select Replicate on Address Change to replicate each time a registration occurs that changes the database.
Where do I specify the Backup Directory?	In the Database Backup Path box, on the Advanced WINS Server configuration dialog box.
Can WINS replicate with a WINS Server that is not a replication partner?	Yes, uncheck the Replicate Only With Partners box, and specify the WINS Server.
How often does WINS back up, once the directory is set?	Every 24 hours.

To type static mappings in a dialog box, open WINS Manager and the Mappings Menu (see Figure 8-7). Click Static Mappings to open the dialog box. Next, click Add Mappings, and, in the Name Box, type the computer name of the system for which you are adding a static mapping (see Figure 8-8). WINS Manager automatically adds the two backslashes (\\), which normally precede the entry of a computer name. In IP Address, type the address for the computer, and in Type, click to indicate whether this entry is a unique name or a group with a special name, and then click Add. The mapping entry is immediately added to the database, and the check boxes are cleared so that you can add another static mapping entry.

The Unique Type is used for a unique name in the WINS database and permits only one address per name. The unique name is the WINS Client's computer name. The Group Type indicates a normal group for which the IP addresses of the individual clients are not stored. A normal group is the name to which broadcasts are sent and is the domain name used for browsing

Static Mappings dialog box

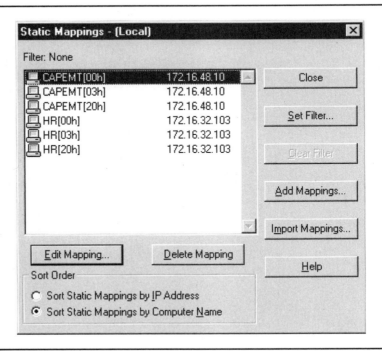

FIGURE 8-8

Add Static Mappings
dialog box

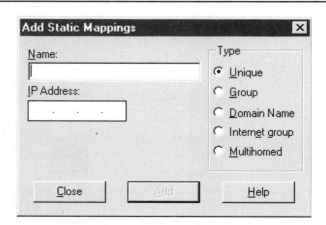

purposes. A normal group name does not have an IP address associated with it and can be valid on multiple networks and registered with multiple WINS Servers. When a WINS Server receives a request for the group name, the WINS Server returns the broadcast address 255.255.255.255, which the Client will then use to broadcast to the network.

The Internet Group is a group that contains the IP addresses for up to 25 primary and backup domain controllers for the domain. The Internet group name is another instance of the domain name being registered; however, this instance is used for the domain controllers in the domain to communicate with each other. The Multihomed Type is similar to a unique name in that it is the WINS Client's computer name; however, it can have up to 25 addresses and is for use by multihomed systems. A multihomed system is a system with more than one network interface and more than one IP address. If Internet Group or Multihomed is selected under Type, the dialog box shows additional controls for adding multiple addresses.

Entries for static mappings of unique and special group names can be imported from any file with the same format as the LMHOSTS file. Scope names and keywords other than #DOM are ignored. Static Mappings for normal group and multihomed names can be added only by typing entries in the Add Static Mappings dialog box.

To import a file containing static mapping entries, in the Static Mappings dialog box, click Import Mappings. In the Select Static Mapping File dialog box, enter the name of the file containing the names to be mapped. The specified file is read, and then a static mapping is created for each computer name and address. If the #DOM keyword is included for any record, an Internet group is created, and the address is added to that group.

CERTIFICATION OBJECTIVE 8.04

WINS Proxy Server

A WINS Proxy Agent or Server (see Figure 8-9) extends the name resolution capabilities of WINS to non-WINS Clients, such as UNIX machines. The Proxy will listen for broadcasts for Name Registration and Name Resolution, and will then forward them to a WINS Server. These names are not fully registered with WINS, but are checked against the database. The Proxy can send a Negative Name Registration Response to the non-WINS Client so that there will not be duplicate names, but this is not the default setting.

The Proxy must differentiate between local subnet queries and remote name queries. By checking the IP address and subnet mask of the broadcasting computer, the Proxy can tell whether or not it should respond to the request. If the Proxy's subnet matches that of the broadcaster, it will not respond to the broadcast. This guarantees that the Proxy will not respond to queries for names local to the subnet.

If the name is found in the Proxy's remote name cache, a response is sent to the non-WINS Client. If the name cannot be found, the WINS Server is queried and the name is entered into the remote name table in a "resolving" state. Should another query come in for the same name before the WINS Server has responded, the Proxy will not query the WINS Server again. When the response is returned from the WINS Server, the remote table entry is updated with the correct address and the state is changed to "resolved." When the next name query comes in for that name, a response is sent to the client.

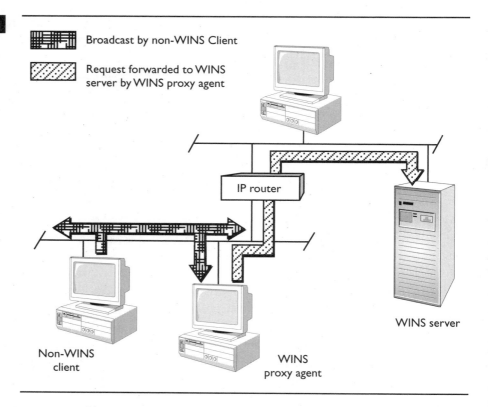

FIGURE 8-9

WINS Proxy
Agent (Server)

In order to reduce duplicate traffic, it is recommended that only one or two Proxies be active on a subnet. Since the Proxy knows the WINS Server's IP Address, this method can make WINS available to non-WINS Clients across routers. The Proxy must be a WINS Client but cannot be a WINS Server. To configure a Proxy, open the following registry key:

HKEY_LOCAL_MACHINE\System\CurrentControlSet\Services\NetBT\ Parameters

and set the EnableProxy parameter to 1 (REG_DWORD). The computer must then be rebooted for the change to take effect.

exam
ⓦatch

Proxies do not register names. They just aid in the resolution process by listening for name resolution broadcasts from non-WINS Clients. Again, these broadcasts will not cross a router, so placement of the Proxy is critical.

`EXERCISE 8-4`

Installing a WINS Proxy Agent

For this exercise to work, a network that has two subnets must be set up. The WINS Server needs to be on a separate subnet from the non-WINS Client and WINS Proxy. Be certain to delete the WINS IP addresses on the TCP/IP Properties, WINS Address tab. Delete the LMHOSTS and HOSTS files on the non-WINS Client from the %systemroot%\system32\drivers\etc folder. It may be wise to clear the NetBIOS Cache as well, by opening a command prompt and typing nbtstat –R. These steps guarantee that no name resolution is available to the computer other than a broadcast.

Configure a WINS Proxy Agent
In this procedure, you will configure one computer on each subnet to function as a WINS Proxy Agent. To be a WINS Proxy, the Client must first be configured as a WINS Client.

1. Click Start and then click Run.

2. In the Open box, type **regedt32.exe** and then click OK. The Registry Editor window appears.

3. Maximize the HKEY_LOCAL_MACHINE window.

4. Open the following registry key: SYSTEM\CurrentControlSet\Services\NetBT\Parameter.

5. Double-click the EnableProxy value. The DWORD Editor dialog box appears.

6. In the Data box, type **1**.

7. Click OK.

8. Close the Registry Editor.

9. Access the TCP/IP Properties dialog box.

10. Click the WINS Address tab.

11. In the Primary WINS Server box, type the IP Address of the WINS Server.

12. Click OK.

13. Click Close. You will be prompted to restart the computer.

14. Click Yes. You now have a WINS Proxy started.

Test Remote NetBIOS Name Resolution with a WINS Proxy
In this procedure, you will test name resolution of a remote NetBIOS host without a mapping in the local LMHOSTS or HOSTS files, but with a WINS Proxy Agent configured on each subnet.

1. Try to browse resources on the WINS Server, which is on a different subnet.

2. Was the resolution successful? Why or why not?

Even though the WINS Server is a remote host, resolution was successful using the WINS Proxy Agent, because the Name Query Request was broadcast and received by the Proxy.

Remove the WINS Proxy

1. Click Start and then click Run.

2. In the Open box, type **regedt32.exe** and then click OK. The Registry Editor window appears.

3. Maximize the HKEY-LOCALMACHINE window.

4. Open the following registry key:
SYSTEM\CurrentControlSet\Services\NetBT\Parameter.

5. Double-click the EnableProxy parameter. The DWORD Editor dialog box appears.

6. In the Data box, type **0**.

7. Click OK.

8. Close the Registry Editor.

9. Access the TCP/IP Properties dialog box.

10. Click the WINS Address tab.

11. In the Primary WINS Server box, clear the IP address.

12. Click OK.

13. Click Close. You will be prompted to restart the computer.
14. Click Yes.

WINS Registration Across Networks

To register NetBIOS names across networks with a WINS Server, the prospective Clients must know the IP address of the WINS Server. Clients can receive this information in two ways, dynamically through DHCP or statically through TCP/IP Properties.

Obviously, it is easier to use DHCP to tell each client the WINS Server address. This is also handy if a secondary WINS Server is added later, or if the IP address changes. One change in the DHCP configuration will change all DHCP Clients the next time they reboot. Without DHCP, each WINS Client must be configured individually. This can be a time consuming process, especially as the network grows and Servers move.

For non-WINS Clients, the Proxy allows Name Resolution across networks and routers, but Name Registration will not occur. Proxies allow names to be checked only for active status, previously registered, not actual registration.

CERTIFICATION OBJECTIVE 8.05

Configuring WINS Client

A WINS Client is any computer that requests name resolution from a WINS Server. The Client can use any of these operating systems:

- Windows NT Server or Workstation 3.5 or later
- Windows 95, or later
- Windows for Workgroups 3.11 running MS TCP/IP - 32
- MS Network Client for DOS
- LAN Manager 2.2c for DOS

Please note that a computer running under UNIX cannot be a WINS Client, but may access WINS through a proxy. In addition, the Client must be configured for WINS.

WINS Clients are set up and configured differently than WINS Servers. Setup does take place through the Network icon, but it only requires that the WINS Server IP Address is given to the Client.

TCP/IP Properties Page

Again, both the primary and secondary WINS Server addresses may be input through Network Properties, under the TCP/IP Protocol, Properties Button, WINS Address tab. Be careful here, mistyping an entry will not allow the Client to find the WINS Server. Any manually input addresses will override the settings obtained from the DHCP Server.

The WINS Address Tab contains several important options (see Figure 8-10). First is the adapter box. Choose the appropriate network adapter, if more than one is present. Next are the IP address boxes that are used to manually input the WINS Server addresses that the specified adapter should use. The two check boxes that follow tell NT whether or not to use DNS and / or LMHOSTS files for WINS resolution. Only after the NetBIOS cache, the WINS Server, and a broadcast, will NT use LMHOSTS. DNS is used if the LMHOSTS and HOSTS files are unsuccessful in resolving the name. The scope ID is usually left blank. It can be used if a DNS Server is not present for Host Name Resolution.

DHCP Option

DHCP allows its Clients to obtain IP addresses and other information upon bootup. DHCP gives out IP addresses on a lease assignment basis. Each lease is good for a set time period, 6 days by default. DHCP can provide WINS Server addresses, as well as NetBIOS Node Type settings. Other settings that might be obtained by DHCP include router information for Gateways, Option 003, DNS Server address, Option 006, and NetBIOS Scope ID, Option 047. These are the only options that a Microsoft DHCP client can accept.

WINS Address Tab

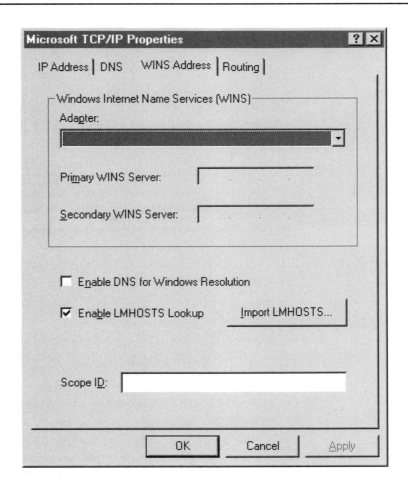

Option 044 – Names of WINS Servers

One of the most useful of all the DHCP options, Option 044 allows a DHCP Client to receive the IP addresses of both a primary and secondary WINS Server. The IP addresses that you configure in both the primary and secondary

WINS Server boxes will take precedence over those received through DHCP. An advantage of DHCP is that correct configuration information ensures correct configuration. Many difficult-to-trace network problems can be eliminated by correct use of DHCP.

Option 046 – NetBIOS Node Type

DHCP Option 046 sets the NetBIOS Node type, or the means of name-to-IP address resolution. There are four possible entries here, with h-node being the best choice for WINS:

- **B-NODE**   Broadcast nodes communicate using a mix of UDP datagrams (both broadcast and directed) and TCP connections. They interoperate with one another within a broadcast area but cannot interoperate across routers in a routed network. B-nodes generate high-broadcast traffic. Each node on the LAN must examine every broadcast datagram.

- **P-NODE**   Point-to-point nodes communicate using only directed UDP datagrams and TCP sessions. They relay on NetBIOS name servers, local or remote. If the name server is down, the p-node cannot communicate with any other system, even those on the same local network.

- **M-NODE**   Mixed nodes are p-nodes that have been given certain b-node characteristics. M-nodes use broadcast first, to optimize performance, assuming that most resources reside on the local broadcast medium, for name registration and resolution. If this is unsuccessful, point-to-point communication with the name server is used. M-nodes generate high-broadcast traffic, but can cross routers and continue to operate normally if the name server is down.

- **H-NODE**   Hybrid nodes are also a combination of b-node and p-node functionality. H-node uses point-to-point communication first. If the NetBIOS name server cannot be located, it switches to broadcast. H-node continues to poll for the name server and returns to point-to-point communication when one becomes available.

When using the h-node setting, the Client first checks its NetBIOS cache, and then the WINS Server. If the WINS Server is not found, a broadcast is sent out. This is the most efficient setting for WINS, because it allows for both fast name resolution and minimum network traffic. The cache is the fastest way for resolution, and a direct exchange with the WINS Server uses the least amount of network resources. Only if the WINS Server fails will a broadcast (that all computers on the subnet must receive and process) be sent.

EXERCISE 8-5

Configuring a DHCP Server for WINS

In this exercise, you will configure the DHCP server to supply the appropriate WINS Server addressing information to DHCP Clients.

First, a server must be running DHCP. Install DHCP by following the instructions for Lab 8-1, but substitute DHCP for WINS. For this exercise to be utilized completely, the DHCP and WINS Servers must run on separate computers that are networked with a third computer configured as a DHCP Client.

Start the DHCP Server service, if it is not already running.
Note: Complete this procedure from the DHCP Server only.

1. Click Start, point to Settings, and click Control Panel.
2. Double-click Services. The Services dialog box appears.
3. Click Microsoft DHCP Server and then click Start.
4. Click Startup. The Service dialog box appears.
5. Click Automatic and then click OK.
6. Click Close.
7. Close Control Panel.

Configure the DHCP Server to Assign WINS Server Addresses
In this procedure, you will configure the DHCP Server to automatically assign the WINS Server address and NetBIOS node types to DHCP Clients.
Note: Complete this procedure from the DHCP Server only.

1. Click Start, point to Programs, Administrative Tools, and then click DHCP Manager. The DHCP Manager window appears.

2. Double-click *Local Machine*. The local scope IP address appears.

3. Click the local scope's IP address. The local scope options appear under Option Configuration.

4. On the DHCP Options menu, click Scope. The DHCP Options: Scope dialog box appears.

5. Under Unused Options, select 044 WINS/NBNS Servers, and then click Add. A DHCP Manager message box appears, indicating that for WINS to function properly, you must add the option 046 WINS/NBT node type.

6. Click OK. The 044 WINS/NBNS Servers option moves under Active Options.

7. Click Value. The DHCP Scope: Options dialog box expands to add the NBNS Addresses in priority order values box.

8. Click Edit Array. The IP Address Array Editor dialog box appears.

9. Under New IP Address, type your IP address, and then click Add. The new IP address appears under IP Addresses.

10. To return to the DHCP Options: Scope dialog box, click OK.

11. Under Unused Options, select 046 WINS/NBT Node Type and then click Add. The 046 WINS/NBT Node Type option moves under Active Options.

12. Under Byte, type **Ox8** and then click OK. The DHCP Manager window appears with active scope options of 003 Router, 044 WINS/NBNS Servers, and 046 WINS/NBT Node Type listed under Option Configuration.

13. Exit DHCP Manager.

Update the DHCP Client
In this procedure, you will renew your DHCP lease, which automatically assigns the new DHCP scope options of WINS Server addresses and node type to the client.

Note: Complete this procedure from the DHCP Client only.

1. Open a command prompt, type **ipconfig /all**, and then press ENTER. The Windows IP Configuration settings appear. The Node Type is listed as broadcast and the primary WINS Server is not listed.

2. Access the TCP/IP Properties dialog box.

3. Click Obtain an IP address from a DHCP Server. A message box asks you to confirm the installation of DCHP.

4. Click Yes.

5. Click OK.

6. Click OK.

7. Switch to a command prompt, type **ipconfig /all**, and then press ENTER. The Windows IP Configuration settings appear. The Node Type and primary WINS Server parameters are updated.

CERTIFICATION OBJECTIVE 8.06

WINS Database Replication

When multiple WINS Servers are used, either for load sharing or redundancy, a method must be implemented to ensure that all resolution requests are handled by up-to-date databases. This method of sharing database information is known as *replication*. Replication can be a resource intensive operation, but there are several ways to reduce its overall impact on a network. Replication of registered names to all WINS Servers is necessary to allow resolution of names registered to different servers.

Each WINS Server will be given at least one replication partner, and be designated as either a push or pull partner. Eventually, through these partnerships, replication will occur across the entire network. Remember, networks with fewer than 10,000 clients require only one WINS Server and one Backup, so all databases are accurate after one exchange. Since there is no upper limit to the number of WINS Servers, replication partners must balance the issues of accuracy, availability, server load, and network traffic usage.

Replication Process

The replication process is configured in WINS Manager. Each WINS Server will be assigned one or more replication partners. These partners are defined as being either a push or pull partner. A *pull partner* is a WINS Server that pulls

FROM THE CLASSROOM

WINS Database Replication

There are four ways in which replication of the WINS database gets triggered:

1. When the WINS Server service is started. This occurs when each configured WINS server initializes during startup.
2. When the specified time occurs. Pull partners will query other WINS Servers for updates at a specified time.
3. When the value of the threshold for the number of changes has been reached.

Push partners will advertise updates when the threshold is reached.

4. When an administrator manually requests that the database be replicated. Through the WINS Manager an administrator can request an immediate replication.

—By D. Lynn White, MCT, MCSE

in replications of database entries from its partner by requesting and then accepting the replications. A *push partner* is a WINS Server that sends update notification messages to its partner when its WINS database has changed. This configuration ensures that the WINS database on each server contains the names and addresses for every network computer. In larger networks, with multiple WINS Servers, one WINS Server may be defined as the Central WINS Server, and all others will be its push or pull partners.

Figure 8-11 shows the Replication Partners box. Each WINS Server is listed by IP address, and can then be assigned as either a push or pull partner. The administrator can force replication between partners at any time by using the Replicate Now button. The Configure buttons allow the partnerships' Replication Options to be defined.

Once implemented, replication is a very straightforward process. One WINS Server will notify its partners of a change to its database. After the notification, the actual update will occur. The update will either be pushed to a WINS Server, or a WINS Server will pull the updates from the source WINS Server.

FIGURE 8-11

WINS Manager Replication
Partners box

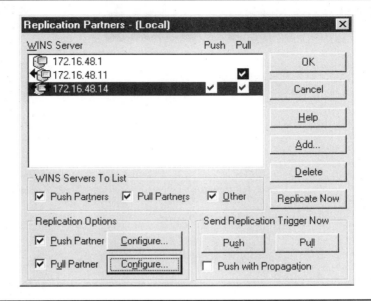

Push or Pull

Each WINS Server will be either a push or pull partner. A pull partner is a
WINS Server that requests new database entries from its push partners. This is
done by requesting entries with a higher version number that the last entry it
received during the last replication. Please note that only the new entries are
updated. This reduces replication traffic on the network.

A push partner is a WINS Server that sends a message to its pull partners
notifying them when its WINS database has changed. When a WINS Server's
pull partners respond to the message with a replication request, the push
WINS Server sends a copy of its new database entries to the requesting
partner. Again, only the changes or additions are actually replicated.

When replication is configured between two WINS Servers, it is
recommended that both servers be push and pull partners of the other. The
Primary and Secondary WINS Servers of any network must have a push and
pull relationship with each other. In general, NetBIOS names are presented
as a flat namespace. Attempts to impose a hierarchy on this namespace

through one-way replication schemes result in problems with name uniqueness and resolution.

PULL PARTNERS   Pull partners are given a set time interval to request updates, if updates are not announced by push partners. In the example shown in Figure 8-12, the pull partner will request updates every 6-½ hours, beginning at midnight. This is done by requesting entries with a higher version ID than the last entry received from a partner during the last replication. Pull partners can and should be used between sites, especially across slow WAN links, because of the ability to designate a time for the update. The update should occur at times when the WAN is least used, usually at night, to conserve network resources.

PUSH PARTNERS   A push partner can be configured to notify its pull partners by setting the update count, or by turning on replicate on address change. The update count has a minimum value of 5. When configured to Push With Propagation, these WINS Servers will tell their pull partners when they have received changes from another source. These partners will then pull the changed entries.

The Update Count box contains the minimum number of changes that must occur before the push partner notifies its pull partners to replicate. WINS Servers that handle large numbers of name registrations when users first log on should not be configured to replicate a small number of registrations.

FIGURE 8-12

Pull Partner Properties

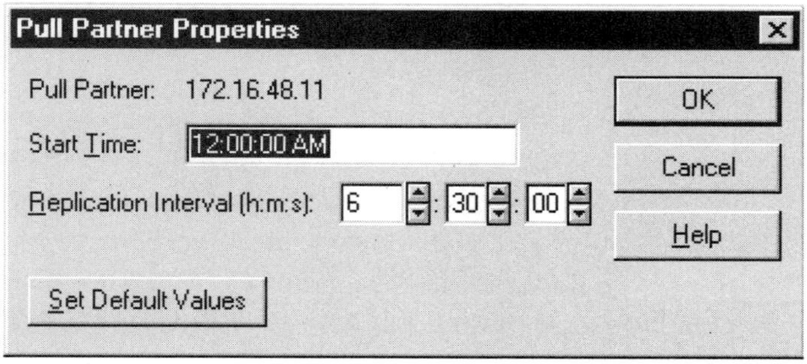

Notification

Notification occurs when a push partner tells its pull partner, or partners, that the database has changed, and an update is due. This notification is set to occur after a set number of changes have happened in the database, and is configured in the Push Partner Properties box (see Figure 8-13). Obviously, a smaller update count number will cause more updates. More updates lead to more accurate name resolution, but can be detrimental to overall network performance.

Most changes happen when computers are started, usually when a shift begins, or after a meal break. If one WINS Server handles all these registrations, then an update is almost sure to be needed, and a notification will be sent out. As we will see, registrations are kept in the database even after being released because a name release will not propagate as fast as a name registration. This is necessary because it is common for names to be released and then reused with the same mapping as PCs are rebooted or turned off for the evening or the weekend. Replicating each of these releases would unnecessarily increase the network load of replication. If a client node crashes or is simply powered off, the registered name is not cleanly released by a NetBIOS Name Release datagram. Therefore, the presence of a name-to-address record in the WINS database does not necessarily mean that the node is running. It only means that at some reasonable time in the past, that node claimed the IP address.

FIGURE 8-13

Push Partner Properties

Push Partner Properties

| Push Partner: | 172.16.48.14 |
| Update Count: | 100 |

Set Default Value

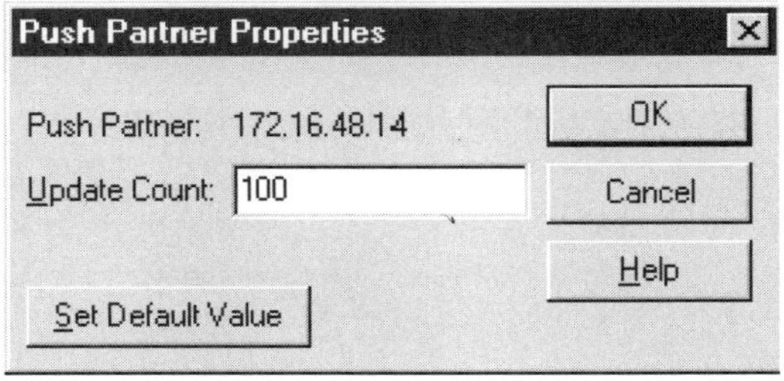

Update

After being notified, a pull partner will begin the update process by making a request from its partner. When the push partner receives a request from another WINS Server it retrieves the required records from its local database and sends them the response. It retrieves the records by seeking the record that starts the range, and then moving sequentially over the records until the last one in the range has been retrieved. When the data is received from the push partners, the pull partner updates its database.

All entries with version IDs higher than those in the pulling database get replicated. However, not every change to a database causes the version ID of a record to be incremented. Records in the WINS database contain state and ownership information. Records may be in an active, released, or extinct state. They are owned by the local database or are replicas from another WINS Server. A record is also static or dynamic.

When names are registered with a WINS Server, they are entered in the database in an active state and Time Stamped with Current Time + Renewal Interval. The version ID is taken from the version ID counter, which is then incremented. If a name is explicitly released or fails to refresh during the Renewal Interval, it enters the released state. The entry is Time Stamped with Current Time + Extinction Interval. The version ID is not changed. Therefore, records in the released state will not be replicated. If a record remains in the released state for more than the Extinction Interval, it enters the extinct state. It is Time Stamped with Current Time + Extinction Time-out, and receives a new version ID to cause it to be replicated. If a record remains in the extinct state for more than the Extinction Time-out, it is deleted from the database.

Only records in the active or extinct states are replicated. In the replica database these records are entered with the fields received from the owner database with the exception of ownership and Time Stamp. The ownership field is taken from the local IP address' Owner ID mapping table. The ownership of the replica does not change. It means that the value used to represent a particular WINS Server differs from server to server. For example, a 2 on WINS_B and a 3 on WINS_A might represent WINS_D. An active record is Time Stamped with (local) Current Time + Verify Interval. An extinct record is Time Stamped with (local) Current Time + Extinction Time-out.

Configuring the Replication Process

Configuring the replication process can be an important issue for networks with thousands of name registrations. Even though only changes are actually sent across the network, a large number of changes, sent to many WINS Servers, will slow down an entire network. Updates across slow links, especially WANs, should be keyed to occur when the network load is lightest, usually at night, unless the need for more current databases is required.

Due to the time differences between name registration and name release, computers that don't change IP addresses will usually never be updated in the database. This alone reduces the need for many updates. In some cases, updating may need to occur only daily; in others, replication may be needed hourly. Each network will be unique, but the settings, which are all made in the WINS Manager, depend on network size, usage, and configuration.

Conflicts During Replication

Name conflicts are normally handled at the time of name registration. However, it is possible for the same name to be registered at two different WINS Servers. This could happen if the same name was registered at a second WINS Server before the database from the first WINS Server had been replicated. In this case, the conflict will be noted and resolved at replication time.

Conflicts at replication can occur between two unique entries, between a unique entry and a group entry, or between two group entries.

There are three criteria used for resolving conflicts between unique entries. The first is the state of the entries. While the database entry can be in the active, released, or extinct state, the replica can be either in the active or extinct state. An active record takes precedence over an extinct one.

Ownership of the entries is the second criterion for conflict resolution. The WINS Server may or may not own the database entry. The final criterion checked is the actual addresses of the entries. These addresses may or may not be the same.

When the conflict is between a unique entry and a group entry, the group entry is kept. Finally, if the conflict is between two group entries, the replica replaces the database record, unless the database record is active. If it is active, its version ID is incremented so that the record gets propagated at replication time. If the replica is also in the active state, the member list of the database record is updated with any members in the replica that are not already present. If the list of members in the active state grows to more than 25, the extra members are not inserted.

exam
ⓌatcH

Replication is the most network-intensive part of WINS. Be certain that you configure replication to occur so that it will not overwhelm the network. Slow links will definitely need to be replicated when they are least used by other network communication.

EXERCISE 8-6

Configuring WINS for Replication

In this exercise, you will configure the WINS Server to perform database replication with another WINS Server. To be effective, two WINS Servers are required.

Configure the WINS Client
In this procedure, you will configure the WINS Client (this is necessary for the WINS Server to work correctly).

1. Access the TCP/IP Properties dialog box.
2. Click the WINS Address tab.
3. Type your IP address in the Primary WINS Server box.
4. Click OK.
5. Click Close. You will be prompted to restart the computer.
6. Click Yes. The computer will restart.

Configure WINS Replication Partners
In this procedure, you will configure another WINS Server as a replication partner.

1. On the Server menu, click Replication Partners. The Replication Partners dialog box appears showing the local WINS Server.
2. Click Add. The Add WINS Server dialog box appears.

3. In the WINS Server box, type Server #2's IP address and then click OK. The Replication Partners dialog box appears with that IP address added to the list of WINS servers.
    Important: The other Server (#2) must also add your WINS Server (#1) as a replication partner, by repeating the first three steps.

4. Under WINS Server, click the Server #2's IP address.

5. Under Replication Options, click Configure next to Pull Partner.

6. The Pull Partner Properties dialog box appears. The replication interval is set for 30 minutes.

7. Click OK.

Force Replication

In this procedure, you will force WINS to replicate the WINS database.

1. From the Replication Partners dialog box, click Replicate Now. A WINS Manager message box appears indicating the replication request has been queued.

2. Click OK.

3. Click OK to return to the WINS Manager window. The WINS Manager window appears with Server #2's IP added as a WINS Server.

4. Under WINS Servers, select the local WINS Server.

5. On the Mappings menu, click Show Database.

6. The Show Database dialog box appears. Under Select Owner, notice the addition of all WINS addresses that the replication partner (Server #2) knows about.
    Note: If the replicated WINS database shows a version ID of 0, repeat steps 1 through 3 again to force replication.

7. Under Select Owner, select 131.107.2.200.

8. Under Mappings, the listing of registered names for the instructor's WINS Server appears.

9. View the information in other WINS Server databases, and then click Close to return to WINS Manager.

CERTIFICATION OBJECTIVE 8.07

WINS Database Maintenance

The WINS Database is actually composed of four files (see Figure 8-14), all located in the \systemroot\system32\WINS directory. These files must not be removed or changed, except when restoring a corrupted database.

The WINS Database can be maintained from the WINS Manager. The ability to view the actual entries, and search for specific entries, is provided under the Mappings menu. The WINS database actually consists of two tables: the IP Address - Owner ID Mapping Table and the Name to IP address mapping table.

The IP Address - Owner ID Mapping Table contains a row for each WINS Server that has entries in the Name to IP Address Mapping Table. A row gives the mapping between the IP address of a WINS Server and its identifier as stored in the Owner ID. The Name to IP Address Mapping Table stores the name to IP address mappings. The entries in this table are created as a result of name registration requests received from NetBIOS over TCP/IP nodes and replicas received from other WINS Servers.

FIGURE 8-14 WINS Database Files

File	Description
wins.mdb	The WINS database file.
winstmp.mdb	A temporary file that is created. It may remain after a crash.
j50.log	A log of all transactions done with the database. This file is used to recover data.
j50.chk	A checkpoint file.

The Show Database box shows these mappings in an easy-to-read format. Each row contains the NetBIOS name, IP Address, the entry's state, an Expiration Date and Time, and the Version ID.

Another means to look at the database is to use Winsdmp. Winsdmp is a command-line interface tool to dump a comma-separated list of the WINS database entries. This tool is part of the Windows NT Resource Kit. These are the comma-separated value fields output by Winsdmp:

- Owner IP address
- Name
- 16th character of name in hexadecimal
- Name length
- Type of record (unique/multi-homed/special group/normal group)
- State of record (active/released/extinct)
- Version ID (high-order word)
- Version ID (low-order word)
- Static/dynamic flag
- Time stamp
- Number of IP addresses
- IP addresses

Backing Up and Restoring The WINS Database

As with any other system file, it is important to back up the WINS Database in case of failure or corruption. By default, NT will not back up the database; it must be started manually the first time. Once started, backups occur every 24 hours.

To start the first backup, open the WINS Manager Mappings menu and select Back Up Database. Specify a location for the backup, and exit. The Registry entries for WINS can also be backed up. These entries are located in:

HKEY_LOCAL_MACHINE\SYSTEM\CurrentControlSet\Services\WINS.

Open this key in the registry editor, regedt32, and choose Save Key from the Registry menu. Again, specify a location for the saved key.

There are two methods to restore the Database if it becomes corrupted. The first requires you to stop and restart the WINS Server. If the WINS Server detects a corrupt database, it automatically restores a backup. To restore a backup, even if the current database is not corrupt, use the Restore Database command on the WINS Manager Mappings menu. This method will allow you to choose the location of the backup to be restored.

Jetpack

Windows NT Server includes a utility called *Jetpack*, which can be used to compact a WINS or DHCP database. Microsoft recommends that you compact the WINS database whenever it approaches 30MB. The biggest benefit of a compacted database is speed. A smaller database increases the resolution speed, the replication speed, and the backup speed.

To use Jetpack, the WINS Server Service must be stopped, from either Control Panel, or at the command prompt. Jetpack is then run from the command prompt using this syntax:

```
JETPACK.EXE <database name> <temp database name>
```

Figure 8-15 shows an example of how to compact the WINS database from the command prompt. In this example, tmp.mdb is a temporary database that is used by Jetpack, and wins.mdb is the WINS database.

Jetpack compacts the WINS or DHCP database by copying the database information to a temporary database file called Tmp.mdb. The original database is then deleted. The Tmp.mdb database, which is a compacted version of the original, is renamed to the original filename. Jetpack creates another temporary file called temp.mdb during the compacting process. Temp.mdb is removed when the compact process is complete.

Therefore, do not specify a filename of temp.mdb on the Jetpack command line. A duplicate file error message appears if temp.mdb is used. Also, make sure you do not have a file called temp.mdb in your WINS or DHCP folder.

Microsoft Windows NT Server 4.0 WINS and DHCP Server Services have a new feature that dynamically compacts their databases. This is in addition to,

FIGURE 8-15   Using Jetpack to compact the WINS database

```
cd %systemroot%\system32\wins

net stop wins

jetpack wins.mdb tmp.mdb

net start wins
```

and not a replacement for, the Jetpack utility. Windows NT 4.0 dynamic compacting decreases the frequency for which the Jetpack utility is needed by compacting the database as it is written.

CERTIFICATION SUMMARY

WINS is Microsoft's NetBIOS name server. WINS takes the place of local LMHOSTS files that can quickly become outdated and are difficult to maintain. Since DHCP dynamically distributes IP addresses, WINS is needed to resolve them. This simplifies the duties of the network administrator who no longer has to manually update NetBIOS name mappings. Network traffic is reduced because queries are directed to the WINS Server, not broadcast.

WINS provides a method for maintaining names and resolutions within an ever-changing network. Since registrations happen dynamically, WINS is always accurate, and, via replication, several WINS Servers can be used when needed. The simple process of Request, Registration, Renewal, and Query does not adversely affect even the largest networks. Proxies allow non-WINS Clients to gain the use of a WINS Server for name resolution.

Installation and maintenance of a WINS Server are relatively easy. Because it runs as a background service, little, if any, day-to-day upkeep is needed. After proper configuration at installation, WINS will do its job with little input required. Backups, replications, and most compressions occur automatically. DHCP can be used to automate configuration of WINS Clients. This includes the distribution of the WINS Server IP address and Node type for name resolution.

Replication occurs between partners. Each partner, whether push or pull, can initiate the process, or the administrator can force a replication. This is the most network-intensive feature of WINS, and should be scheduled around peak network use.

The Jetpack utility, which is included with NT Server, should be used to keep the database compacted. The maximum recommended database size is 30MB.

TWO-MINUTE DRILL

- ❑ A WINS Server eliminates the need for many network broadcasts, and therefore reduces network usage.
- ❑ The WINS Server is any Windows NT Server on a TCP/IP network.
- ❑ The WINS Server maintains a database of mappings for IP addresses to NetBIOS names.
- ❑ A WINS Client is the machine that requests a NetBIOS mapping.
- ❑ The LMHOSTS file contains mappings of IP addresses to NetBIOS names. Its greatest limitation is that it is a static file.
- ❑ Remember that an LMHOSTS file is used for NetBIOS name mappings and a HOSTS file is for host name mappings. These roughly correspond to a WINS Server and a DNS Server. You need to know which file corresponds to which server.
- ❑ WINS provides a distributed database for registering and querying dynamic NetBIOS names to IP address mappings in a routed network environment.
- ❑ WINS provides for Point-to-Point name resolution, in that a computer requests an IP address mapping directly from the WINS Server.
- ❑ The WINS process is relatively simple, and, when implemented properly, will not significantly affect network utilization.

❑ The first step in the WINS process is the Name Registration Request.

❑ It is the Client's responsibility to renew its names.

❑ The real function of WINS is the Name Lookup or Name Query.

❑ Once a computer registers a name, the host owns the name until it releases it.

❑ Very little optimization is needed for WINS as it typically accounts for less than 1% of all network traffic.

❑ Keep each of the optimization tips in mind when determining proper placement and configuration of WINS. Know which methods work best in both large and small networks.

❑ For WINS to work, there must be at least one WINS Server. To provide for fault tolerance, and load sharing, two or more WINS Servers may be ideal.

❑ To install the WINS Server Service, log on with Administrator privileges and open Network Properties either through the Control Panel or Network Neighborhood icon. On the Services tab, choose install Windows Internet Name Service.

❑ The WINS Configuration Manager is automatically installed and added to the Administrative Tools (Common) group when WINS is installed on an NT Server.

❑ A WINS Proxy Agent or Server extends the name resolution capabilities of WINS to non-WINS Clients, such as UNIX machines.

❑ Proxies do not register names. They just aid in the resolution process by listening for name resolution broadcasts from non-WINS Clients. These broadcasts will not cross a router, so placement of the Proxy is critical.

❑ Clients can receive this information in two ways: dynamically through DHCP or statically through TCP/IP Properties.

❑ A WINS Client is any computer that requests name resolution from a WINS Server.

❑ Both the primary and secondary WINS Server addresses may be input through Network Properties, under the TCP/IP Protocol, Properties Button, or WINS Address tab.

❑ DHCP allows its Clients to obtain IP addresses and other information upon bootup.

❑ When multiple WINS Servers are used, either for load sharing or redundancy, a method must be implemented to ensure that all resolution requests are handled by up-to-date databases. This method of sharing database information is known as *replication*.

❑ A *pull partner* is a WINS Server that pulls in replications of database entries from its partner by requesting and then accepting the replications.

❑ A *push partner* is a WINS Server that sends update notification messages to its partner when its WINS database has changed.

❑ Replication is the most network-intensive part of WINS. Be certain that you configure replication to occur so that it will not overwhelm the network. Slow links will definitely need to be replicated when they are least used by other network communication.

❑ The WINS Database is actually composed of four files all located in the \systemroot\system32\WINS directory.

❑ It is important to back up the WINS Database in case of failure or corruption.

❑ Windows NT Server includes a utility called *Jetpack*, which can be used to compact a WINS or DHCP database.

SELF TEST

The following Self Test questions will help you measure your understanding of the material presented in this chapter. Read all the choices carefully, as there may be more than one correct answer. Choose all correct answers for each question.

1. What is the first step in the name resolution process?

   A. WINS

   B. LMHOSTS File

   C. NetBIOS Cache

   D. DNS

2. What is not a disadvantage of the LMHOSTS file?

   A. Dynamic

   B. Manual update

   C. Static

   D. Preloads the cache

3. What is not a characteristic of a broadcast for name resolution?

   A. All computers must process

   B. Can't cross routers

   C. Used by WINS Proxies

   D. Sent directly to WINS Server

4. Which is not a benefit of WINS?

   A. Needs more administration

   B. Automatic name registration

   C. Provide internetwork and interdomain browsing

   D. Eliminate the need for local LMHOSTS

5. (True/False) Only DHCP can configure a WINS Client.

6. How many WINS Servers are required for a network with 15 subnets and 1000 users?

   A. 1

   B. 2

   C. 3

   D. 4

7. Which methods can a non-WINS Client use to resolve names?

   A. WINS Proxy

   B. LMHOSTS

   C. Broadcast

   D. WINS Server

8. (True/False) Every subnet on a network, that does not have a WINS Server, must have a WINS Proxy.

9. WINS network traffic accounts usually accounts for __ % of total network traffic.

   A. 1

   B. 2

   C. 5

   D. 10

10. The first step in the WINS process is

   A. Name Query Request

   B. Name Request

C. Name Registration Request

D. Name Lookup

11. The default TTL for a registered name is

A. Six days

B. One week

C. Six weeks

D. Until the computer is turned off

12. How many attempts to a Primary WINS Server will a Client make, before using the Secondary, for Name Resolution?

A. 1

B. 3

C. 5

D. 7

13. How often, after a default installation, does WINS back up the database?

A. Every three hours

B. Daily

C. Weekly

D. Never

14. How many pairs of WINS Servers and Backups are needed for a network with 150 subnets, each subnet having over 100 Clients?

A. 1

B. 2

C. 5

D. 10

15. (True/False) WINS is installed through Add/Remove Programs in Control Panel.

16. (True/False) WINS Manager can manage any number of WINS Servers.

17. Which of the following would need a permanent, static, IP address?

A. DHCP Server

B. WINS Server

C. File And Print Server

D. Application Server

18. (True/False) A WINS Proxy Server cannot be a WINS Client.

19. Which of the following operating systems cannot use WINS?

A. MS Network Client for DOS

B. UNIX

C. Windows for Workgroups 3.11 running MS TCP/IP 32

D. Windows 95

20. A WINS Client should use which node type for name resolution?

A. B Node

B. H Node

C. M Node

D. P Node

21. (True/False) Replication can be initialized only by a push partner.

22. (True/False) Once a computer is turned off, its registered names are not immediately available to other computers.

23. To start automatic, daily backups of the WINS Database, you must

A. Check the Start Backup box in WINS Manager

B. Configure Backup from TCP/IP Properties

C. Run NT Backup

D. Specify a location for the backup

24. Jetpack should be run when the WINS Database reaches what size?

A. 10MB

B. 25MB

C. 30MB

D. 50MB

25. All of the following will speed up WINS, except:

A. Add a second processor

B. Increase WINS runtime priority

C. Reduce the default registration TTL from 6 days to 3 days

D. Turn off logging

MICROSOFT CERTIFIED SYSTEMS ENGINEER

9

TCP/IP Host Names and Browsing the Network

A number of network architectures utilize some type of naming system to facilitate the usability and manageability of the network. TCP/IP uses *host names*, which are simply names assigned to network devices such as servers, workstations, printers, and routers. The host name implementation for TCP/IP is scalable due to its hierarchical structure.

The naming functionality for some other types of networking, such as Novell and Microsoft networks, is less scalable. However, when TCP/IP is used with these networks, they also can benefit from the advantages of its powerful naming system. In fact, each new version of Microsoft and Novell network operating systems relies more on TCP/IP than the previous version. It is likely that future versions of these operating systems will employ only TCP/IP naming in an effort to standardize with the Internet protocols and simplify network administration.

Microsoft networking uses *NetBIOS names*, commonly called computer names. Although the TCP/IP host name and the NetBIOS name of a Microsoft computer are often the same, they are not required to be identical. Microsoft networks also use *browsing*, which enables users to easily find other computers by their NetBIOS name on the network. In an internetwork environment, browsing across the entire network requires the use of Windows Internet Name Service (WINS), or carefully designed and managed LMHOSTS files so that computers can find the IP addresses of other computers to participate in browsing.

This chapter will discuss TCP/IP host names, the HOSTS file, and internetwork browsing and the configurations that make it work.

CERTIFICATION OBJECTIVE 9.01

Host Names

Each device on a given TCP/IP network has a unique IP address, such as 146.115.28.75, and a unique name, such as www.syngress.com. Connections to network hosts on a TCP/IP network can be made by using either the name or the IP address, although using the host name is certainly preferable in most instances.

When connecting to a computer by its host name, the host name must be *resolved* to an IP address by either one of two ways. Most commonly, the host name is resolved by Domain Name System (DNS), the topic of the next chapter. DNS is a distributed database of host names and IP addresses, and is used on most TCP/IP networks. The second method is by the HOSTS file, a text file on the local computer that contains entries for host names and IP addresses.

TCP/IP Requirements

Networks that are connected to the Internet must register their domain name with the *InterNIC*, an organization that sets and maintains standards on the Internet. This ensures that each domain name is unique, which is absolutely necessary for the Internet to function properly.

The administrators of a given domain, on the other hand, must take care to secure unique host names for each device on their network. Since the domain name is guaranteed to be unique by the InterNIC, network administrators do not need to be concerned about the host names on other domains. If the InterNIC and the local administrator have been diligent, each device on the Internet will have a completely unique *fully qualified domain name*. Table 9-1 summarizes these responsibilities for creating unique names.

TCP/IP domain and host names are subject to certain rules that are necessary to ensure that reliable software and hardware can be developed to handle the various implementation and management details. TCP/IP names, in general, can use alphanumeric characters and the dash (minus sign). Some IP software, including Microsoft's DNS server, also allows the use of the

TABLE 9-1	Object	Example	Responsible for Unique Name
Responsibility for Host and Domain Names on the Internet	host name	www	network admin
	domain name	syngress.com	InterNIC
	fully qualified domain name	www.syngress.com	InterNIC & network admin

underscore character to support versions of BIND (Berkeley Internet Name Domain) released before version 4.94.

Host Names and TCP/IP Utilities

Most TCP/IP utilities can be run using either a local host name, a fully qualified domain name, or an IP address to establish and test network connections with other network hosts. When used with a name, the utility will use either DNS or the HOSTS file to resolve the other host's IP address and then use the IP address to establish communications.

Ping

Almost all TCP/IP software includes a Ping utility. Ping is a simple tool that uses the Internet Control Message Protocol (ICMP) to send an echo request to an IP address, as shown in Figure 9-1. When the device that was pinged replies, the Ping program displays information about the replies such as the size and the time it took to reply. Ping needs an IP address to work, so if you ping a host name, it will first resolve the name and then it will go to work carrying out the ping request. If the wrong IP address is returned for the requested name, then the Ping utility will dutifully ping that incorrect address. Always confirm that Ping is using the correct IP address of the device you want to ping.

Some Ping programs will provide additional information such as statistics for the entire ping session. Windows 95 and Windows NT 4.0 do not provide any stats with their Ping utilities, but beta versions of Windows NT 5.0 have an enhanced ping utility that provides extended information that is commonly found on UNIX versions of Ping.

Telnet

Telnet is a utility used to establish remote command sessions on computers, routers, print servers, and other devices. Like Ping, Telnet can be used with either the host name or the IP address of the remote host. When the host name is used, correct address resolution is required, just as it is for Ping.

FIGURE 9-1

The Ping utility can be used with either an IP address or a host name

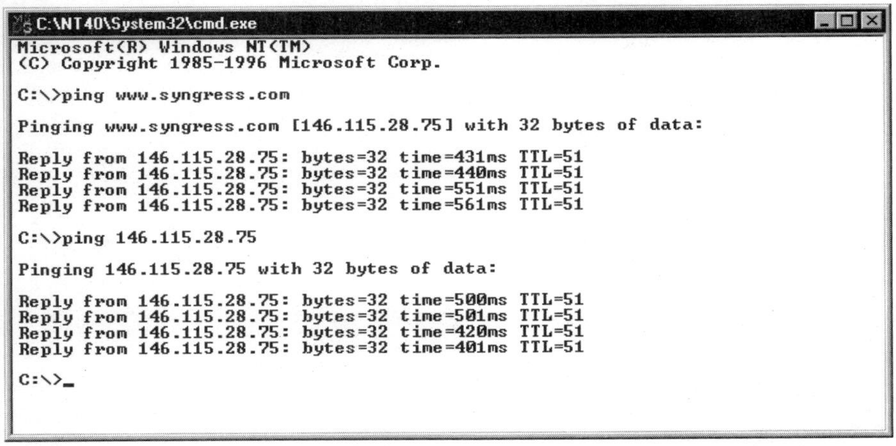

```
 C:\NT40\System32\cmd.exe                                    _ □ ×
Microsoft(R) Windows NT(TM)
(C) Copyright 1985-1996 Microsoft Corp.

C:\>ping www.syngress.com

Pinging www.syngress.com [146.115.28.75] with 32 bytes of data:

Reply from 146.115.28.75: bytes=32 time=431ms TTL=51
Reply from 146.115.28.75: bytes=32 time=440ms TTL=51
Reply from 146.115.28.75: bytes=32 time=551ms TTL=51
Reply from 146.115.28.75: bytes=32 time=561ms TTL=51

C:\>ping 146.115.28.75

Pinging 146.115.28.75 with 32 bytes of data:

Reply from 146.115.28.75: bytes=32 time=500ms TTL=51
Reply from 146.115.28.75: bytes=32 time=501ms TTL=51
Reply from 146.115.28.75: bytes=32 time=420ms TTL=51
Reply from 146.115.28.75: bytes=32 time=401ms TTL=51

C:\>_
```

Telnet is a heavily used utility with UNIX computers, and is used for everything from e-mail to editing remote files to network administration. Windows NT Server is capable of hosting Telnet sessions as well, and the usefulness of Telnet is becoming appreciated within the Windows NT community. A Telnet server is included with the Windows NT Server Resource Kit, along with another utility, Remote Command Server, that functions somewhat like Telnet but works from the Windows NT command line.

To test the connectivity between two remote computers, an administrator can Telnet to one of the computers, and ping the other computer from within the Telnet session. A Telnet client is included with the TCP/IP connectivity software in both Windows 95 and Windows NT.

FTP

File Transfer Protocol (FTP) is a TCP/IP utility that exists solely to copy files from one computer to another. Like Telnet and Ping, FTP can establish a connection to a remote computer using either the host name or IP address, and must resolve host names to IP addresses to establish communication with the remote computer. As you read in Chapter 1, Windows NT includes an

FTP server in its Internet Information Server software. Windows NT and Windows 95 computers each include a command-line FTP client with their TCP/IP protocol software. Although it is not widely known, the Windows FTP client supports scripting, which enables users to automate repetitive FTP tasks.

There are a number of third-party graphical user interface (GUI) FTP clients for all versions of Windows computers. If you use FTP a lot, a GUI FTP client may save you a lot of time and frustration.

CERTIFICATION OBJECTIVE 9.02

HOSTS File

The HOSTS file is a text file that contains IP address to host name mappings. Each HOSTS file entry is entered on a separate line. The format for host entries is to list the IP address followed by one or more spaces, and then the host name. If you wish to add comments, put a pound sign (#) after the host name followed by the comment.

By default, the HOSTS file is located in the %SystemRoot%\System32\Drivers\Etc directory. Most networks are designed to have client computers use DNS for host name resolution, so HOSTS files are used sparingly. When DNS is in use, the HOSTS file on a DNS server is populated with all host name to IP address mappings for the domains it serves.

Remote and Local Host Entries

When adding hosts to the HOSTS file, it is necessary to use the fully qualified domain name of any host that is in a different DNS domain. For hosts that are in the same DNS domain, it is necessary to add only the host name. This rule is necessary so that duplicate names won't appear in the file, while making it unnecessary to use the fully qualified domain name for every host on the local DNS domain. The example in Figure 9-2 shows an entry for a host named "multia" that is in the same DNS domain, and an entry for "www.syngress.com" that is in a different DNS domain.

FIGURE 9-2

A HOSTS file containing entries for local and remote networks

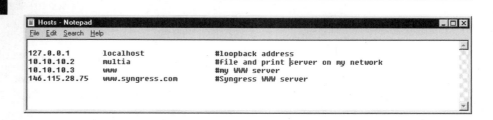

```
Hosts - Notepad                                                          _□×
File  Edit  Search  Help
127.0.0.1        localhost            #loopback address
10.10.10.2       multia              #file and print server on my network
10.10.10.3       www                 #my WWW server
146.115.28.75    www.syngress.com    #Syngress WWW server
```

Host Name Resolution

Three steps occur when a host name is resolved using the HOSTS file:

1. A command is entered at Computer 1 using the host name of Computer 2.

2. Computer 1 parses its HOSTS file until it finds the entry for Computer 2, which contains the IP address of Computer 2.

3. Address Resolution Protocol (ARP) is used to find the hardware address of Computer 2 if Computer 2 is on the local subnet. Otherwise, ARP will be used to provide the hardware address of the default gateway for the route to Computer 2.

EXERCISE 9-1

Configuring and Using a HOSTS File

1. Run the Notepad utility.

2. For Windows NT computers, open %SystemRoot%\System32\Drivers\Etc\hosts. For Windows 95 computers, open %windir%\hosts. If the specified file does not exist, open the hosts.sam file and change its name to hosts.

3. Add an entry for a computer on your network. Enter the IP address at the start of the line, leave a few spaces, followed by the host name. If you don't have another computer on the network, you can make up any valid host name and enter the IP address of your computer just for testing purposes.

4. Run a command prompt and run the ping utility using the host name entered in step 3.

Troubleshooting Host Name Resolution Errors

If host name resolution fails, the following items must be checked:

- The HOSTS file does not have an entry for the requested host.

- The host name is misspelled in the HOSTS file. This includes capitalization errors since host names are case sensitive.

- The IP address for the host entry in the HOSTS file is incorrect.

- Multiple entries for a particular host name are listed in the HOSTS file.

- A NetBIOS computer name was used in the HOSTS file instead of the TCP/IP host name.

CERTIFICATION OBJECTIVE 9.03

Internetwork Browsing

Users must be able to easily find servers, files, and printers on a network and Microsoft networks implement browsing to accomplish this. Browsing enables a user to "drill down" through the Windows NT domains and servers to find specific files or printers they need. Browsing uses the NetBIOS name of computers, and when used with TCP/IP, this type of communication is known as NetBT (NetBIOS over TCP/IP).

The NetBIOS names inherent with Windows networking are 15-character names with a non-printing character available as the 16th character.

A computer can belong to a Windows NT domain or Windows workgroup, which enables users to browse computers by either of those logical groupings. NetBIOS computer names and Windows NT domain names are not regulated in any way outside of the businesses and organizations that are setting the names for their own networks. This means that uniqueness cannot be guaranteed across disparate entities unless they have collaborated. This is why NetBIOS naming is not an appropriate method of accessing computers on the Internet, and why Windows NT is becoming more DNS-centric with each new version of the operating system.

Microsoft Network browsing is a simple process when it occurs on only one local network and requires no special configuration. When browsing is extended across a TCP/IP internetwork, however, it becomes more complex and it requires specific steps to make it work correctly. WINS or LMHOSTS files must be configured for internetwork browsing to function. When one or both of these components are put in place, the Microsoft browsing service will take care of the details, including the election of domain master, master, and backup browsers. A third alternative that is not recommended is to configure the routers to forward UDP port 137 traffic. UDP port 137 is used by the browser service to carry out its communications on local networks.

Browser Functions

Windows NT computers elect among themselves computers, called browsers, to collect and distribute lists of shared resources on the network. Whenever a client browses the network, they request and receive these lists from a browser. There are three types of browsers: 1) domain master browsers; 2) master browsers; and 3) backup browsers. All three are necessary for internetwork browsing and will be automatically elected if either WINS or LMHOSTS is correctly configured. For browsing to work on a local network only, however, the domain master browser is not necessary, and neither WINS nor LMHOSTS need to be configured. Knowing the role that each browser plays is essential to understanding how internetwork browsing works. The distinction between local network browsing and internetwork browsing is summarized in Table 9-2.

Browsing uses computer NetBIOS names, not DNS names, so whenever "names" and "browsing" are mentioned together, it is safe to assume that the reference is to a NetBIOS name. Browsing requires special designations, such as domain master, browser, and master browser, to be associated with computer names. DNS currently does not have the capability to fulfill this requirement so it cannot be used to implement internetwork browsing.

Non-Browser

Computers that have been configured specifically not to become a master or backup browser are called *non-browsers*. Configuring most client PCs to be

TABLE 9-2	Local Network	Internetwork
Browsing Components Necessary for Local and Internetwork Browsing	Master Browser	Domain Master Browser
	Backup Browsers	Master Browsers
		Backup Browsers
		WINS, LMHOSTS, or Routers Configured to Forward UDP Port 137

non-browsers will reduce the possibility of having browsing problems. To configure a computer to be a non-browser, the registry setting MaintainServerList is set to "no" (see Table 9-3).

Potential Browser

A *potential browser* is a computer that can become a master or backup browser. In order for it to become a backup browser, the master browser must designate it as such. If there is no master browser, a potential browser will force an election.

Master Browser

A *master browser* is responsible for collecting information about the servers in its workgroup or the servers in its domain that are on the same subnet. When a server is started, it announces itself to the master browser with a directed datagram called a *server announcement.* Windows NT Server, Windows NT Workstation, Windows for Workgroups, Windows 95, and LAN Manager servers all send server announcements at startup. If a domain spans more than one subnet, the master browser will maintain the resource list *only* for the

TABLE 9-3	Value	Description
Values for \HKEY_ LOCAL_MACHINE\ System\CurrentControl Set\Services\Browser\ Parameters, MaintainServerList	No	This computer will not be a browser.
	Yes	This computer will be a master or backup browser. This is the default setting for Windows NT Server.
	Auto	This computer will become a browser if needed. This is the default setting for Windows NT Workstation.

portion of the domain on its subnet. Master browsers also send resource lists to backup browsers and provide lists of backup browsers to clients.

Domain Master Browser

A *domain master browser* receives lists of resources from each master browser in the internetwork, which enables it to compile a list of all resources available on the internetwork. This complete list is then distributed back to the master browsers. The domain master browser is always a primary domain controller (PDC), and is very likely to be the master browser of its own subnet.

The master browsers announce themselves to the domain master browser with a MasterBrowserAnnouncement directed datagram. The domain master browser then issues a remote NetServerEnum API call to each master browser about which it knows. This is a request for the master browser to send the resource list that it is maintaining. By default, this call is repeated every 15 minutes, making sure that the resource lists are reasonably current. The domain master browser thus collects the browser list from each master browser on the internetwork and compiles the complete list of resources available.

Each master browser in turn issues the NetServerEnum request to the domain master browser, collecting the entire list of resources on the internetwork. As this information is then distributed to backup browsers, clients are able to browse the entire internetwork.

Backup Browser

A *backup browser* receives the resource list from the master browser and fulfills browse requests from the clients in its domain or workgroup. If a Windows NT domain controller is not a master browser, it will automatically become a backup browser. If there are not enough Windows NT Server computers to fill the needed backup browser roles, Windows NT Workstation, Windows for Workgroups, and Windows 95 computers can perform the duties of backup browser.

Backup browsers contact the master browser every 15 minutes to get the latest list of resources. Whenever a client sends a NetServerEnum request to a backup browser, the backup browser forwards the list of resources to the client. If a backup browser cannot find the master browser, it forces an election, and a new master browser is designated.

The number of backup browsers that exist for a given domain or network segment depends on the number of computers in the domain or segment, as shown in Table 9-4. In some instances, these numbers will vary since BDCs are automatically backup browsers. For example, if a network with fewer than 31 computers has two BDCs, there will be two backup browsers instead of just one. The standards in Table 9-4 can also be broken if the MaintainServerList registry entry is manually set to "yes" on computers.

Browser Elections

A browser election is a process to determine which computer will be the master browser. There are four circumstances that will force a browser election to take place:

- A client or backup browser cannot find a master browser.
- A server with MaintainServerList set to "yes" is started.
- A Windows NT primary or backup domain controller is started.
- A Windows NT computer with IsDomainMasterBrowser set to "yes" is started.

When any of these situations arises, the computer initiating the election sends out an *election datagram*. All browsers receive this datagram and examine its *election criteria*. If the receiving computer's election criteria are better than the sender's criteria, the receiver enters into an *election-in-progress* state and issues its own election datagram. Otherwise, it will try to determine which computer is the new master browser. A number of criteria, listed in Table 9-5, are used to determine which computer wins the browser election.

TABLE 9-4	**Computers**	**Backup Browsers**
The Number of Backup Browsers Designated Depends on the Number of Computers in the Domain or on the Network Segment	1	0
	2 - 31	1
	32 - 63	2
	63+	+1 for each additional 32 computers

	Election Datagram	Description
TABLE 9-5 The Master Browser Is Elected after Comparing Each Browser's Election Criteria	0xFF000000	Type of Operating System
	0x01000000	Windows for Workgroups/Windows 95
	0x10000000	Windows NT Workstation
	0x20000000	Windows NT Server
	0x00FFFF00	Election Version
	0x000000FF	Criteria Per Version
	0x00000080	Primary Domain Controller
	0x00000020	WINS Client
	0x00000008	Preferred Master Browser
	0x00000004	Currently a Master Browser
	0x00000002	MaintainServerList Set to Yes
	0x00000001	Currently a Backup Browser

For example, the election datagram of a Windows NT Server computer that has been configured as a preferred master browser will be 0x00000008. A computer that is currently a backup browser will receive this datagram and notice that its own election criteria are better. Therefore, it will send out its own election datagram and enter into the election-in-progress state.

As you may have realized, there is likely to be more than one backup browser on the network, and there must be some way to "break the tie" since the backup browser criteria are the highest election criteria specified. In this case, two rules will be followed to select the new master browser: 1) the browser that has been running the longest will win, and then 2) the browser with the lowest name alphabetically will win. The chances of an election being decided by the alphabetical criteria are miniscule.

After a browser has determined that it has won the browser election, it enters into the *running election* state. During this time it sends out an election request after a short pause. The length of the delay depends on the browser's role:

- Primary domain controllers and master browsers pause for 100 microseconds.

■ Backup domain controllers and backup browsers delay for 600 and 200 microseconds.

■ Other browsers delay between 800 and 3000 microseconds randomly.

This delay is implemented so that browsers that are less likely to win elections won't end up sending election datagrams. This reduces network traffic and the number of election packets that must be analyzed by each browser. The pause also keeps browsers from actually becoming the master browser before all of the other browsers have had time to broadcast their election criteria.

A browser sends up to four election datagrams, and is promoted to master browser if no greater election criteria are received from other computers. If it is currently the master browser and receives better criteria from another browser, it will demote itself to backup browser. Events are recorded in the Event Viewer's System log on a Windows NT computer when it forces an election, including separate events for each protocol on which the browser service forces the election.

Browsing Across a WAN

Now that you understand how browsing works, we will take a look at how browsing operates in a WAN environment. On a given TCP/IP network segment, the browsing service uses UDP port 137, which will not be forwarded by routers unless they are specifically configured to do so. Having routers forward browser traffic on large WANs will likely cause some problems, including much too frequent browser elections.

The browsers on each segment will elect a master browser for that segment. This master browser will assign backup browser duties to an appropriate number of computers. The master browser will also send a MasterBrowserAnnouncement datagram to the domain master browser. The election process is illustrated in Figure 9-3. The domain master browser will usually be across a router, which is why WINS or LMHOSTS must be in place for TCP/IP WAN browsing to function—or less desirably, UDP port 137 datagrams must be forwarded by the routers.

FIGURE 9-3

The master browser of each subnet sends its resource list to the domain master browser, and in turn receives a list of all internetwork resources from the domain master browser

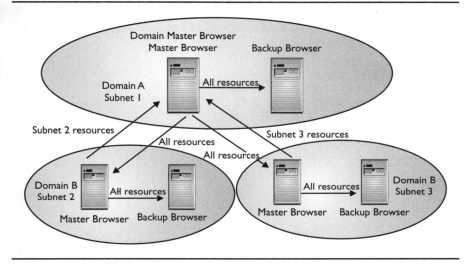

WAN Browsing Using WINS

Microsoft recommends that TCP/IP WAN networks implement WINS, which was discussed in the previous chapter. Deploying WINS is the preferred way to accomplish WAN browsing since it requires less manual configuration, automatically adjusts to reflect changes in the network resources, and is less susceptible to human error.

Computers that are serving as browsers will register special names, shown in Table 9-6, with the WINS service that will identify them as potential browsers, master browsers, and domain master browsers. The 16th byte is used to designate the type of browser the computer is.

Once WINS is in place, the browser service will use it without any special configuration. WINS enables master browsers to determine which computer is the domain master browser, even though it may be on different network segment. It also enables the domain master browser to easily locate all browsers and potential browsers. Client computers must be WINS-enabled as well for them to be able to browse the internetwork. A client can then locate the master browser for its domain by querying the WINS server.

TABLE 9-6	Registered Name	Description
Special Browser Entries Registered in WINS-Enable Browsers and Clients to Find Browsers on Other Subnets	\\<domain_name>[1B]	This name is registered by the Windows NT system that is the domain master browser, and allows remote browsing of domains. A WINS Server returns the IP address of the system that registered this name when a client queries for this name.
	\\2--__MSBROWSE__[01]	This name is registered by the master browser and is used to broadcast and receive domain announcements on the local subnet. It is through this name that master browsers for different domains learn the names of different domains and the names of the master browsers on those domains. When a WINS Server receives a name query for this name, the WINS Server will always return the subnet broadcast address for the requesting client's local subnet.
	\\<domain_name>[1E]	All browser and potential browsers in a domain or workgroup register this name. Master browsers use these entries for announcement requests in order to fill up its browse lists and for election requests.

exam
ⓦatch

Be sure you understand the three types of browsers, how to configure browser registry entries, and the three methods of implementing internetwork browsing.

WAN Browsing Using LMHOSTS

Another way that computers can find each other based on NetBIOS names in an internetwork is to configure the LMHOSTS file for each computer. This is similar to the HOSTS file, except it is for NetBIOS names instead of TCP/IP names.

The LMHOSTS file is a text file located by default in the \<*winnt_root*>\ System32\drivers\etc directory. A sample file, LMHOSTS.SAM, is installed whenever TCP/IP is installed on a Windows NT computer. For internetwork browsing to function using LMHOSTS, there are a number of LMHOSTS entries that need to be present:

- The NetBIOS names and IP addresses of all browsers must be listed in the LMHOSTS file of the domain master browser.

- The PDC for each domain must be entered with the #DOM tag into the LMHOSTS file on each master browser.

- Each master browser's LMHOSTS file must have an entry for the domain master browser, including the #PRE and #DOM extensions.

As you can see, using this method to enable WAN browsing requires a great deal of manual configuration, and must be updated whenever a domain or network segment is added or removed. The #INCLUDE function in the LMHOSTS file can alleviate most of the work, but you will still have to manually maintain a central LMHOSTS file.

EXERCISE 9-2

Browsing with LMHOSTS File

1. Use the browstat.exe utility to find all of the browsers on each segment and domain of your network.

2. Add entries for all browsers to the LMHOSTS file of the domain master browser.

3. Add entries to the LMHOSTS file on each master browser for the PDC of each domain using the #DOM tag.

4. Add an entry for the domain master browser, using the #PRE and #DOM tags, to each master browser.

5. After the computers have time to collect and distribute resource lists, run Explorer and browse through the available domains.

WAN Browsing Using UDP Port 137

The NetBT Name Service uses UDP port 137, as defined in RFCs 1001 and 1002. Routers typically filter this traffic because it is used for hardware and subnet broadcasting. Some routers are capable of being configured to forward

UDP port 137, and doing so will allow browsing to function without the use of WINS or LMHOSTS. This method is not recommended for a number of reasons.

- Browser elections will not function correctly if computers across slow links cannot respond in a timely manner.

- Browser elections will involve a greater number of computers, thus generating more browser traffic that will hit every segment of the WAN.

- Browsing will be slower since computers will have to communicate across routers to supply resource lists to clients.

Browser Monitoring

Two utilities come with the *Windows NT Server Resource Kit* that enable you to view browser information, force elections, and stop master browsers. These utilities will be invaluable if you have trouble with internetwork browsing.

Browmon.exe is a GUI tool that allows you to see the master and backup browsers for specified domains. If more than one transport protocol is in use, the browsers for each protocol will be listed. Browmon also provides statistics about the number of server announcements, domain announcements, election packets, and other information.

Browstat.exe is a command-line utility that gives you the ability to force elections and stop master browsers, which also forces an election. Documentation for these two tools is included in the Resource Kit books and Help files.

CERTIFICATION SUMMARY

In order for users and applications to make use of TCP/IP host names, the host names must be resolved to IP addresses. This can be accomplished by either DNS or the local HOSTS file. The HOSTS file is a text file containing entries that associate IP addresses with host names. When supplied with a host name, the computer parses its HOSTS file and returns that host's IP address to the application. HOSTS files are not used on most client PCs since DNS is a more manageable solution for host name resolution.

Microsoft networking uses NetBIOS name browsing to enable users to easily find files and printers located on other computers. The resource lists for a network are gathered and distributed by three types of browser computers: master browsers, backup browsers, and domain master browsers.

Since browsing uses UDP port 137, which by default is not forwarded by routers, you must configure the network in one of three ways to enable internetwork browsing. The best way to implement internetwork browsing is to use WINS servers. Browsers register their names with specific 16th byte characters identifying their browsing role. This enables the domain master browser to find all of the master browsers on an internetwork to coordinate the collection and distribution of resource lists.

The second way to make internetwork browsing function is to configure the LMHOSTS files on all browser computers with the appropriate entries. This is a manual process, subject to human error.

The third and least recommended way is to configure the routers on the network to forward UDP port 137 traffic. This will cause more network traffic on each segment of the network and may cause problems with browser elections if low-speed WAN links are in use. This method would be considered in only the smallest routed network environments.

 # TWO-MINUTE DRILL

- Each device on a given TCP/IP network has a unique IP address, such as 146.115.28.75, and a unique name, such as www.syngress.com.

- When connecting to a computer by its host name, the host name must be *resolved* to an IP address by either one of two ways:

  - The host name is resolved by Domain Name System (DNS) or by the HOSTS file, a text file on the local computer that contains entries for host names and IP addresses.

- Networks that are connected to the Internet must register their domain name with the *InterNIC*.

- Most TCP/IP utilities can be run using either a local host name, a fully qualified domain name, or an IP address to establish and test network connections with other network hosts.

- Ping is a simple tool that uses the Internet Control Message Protocol (ICMP) to send an echo request to an IP address.

- Telnet is a utility used to establish remote command sessions on computers, routers, print servers, and other devices.

- File Transfer Protocol (FTP) is a TCP/IP utility that exists solely to copy files from one computer to another.

- The HOSTS file is a text file that contains IP address to host name mappings.

- When adding hosts to the HOSTS file, it is necessary to use the fully qualified domain name of any host that is in a different DNS domain.

- Users must be able to easily find servers, files, and printers on a network and Microsoft networks implement browsing to accomplish this.

- Browsing enables a user to "drill down" through the Windows NT domains and servers to find specific files or printers they need.

- There are three types of browsers: 1) domain master browsers; 2) master browsers; and 3) backup browsers.

- Computers that have been configured specifically not to become a master or backup browser are called *non-browsers*.

- A *potential browser* is a computer that can become a master or backup browser.

- A *master browser* is responsible for collecting information about the servers in its workgroup or the servers in its domain that are on the same subnet.

- A *domain master browser* receives lists of resources from each master browser in the internetwork, which enables it to compile a list of all resources available on the internetwork.

- A *backup browser* receives the resource list from the master browser and fulfills browse requests from the clients in its domain or workgroup.

- A browser election is a process to determine which computer will be the master browser.

- Microsoft recommends that TCP/IP WAN networks implement WINS.

- Be sure you understand the three types of browsers, how to configure browser registry entries, and the three methods of implementing internetwork browsing.

- Another way that computers can find each other based on NetBIOS names in an internetwork is to configure the LMHOSTS file for each computer.

- Two utilities come with the *Windows NT Server Resource Kit* that enable you to view browser information, force elections, and stop master browsers.

SELF TEST

The following Self Test questions will help you measure your understanding of the material presented in this chapter. Read all the choices carefully, as there may be more than one correct answer. Choose all correct answers for each question.

1. By which methods can TCP/IP host names be resolved to IP addresses?

   A. LMHOSTS file

   B. HOSTS file

   C. WINS

   D. DNS

2. Which method is the most recommended way to enable internetwork browsing?

   A. Configure routers to forward UDP port 137 traffic

   B. Configure LMHOSTS files on all servers and clients

   C. Configure HOSTS files on all servers

   D. Implement WINS

3. Which type of browser services client requests for resource lists?

   A. Domain master browser

   B. Master browser

   C. Backup browser

   D. WINS server

4. Which of the following statements are true?

   A. The domain master browser will always be a primary domain controller.

   B. The domain master browser cannot be a master browser.

   C. The domain master browser will always be a backup domain controller.

   D. The domain master browser sends resource lists to master browsers.

5. Which events will cause a browser election to occur?

   A. A computer cannot find a master browser.

   B. A Windows NT domain controller is started.

   C. A backup browser is shut down.

   D. A preferred master browser is started.

6. Which of the following occur when routers forward UDP port 137?

   A. Browsing traffic is reduced.

   B. Browsing traffic is increased.

   C. WINS and LMHOSTS files are not needed for browsing.

   D. Slow WAN links may cause browser election problems.

7. Which of the following are valid TCP/IP host names?

   A. www

   B. one-zinger

C. !ohno!

D. 123inarow

8. Which entries must be made in LMHOSTS files for internetwork browsing to function without WINS or UDP port 137 forwarding?

   A. Each master browser's LMHOSTS file must have an entry for the domain master browser, including the #PRE and #DOM extensions.

   B. LMHOSTS files on client computers must contain entries for all backup browsers on their subnet.

   C. The NetBIOS names and IP addresses of all browsers must be listed in the LMHOSTS file of the domain master browser.

   D. The PDC for each domain must be entered with the #DOM tag into the LMHOSTS file on each master browser.

9. Which entity regulates Internet domain names?

   A. The IEEE

   B. Microsoft

   C. The ISO

   D. The InterNIC

10. Which of the following is a fully qualified domain name?

    A. ftp.microsoft

    B. \\FTP

C. ftp.microsoft.com

D. microsoft.com

11. Which of the following statements are correct?

    A. NetBIOS names and TCP/IP host names must be the same on a given computer.

    B. NetBIOS names and TCP/IP host names are unrelated and can be the same or different on a given computer.

    C. WINS is a method of resolving TCP/IP host names to IP addresses.

    D. The HOSTS file can be used to resolve TCP/IP host names.

12. Comments in the HOSTS file can be added after what symbol?

    A. #

    B. @

    C. $

    D. %

13. Which TCP/IP protocol is used to find the hardware address of host or router after the host name has been resolved to an IP address?

    A. UDP

    B. HTTP

    C. ARP

    D. BOOTP

14. Which of the following choices will cause host name resolution to fail using the HOSTS file?

   A. Multiple entries for a particular host name are listed in the HOSTS file.

   B. The HOSTS file was moved from the %SystemRoot%\System32\Drivers\ Etc directory.

   C. The host name is mis-capitalized in the HOSTS file.

   D. A NetBIOS computer name was used in the HOSTS file instead of the TCP/IP host name.

15. A network segment with 120 computers will have how many backup browsers?

   A. 6

   B. 5

   C. 4

   D. 3

10

Domain Name Service

Since NT 3.5x, the TCP/IP protocol has become more important and in NT 4.0, TCP/IP is the required base protocol. With the ever growing commercial success of the Internet, NT developers have swung on board and offer many of the excellent services that are inherent with TCP/IP. One service that is used throughout the Internet is the Domain Name Server Service (DNS).

All IP-based traffic requires the IP address of the destination. DNS is one method of resolving a host name to a given IP address.

As the size of the Internet grew, a central HOSTS file became inadequate. DNS is not one central service like the original HOSTS file. DNS is much more robust and reliable. Every domain name could represent a DNS service zone containing the local hosts and their associated IP addresses. DNS provides a segmented service of small local databases that can pass, along a hierarchical chain, any requests for host name resolution that cannot be resolved locally.

All client machines require the IP address of the server and the name of the zone to which this server is the *authority*. Optionally, you can configure a client with the IP address of backup (secondary) servers. A secondary server has a local read-only copy of the primary server data and is available as an alternate site for name resolution of the specified domain or zone.

The hierarchical design of DNS is similar to a file tree structure. The root servers provide resolution to the same layer and the next below. Any further layers provide localized data zone authorities. In a private intranet, the domain servers can have any names. In the Internet, the root server names have been around a long time and are expanded all the time to allow for the exponential growth seen in the last few years.

For a Fully Qualified Domain Name, FQDN, like bicycles.phnx.ar.us, this can be interpreted to mean there is a root server somewhere that manages the .us root zone. The next layer of zones is the two-letter state monikers. In this case, ar is for arizona. The next layer represents a short form for the major cities, in this case Phoenix. The left-most part is the host in question, bicycles in Phoenix, Arizona, USA. Note that the names are delimited by periods similar to the format in a file system.

To enable a machine to be a DNS server, you must install the service in the Network applet of the Control Panel. Once installed, you need to create the zone file for the domain being managed and the reverse lookup records. You add one record for each name and IP address, as well as some specialized records for mail, synonyms, etc.

All clients will automatically use DNS when they request a host name for an IP address that is not known locally. The host name request is passed to DNS, which will use all known resources to try to resolve the host name to an IP address. Optionally, you can configure the NT version of DNS to query any configured WINS servers. To configure a WINS server, you must add the WINS server IP address to the properties of the zone file.

FROM THE CLASSROOM

WINS and DNS

On the certification exam you will need to clearly know the difference between WINS and DNS.

	WINS	**DNS**
Purpose	Resolve NetBIOS name to an IP address	Resolve host name to an IP address
Names	Flat in structure and limited to 15 characters	Hierarchical structure and limited to 255 characters
Name registration	Dynamic and happens automatically	Static and must be done manually
Replication of	Changes are replicated	Whole database is replicated

—By D. Lynn White, MCT, MCSE

Understanding Name Resolution and DNS

Every network interface card or connection has a unique 48-bit numeric ID called a Media Access Control (MAC) address, commonly displayed as six hexadecimal values. The transport protocols like NetBEUI, TCP/IP, and IPX/SPX hide the MAC address by associating a name and/or number with the host.

The TCP/IP protocols use a 32-bit numeric identification, such as 221.123.34.65, for every host on the network. To make the 32-bit number easier to remember, the 32 bits are split into parts each containing 8 bits. These 4 parts are each separated by a period. Each 8-bit segment can range between 0 and 255. As we learned in Chapter 3, Internet Addressing, there are many rules and restrictions on the number ranges.

Role of the Name Resolver

Most machines have a host name assigned as well as an IP address. If you use the host name, it must be translated to the IP address for the communication protocols to work. The function of the resolver is to pass a name request to the name server. The name servers take the request and resolve the name to an IP address.

Basic Routing

The final requirement of a WAN protocol is to provide full routing capability. Routing is a way for the software to know whether the requested remote host is on the same LAN or on a remote LAN. This is determined based on the Network Mask value, which isolates the bits that represent the network portions from the local and remote hosts' IP addresses. If these two network portion values are the same, then the remote host can be reached on the local media connection. If the two network portion values are different, then the remote host is reachable through the default gateway, sometimes referred to as the router port. Routers provide a method of forwarding requests between different networks. The default gateway is a local connection point on the network that provides a shuttle service of the packet to another network where it can continue on to the requested host.

Packet Communication

The actual packet communication between machines is done at the MAC layer and requires the software to resolve the IP address to a MAC ID. This is accomplished with the Address Resolution Protocol (ARP) request.

To communicate with another machine, you need its MAC address. In most protocols, you associate a name with the node or the IP address number. This requires translation from the name or IP address to the MAC address of the remote host. The TCP/IP software can also use a broadcast method to locate the MAC address associated with the remote host, but only if the address is on the same local area network.

Accessing Another Host

To access another host, you need to know its IP address or host name. As the number of network addresses increased, there were more and more IP addresses and host names to remember. Thus the need developed for automated name resolution.

For example, rather than have you remember the IP address of the host corpHQftp, you can use the host name:

```
User command                    After name resolution
telnet  corpHQftp               telnet 230.54.36.78
ping                            ping xxx.yyy.zzz.ccc
```

One of the first TCP/IP name resolution systems was the HOSTS file.

The HOSTS File as Name Resolver

Within a TCP/IP network, each host has at least one host name and one or more IP addresses assigned to each network connection. When a user wants to telnet or ftp to another host, the other host is usually referred to by name. This remote request requires that the system resolve the specified host name to an IP address.

Host Names

Most workstations have just one network connection and one host name. However, you can have more names if desired. Some servers provide many services for many networks and hence require multiple IP addresses, at least one for each port. Optionally, a server may provide more than one network service and each service may have a name associated with it, such as FTP and WWW.

In early TCP/IP networks, all known host names and their associated IP addresses were stored in a simple text file called *hosts*. In most UNIX installations, the HOSTS file is located in the /etc directory and is also commonly referred to as /etc/hosts.

The HOSTS file contained one line for each IP address and at least one associated name. The HOSTS file design allowed for multiple names for the same IP address, all on one line. Shown next is an example of some HOSTS files.

```
206.197.150.11      bigsun      BIGSUN      ftp       www
206.197.150.51      host51      HOST51      jan
206.197.150.52      host52      HOST52      shamir
206.197.150.53      host53      HOST53      diane
206.197.150.54      host54      HOST54      ray
206.197.150.55      host55      HOST55      pat
```

The HOSTS file provides a static lookup of a host name for the associated IP address. Notice also that the HOSTS file is flexible, in that multiple names can be associated with one IP address. In the first line of the previous example, there are four names associated with the one IP address on the left. This allows a network user the option of using bigsun, BIGSUN, ftp, or www as reference host names to reach the machine with the IP address 206.197.150.11.

To describe the design and functionality of DNS, our example will be the largest public network in the world, namely the Internet.

Sharing the HOSTS File

Each isolated TCP/IP network has to maintain its own HOSTS file and make it available, by some copy method, to every other host on the network. In a small network of, say, less than a hundred, this can be managed centrally by paper and pencil. This design becomes cumbersome if the network is larger than a few hundred. You could not change a host name or IP address without updating the HOSTS file on every other host in the network.

Limitation of HOSTS File

As networks became more and more complex, not only topologically and geographically, there was a corresponding need to simplify name resolution. In small offices, a host name might reflect the name of the user; the server may reflect the name of the company. But when there are hundreds of servers, spread out in many office locations, and thousands of users pressing the need for central management, the HOSTS file system revealed its limitations.

Internet Growth

As the Internet grew, every time a host was added, every other machine had to add that name to its host file. When this became too cumbersome, the host files were trimmed down to directly reachable hosts. These hosts would then pass the requests on, if they were not destined locally, to the remote hosts of all the other networks that could possibly get the packet to the eventual host. This was like a drop on water, creating a wave of packets heading out in all directions from the server. Since some hosts knew about others who knew about them, the packets sometimes ended up in a circle, routing. This routing loop was controlled with a Time To Live (TTL) value included in each packet.

Example of Selective Entries in a HOSTS File

For example, at a university connected to the Internet, the local administrator would keep a central HOSTS file that would be propagated out to all other hosts. This file would contain all local host IP addresses as well as some well known or often-used remote network addresses of other schools or government resources needed by the local users. Imagine if they tried to keep a file of every known network address. Now imagine having to coordinate this with thousands of schools.

In the imaginary set of university names in Figure 10-1, the campus referred to as und has a HOSTS file that contains all the local hosts and additionally all important hosts from some selected other campuses: unc, ubc, usc, umd, ufs, unv, and udc. This same scenario is repeated at every other campus shown.

How would a user on a host at the umm campus connect to the ftp server at und, if the host IP is not in the local HOSTS file and is generally unknown? Each host in the list can resolve to the next host. The user could connect to a host in uma, from there connect to uws, from there connect to umd, and from there get to the ftp site on und. The point of this example is that there are tens of thousands of possible connections and the administrators cannot keep track of every other host in their HOSTS file.

NIS

An early implementation of distributing a set of system files was called Yellow Pages. This service is now called Network Information Services (NIS). NIS provides a centrally managed file distribution system for mainly UNIX based hosts, although there are versions of NIS for other platforms.

NIS had a master domain server, much like the Primary Domain Controller in NT, that maintained the master copy of the files. All other hosts got a local read-only copy. As you can imagine, these networks grew to thousands of users and hosts, and the distribution of one or more very large files became cumbersome and network-intensive.

HOSTS File Too Large!

The HOSTS file remained the only central location for host name resolution until it became apparent that this centralized management was too inefficient and error-prone with such a large community of networks. However, it is still effective in smaller networks.

Imaginary Internet of campuses example

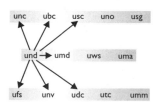

Sequential Search vs. Indexed Search

The HOSTS file is simply a long flat file of single-line entries. Each entry represents one IP address and one or more names. Every search of this file starts at the beginning and reads every record until one is matched (or not matched).

The DNS hierarchy is patterned after the file system with smaller, better organized groups. Using directories or folders allowed for easy expansion and no limits to the design. Rather than one big file, records were grouped into common zones of management, something like the groups of files or folders that are the current standard in many file systems like FAT, HPFS, and NTFS.

Introducing DNS

DNS distributes the information in a standardized hierarchical structure that provides an indexed search path rather than a sequential search of one large file. DNS uses a sequential set of records in data files containing various types of records. Each record represents one host name, one IP address, and the type of record. Some record types allow for more information. This record design allowed for flexibility and extensibility.

Domain Names in a Nutshell

A DNS record consists of a name, record type, and an IP address. A set of these records can be associated with a grouping called a *domain*. The Fully Qualified Domain Name (FQDN) is the name of the host suffixed by a period, followed by the domain name.

For example, the ftp server in the domain mycomp.com would have an FQDN of ftp.mycomp.com. If the IP address is 12.34.56.78, then the DNS record would consist of the FQDN, the IP address, and a record type, in this case an address record type of A:

```
A   12.34.56.78
```

Each local database maintains one or more records for a host name and an associated IP address. This adds the flexibility of duplicate names for the same IP address.

As an additional feature, there can also be secondary servers with read-only copies of the database from the primary server.

DNS is not a dynamic service like WINS or DHCP.

CERTIFICATION OBJECTIVE 10.02

DNS Architecture

DNS is a system of interconnected data files representing local host names and their IP addresses. The design provides a well defined hierarchical structure that provides a local name resolution service or the service passes the request up the hierarchical tree. The structured combination of these smaller data files provides the entire set of names of all registered host machines on the network.

All the host names are grouped into smaller, locally managed databases. Each of these databases knows about the parent servers above them, called *root servers*.

The most popular implementation of the DNS protocol was developed at the University of California at Berkeley, and is appropriately called Berkeley Internet Name Domain (BIND). The specifications for DNS are defined in RFCs 974, 1034, and 1035.

Figure 10-2 shows the three basic levels of DNS. The root servers are named A, B, C, etc. The top-level domains are .com, .edu, .gov, and there are many more.

FIGURE 10-2

Selected DNS hierarchical structure from the Internet

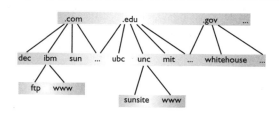

There is a file supplied with the DNS installation that contains a few records for some of the common root servers. The file and path is:

%systemroot%\system32\DNS\samples\cache

The second level or layer represents the distributed DNS servers for each zone. Each zone maintains its own set of local host records. For instance, the ibm.com domain shows the host and the host names. These are just the registered host records and may or may not be separate physical machines. These records are maintained on the DNS server that manages the ibm.com zone.

DNS SERVER LOCATION   The DNS server and the domain are not necessarily one machine. A DNS server may support multiple domains or zones. The DNS hierarchy is just the structure of how the data is supported. The actual DNS server machine is not indicated within the DNS hierarchy. Any machine could provide this DNS domain service for one or more zones.

DNS SEARCH PATTERN   This hierarchical design for DNS provides an indexed search pattern that does not require looking at every host record. Each domain or zone database has records that point to at least the named root server and possibly other root servers. The local server provides an indexed search of its cached records or its database of records and passes the request up the hierarchy only if needed.

Root Domains

Root domains represent the upper indexed pointers to other DNS servers.

.COM   This is the commercial organizations group and is by far the largest group. Almost everyone wants to be here because it is the first default extension for all commercial organizations like DEC, SUN, IBM, Microsoft, etc.

.ORG   This is for non-commercial organizations.

.NET   This is for networking organizations like island.net, nfs.net, and Internet Service Providers like tiac.net.

.MIL   This is for military organizations like army.mil and navy.mil.

.GOV   This is for the government offices of the U.S. only.

.COUNTRIES' DOMAIN NAMES   The Internet started in the U.S. and as such, the organizations normally are located in this country. For the rest of the world, there are country servers based on a two- or three-letter shortcut. Every country has one, including the U.S.

- Canada has the .ca root domain.
- United Kingdom uses .uk.
- Ireland uses .ie.
- U.S. uses .us.

Top–Level Domain Servers

The root servers are used to route the request to the next correct server, as shown in Figure 10-3.

The root server for Canada, .ca, has another root server or subdomain for each province. A provincial server may or may not have further nested subdomain servers, as required. In other countries, the root servers may have city-based nested subdomains.

Within the .us and .ca root servers are another set of servers for each state / province / region and from there possibly many cities. For example, dallas.tx.us for Dallas, Texas and vancouver.bc.ca for Vancouver, British Columbia,

FIGURE 10-3

Selected top-level servers around the world

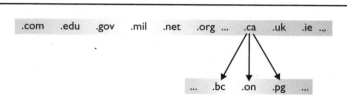

Canada. These are just the domain names. The host names append to these like an information center. For example, the city of Vancouver in British Columbia, Canada could be reached with info.vancouver.bc.ca or www.vancouver.bc.ca. Normally, DNS names are displayed in lowercase. However, most DNS services are not case sensitive.

There are many root servers, but the .com server is by far the largest and most overloaded. The other root servers offer local access with faster response for local users and make it easier to get a domain name that is not already used by another DNS service.

Root Servers

The root servers provide addresses to the domain servers associated with that root. For example, the .com root server maintains IP address pointer records for all the *name*.com DNS servers. In turn, each of these *name*.com domains contains records for all of their local machines only. The root DNS database is maintained locally by a specific authority.

The .com root server knows the .edu, .mil, and all the other root server addresses. When a host name request comes in to a root server, it simply looks at the root portion of the name and passes the name off to this root server. This second root server would then look up the domain name in its database and send the packet on to that specific domain name service. This specific domain name would then provide an answer or an error if nothing was found.

In Figure 10-4, the arg.com server maintains the DNS database of records for its local machines, in this case classroom, sugar, ftp, and www. These are four of possibly hundreds of records. The IP addresses they represent may or

FIGURE 10-4

Domain name structure from selected root servers

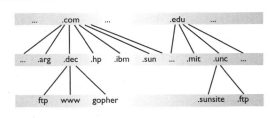

may not be different from one another; these are just names in the database. All four host names could be the same or different servers.

Resolving Host and Domain Names

When a program requests a host by a single name, like sunsite, the network protocol has a sequence of steps to resolve the name. If the client is DNS-aware, then the DNS service request will append the local domain name to the end of the requested host name and try to resolve this within its database. If this first domain name fails and there are other suffix names configured within DNS, then the name will be appended to each of them successively and tried within the specified DNS service again.

If a Fully Qualified Domain Name (FQDN) is supplied, then the DNS service is queried directly first.

DNS Request Sequence Example

Let's say a host named classroom.arg.com wants to reach sunsite.unc.edu (see Figure 10-5). This will generate many smaller requests. The first request goes to the local DNS server for arg.com. The host named classroom must have the address of this DNS server already configured in the TCP/IP Protocol information.

FIGURE 10-5

DNS resolving process

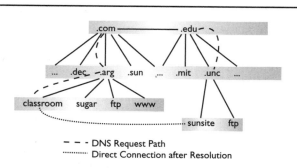

Primary DNS Server

The primary DNS server for arg.com first tries to resolve the request locally by checking its own records. The DNS server may have more than one zone database and the TCP/IP protocol properties for alternate suffix search names would have to reflect these alternate domain names.

Some specialized servers are configured to maintain a cache of previous hits so that common requests may not have to repeat the longer full-request process.

Search DNS Servers

If the local DNS server could not provide an address resolution, then it passes the request "up the ladder" to the .com server, which looks in its local databases. If it does not find the IP address for the host, it passes the record on to the root server of the remote host name, in this case, the .edu root server.

Return to Resolver

The .edu server passes the request on to the unc.edu DNS zone server, which hopefully has the IP address. The found IP address then passes back through the same chain to the original host. At this point, the original host is finally able to send packets directly to the remote host.

DNS Files

All DNS information that is maintained in the registry can also be maintained in text file format, if you select Update Data Files from the DNS Menu of DNS Manager. If you are using files from a UNIX BIND version of DNS, you can force the DNS server to not read the registry and just use the files ported over from UNIX. Be aware that the UNIX BIND files may contain some commands that NT DNS will not understand.

The files are located in:

```
%systemroot%\system32\DNS
```

After installation, this directory contains the files boot and CACHE.DNS as well as the directory SAMPLES.

CACHE   The cache is used for additional name resolution. The cache file contains Name Server (NS) type records for additional name servers. This file can be updated from a central file maintained by the Internic (www.internic.net).

The cache file needs to point to other Internet related sites only if you are joining the Internet. If you are just creating your own intranet, then you should change the entries in this file to reflect your own root domain servers.

REVERSE LOOKUP   In most cases, users request a host by name. This results in what is a *forward lookup*. A remote server gets a packet with the source and destination IP addresses. If the server needs to look up the name of the original source machine, then it sends a request for the host name based on a given IP, the one supplied in the packet received. This is referred to as a *reverse lookup request*.

To handle reverse lookup requests, a special database, in-addr.arpa, is created for the reverse lookup records. We'll discuss reverse lookups in more detail later in this chapter.

CERTIFICATION OBJECTIVE 10.03

Installing and Configuring DNS Servers

This section will take you through the steps for installing the DNS service and give you some important secondary information that may be required by some sites.

Preparing the Server for Installation

Your server must already be using TCP/IP and the IP address must be static. You can use DHCP but the IP address would have to be a fixed reservation.

You need to know the IP addresses of any other DNS servers that will be installed as primary or secondary servers and the domain names of the authority they will be servicing.

Installing the Service

From Control Panel go to Network Applet to begin the installation process.

1. Double-click Network Icon to bring up the Network Settings Control Screen.

2. Click the Services tab. This will display the Services panel and all currently installed services. The Add button can be used to add another service such as Microsoft DNS Service.

3. Click the Add button to add another service.

4. After a few seconds, the Select Network Service display appears. Click Microsoft DNS Server to select it and then click the OK button to start the installation.

5. A Windows NT Setup captioned input control prompts you for the location of the files if it has changed from when you first installed NT.

During the installation of NT 4.0, the system stores the location of the installation files in the registry. Every time you add another service or update a service, the system will want to verify that the location of the installation files has not changed. Make sure the location is correct and then click Continue.

A display box indicating progress appears for a short time while files are copied to your machine.

Your Services panel now shows the service installed. At this point you have completed the installation of the actual service files for DNS. The network bindings still need to be determined and then a reboot is required.

EXERCISE 10-1

Client DNS Configuration Parameters

This exercise assumes that this is a first-time setup of a client to use your DNS Service, and that you will be using the 'mycomp.com' domain. You must know the IP address of your machine where DNS is installed for this domain.

1. Start the Network applet in Control Panel.

2. Click the Protocols panel.

3. Click TCP/IP and then select Properties.

4. Click DNS.

5. In the Domain box enter **mycomp.com.**
6. Click the Add button to add the IP address of your DNS server.

Additional TCP/IP Setup for DNS

Before rebooting, there is some further installation required to finish the DNS setup. You need to configure your TCP/IP protocol settings to point to the DNS service and to indicate the domain name that this DNS service provides.

Still within the Network applet of Control Panel, go to the Protocols panel and click TCP/IP protocol.

You need to click the Properties button to get the Microsoft TCP/IP Properties panel. The TCP/IP Properties setup window has five panels. A sample DNS panel with some input values entered is shown in Figure 10-6.

Click the DNS tab at the top of the TCP/IP Properties Control sheet to get to the DNS setup panel.

DNS CLIENT SETUP   If you are a client only of the DNS service, you would need to enter the domain name and the IP address of the DNS service. Click the Domain box and enter your domain name, as in arg.com shown in Figure 10-6. You also need to enter the IP address of this service in the DNS Service Search Order table. These are the minimum requirements to be a client of a DNS service.

DNS CLIENT SETUP WITH SECONDARY SERVER   A secondary DNS server is a backup server with a copy of the zone information from the master server. If there is one or more Secondary DNS servers for this domain, you would enter one or more additional IP addresses in the DNS Service Search Order table of entries the same way you add the primary DNS server IP address. Click the Add button within this area.

The DNS Service Search Order is a fail-over list, not an additional location. Only if the first one fails to respond after a nominal timeout period is the next DNS server service list tried with the same request, and so on. These secondary servers must have a valid domain zone file for this to work.

FIGURE 10-6

DNS setup panel in TCP/IP Properties Input Control window

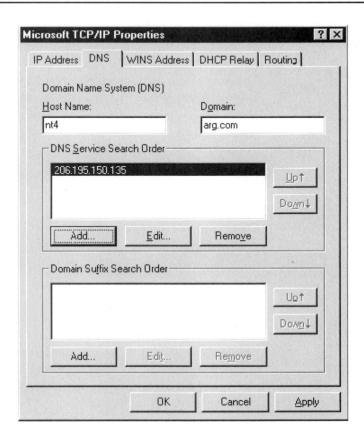

exam
ⓦatch

There are two Add buttons on this panel; the lower one is used to add additional suffix names. The upper one adds the IP address of your primary server.

DNS Server Setup

Even though the machine is the DNS server, you still need to establish your domain name and IP address information here for this machine to use DNS.

The NetBIOS name of your machine becomes the host name equivalent. Although you can change this to anything, it is not recommended; DNS can do that for you with multiple name entries.

The host name for a machine defaults to the NetBIOS name as originally configured during installation.

DNS DOMAINS AND THE INTERNET The Internet is an established network. If you are joining the Internet, you will have to check that the domain name you want to use is not already in use. This can be done through InterNIC at www.internic.org.

DNS Server Domain Setup

You need to add the domain name that represents the data being managed by this DNS and the IP address for the DNS service.

In our example the arg.com domain is being managed. The IP address of the server managing arg.com is 206.195.150.135, the same IP address as the current host.

This is the minimum basic installation for both the client and the server as client to use DNS. You need a host name, domain name, and the IP address of the DNS primary server for this domain. Optionally you can add secondary server IP addresses and alternate suffix search orders, additional domains, and subdomains managed at the same server.

Adding to the Domain Suffix Search Order

If your DNS service will be splitting up the domain information into subdomains like sales.arg.com, mis.arg.com, and staff.arg.com, then you need to add these additional domain suffixes to this list. The request for a single host name with no domain qualification, no periods in the name, will iterate through the main domain suffix and then try each of these additional suffixes to try to resolve the name to an IP address.

To add each additional domain suffix to the list, click the lower Add button in the DNS setup panel. Enter each path with the full domain name structure.

No leading period is required; the period will be supplied when the suffix is appended after the host name. Figure 10-7 illustrates the additional three Domain Suffix Search Order entries.

Example Network

The domain and server names shown in the next table were used in the figures throughout this chapter.

FIGURE 10-7

Client setup panel with additional Domain Suffix Search Order entries

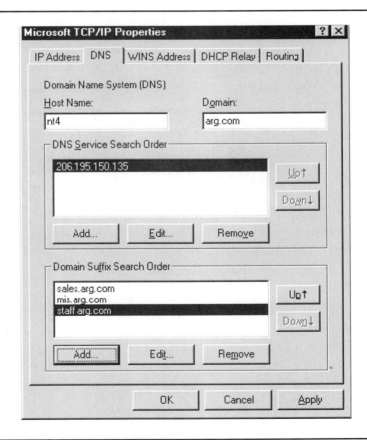

For example, the arg.com zone data may be subdomained as follows:

Subdomain	Hosts FQDN in Subdomain
sales.arg.com	NT01SSvr.sales.arg.com, (.140)
	PC141S.sales.arg.com, PC142S.sales.arg.com
	PC143S.sales.arg.com, PC144S.sales.arg.com
staff.arg.com	NT02TSvr.staff.arg.com, (.150)
	PC151T.staff.arg.com, PC152T.staff.arg.com
	PC153T.staff.arg.com, PC154T.staff.arg.com
	PC155T.staff.arg.com, PC156T.staff.arg.com
mis.arg.com	NT03MSvr.mis.arg.com, (.160)
	PC161M.staff.arg.com, PC162M.staff.arg.com
	PC163M.staff.arg.com, PC164M.staff.arg.com

Add Domain Suffix

The input display to add domain suffixes has an input box called Domain Suffix. Enter each suffix and click the Add button for each one. You should order these suffixes by "most often used" to "least often used" as they are sequentially checked.

After all subdomains are added, the DNS panel looks like Figure 10-7.

Click the OK button of the DNS panel to finish setup.

You are returned to the Network Applet - Protocols Panel. Click Close to complete the installation.

The bindings screens will flash across the screen showing a progress bar as each binding set is completed. A *binding* is the list of protocol layer pieces, the path a request might possibly take through all the layers of the network software, starting from the requesting interface software and ending at the MAC layer interfaces.

Finally, you are asked to reboot. Click Yes to reboot.

At this point, the installation of the DNS server is complete. After the reboot, you will need to start up the DNS manager so that you can add your zone or zones and sub-zones, and to add records to the various zones as needed.

Installing DNS Service on the DNS Server

Install the DNS Service from the Network Services panel in Network Applet of Control Panel.

1. Start the Network applet in Control Panel.

2. Click the Services panel.

3. Click Add to add a service.

4. Click DNS Service and then click OK.

5. If the location for the NT 4.0 files is incorrect or has changed, then enter the correct path.

6. Click OK and then close. The network bindings will be re-established.

7. Click OK to reboot the machine.

CERTIFICATION OBJECTIVE 10.04

Adding Primary Domain Zones

The first database needed is the Primary Zone for your domain. The database represents the records that are managed at this zone of authority. The zone represents the database query object that responds to the Domain name queries. The domain name is something like arg.com or 2dt.com. These are the domains that are referred to as *zones of authority*.

Start the DNS Manager Utility

You can start the DNS Manager utility from the Administrative Tools Menu as follows:

Start | Programs | Administrative Tools | DNS Manager

When the Domain Name Service Manager screen appears, the only icon in the display is a Globe with the caption Server List to the right of it. This will always appear in every view of the DNS Manager.

You need to point the manager at a DNS server, including the one on the local machine, by IP address.

Add a New Server

To add a new server, you click the New Server option on the DNS menu. You are prompted for the name or IP address of the DNS server to add to the list.

For example, to add the server at IP address 206.195.150.135, enter this IP address in the DNS Server input box and click OK.

This should bring up a running service if the DNS installation worked correctly.

EXERCISE 10-3

Configuring DNS with DNS Manager

1. Start the DNS Manager by going to:

   Start | Programs | Administrative Tools | DNS

2. Click the DNS menu and the first option, New Server. Enter the host IP address.

This should bring up the IP address to represent the DNS service and a cache service.

Creating a Primary Zone

You must click the IP address of the DNS service first. The options on the DNS service are related to the object. Alternatively, using the second mouse button will bring up the content menu for the server and you can select the New Zone option. Using the secondary mouse button bring up the content menu and select New Zone.

This menu will use the Create Zone Wizard to add a New Zone database.

This first wizard screen allows you to create either a primary or secondary zone. A primary zone has local unique records making the primary or master source of a zone. A secondary zone is an alternate copy of the same zone data information located on another DNS server. It acts as a backup service to the primary. There does not need to be a secondary server but there can be one or more secondary servers for any zone. However, to provide a DNS service on the Internet, you must provide at least one secondary DNS server service for the domain you manage. This is a requirement of joining and hosting a DNS service on the Internet.

In the second screen, you enter the name of the domain you want to create. Assuming you are joining the Internet and you have decided to create the local zone called 2dt under the .com root server, you would enter **2dt.com** as the zone name.

If you press the TAB key to get to the next field, the wizard automatically enters the normal data file name which is a suffix of '.dns' added to the original zone name, in this case 2dt.com.dns as shown in Figure 10-8.

Click the next button to continue creating this zone. The zone data file will be created in the following directory with the name entered in the screen shown in Figure 10-8:

%systemroot%\system32\DNS

FIGURE 10-8

Zone name and associated data file name for a primary zone

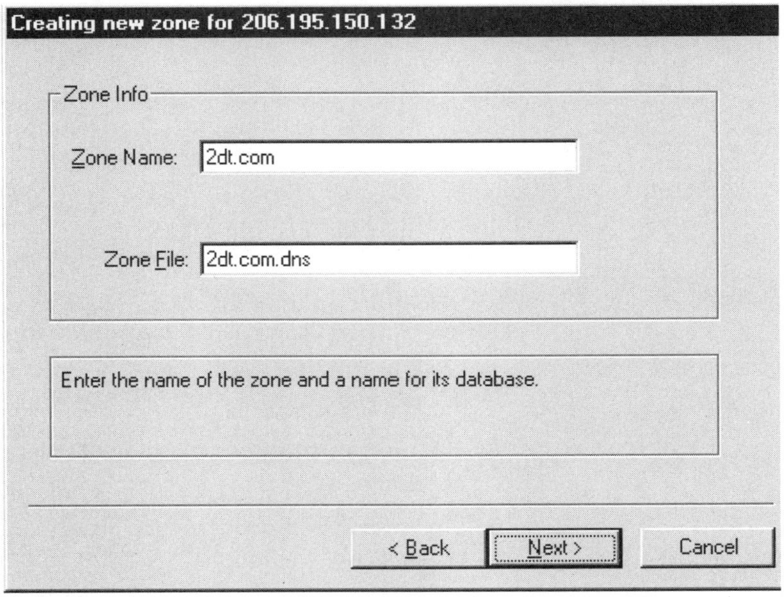

Creating new zone for 206.195.150.132

Zone Info

Zone Name: 2dt.com

Zone File: 2dt.com.dns

Enter the name of the zone and a name for its database.

< Back   Next >   Cancel

The directory listing will look something like this after creating the zone 2dt.com and the data file would be 2dt.com.dns:

```
==================== From Command Prompt====================
C:\SVR\system32\DNS > dir
 Volume in drive C has no label.
 Volume Serial Number is A447-C2B2

 Directory of C:\SVR\system32\DNS

01/30/98  11:41a        <DIR>          .
01/30/98  11:41a        <DIR>          ..
01/30/98  11:41a                   532 2dt.com.dns
01/30/98  11:41a        <DIR>          backup
01/30/98  11:41a                   754 boot
08/08/96  09:30p                 2,144 CACHE.DNS
01/30/98  11:41a                   851 in-addr.arpa.dns
01/30/98  07:54a        <DIR>          SAMPLES
                8 File(s)          4,281 bytes
                            316,315,136 bytes free
================== From Command Prompt ==================
```

The last wizard screen simply allows you to either finish and create the zone, cancel creation of the zone, or go back and make changes. Use the Back button on any of the previous screens to make changes.

EXERCISE 10-4

Creating Primary Zone File

Create the Primary Zone mycomp.com. on the host 213.88.77.16.

1. Start the DNS Manager by going to Start | Programs | Administrative Tools | DNS Manager.

2. If no server is listed, click the DNS Menu and click New Server. Enter server IP address.

3. Click the IP address object displayed in DNS Manager, then click DNS menu, New Zone.

4. The Creating New Zone for 213.88.77.16 Network appears.

5. Select Primary, then click Next.

6. Enter **mycorp.com** in the Zone Name input field and press TAB to go to the next field.

7. Take the default name provided, mycorp.com.dns; click Next.

8. Click the Finish button to create the zone.

Adding Reverse Lookup Zones

The primary zone also requires a reverse address zone to store reverse order records, called *PTR records*. These records provide host names for a given IP address. The order is reversed so the search mechanism remains the same.

Every DNS server requires the special reverse lookup zone. The name of this zone is in-addr.arpa or z.y.x.in-addr.arpa for a single zone server representing the x.y.z network. The network number order is reversed.

Create Associated PTR Record

The reverse lookup zone contains an additional record for each registered host record in all locally managed zones. During the creation of the host records, the wizard will create a regular host to IP record in the domain zone and can also create one reverse lookup record in the reverse lookup database. Click on the box to create the Associated PTR Record for automatic record creation. This box appears in both the Add Host and Add Record input screens.

Reverse Lookup Zone Record

A reverse lookup record has the fields in a different order; the IP address is first, then the pointer type, usually PTR, and then the host name.

A normal host record for zone domain.com would look like this:

```
www      A      x.y.z.n
```

The corresponding reverse lookup record would look like this:

```
x.y.z.n      PTR      www.domain.com
```

Default Reverse Lookup Zone Name

There is only one reverse lookup zone needed for all zones managed by the local service. By using the default name of in-addr.arpa all zones can create reverse lookup records there.

If you want to keep them separate, then you need to follow the standard naming convention of reversing the network number in dotted notation followed by in-addr.arpa.

Separate Reverse Lookup Zone Naming Convention

To separate the reverse lookup zones, you need to name these zones according to their IP network number. For instance, if you are creating zones for corp1.com and corp2.com and their IP network addresses are 199.72.26.0 and 199.72.45.0 respectively, then the reverse lookup zones would be named as follows:

Zone	Network IP	Reverse Database Name
corp1.com	199.72.26.0	26.72.199.in-addr.arpa
corp2.com	199.72.45.0	45.72.199.in-addr.arpa

Create Reverse Lookup Zone

You create the reverse lookup zone file as a primary type zone as illustrated previously.

The second wizard screen (see Figure 10-9) asks for the zone name; in this case enter **in-addr.arpa** as the general default reverse lookup zone name. You could be more specific and use the reversed network number prefix if so desired.

You complete reverse lookup zone information as previously explained. Simply press the TAB key to get to the next field. The wizard will fill in the file name automatically for you. You can change this name if you wish but it is not necessary. Click Next and then the Finish button on the last screen to complete the zone creation.

DNS Data in Registry of NT

In a conventional UNIX version of DNS, all of this information is maintained in local text-based data files. You can have the DNS Manager write this data

FIGURE 10-9

Reverse lookup zone and
data file creation

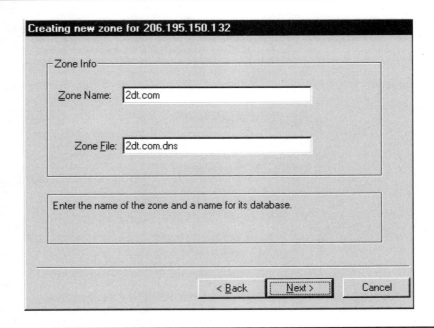

```
Creating new zone for 206.195.150.132

  ┌─Zone Info──────────────────────────────────────────
  │
  │    Zone Name:  │2dt.com                          │
  │
  │
  │    Zone File:  │2dt.com.dns                      │
  │
  └────────────────────────────────────────────────────

  ┌────────────────────────────────────────────────────
  │  Enter the name of the zone and a name for its database.
  │
  └────────────────────────────────────────────────────


                    [ < Back ]  [  Next >  ]   [ Cancel ]
```

into data file format as a precaution or as a means of transferring the data to
another server at a later time.

To write the data to local disk files in the normal DNS directory, from
the DNS Manager, click the DNS Menu item and then click Update Server
Data Files.

Creating Reverse Lookup Primary Zone File

Create the in-addr.arpa zone for mycomp.com on the host 213.88.77.16.

1. Start the DNS Manager by going to Start | Programs | Administrative
   Tools | DNS Manager.

2. If no server is listed, click the DNS Menu and click New Server. Enter
   server IP address. The IP address should be 213.88.77.16 for this
   exercise.

3. Click the IP address object displayed in DNS Manager, then click DNS
   menu, New Zone.

4. The Creating New Zone for 213.88.77.16 Network appears.

5. Select Primary, then click Next.

6. Enter **in-addr.arpa** in the Zone Name input field and press TAB to go to next field.

7. Take the default name provided, in-addr.arpa.dns, and click Next.

8. Click the Finish button to create the zone.

Creating a Domain or Sub-Zone

You can also select the zone and then add a sub-zone (or domain as it is called here). To add a domain (sub-zone) click the DNS Menu option and then click Add Domain.

The input screen simply asks for the domain name, subdomain. Enter in the name desired and click the OK button. You do not need a fully qualified name entered here.

This adds a nested domain to the main zone file, and looks like a subdirector of the zone directory.

In Figure 10-10, three subdomains were added to the arg.com zone called mis, sales, and staff.

Figure 10-10 shows a basic installation of a single zone with three sub-zone domains. All of this information is maintained in the same zone database.

After adding a few records to each subdomain, the data files look like Figure 10-11.

Updating Server Data Files

All information added through the DNS Manager is stored in the registry of NT 4.0.

Make sure that you update the data files from the registry. Select Update Server Data Files from the DNS Menu Options.

Your DNS server is now ready to be tested before going into production. You should test at each step of the installation to ensure proper functioning. You can test the data using the nslookup utility, detailed later in this chapter. The nslookup utility is supplied with the TCP/IP protocol installation on NT 4.0. An actual application to test your DNS service would be the telnet service to a multiuser host like a UNIX host and/or try the ping utility to connect via an FQDN to a registered host.

FIGURE 10-10

DNS Manager showing
sub-domains to main zone
and reverse lookup
sub-domains with PTR
records

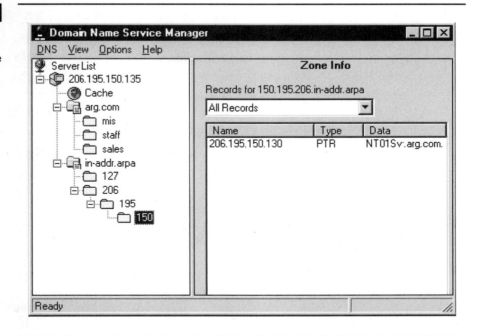

FIGURE 10-11

Subdomain host address
records and subdomains of
in-addr.arpa zone

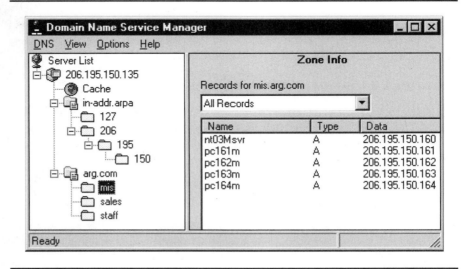

Configure Client for Secondary Name Server

To allow any DNS client to use a backup or secondary server, you need to add the alternate server IP address or addresses to the DNS setup of TCP/IP.

From the Network Icon in Control Panel, click on the DNS panel.

In the section marked DNS Server Search Order, click the Add button to add each secondary server in the order of precedence. Precedence may be given to the closest server or the one with the most reliable network access path to it.

This does not preclude this machine from being a secondary server to another zone.

CERTIFICATION OBJECTIVE 10.06

Connecting DNS to Other DNS Servers

The DNS Manager Utility can manage a local or remote server(s) or just remote servers. You do not have to set up a domain locally. You can use DNS Manager to manage other servers on the network.

Although it would be a nice feature to work with all DNS servers, the DNS Manager Utility is capable of managing only another NT 4.0 DNS service. Like many UNIX flavors, their DNS services may be proprietary, as is this NT 4.0 version.

Connect to Another New Server

To add management of another server service you must input the IP address of the new server. If your credentials are accepted, you will be able to manage the other server as if it were local from the DNS Manager Utility.

Add Another Server Service to Manage

Select New Server from the DNS Menu and enter the IP address of the other machine in the input box (see Figure 10-12). Click OK when done.

The DNS manager will then try to connect to that service's IP address. If this is on a remote network, it may take some time. A red question mark will

FIGURE 10-12

Add DNS Server - Additional Service to Manage

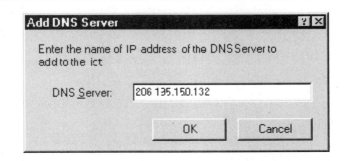

appear during the query. A red X will appear on the server icon if the service is not reachable.

CERTIFICATION OBJECTIVE 10.07

Adding Records to Zones

You can use the DNS Manager Utility to add records to either a primary or a secondary zone. The only difference is that the record is stored permanently only in the primary zone.

Zone Records

A basic record in a DNS zone file is one host name, one IP address, and a record type. There are many record types for things like mail and other services that are not discussed here. The basic record type used is the address record denoted by an "A" in the data file and a reverse lookup record type denoted by "PTR" in the reverse lookup data file of the zone.

Creating DNS Records

There are many ways to create records depending on the object chosen in the DNS Manager. You must click a zone (domain name) to add records. You can right-click this object to get a menu specific to the zone or you can select the DNS menu item.

When you create a record, you have the option to create the reverse record at the same time through either of the input screens.

Two Different Formats for Creating Records

There are two different formats to add records to a zone file. The simple format is called New Host, which allows you to simply enter a host name and the associated IP address. This creates a standard address or A type record. This format also allows for automatic creation of the Associated (Reverse) Pointer Record.

The other format type, New Resource Record, allows for all types of records to be added to the zone file.

New Host Format

The simplest way to add new records to any zone is to click the zone name in the DNS Manager, then click the DNS Menu and select the New Host option. Alternatively, you could right-click the zone name in DNS Manager and a menu will pop up with similar options.

The simple format for New Host is displayed in Figure 10-13. This is one way to add a host entry as an A type record. Make sure the Create Associated PTR Record box is selected before clicking the OK button. This will create the reverse lookup record for this file in the in-addr.arpa or z.y.x.in-addr.arpa file, whichever is present. If one of these files is not present or incorrectly named, then an error message will appear indicating this reverse lookup record did not get created. You can create it using the New Resource Record format later if desired.

Figure 10-13 shows an entry for the www.2dt.com host. This is an incorrect entry. The proper entry would not contain any period characters, which imply some or all of the domain name itself.

You will get an error message if your entry is incorrect because it contains some or all of the domain name. You need to add only the host part of the name; the rest is implied by the zone itself.

FIGURE 10-13

Correct and incorrect
entries

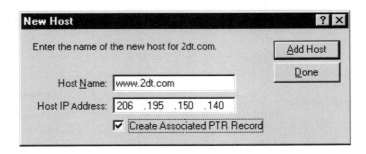

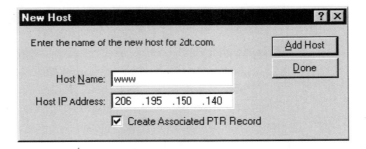

The error message would read:

The 'Host Name' field can not contain any '.' characters.

The host name is always relative to the currently selected domain. The host name will be combined with the domain to form the fully qualified domain name for this record.

Click the OK button.

A correct entry would look like the second screenshot in Figure 10-13 and would add the www host to the 2dt.com zone file and create the associated reverse lookup record.

You can continue to add records from this dialog box as it will clear between each record.

Click the Done button, or press the ESCAPE key, to end input.

New Resource Record Format

To add any type of record, including the default A (Address) record type, you can use the more detailed New Resource Record format. Either right-click the zone name in DNS Manager, or from the DNS drop-down menu select New Record.

The DNS Manager Utility will display the zone information after you are done adding records. The information is in the registry and you may need to refresh the screen using the F5 key.

If you double-click a record line in the right-side panel, you can get an input screen that allows you to make changes to the record, as shown in Figure 10-14.

If you double-click the Delta2 entry, you are presented with a screen similar to the New Record entry shown in Figure 10-15.

Displaying Records - Refresh Screen

All records added in the NT version of DNS are stored in the registry and the DNS Manager may not display the record information after an entry is added. You can refresh the screen at any time by pressing the F5 Function Key. You must click each yellow zone display and press F5 to refresh all displays from all associated registry data.

FIGURE 10-14

DNS Manager with two servers being managed

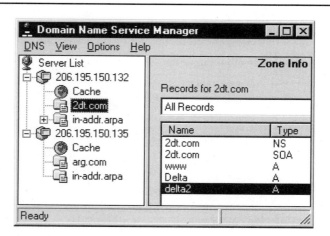

FIGURE 10-15

Record Properties sheet
(Can change only IP
address and enable PTR
record)

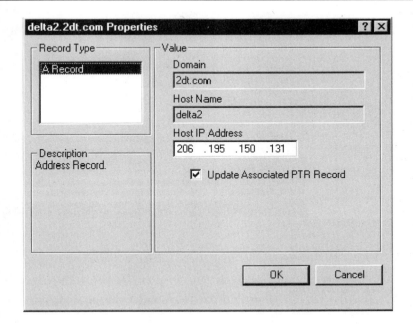

Double-click the zone to check for the record; both zones should be
checked.

The reverse lookup screen will probably need a Refresh from the data so
press F5.

EXERCISE 10-6

Adding a Host Record

Add a record for www with the IP address of 213.88.77.17.

1. Start the DNS Manager.

2. Right-click the zone object. Select New Host from the menu.

3. Enter **www** for the host name. Press TAB.

4. Enter **213.88.77.17** for the host IP address.

5. Enable Create Associated PTR Record by clicking in the associated
   box.

6. Click the Add Host button. Then click Done.

Primary and Secondary Zones in DNS Manager

If you are managing two different primary zones, you can also make each the backup or secondary service provider for the other. In Figure 10-16, there are two zones being managed. You could create the secondary zone for the 2dt.com zone on the other server and vice versa.

The DNS Manager shown in Figure 10-16 has two DNS services. If these servers are within the same company, then they could each also act as backup service to the other server by creating a secondary zone to the primary zone on the other server.

In Figure 10-16, 206.195.150.132 manages the 2dt.com zone and could potentially be the secondary server for arg.com on the 206.195.150.135 server. And conversely, the 206.195.150.135 server could have a secondary service for 2dt.com from 206.195.150.132.

Never hit the delete key on a record in a zone; it may delete the reference to the data file in the registry. You lose *everything* you entered for that zone. The delete action does warn of this impending disaster, but sometimes you may be too quick to hit another OK button, so be careful.

FIGURE 10-16

Two independent zones showing only one primary zone each

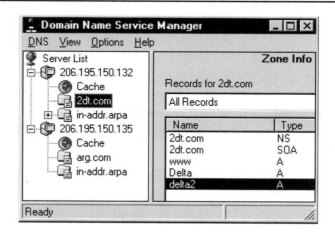

Primary and Secondary Zones in DNS Manager

The secondary zone looks the same in the DNS manager except for the caption in the lower right corner, shown in Figure 10-17. The caption reads Secondary Zone when that zone is highlighted.

Figure 10-17 shows a secondary zone service for the arg.com zone on the 206.195.150.132 server. For clients to use this feature, their TCP/IP Protocol | DNS setups would require a second IP entry in the DNS server list to reflect this backup service for the same domain, arg.com, as indicated earlier in this chapter.

CERTIFICATION OBJECTIVE 10.08

Adding Secondary Zones

The DNS manager can connect to other DNS servers and act as a backup server. This is referred to as a secondary zone within DNS. The secondary zone

FIGURE 10-17

Secondary zone indicated in lower right corner

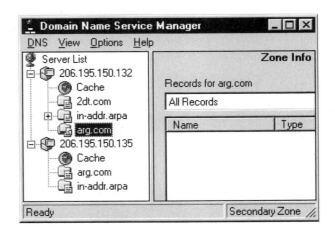

appears the same and is manipulated the same as the primary zone. The only difference is that all changes are made in the primary zone file and then passed along to all secondary zone servers as read-only copies of the data.

To create a secondary zone, the same Creating New Zone Wizard is used from the DNS Menu of the DNS Manager Utility as shown in Figure 10-18.

To create a secondary zone to the other machine, you need to know the name of the zone and the IP address of the host server.

In Figure 10-18, the zone on the other host is called arg.com and the host has an IP address of 206.195.150.135.

Click the Next button when the information is correct.

The secondary zone has a specific file that represents the database of records. You enter the name of the zone and then TAB to the next field. The wizard will enter a default name based on the zone name. If this is incorrect, change the zone filename to the correct one.

Creating a secondary zone

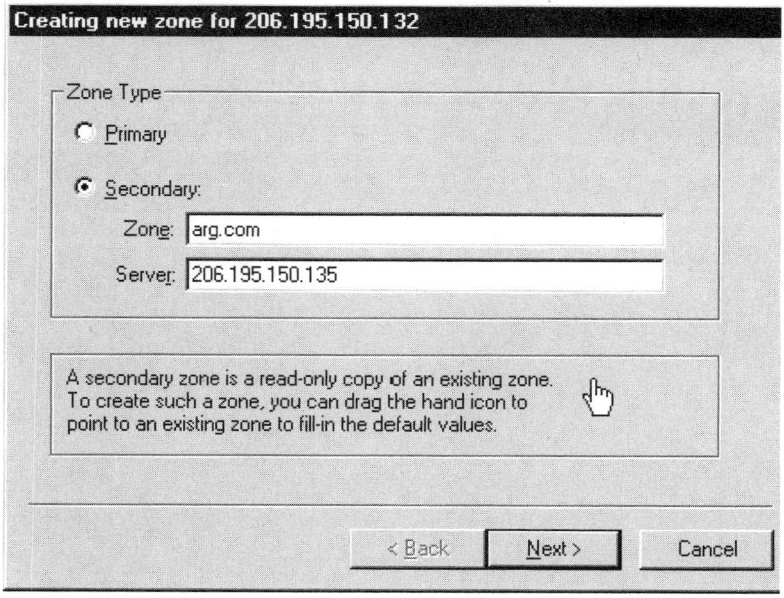

In our example, the zone is called arg.com and the associated data file would be arg.com.dns by default.

Click Next to continue with the setup.

The secondary zone needs an IP master; use the address of the DNS service.

In this case, the IP master is the same IP as the other DNS service, 206.195.150.135.

Click Finish to update the local zone file with the information. This is actually just a record in the zone file that points to the other service.

Creating Secondary Zone File

Attach to the secondary zone file yourcomp.com on the host with IP 213.56.79.23.

1. Start the DNS Manager by going to Start | Programs | Administrative Tools | DNS Manager.

2. If no server is listed, click the DNS Menu and click New Server. Enter server IP address.

3. Click the IP address object displayed in DNS Manager, then click DNS menu, New Zone.

4. The Creating New Zone for 213.88.77.16 Network appears.

5. Select Secondary; then click Next.

6. Enter the name of the zone in the Zone field; type **yourcomp.com**.

7. Tab to the next field. Enter the IP address of the other zone. Type **213.56.79.23**, and click Next.

8. The Zone Name input field defaults to yourcomp.com. Press TAB.

9. The Zone File input field defaults to yourcomp.com.dns. Click Next.

10. The IP Master(s) input panel appears. Enter **213.56.79.23** and click Add.

11. Finally, click Next, and then the Finish button.

DNS DATA FILE FORMAT AND SECONDARY SERVERS

There is a supplied sample boot file that shows the record for a secondary service. This example has been updated with the local information for the sample DNS network used in this chapter.

Managing Multiple Zone Files

The DNS manager can manage any number of DNS services (assuming you are authorized). You can add more DNS servers by clicking the DNS Menu in the DNS Manager and selecting the first option, New Server. You will have to supply a valid username and password for the remote server to get access.

You can add records to the other DNS servers only as the master control, not through the secondary control. The display will show only ghost connections to the secondary service. The zone properties from the secondary server are greyed out as shown in Figure 10-19; you cannot make changes.

To display information about the secondary zone, right-click Secondary Zone and select Properties, as shown in Figure 10-20.

Properties View of a Managed Service

You can view the properties of a managed service from the DNS Menu or right-click the service and select the Properties option. First select the service to be viewed.

The Properties display has four panels: General, SOA (Start Of Authority), Notify, and WINS Lookup.

If you select the Notify panel, you can add additional servers by their IP addresses to be notified in an emergency.

FIGURE 10-19

Cannot update secondary zone

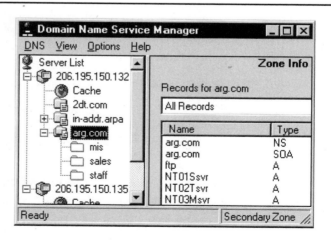

FIGURE 10-20

Zone Properties input sheet

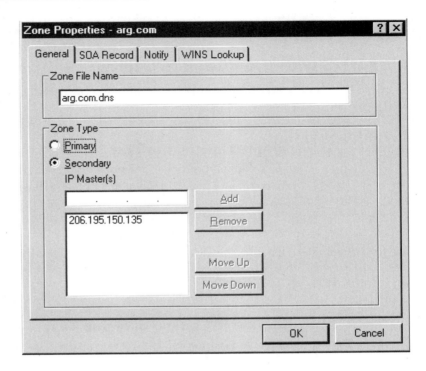

Every DNS zone file contains a first SOA (Start Of Authority) record which includes the name of the keeper of the DNS service. For NT DNS, this is usually the administrator account. Additional information may include a contact phone number.

WINS Lookup from DNS

The last option of the Zone Properties for a given domain allows a last resort search through any configured WINS servers if the DNS searches all fail. Add at least the IP address of the primary WINS server and optionally add any secondary server IP addresses as well.

If the DNS search fails, and WINS Lookup is enabled and a primary WINS server IP is configured properly, then the DNS service will pass the host name only, no domain name suffix, to WINS. If WINS can resolve the name to an IP address, this is passed back to the requesting host.

Testing DNS with the nslookup Utility

At a command prompt, we can test our service using the Name Server Lookup Utility, nslookup.

Simple Host Name Test

The nslookup utility has two operation modes, interactive and single query, at the command line. The following example shows a single query for the www host record using nslookup.

```
c:\ > nslookup www
Server: Delta.2dt.com
Address: 206.195.150.132
Name: www.2dt.com
Address: 206.195.150.140
```

Reverse IP Lookup of Name Test

Similarly, you can test the reverse lookup of an IP address to a host name with nslookup as follows:

```
c:\ > nslookup 206.195.150.140
Server: Delta.2dt.com
Address: 206.195.150.132
Name: www.2dt.com
Address: 206.195.150.140
c:\ >
```

If any errors occur, then the service is not correctly configured. If you get a response that the server itself is unknown, then you probably do not have a record for the DNS server itself in either the domain zone data or the reverse zone data. You can add these records via the DNS Manager and try your query again.

EXERCISE 10-8

Using nslookup to Test DNS

Test for the www record entered in the domain for forward and reverse name resolution.

1. Start a command prompt.

    Start | Programs | Command Prompt

2. Enter the command to test for the host named www:

    > nslookup www

    (This should provide the server name, server IP address, then the fully qualified host name and host IP address.)

3. Enter the command to test for the IP address 213.88.77.17:

    > nslookup 213.88.77.17

    (This should provide the server name, server IP address, then the fully qualified host name and host IP address.)

4. Type **EXIT** to quit the command prompt.

Adding DNS Option to DHCP Service

If you are using the Dynamic Host Configuration Protocol (DHCP) service, you can add the option 006 name server with the value of your DNS IP address as a scope or global option. You would need to release and renew all clients for this option to take effect for that scope.

EXERCISE 10-9

DHCP DNS Options

If the DHCP service is running and you are familiar with DHCP options, you can specify the DNS server IP address for the clients of DHCP.

1. Start the DHCP Manager.

2. Double-Click Local Machine object.

3. Click a Scope (create a scope if none available).

4. Click DHCP Options Menu then Scope option in the drop-down list.

5. In the Unused Options box, click 006 DNS Servers.

6. Click Value >>> on the right side.

7. Click Edit Array...

8. Enter the IP address for this DNS server: **213.88.77.16**.

9. Click OK.

10. Now force every client to renew their lease to get the new option:

   At a command prompt type:
   > **IPCONFIG /RELEASE**
   > **IPCONFIG /RENEW**

CERTIFICATION SUMMARY

DNS is one of the new services added since NT 3.5x and is now an integral part of the network services. DNS provides an elegant method of decentralizing host name resolution by letting the administration of the host records fall on the system administrator of each attached network rather than on one central authority.

In this chapter, you have been introduced to the DNS Service for NT and some of the aspects of managing and maintaining this service. We saw the basic hierarchy and installation of the DNS service. We discussed the concept and creation of both a primary and a secondary zone, as well as sub-zones, which are referred to as a domain by the DNS Manager. We learned how to create a reverse lookup zone, how to add basic and advanced records to any zone or sub-zone, and how to create the text files that represent the zone information created in the DNS Manager. Finally, we discussed how to manage more than one primary domain from the DNS Manager Utility.

TWO-MINUTE DRILL

❑ Every network interface card or connection has a unique 48-bit numeric ID called a Media Access Control (MAC) address, commonly displayed as six hexadecimal values.

❑ The function of the resolver is to pass a name request to the name server.

❑ The final requirement of a WAN protocol is to provide full routing capability.

❑ To access another host, you need to know its IP address or host name.

❑ Most workstations have just one network connection and one host name.

❑ Each isolated TCP/IP network has to maintain its own HOSTS file and make it available, by some copy method, to every other host on the network.

❑ NIS provides a centrally managed file distribution system for mainly UNIX based hosts, although there are versions of NIS for other platforms.

❑ The HOSTS file remained the only central location for host name resolution until it became apparent that this centralized management was too inefficient and error-prone with such a large community of networks.

❑ DNS distributes the information in a standardized hierarchical structure that provides an indexed search path rather than a sequential search of one large file.

❑ A DNS record consists of a name, record type, and an IP address.

❑ The Fully Qualified Domain Name (FQDN) is the name of the host suffixed by a period, followed by the domain name.

❑ DNS is not a dynamic service like WINS or DHCP.

❑ DNS is a system of interconnected data files representing local host names and their IP addresses.

❑ The root servers provide addresses to the domain servers associated with that root.

❑ A secondary DNS server is a backup server with a copy of the zone information from the master server.

❑ The minimum basic installation for both the client and the server as client to use DNS is: a host name, domain name, and the IP address of the DNS primary server for this domain. Optionally you can add secondary server IP addresses and alternate suffix search orders, additional domains, and subdomains managed at the same server.

❑ The first database needed is the Primary Zone for your domain.

❑ The primary zone also requires a reverse address zone to store reverse order records, called *PTR records*.

❑ To allow any DNS client to use a backup or secondary server, you need to add the alternate server IP address or addresses to the DNS setup of TCP/IP.

❑ The DNS Manager Utility can manage a local or remote server(s) or just remote servers.

❑ You can use the DNS Manager Utility to add records to either a primary or a secondary zone.

❑ A basic record in a DNS zone file is one host name, one IP address, and a record type.

❑ The DNS manager can connect to other DNS servers and act as a backup server. This is referred to as a secondary zone within DNS.

SELF TEST

The Self Test questions will help you measure your understanding of the material presented in this chapter. Read all the choices carefully, as there may be more than one correct answer. Choose all correct answers for each question.

1. From where is the DNS Service installed?

   A. Add Software Wizard In Control Panel

   B. Services Applet in Control Panel

   C. System Applet in Control Panel

   D. Network Applet in Control Panel

2. In what order is a basic DNS record entry?

   A. IP Address, Record Type, Host Name

   B. Host Name, Record Type, IP Address

   C. IP Address, Record Name, Host Type

   D. IP Address, Host Name, Record Type

3. What is a PTR record?

   A. Position Translator Record

   B. Reverse Pointer Record

   C. Path Transfer Record

   D. Pilot Term Record

4. What is the default data file name for the zone urcorp.net?

   A. urcorp.net

   B. urcorp.net.com

   C. urcorp.net.dns

   D. urcorp.dat

5. How do you configure a DNS domain to use WINS?

   A. Click the Cache object, click DNS Menu, then select Properties.

   B. Click the domain object, right-click the Options Menu, select WINS.

   C. Click the domain object, click the DNS menu, select Properties.

   D. Click Network Icon in Control Panel, click services, click WINS, then click Properties.

6. What is the name of the general (default) Reverse Lookup zone as displayed in the DNS Manager?

   A. in-addr.arpa

   B. cache

   C. place.dom

   D. reverse.dns

7. What is the name of the specific Reverse Lookup zone for the domain place.dom representing the network 219.145.86.0 when displayed in the DNS Manager?

   A. 219.145.86.0.cache

   B. 86.145.219in-addr.dns

   C. place.dom.219.145.86

   D. 219.145.86.reverse.dns

8. What is the information needed by a client to use DNS? Select all that apply.

   A. in-addr.arpa

   B. domain name

   C. IP address of server

   D. Optional subdomain names

11

TCP/IP Services and Tools

U NIX connectivity is an important issue in many enterprise networks. FTP and WWW access are based on basic UNIX connectivity as are many other Internet facilities. In this chapter, we'll look at RAS (Remote Access Service), the Windows NT facility that connects machines together. Most RAS connections use modems or ISDN adapters. We'll also discuss Network Monitor, which is a tool used to view packets on the network.

UNIX Connectivity

Because TCP/IP was first designed for UNIX, there are many services on UNIX platforms that Windows NT needs access to. Therefore, it is necessary to develop UNIX connectivity solutions.

Determining When UNIX Connectivity Is Required

On a daily basis, users are connecting to UNIX platforms without even realizing it. In fact, until recently nearly every FTP and WWW server on the Internet was a UNIX system. The most common uses of UNIX connectivity are for FTP and WWW services.

FTP

FTP (File Transfer Protocol) enables file transfer from an FTP server to a local workstation. Traditionally FTP servers are UNIX servers, but recently FTP servers have been developed for Windows NT and other operating systems. FTP uses port 21 for its initial communication, or control port. An FTP server service is included with Microsoft Internet Information Server, which is included in Windows NT Server 4.0.

WWW Access

Similar to FTP, WWW originated in the UNIX community, and has since been integrated onto nearly every platform, including Windows NT. WWW traffic uses the HTTP (Hyper Text Transport Protocol) to complete transfers requested by users. HTTP uses port 80 to accomplish these transfers.

LPD Printing Service

LPD (Line Printer Daemon) Printing Service allows printing from operating systems that would normally not be able to print to Windows NT Server. For example, LPD allows a UNIX workstation to print through a Windows NT Server.

Configuring LPD Print Service

LPD is fairly easy to configure:

1. Open Network Control Panel.
2. Select the Services Tab.
3. Click Add.
4. Select Microsoft TCP/IP Printing.
5. Enter the Path to the Windows NT Server CD.
6. Restart the Server.

Once this has been installed, any workstation can print to the LPD print service by specifying the NT Server's IP address followed by a colon and the share's name.

CERTIFICATION OBJECTIVE 11.02

RAS Connectivity

RAS (Remote Access Service) connects a remote workstation to a RAS server using a non-Ethernet connection. RAS is Windows NT's implementation of Dial-up Networking. RAS is most commonly used with modems or ISDN adapters. RAS clients can connect to services provided by the RAS server and, if the RAS server is configured to allow it, any resources on the network to which the RAS server is connected.

Point-to-Point or SLIP

The most common RAS connections are PPP (Point-to-Point Protocol), or SLIP (Serial Line Internet Protocol). Both PPP and SLIP can connect RAS clients to a RAS server via modem / telephone line. PPP, however, is replacing SLIP because it is more robust, and guarantees cross-platform connectivity. Because SLIP is declining in popularity, RAS is capable of using SLIP only for dial out, not for dial in.

Connect to NT or UNIX Using PPP

PPP is a cross-platform protocol that can be used to connect to both NT and UNIX systems. By utilizing the PPP protocol, an NT workstation can be connected to a UNIX server and vice versa. When the PPP protocol is used, the server and workstations are not required to be running the same operating systems.

TCP/IP Address Assignment

As with any TCP/IP connection, RAS connections are required to have TCP/IP addresses. These addresses can be assigned manually or automatically. Automatic address assignment is usually referred to as dynamic and manual is referred to as static.

A Specific Pool of Addresses

Each RAS connection requires an IP address, which is taken from a designated range of IP addresses, called a *pool*. Each RAS connection will obtain an address from this pool.

Manual Assignment

Assigning IP addresses manually is tedious and error-prone. When manually assigning addresses to RAS ports, each assignment must be tracked to avoid duplicate address assignments.

Using DHCP

DHCP (Dynamic Host Configuration Protocol) dynamically tracks the assignment of IP addresses. DHCP automatically assigns an IP address to each machine, and tracks the machine's usage of this IP address. After the machine no longer uses the IP address, it can be returned to the address pool for reassignment at a later time.

All RAS Clients Use Assigned Addresses

If RAS clients each use an assigned address, it is necessary to track the usage of these IP addresses and maintain a list of all active IP addresses in order to avoid possible duplicate IP address assignment.

All RAS Clients Use DHCP

If RAS is configured to use DHCP addresses for each RAS client, a great deal less work is required. DHCP automatically assigns an IP address to each port of the RAS server and no additional configuration is required.

Mix of Both

A combination of DHCP assigned addresses and statically configured IP addresses can be used. The primary reason for using a manually assigned IP address in a mixed environment is to establish a link to another network where it is important that the IP address not be changed. A good example of this is when a RAS connection is used as a permanent link to the Internet, in which case it would be desirable for the IP address not to change.

exam
ⓦatch

It is important to remember that RAS clients can use statically assigned IP addresses, dynamically assigned IP addresses, or a combination of both. The most common configuration is dynamic assignment using DHCP.

EXERCISE 11-2

Configuring TCP/IP Parameters for RAS Clients

When RAS clients are configured for dial-in, they must be configured properly in order to communicate.

1. Verify that DHCP Server is configured properly for WINS, DNS, and Gateway.

2. Install the RAS client.

3. Verify that the RAS client is configured to use DHCP for its IP address and other settings.

4. (optional) Manually define WINS servers on the RAS client. (This will allow a mobile user to access your servers from anywhere in the world.)

CERTIFICATION OBJECTIVE 11.03

Network Monitor

Network Monitor is a utility that shows network activity. Network Monitor can be used with any protocol, not just TCP/IP. There are two different versions of Network Monitor available. The version that ships with Windows NT Server 4.0 is only capable of viewing packets to and from the server that acts as the network monitoring agent. Another version of Network Monitor that ships with SMS (Systems Management Server) is capable of viewing all data transmitted on the network.

exam
Watch

There are two different versions of Network Monitor. One can view only the traffic to and from the server that the network monitoring agent is installed on and the other one can view all traffic on the network. These versions of Network Monitor ship with Windows NT Server 4.0 and Systems Management Server, respectively.

Installing and Using Network Monitor Tools and Agent

The installation of Network Monitor is a simple process. You need to add it through the services tab of the Network Control Panel. Actually using Network Monitor is a bit more involved. The amount of information that can be acquired through Network Monitor's facilities is enormous.

Capturing Data

To capture data with Network Monitor, click Capture and then Begin. Network Monitor requires very little work on your part. When capturing data it is important to remember that every packet that is transmitted on the network will be added to your capture. You can lessen the amount of data that you will receive by creating a filter: click Capture and Filter.

Viewing and Interpreting Data

Interpreting the results of Network Monitor is a skill that can only be honed by practice. Once you are satisfied with the quantity of data that you have captured, click Capture, then Stop and View Data. A summary of all packets that were captured will then be presented. From this summary you can double-click any one that interests you.

The middle window that is displayed shows the information that we are primarily interested in. There are many different sections that are usually displayed. We are primarily concerned with the Frame, Ethernet, and IP sections.

Frame Information

The Frame information section gives us information about the capture of the frame, which usually includes the time at which the frame was captured, the point in time that the frame was captured, and the total length of the frame.

EXERCISE 11-3

Installing and Configuring Network Monitor

Network Monitor is a utility that can be used to provide assistance in troubleshooting. Installation and configuration of Network Monitor is extremely simple.

1. Open the Network Control Panel.
2. Select the Services Tab.
3. Click Add.
4. Select Network Monitor Agent and Tools.
5. Enter the path to the Windows NT Server CD.
6. Restart the Server.

Hardware Ethernet Frame

The Hardware Ethernet Frame gives us information such as the source and destination MAC addresses. This information can be used to pinpoint exactly where packets are coming from and going to, since in general MAC (media access control) addresses are unchangeable addresses.

e x a m
ⓦa t c h

Remember that the MAC address is an address assigned to a network interface card by the hardware manufacturer. This address cannot be changed on most current network interface cards.

IP Address Frame

The IP section gives us information such as the Source and Destination addresses, the version of IP that was used to create the packet, a packet identification number, a Time to Live for the packet, along with some additional information that is not often used.

Monitor TCP/IP Frames

As we discussed earlier, Network Monitor allows you to view all of the frames that have been sent across the network. Most of the packets are somewhat self-explanatory. There are some packets that are of special interest to us.

DHCP Messages

DHCP packets contain messages that are used between DHCP servers and clients during communications to establish and manage a lease for an IP address and related information. In Network Monitor, these packets will be of type DHCP. Since you can see the DHCP conversation between the client and server with Network Monitor, it is a useful way to troubleshoot DHCP problems.

Point-to-Point Messages

Point-to-Point messages are usually messages between a RAS server and a RAS client pertaining to the connections status.

WINS Messages

WINS messages are between the WINS server and clients. There are primarily three different types of WINS messages: broadcast, announce, and request. A broadcast is a standard broadcast message used by a workstation or server to announce its existence. These are standard broadcasts that will occur with or without the presence of a WINS server. If a WINS server is present, the server will use these broadcasts to help maintain the WINS database. An announce message is sent to the WINS server announcing the existence of a client. This message is sent repeatedly for a predefined period of time. A request message is when a client requests the IP address of another client from the WINS server in order to resolve a NetBios name.

DNS Messages

The only type of DNS message is a request from a client. When a client requests that a DNS name be resolved by the DNS server, the DNS server responds with the target IP address.

EXERCISE 11-4

Viewing TCP/IP Packets with Network Monitor

Viewing packets provides information about the performance of your network. Network Monitor not only provides information about packets, but also includes the packets. For this reason, it is important to use Network Monitor with the utmost care and integrity.

1. Open Network Monitor from the Administrative Tools Menu.
2. Click Capture, and click Start to begin capturing transmitted packets.3.
   Once a sufficient number of packets have been captured, click Capture and Stop and View.
4. A summary of packets will be displayed., From this summary you can select a packet to view by double-clicking it.
5. Information about the packet, such as the source and destination addresses and the protocol used, will be displayed in the middle frame.
6. The actual packet will be displayed at the bottom of the screen.

Ethics of Network Monitor

Network Monitor is undoubtedly the most powerful device to track network usage. Unfortunately with this great ability comes a bad side. Network

Monitor can literally see everything. Network Monitor is capable of viewing the contents of every packet that crosses the network. This ability can be a bit humbling at times, and can give you the power to truly implement the "Big Brother is Watching" security system. Using Network Monitor to do anything other than troubleshooting a specific network problem is entirely unethical.

A simple standard to follow, that seems to be acceptable to the judicial system and to the corporate world, is that you are not at any time permitted to view the contents of user-generated packets. Any machine-generated packet is fair game for your viewing pleasure. A machine-generated packet is further defined as a packet that the machine generates without any specific interaction on the user's part, while a user-generated packet is one that is generated by an action of the user or an application that the user is running. Table 11-1 gives some examples of user- and machine-generated packets.

Unfortunately, no matter how well defined a system you have, the correct use of Network Monitor is still a gray area. As a Network Administrator it is important to be very careful how you use Network Monitor and verify that its use is permitted within your organization. Table 11-2 gives some typical scenarios you may encounter as a Network Administrator.

TABLE 11-1	User-Generated	Machine-Generated
User- and Machine-Generated Packets	POP3 transfer	ARP request for mail server's IP Address
	FTP transfer	Keep alive Message
	SMTP transfer	Ping
	SMB transfer	DHCP
	HTTP transfer	WINS
		Broadcasts

QUESTIONS AND ANSWERS

I have this problem	Is the use of Network Monitor Ethical?
Two machines have been assigned the same IP address and I am unable to manually find the offending computers.	Yes, IP address conflicts are machine-generated problems.
I think my boss is trying to fire me, I'll bet I could find out more information from his e-mail.	No, intentionally reading anyone's e-mail is undoubtedly unethical, and possibly illegal.
A user is browsing sites that are considered inappropriate during the workday. I can use Network Monitor to prove this.	Maybe, viewing the contents of user's HTTP packets is generally considered unethical. This may be allowable by company policies but you should consult your company's lawyers.
DNS requests are being made by workstations, but are not being answered by the server. I suspect there is a configuration error.	Yes, DNS messages are machine-generated and could be used to troubleshoot network problems.

CERTIFICATION SUMMARY

Connectivity to UNIX servers is crucial to connect to hosts on the Internet. In addition many companies have UNIX servers that users benefit from being able to connect to. Services such as FTP and WWW traditionally have been located on UNIX servers. FTP and WWW services are now being provided by other platforms, including Windows NT.

Remote Access Service (RAS) helps to connect a RAS workstation to a RAS server using non-Ethernet media. Common media for RAS connections are modems and ISDN adapters. These connections are usually made using either the Point-to-Point Protocol (PPP) or Serial Line Interface Protocol (SLIP). RAS servers can be configured either to provider a pre-assigned pool of IP addresses or to use DHCP to assign IP addresses to RAS clients. DHCP is most commonly used.

Network Monitor is used to view the activity of a network. Network Monitor can be used with any protocol, not just TCP/IP. Network Monitor, as it is shipped with Windows NT Server 4.0, captures all packets that are sent to and from the server that is being monitored. Network Monitor is capable of extracting information from the packets such as source and destination IP and MAC addresses. Network Monitor is a powerful tool that could be used in an unethical manner. It is important to determine if Network Monitor is being used ethically in each particular situation.

TWO-MINUTE DRILL

- ❏ Because TCP/IP was first designed for UNIX, there are many services on UNIX platforms that Windows NT needs access to.

- ❏ The most common uses of UNIX connectivity are for FTP and WWW services.

- ❏ LPD (Line Printer Daemon) Printing Service allows printing from operating systems that would normally not be able to print to Windows NT Server.

- ❏ RAS (Remote Access Service) connects a remote workstation to a RAS server using a non-Ethernet connection.

- ❏ The most common RAS connections are PPP (Point-to-Point Protocol) or SLIP (Serial Line Internet Protocol).

- ❏ PPP is a cross-platform protocol that can be used to connect to both NT and UNIX systems.

- ❏ RAS connections are required to have TCP/IP addresses.

- ❏ DHCP (Dynamic Host Configuration Protocol) dynamically tracks the assignment of IP addresses.

- ❏ DHCP automatically assigns an IP address to each machine, and tracks the machine's usage of this IP address.

- ❏ It is important to remember that RAS clients can use statically assigned IP addresses, dynamically assigned IP addresses, or a combination of both. The most common configuration is dynamic assignment using DHCP.

❑ Network Monitor is undoubtedly the most powerful device to track network usage.

❑ There are two different versions of Network Monitor. One can view only the traffic to and from the server that the network monitoring agent is installed on and the other one can view all traffic on the network. These versions of Network Monitor ship with Windows NT Server 4.0 and Systems Management Server, respectively.

❑ Interpreting the results of Network Monitor is a skill that can only be honed by practice.

❑ Remember that the MAC address is an address assigned to a network interface card by the hardware manufacturer. This address cannot be changed on most current network interface cards.

❑ DHCP packets contain messages that are used between DHCP servers and clients during communications to establish and manage a lease for an IP address and related information.

❑ Point-to-Point messages are usually messages between a RAS server and a RAS client pertaining to the connections status.

❑ WINS messages are between the WINS server and clients. There are primarily three different types of WINS messages: broadcast, announce, and request.

❑ The only type of DNS message is a request from a client.

❑ As a Network Administrator it is important to be very careful how you use Network Monitor and verify that its use is permitted within your organization.

SELF TEST

The following Self Test questions will help you measure your understanding of the material presented in this chapter. Read all the choices carefully, as there may be more than one correct answer. Choose all correct answers for each question.

1. Network Monitor is capable of monitoring traffic _____.

   A. Only that is passed by a router or switch.

   B. Only that is to or from the server it is installed on.

   C. Of any device on the network.

   D. None of the above are true.

   E. B and C are correct, depending on the version of Network Monitor you have.

2. RAS servers can be configured to assign IP addresses to the RAS clients using any of the following except:

   A. DHCP

   B. WINS

   C. Manual Assignment

   D. A combination of DHCP and Manual Assignment

3. Reading a co-worker's e-mail using Network Monitor is _____.

   A. Unethical

   B. Fine as long as you do not get caught

   C. Possibly illegal

   D. A & C are both true

   E. None of the above

4. What port does the FTP protocol use as its control port?

   A. 23

   B. 21

   C. 119

   D. 80

   E. 110

5. Which port does the HTTP protocol use?

   A. 21

   B. 23

   C. 119

   D. 80

   E. 110

6. What is the address called that is assigned to hardware that can be determined by using Network Monitor to capture packets from the network?

   A. IP Address

   B. Mailing Address

   C. MAC Address

   D. Street Address

   E. Dynamic Address

7. Network Monitor is capable of viewing _____ packets.

   A. only DHCP

B. all

C. only machine-generated

D. only user-generated

E. no

8. RAS. . .

A. provides the ability to connect a remote workstation to a RAS server.

B. is most commonly used with modems and ISDN adapters.

C. clients can access services the RAS server is able to connect to.

D. All of the above are true.

9. RAS is most commonly configured to use a combination of both DHCP and manual assignment . . .

A. when a permanent link to the outside world is being established.

B. if no other method is available.

C. When modem speeds slower than 14.4 Kbps are used.

D. None of the above are true.

10. Which of the following are considered user-generated packets?

A. FTP packets

B. HTTP packets

C. POP3 packets

D. SMB packets

E. All of the above

11. Which of the following is not a type of WINS message?

A. Broadcast

B. Verification

C. Announce

D. Request

E. All of the above

12. PPP is an acronym that stands for

_____.

A. Paper Production Protocol

B. Point Production Protocol

C. Point to Production Protocol

D. Point-to-Point Protocol

13. The acronym SLIP stands for _____.

A. Serial Line Interface Protocol

B. Serial Line Internet Protocol

C. Serial Link Interface Protocol

D. Serial Link Interconnect Protocol

E. None of the Above

14. The IP section of a packet can contain information such as . . .

A. Source IP address

B. Destination IP address

C. Version of the IP protocol that was used

D. Packet Identification Number

E. All of the above

15. The Hardware Ethernet Frame contains information such as . . .

A. Source MAC address

B. Destination MAC address

C. Source IP address

D. Both A & B

E. All of the above

12

Simple Network Management Protocol (SNMP)

H

ave you ever had to configure a router on another floor of your building, or a bridge at a location across town? You may have lost half a day driving back and forth between locations. What if you wanted to know how efficiently a switch in Europe is running, and you are stuck back in North America?

Simple Network Management Protocol (SNMP) makes these routine tasks performed at your desk. SNMP is a full Internet standard that is endorsed and supported by nearly every manufacturer of network equipment and software. SNMP gives client/server functionality to network maintenance and monitoring.

After reading this chapter, you will understand the principles behind SNMP and be able to install and configure it to work with a third-party management system.

CERTIFICATION OBJECTIVE 12.01

Understanding SNMP

Simple Network Management Protocol (SNMP) is an Internet standard defined in RFC 1157. SNMP provides a simple method for remotely managing virtually any network device. A network device could be a network card in a server, a program or service running on a server, or a standalone network device such as a hub or router.

The SNMP standard defines a two-tiered approach to network device management: a central *management system* and the *management information base* (MIB) located on the managed device. The management system can monitor one or many MIBs, allowing centralized management of a network. From a management system you can see valuable performance and operation statistics from network devices, allowing you to diagnose network health without leaving your office.

The goal for a management system is to provide centralized network management. Any computer running SNMP management software is referred to as a management system. For a management system to be able to perform centralized network management, it must be able to collect and analyze many things, including:

- Network protocol identification and statistics
- Dynamic identification of computers attached to the network (referred to as *discovery*)
- Hardware and software configuration data
- Computer performance and usage statistics
- Computer event and error messages
- Program and application usage statistics

Now, you may be thinking, "Can't Windows NT do a lot of this with its built-in functionality?" In most cases, yes. That's one of the reasons Windows NT has become a popular network operating system. But SNMP extends such functionality beyond a server, allowing management of *any* network device that supports SNMP. It is also an open standard, allowing it to manage any device or software manufactured to support it.

Why SNMP?

Would you rather do your network configuration crouched in a cramped wiring closet, or sitting at your desk enjoying a cup o' joe? In a large internetwork, the particular wiring closet you need may be 1000 miles away!

SNMP was originally developed to assist in configuring and managing bridges and routers. As it evolved, it gained more functionality and extensibility. Being an open Internet standard, it didn't take long for manufacturers of a variety of network devices to incorporate it into their products.

SNMP allows large networks to be brought under control from a central location. Reconfiguring a network device from anywhere in the world results in huge cost savings for a company. It may also mean that fewer administrators can effectively manage the network.

Besides allowing network managers to remotely configure network devices, SNMP also allows managers to monitor devices, both passively and actively. In a passive scenario, a network device can signal a problem to the management console, getting the network manager's attention. In an active scenario, the manager may have the management console routinely gather statistics from SNMP-enabled devices. Looking at that data, the manager can make proactive decisions, rather than waiting for a resource to run out and network users to start complaining. SNMP is a popular Internet standard for making large-scale network management possible.

How SNMP Works

An SNMP-managed network requires two things to function: an SNMP management system, and an SNMP agent. The management system allows network managers to view and configure network devices from a central location.

The SNMP agents respond to management system requests, sending information or configuring the network device for the management system. In rare instances, SNMP agents send information to management systems when there is an error or some other problem. When an SNMP agent decides to send information to a management system, it is called a *trap*. A trap can be initiated only by an SNMP agent. Management systems can respond to traps, but they can not issue traps.

SNMP defines *communities*, which are logical groupings of management systems and agents. Communities allow network managers to specify which management systems agents respond to. They also allow the managers to specify which management systems agents should send traps to.

SNMP communities not only allow network managers to logically group SNMP management systems and agents, but also allow them to secure the SNMP system. By default, all SNMP management systems and agents belong to the "public" community. This makes default configuration a snap, but it could lead to problems as the network manager loses control of SNMP access.

SNMP Management System

An SNMP management system is any computer running SNMP management software. UNIX has long been a favorite platform for management software, but Windows NT has made huge inroads into this market. You can now pick just about any platform to be your management system.

Management systems obtain data about network devices and make this information available to a network administrator through textual, graphical, or object-oriented user interfaces. The manager system sends SNMP messages to SNMP agents. A management system can issue three commands to SNMP agents: get, get-next, and set.

The get operation allows the management system to request a specific value. The value could be a fixed value, such as a maximum number of users, or a variable value, such as a current CPU utilization.

The get-next operation simply gets the next value in the hierarchical SNMP object being queried. Typically, a management console will issue one get command to get to the object it is interested in, then simply issue many get-next commands in succession to get all the values it wants.

For instance, an SNMP agent may have an object for performance counters. If the management system wanted to gather all the performance information on the object, it would issue a get command to the agent requesting the first value in the performance object. After that it would simply issue get-next commands repeatedly until the last performance counter was reached.

The set command allows a management system to configure a remote SNMP agent. This can be very handy in a larger internetwork. Most values an agent has are read-only so the set command is rarely carried out.

SNMP Agent

An SNMP agent simply responds to get, get-next, and set commands issued by a management system. Any network device running SNMP agent software is an agent. Usually they are servers and intelligent routers, hubs, and bridges.

The SNMP agent does have one command at its disposal: the trap. An SNMP agent uses the trap command to report events (usually bad ones) to one or more management systems. A trap may be issued if there is a security breach or serious network error.

The trap allows SNMP agents to report errors without waiting for a management console to ask for the information. This is very important to efficiently monitor a network. An error can grow if not caught quickly. Having an SNMP management system constantly querying SNMP agents would be a drain on network resources, not to mention the SNMP agent's resources.

exam
ⓦatch

It is important to know which commands are issued by management systems, and which are issued by agents. Get, get-next, and set are issued only by SNMP management systems. Trap is issued only by SNMP agents.

SNMP Service

Windows NT includes an SNMP agent service with its TCP/IP protocol stack. The Windows NT-based SNMP service is an optional service that is installed after TCP/IP is installed on a Windows NT-based computer. After the SNMP service is installed on a computer, it automatically starts each time the computer is started, as illustrated in Figure 12-1.

WARNING! If you install the SNMP service after installing Windows NT 4.0 Service Pack 2 or higher, you must reinstall the Service Pack for the SNMP service to operate properly. (See Microsoft Knowledge Base article Q163595 for more information.)

The SNMP service allows Windows NT computers to report their status to management systems. It also allows the management system to query Windows NT computers for performance statistics. In fact, the Windows NT Performance Monitor requires SNMP to be installed in order to monitor TCP/IP performance statistics, even if you are not using SNMP to manage your network.

exam
ⓦatch

You must know when SNMP is needed. You cannot perform Performance Monitor monitoring of TCP/IP without first installing the SNMP service.

FIGURE 12-1

SNMP MIB with TCP/IP
Protocols

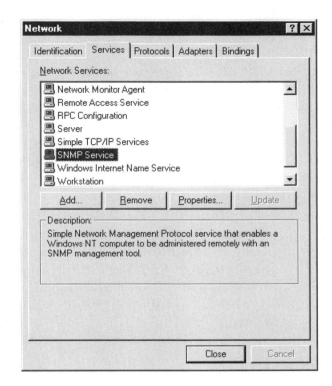

CERTIFICATION OBJECTIVE 12.02

Management Information Bases (MIB)

Management Information Bases (MIB) are the building blocks in any SNMP implementation. MIBs define a hierarchical structure of manageable objects, which define what may be monitored and/or configured on a network device with a management system.

Every device that is to be managed by SNMP must have a MIB to define what can be done with the device. The MIB will define several things about the objects:

- The association between (1) the host hardware or software component (object) and (2) an object name and an object identifier.

- A definition of the data type used to define the object.

- A textual description of the object.

- An index method used for objects that are a complex data type.

- The read or write access that is allowed on the object.

Windows NT includes several MIBs for monitoring and configuring several NT services. The *Internet II MIB* is a standard Internet MIB for common Internet functions, and *LAN Manager II MIB* is for managing Windows NT-based services. The *DHCP MIB* allows management of a Dynamic Host Configuration Protocol service running on Windows NT, and the *WINS MIB* for managing a Windows Internet Name Server service running on Windows NT.

Internet MIB II

The Internet MIB II is an Internet standard MIB defined in RFC 1213 and is a superset of a previous standard, Internet MIB I. Internet MIB II provides a standard set of objects essential to fault tolerance and management in an Internet environment. Internet MIB II defines 171 objects for the management system.

LAN Manager MIB II for Windows NT

The LAN Manager MIB II defines 86 objects for management on a Windows NT system. These include a share, session, user, logon, and statistical information. This MIB would be useful for monitoring Windows NT logon/file/print services.

DHCP MIB

The DHCP MIB allows an SNMP management system to manage and monitor the Dynamic Host Configuration Protocol service running on a Windows NT server. DHCP MIB defines 14 objects for monitoring. This MIB is automatically installed when the DHCP Server service is installed.

WINS MIB

The WINS MIB allows an SNMP management system to manage and monitor the Windows Internet Name Server service running on a Windows NT server. WINS MIB defines 72 objects for monitoring and configuring the WINS Server. This MIB is automatically installed when the WINS service is installed.

Internet Information Server MIB

The Internet Information Server MIB allows an SNMP management system to manage and monitor the Internet Information Server running on a Windows NT server. The Internet Information Server MIB doesn't actually define any objects. The FTP, Gopher, and HTTP Server MIBs are all derived from the Internet Information Server MIB (don't forget that SNMP MIBs are hierarchical). The FTP Server MIB defines 16 objects, the Gopher Server MIB defines 18 objects, and the HTTP Server MIB defines 22 objects for monitoring. These MIBs are automatically installed when these services are installed.

Hierarchical Name Tree

The Simple Network Configuration Protocol defines a hierarchical tree for naming management objects (see Figure 12-2). The structure allows each manageable object to have a unique name in the tree. When a management system queries an agent, it provides an object name or number to tell the agent what object it wants the agent to process.

FIGURE 12-2

SNM hierarchical
name tree

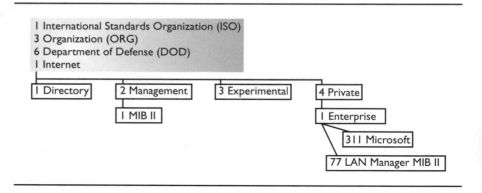

To simplify additions to the name tree, individual organizations may be assigned authority over a single branch, allowing them to control the objects on that branch. In this way, companies can introduce and extend MIBs and have to register only once.

The name tree defines both an English name and a number for each object. When specifying either an object name or an object number, it is listed from the root of the tree to the object, separated by periods. Table 12-1 shows a few examples.

If you look at Figure 12-2, you can see that Microsoft has been assigned number 1.3.6.1.4.1.311 for its use. For example, the DHCP and WINS MIBs both fall under this number. So why does LAN Manager have its own number? Quite simply, it was given a number before Microsoft as a whole received its number.

TABLE 12-1

MIB Names, Object
Names, and Object
Numbers

MIB Name	Object name	Object number
Internet MIB II	iso.org.dod.internet. management.mibii	1.3.6.1.2.1
LAN Manager MIB II	iso.org.dod.internet.private. enterprise.lanmanger	1.3.6.1.4.1.77

Most of the time you do not need to worry about object names and numbers. Instead you will just focus on individual MIBs. However, you will need to acquaint yourself with the hierarchy in case any questions are posed on the exam, or if you need to diagnose your SNMP configuration using the SNMP Utility (covered later in the chapter).

CERTIFICATION OBJECTIVE 12.03

Installing and Configuring **SNMP Service**

Before SNMP can be used on Windows NT, it must be installed and configured. While installation is very easy, configuration is more challenging and requires some preparation. Before installing the SNMP service, an administrator must identify the following information:

- The contact person and location for the administrator of the local computer

- Community names that can be shared by hosts on the network

- IP address, IPX address, or network computer name of the SNMP management console, or consoles, that will be the destination for trap messages generated by computers within a specific community. (Not all SNMP management consoles must also be trap destinations.)

The SNMP service requires a management system to report to. You must have at least one management system on the network in order to use the SNMP service, unless you want to monitor TCP/IP performance statistics using only Performance Monitor.

Installing **SNMP**

The Microsoft SNMP service is not installed by default when the TCP/IP protocol is installed. The SNMP service must be installed manually. It is installed using the Network control panel applet. Follow these steps to install the SNMP service:

1. From the Control Panel, double-click Network.

2. Select Services and click Add.

3. Select SNMP Service from the list and click OK. Windows NT will copy the necessary files.

4. After copying the files, the SNMP Properties page will be displayed, as shown in Figure 12-3.

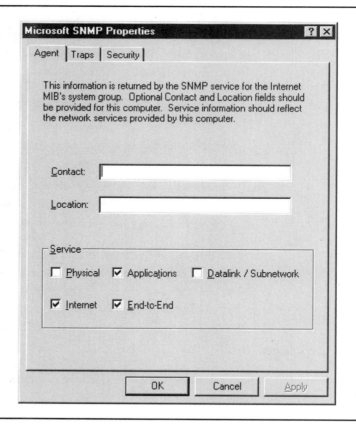

The Contact and Location fields are optional, but can be useful for providing additional information. The Services section allows you to define what services the agent provides, as listed in Table 12-2. Each service provides information regarding activity at different levels of the OSI model. The defaults are Application, Internet, and End-to-End.

exam
ⓦatch

It is important to know how to install the SNMP service. You must know that it is installed from the Services tab of the Network control panel applet.

EXERCISE 12-1

Installing an SNMP Agent

The SNMP agent is installed from Network control panel applet. Click the Start button on the taskbar, select Settings, then select Control Panel.

1. Open the Control Panel and select Network.

2. Click the Services tab to see the currently installed services. If SNMP Service is not listed, click the Add button.

3. A list of NT services that can be installed is shown. Scroll down to SNMP Service and click OK.

4. Windows NT will copy the necessary files and then present the SNMP service configuration dialog.

5. Click OK to finish configuration. You must reboot the computer for the SNMP Service to become active.

TABLE 12-2	Service	Check if the server...
The Five SNMP Services and Their Functions	Physical	Manages Physical layer devices such as repeaters
	Data Link	Manages Data Link layer devices such as bridges
	Internet	Acts as a gateway (like a router)
	End-to-End	Acts as an IP host. Always have this one selected
	Application	Uses TCP/IP applications. Should also always be selected

Identifying Security Parameters

The traps and security tabs of the SNMP service properties sheet allow you to enforce some amount of security in an SNMP managed network. It is important to work out a security plan for SNMP, because by default it is not secure, allowing virtually any management system to make requests, possibly using set in a harmful manner (whether intentionally or not).

SNMP allows security to be controlled by two methods: communities and directed traps. A community is a logical grouping of one or more management systems and one or more SNMP agents. Traps can be directed to specific management systems within SNMP communities.

By default, the SNMP service will respond to commands from, and management systems in, the public community. All management systems and agents are members of this community. You can see how this would diminish the security of SNMP. Therefore it is important to specify the community names of trusted management systems, and remove the public community from the list of accepted communities.

FROM THE CLASSROOM

SNMP Increases Network Security

SNMP can provide you with a sense of security. If your network is connected to the Internet, a firewall should be in place to prevent intrusion from other SNMP management consoles. You can have the SNMP service send a trap to the trap destination when a request does not match your community name. The SNMP service can be configured to accept requests from numerous community names, not just one. A host must belong to a community name on this list to accept requests. To tighten up security even more, you can clear the option to accept packets from every host with a matching community name, and supply a list of hosts within a community to accept requests. Then, even if the community name matches, SNMP screens it before accepting a request.

—*By D. Lynn White, MCT, MCSE*

When configuring security for the Windows NT SNMP service, the traps and security tabs allow you to set the security. The Traps tab (show in Figure 12-4) allows you to specify who to send SNMP traps to. The Security tab allows you to set who the SNMP service will accept requests from.

In the Community Name section, you may add the community names that you want the SNMP service to send its traps to.

You may further refine security by specifying which hosts in a particular community the SNMP service will send traps to. A community may have many management systems, but you may want only a select few to receive

FIGURE 12-4

The Traps tab from SNMP
Properties sheet

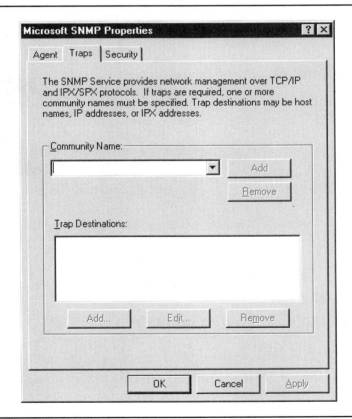

traps from a particular SNMP service. You may set this on the traps properties sheet.

The Security tab (shown in Figure 12-5) allows you to secure the SNMP service from management systems. It allows you to define which SNMP communities the service will accept requests from. To further increase security, the Security tab allows you to specify one or more specific management systems to accept requests from.

The Send Authentication Traps allows the SNMP service to send a trap when a host is not listed in the Accepted Community Names or defined as a host to accept packets from (assuming the service is not configured to accept packets from any host). This way when an unauthorized management system attempts to access the SNMP service, the real management systems can see this and know who attempted the access.

FIGURE 12-5

The Security tab from
SNMP Properties sheet

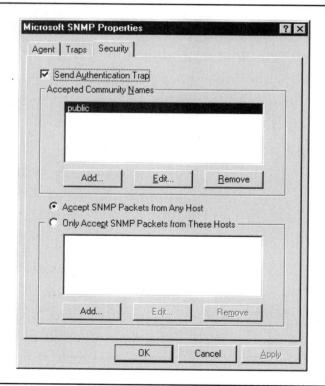

By default, the SNMP service responds to any management system in the public community. This allows virtually any management system to view variables from the SNMP service. You should have private communities defined in an SNMP management system, and use these communities to restrict who may query the SNMP service. Add the community name of any management systems you want to allow to view the SNMP service under the Accepted Community Names section using the Add button.

By default, the SNMP service allows any SNMP management system to send commands. This includes set commands, which could severely affect services on the Windows NT computer. For more security, it is important to change the Accept SNMP Packets From Any Host setting to Only Accept SNMP Packets From These Hosts and give a list of trusted management systems.

Agents can belong to more than one community as well. For example, all of your DCHP Servers may be in a community called *DHCP_server* and all of your WINS Servers may be in a community called *WINS_server*. Usually DHCP and WINS servers are separate machines, but not always. So if you have a machine running both DHCP and WINS, you would want that computer to also list both *DHCP_server* and *WINS_server* in the Accepted Community Names section.

On very large internetworks, there may be several levels of network management with many management systems. To simplify things, there may be several different communities, one for each group of network managers. Agents can pick who manages them from the appropriate communities, picking one or even all of the communities.

exam

ⓦatch

You must know how to configure the SNMP service. Understand what SNMP communities are, how to configure security for SNMP agents, and how to configure traps. Know the three tabs from the SNMP Service properties (Agent, Traps, and Security) and what each one configures.

EXERCISE 12-2

Configuring SNMP Agent Parameters

Once the SNMP service is installed, you will want to configure the parameters to assure proper and secure operation. By default, the SNMP service will respond to requests from any management system in the public community.

This will allow it to function with just about any management system, but only at the sacrifice of security.

1. Open the Network control panel applet. Click the Services tab, select the SNMP Service from the list, and click the Properties button.

2. Configure the Agent properties. The Contact and Location fields are optional, but can be useful for providing additional information. The Services section allows you to define what services the agent provides

3. Click the Traps tab. This section allows you to specify which management systems the SNMP service should send which traps to.

4. Click the Security tab. This section allows you to determine which management systems to accept requests from. On this tab you may also have the SNMP service send a trap if an invalid management system attempts to access the SNMP service.

5. Click OK to accept the changes. You may need to reboot for the changes to take effect.

Having seen how to configure the Windows NT SNMP service, let's try looking at some scenarios and how to resolve them:

QUESTIONS AND ANSWERS

"My management console doesn't belong to the public community..."	On the Security tab, add the proper community under Accepted Community Names.
"I want to make sure unauthorized management consoles don't query my agent..."	Select Only Accept SNMP Packets From These Hosts and enter the trusted management systems address(es).
"If there is an error, I want the SNMP service to report it..."	On the Traps tab, add the community name(s) you want, then add the host names.

SNMP Utility

The Microsoft Windows NT 4.0 Resource Kit contains the program SNMPUTIL.EXE. This utility allows the SNMP service to be verified so that it can communicate with management systems correctly. The SNMP utility allows SNMP commands to be sent to the local SNMP service as though they were issued by a management system and then view the results. The syntax is very straightforward:

```
snmputil command agent community object_identifier_(OID)
```

There are three valid commands that can be used with SNMPUTIL: get, get-next, and walk. Get simply gets the value of the requested object. Get-next requests the next object following the specified object. Walk allows stepping through the MIB branch specified in the OID.

The SNMP utility can be very useful for verifying the SNMP configuration. For example:

```
snmputil getnext DHCPserver Public
.1.3.6.1.4.1.311.1.3.2.1.1.1
```

This command would return the Object ID (OID) and counter value for the OID, in this case the number of IP leases that the DHCP Server name *DHCPserver* has issued.

exam
Watch

Be sure you know which commands are initiated by the management system and which commands are initiated by the agent.

CERTIFICATION SUMMARY

The Simple Network Management Protocol (SNMP) is an Internet standard for monitoring and configuring network devices. An SNMP network is composed of management systems and agents. Management systems monitor agents use get, get-next, and set commands to gather statistics and configure devices. Agents respond to the get, get-next, and set commands. Occasionally agents will issue their own command, trap, to alert management systems to extraordinary events.

The Management Information Base (MIB) defines management objects for a network device. Both management systems and agents understand MIBs and what they define. Windows NT includes several MIBs: Internet MIB II, LAN

Manager MIB II, DHCP MIB, and WINS MIB. The Internet Information Server MIB doesn't define any objects itself, but the HTTP, FTP, and Gopher MIBs are derived from it.

The Windows NT SNMP service allows you to configure a variety of parameters: which communities it belongs to, whether to accept SNMP queries from all hosts or only certain ones, and what communities and hosts to send traps to. The service can also be told what roles (router, server, etc.) the NT computer fills and report only pertinent information regarding those roles. The Windows NT 4.0 Resource Kit includes tools such as SNMPUTIL.EXE for verifying the configuration of the SNMP service.

TWO-MINUTE DRILL

- ❑ *Simple Network Management Protocol* (SNMP) provides a simple method for remotely managing virtually any network device.

- ❑ The SNMP standard defines a two-tiered approach to network device management: a central *management system* and the *management information base* (MIB) located on the managed device.

- ❑ SNMP allows large networks to be brought under control from a central location.

- ❑ An SNMP-managed network requires two things to function: an SNMP management system, and an SNMP agent.

- ❑ An SNMP management system is any computer running SNMP management software.

- ❑ An SNMP agent simply responds to get, get-next, and set commands issued by a management system.

- ❑ It is important to know which commands are issued by management systems, and which are issued by agents. Get, get-next, and set are issued only by SNMP management systems. Trap is issued only by SNMP agents.

- ❑ The Windows NT-based SNMP service is an optional service that is installed after TCP/IP is installed on a Windows NT-based computer.

❑ If you install the SNMP service after installing Windows NT 4.0 Service Pack 2 or higher, you must reinstall the Service Pack for the SNMP service to operate properly.

❑ You must know when SNMP is needed. You cannot perform Performance Monitor monitoring of TCP/IP without first installing the SNMP service.

❑ *Management Information Bases* (MIB) define a hierarchical structure of manageable objects, which define what may be monitored and/or configured on a network device with a management system.

❑ Internet MIB II provides a standard set of objects essential to fault tolerance and management in an Internet environment.

❑ The LAN Manager MIB II defines 86 objects for management on a Windows NT system. These include a share, session, user, logon, and statistical information.

❑ The DHCP MIB allows an SNMP management system to manage and monitor the Dynamic Host Configuration Protocol service running on a Windows NT server.

❑ The WINS MIB allows an SNMP management system to manage and monitor the Windows Internet Name Server service running on a Windows NT server.

❑ The Internet Information Server MIB allows an SNMP management system to manage and monitor the Internet Information Server running on a Windows NT server.

❑ The Simple Network Configuration Protocol defines a hierarchical tree for naming management objects.

❑ The SNMP service must be installed manually.

❑ It is important to know how to install the SNMP service. You must know that it is installed from the Services tab of the Network control panel applet.

❑ The traps and security tabs of the SNMP service properties sheet allow you to enforce some amount of security in an SNMP managed network.

❑ You must know how to configure the SNMP service. Understand what SNMP communities are, how to configure security for SNMP agents, and how to configure traps. Know the three tabs from the SNMP Service properties (Agent, Traps, and Security) and what each one configures.

❑ The SNMPUTIL.EXE. utility allows the SNMP service to be verified so that it can communicate with management systems correctly.

❑ Be sure you know which commands are initiated by the management system and which commands are initiated by the agent.

SELF TEST

The Self Test questions will help you measure your understanding of the material presented in this chapter. Read all the choices carefully, as there may be more than one correct answer. Choose all correct answers for each question.

1. What command is not available to an SNMP management system?

   A. get

   B. get-next

   C. trap

   D. set

2. The Windows NT SNMP service must be loaded in which situation?

   A. Monitoring TCP/IP statistics with Performance Monitor

   B. Identifying boot errors with Event Viewer

   C. Viewing account properties with User Manager for Domains

   D. Viewing TCP/IP packets with Network Monitor

3. What kind of name tree does SNMP use to define manageable objects?

   A. Flat

   B. Parallel

   C. Serial

   D. Hierarchical

4. Which two components make up an SNMP managed network?

   A. SNMP agent and Network Monitor

   B. SNMP management system and SNMP agent

   C. Performance Monitor and Windows NT SNMP service

   D. Network Monitor and Performance Monitor

5. SNMP agents can initiate which command?

   A. set

   B. get-next

   C. trap

   D. get

6. Which one of the following is not a tab from the SNMP service properties sheet?

   A. Security

   B. Management

   C. Traps

   D. Agent

7. What SNMP service setting allows the maximum security from unauthorized access?

   A. Only Accept SNMP Packets from These Hosts

   B. Accepted Community Names

   C. Send Authentication Trap

   D. Trap Destinations

8. Which MIB is defined by the SNMP RFC?

   A. DHCP MIB

   B. LAN Manager MIB II

   C. Internet Information Server MIB

   D. Internet MIB II

9. When setting up an SNMP agent to report traps, what information must be supplied?

   A. TCP/IP address of agent and IPX address of management system

   B. Community name and IPX address of management system

   C. Agent's community name and TCP/IP address

   D. Host name of DNS server

10. Performance Monitor requires which service in order to monitor TCP/IP statistics?

   A. DHCP

   B. Event Log

   C. WINS

   D. SNMP

13

Troubleshooting

N o matter how well implemented a network is, problems will always come up. The problem could be serious, such as losing TCP/IP communication between sites, or minor, such as an end user not having a TCP/IP address. The bottom line is that these problems require your immediate attention. A relatively minor problem may not seem urgent to you, but to the end user it might be critical, affecting his/her ability to effectively perform their job. By the same token, a network-wide crisis, such as the loss of TCP/IP communication between WAN nodes, obviously requires quick resolution. Fortunately, you have a methodical, systematic manner in which to approach all TCP/IP related problems.

Troubleshooting TCP/IP issues requires a good understanding of TCP/IP and awareness of tools and logical procedures designed to assist you. These troubleshooting tools and procedures will augment your network street-smarts. It is also important to grasp the big TCP/IP picture. Together, these elements help you successfully troubleshoot TCP/IP problems.

CERTIFICATION OBJECTIVE 13.01

Standard Troubleshooting Procedures

Network administrators and engineers have been troubleshooting TCP/IP problems for many years. There are some fundamental troubleshooting procedures that allow you to move up the learning curve to quickly identify and resolve your TCP/IP connectivity issues.

Identify the Problem Area

The first step is recognizing that a problem exists. End users will definitely let you know the moment they lose a service. Your WAN is not going to send you a message that the router is no longer passing TCP/IP traffic, but an end user attempting to access a service across your WAN will let you know if it fails. TCP/IP connectivity issues fall into four different categories: network, subnet, host, and service. You will employ different tools depending on the clues you receive from attempting to duplicate problems or from asking the end user questions relating to the failure.

Network

A network TCP/IP problem occurs when data is not being passed between networks. This can be the result of an incorrectly configured default gateway or a router that is failing or not configured to pass TCP/IP traffic to a needed destination. For example, Tom is an end user on your network. He receives instructions to visit a specific URL on your corporate Web site. When Tom types the URL in his Web browser, the page is not loaded. The configurations of Tom's desktop are accurate; he can access any other corporate URL; but your corporate URL fails. After using the PING utility, you discover that your network router is not aware of the network where the requested URL address resides. The router configuration is amended and Tom gets access to the URL.

Subnet

A subnet TCP/IP problem occurs when data is not being passed between hosts on the same subnet. This is usually the result of an incorrectly configured subnet mask on the affected host computer. For example, Sue is an end user on your network. She has a report due that will make or break the company's earning potential for years to come. When Sue realizes that she can't print the report, she immediately notifies you, believing that the printer is malfunctioning. Aware of such issues, you check her TCP/IP configuration and notice that she has the wrong subnet mask entered, which is preventing her from communicating with the network printer. The configuration is changed and Sue is now able to print.

Host

A host TCP/IP problem occurs when a host computer/printer is configured incorrectly, preventing other hosts from communicating with it. This problem could be the result of an incorrect TCP/IP address, subnet mask, or DHCP configuration. For example, Tom changes the configuration of his workstation because he wants his IP address to be 1.1.1.1. Unfortunately, his network address is 200.200.200.0. After running IPCONFIG, you determine that with the IP address Tom specified, his work over the network would not get done. You give Tom the appropriate configuration and he is reconnected.

Service

A service TCP/IP problem occurs when a service such as Telnet, FTP, or DNS is not functioning properly. The problem could be a result of the service not being installed or, in the case of DNS, not returning valid host to IP address information. For example, Sue has just learned the wonders of telneting from machine to machine. She successfully telnets to a UNIX machine on her network but when she attempts the same to the Windows NT server, the connection fails. Unfortunately, in this situation you have not installed the telnet service on your Windows NT server, and Sue cannot use an unimplemented service.

CERTIFICATION OBJECTIVE 13.02

TCP/IP Troubleshooting Utilities

There are several TCP/IP utilities that can assist you in your investigation and troubleshooting of TCP/IP network issues.

PING (Packet Internet Groper)

The PING utility is a fast method to test TCP/IP connectivity and verify that a TCP/IP address is reachable. Ping can be used to test the TCP/IP connection on the local host or to a remote host. Ping sends an ICMP echo_request packet to a destination address that is expected to return an ICMP echo_response packet. The destination host, if reachable, returns an equal reply packet to the originating node. This response signals that you have reached the intended destination TCP/IP address and, in turn, have connectivity between your location and the pinged host. Several PING utilities offer summary information in addition to the echo_response. Summary information can include the number of packets transmitted, the number of packets received, the percentage of packet loss and minimum, and average and maximum packet round-trip time. Figure 13-1 shows an example of pinging the White House.

As seen from another PING utility:

```
>ping www.whitehouse.gov

www.whitehouse.gov is alive.
```

Indeed www.whitehouse.gov sends a reply and the PING is successful. If you receive a message stating *Bad IP address www.whitehouse.gov* or *PING: unknown host www.whitehouse.gov*, your connection attempt failed. It is time to investigate the DNS and/or host file for existence and validity of the failed TCP/IP address to its domain-name.

Ping utilities offer several options, which allow for continuous pinging, varying packet size, and/or a specific number of echo requests to send.

Figure 13-2 shows an example of using command-line options to specify this Windows NT workstation to send five echo_requests [-n 5] of a 128-byte packet size [-l 128].

FIGURE 13-1

Using the PING utility

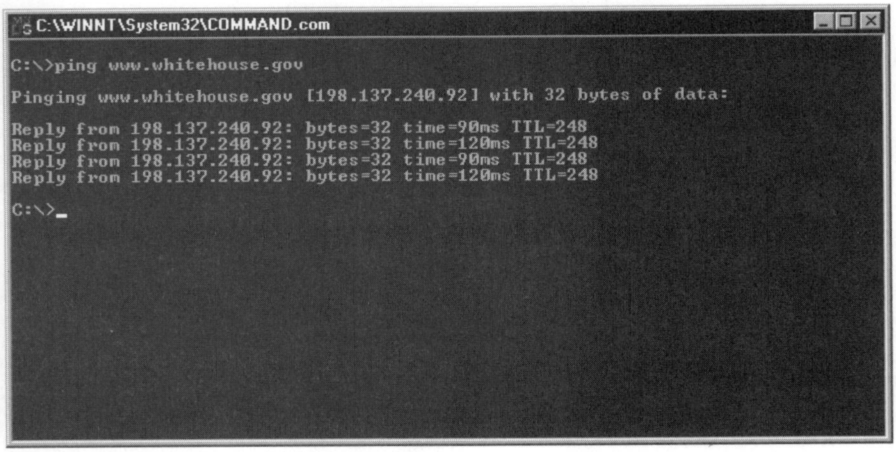

```
C:\WINNT\System32\COMMAND.com

C:\>ping www.whitehouse.gov

Pinging www.whitehouse.gov [198.137.240.92] with 32 bytes of data:

Reply from 198.137.240.92: bytes=32 time=90ms TTL=248
Reply from 198.137.240.92: bytes=32 time=120ms TTL=248
Reply from 198.137.240.92: bytes=32 time=90ms TTL=248
Reply from 198.137.240.92: bytes=32 time=120ms TTL=248

C:\>_
```

Using command-line
options with the
PING utility

```
C:\WINNT\System32\COMMAND.com

C:\>ping www.whitehouse.gov -n 5 -l 128

Pinging www.whitehouse.gov [198.137.240.92] with 128 bytes of data:

Reply from 198.137.240.92: bytes=128 time=321ms TTL=248
Reply from 198.137.240.92: bytes=128 time=230ms TTL=248
Reply from 198.137.240.92: bytes=128 time=351ms TTL=248
Reply from 198.137.240.92: bytes=128 time=100ms TTL=248
Reply from 198.137.240.92: bytes=128 time=451ms TTL=248

C:\>_
```

Here are the ping results from another utility configured to send the same information:

```
> ping -s www.whitehouse.gov 128 5

PING www.whitehouse.gov: 128 data bytes

136 bytes from www1.whitehouse.gov (198.137.240.91): icmp_seq=0.
time=411. ms

136 bytes from www1.whitehouse.gov (198.137.240.91): icmp_seq=1.
time=292. ms

136 bytes from www1.whitehouse.gov (198.137.240.91): icmp_seq=2.
time=165. ms

136 bytes from www1.whitehouse.gov (198.137.240.91): icmp_seq=3.
time=157. ms

136 bytes from www1.whitehouse.gov (198.137.240.91): icmp_seq=4.
time=89. ms
```

```
----www1.whitehouse.gov PING Statistics----

5 packets transmitted, 5 packets received, 0% packet loss

round-trip (ms) min/avg/max = 89/222/411
```

Using PING to Troubleshoot

The PING utility comes in handy to quickly troubleshoot TCP/IP network connection issues.

Troubleshooting Scenario Using PING

1. Log on as Administrator to a system that has TCP/IP installed.
2. Click the Start button and select Programs | Command Prompt.
3. At the prompt type **ping 127.0.0.1**, the loopback address.
4. You receive replies verifying that TCP/IP is installed properly.
5. At the prompt type **ping 200.200.200.10**, the IP address of a printer on your subnet.
6. You do not receive a reply and decide to use IPCONFIG to explore the possibility of a configuration issue.

The following procedures are general examples of how PING can be implemented to determine TCP/IP connectivity failures on your network.

The first step is to send an echo_request to TCP/IP address 127.0.0.1. A fail response from the loopback address, 127.0.0.1, indicates that TCP/IP is not properly installed/configured on your computer. A reply from the loopback address confirms that TCP/IP is installed properly and that you should investigate further.

The second step identifies computers on your subnet. Ping the TCP/IP address of a neighboring computer or printer. A fail response is typically due to a typo or invalid subnet address in your TCP/IP configuration. If you receive a reply from the neighboring address, then you should plan to investigate deeper.

The third step checks for a response from the near-side interface of your router, necessary for internetwork communication. Ping your network default gateway. A fail response from the default gateway could mean that the router interface is down; start troubleshooting your router!

The fourth step checks for a response from the far-side interface of your router. Ping the far-side of the router. This ensures that your router has routed the echo_request to the correct interface. If the PING fails, troubleshoot the router again.

The fifth step verifies connection to a remote host and segment. Ping a well-known (reachable) remote host. It is possible you decided to skip pinging the router near and far interfaces, and went right for the glory of pinging the remote host after that successful local host reply. Without an echo_response, odds are that you could have an invalid default gateway setting in your machine's TCP/IP settings.

exam
⒲atch

When attempting to troubleshoot a connectivity issue, ping in successive order: the loopback address, a local host, the default gateway, the far-side of the router, and finish by pinging the remote host.

ARP

The ARP utility is used to view and make changes to IP address to MAC address translation tables. ARP uses these tables to determine how your machine will resolve the IP address of transmitted packets to their MAC address. In order to view your computer's ARP cache, type **arp -a**, as shown in Figure 13-3.

The ARP utility can be used to add and delete entries in your machine's arp cache. The command-line option [-d] deletes an arp cache entry and option [-s] adds a static entry to your arp cache, as shown in Figure 13-4.

Using ARP to Troubleshoot

The ARP utility is useful to determine the IP address to MAC address translation of transmitted packets on your computer.

Using arp -a will detail the IP address to MAC address information present in your machine's arp cache. If the MAC address destination of the packet to

A computer's ARP cache

```
C:\WINNT\System32\COMMAND.com                                          _ □ X

C:\>arp -a

Interface: 204.241.179.155 on Interface 2
  Internet Address       Physical Address       Type
  204.241.179.1          00-60-5c-49-de-80      dynamic
  204.241.179.57         00-20-af-40-e7-7b      dynamic
  204.241.179.127        00-a0-24-dd-cf-a5      dynamic
  204.241.179.151        00-60-b0-27-5b-3f      dynamic

C:\>_
```

transmit matches an entry in this cache, then your transmission will resolve the
IP address. If the destination MAC address is not in the ARP cache, then ARP
sends an ARP request packet to hosts on your subnet. Should a host reply,
then the MAC to IP address is resolved., If not, another ARP request packet is

Using arp -s to add a static
ARP cache entry

```
C:\WINNT\System32\COMMAND.com                                          _ □ X

C:\>arp -s 204.241.179.130 08-00-09-4f-78-d1

C:\>arp -a

Interface: 204.241.179.155 on Interface 2
  Internet Address       Physical Address       Type
  204.241.179.1          00-60-5c-49-de-80      dynamic
  204.241.179.3          00-80-5f-50-b7-32      dynamic
  204.241.179.127        00-a0-24-dd-cf-a5      dynamic
  204.241.179.130        08-00-09-4f-78-d1      static
  204.241.179.151        00-60-b0-27-5b-3f      dynamic
  204.241.179.254        00-a0-24-ec-a0-66      dynamic

C:\>
```

sent to the subnet's default gateway (router) to be routed to a remote network for host resolution.

NETSTAT

The NETSTAT utility is useful for relating protocol statistics and current active connections utilizing TCP/IP. Local addresses are shown as IP address and port number of the connection. Foreign addresses are shown as IP address and port number of the connection. Host names may take the IP address place when HOSTS file entries are present. Asterisks (*) may also appear, denoting an unassigned port. To view your computer's current connections, type **netstat -a**, as shown in Figure 13-5.

Using command-line options, NETSTAT offers many ways to personalize the statistics you are given. The [-e] option relates Ethernet information, the [-s] option is used to specify which protocol's statistics you are interested in observing, and the [-r] option relates the NETSTAT routing table.

Figure 13-6 shows an example of Ethernet statistics derived by using the command netstat -e.

FIGURE 13-5

Output from the NETSTAT utility

```
C:\WINNT\System32\COMMAND.com

C:\>netstat -a

Active Connections

  Proto  Local Address          Foreign Address        State
  TCP    ducati:1025            localhost:1026         ESTABLISHED
  TCP    ducati:1026            localhost:1025         ESTABLISHED
  UDP    ducati:1027            *:*
  UDP    ducati:echo            *:*
  UDP    ducati:discard         *:*
  UDP    ducati:daytime         *:*
  UDP    ducati:1039            *:*
  UDP    ducati:qotd            *:*
  UDP    ducati:chargen         *:*
  UDP    ducati:135             *:*
  UDP    ducati:snmp            *:*
  UDP    ducati:nbname          *:*
  UDP    ducati:nbdatagram      *:*

C:\>
```

FIGURE 13-6

Output of ethernet
statistics generated with
netstat -e

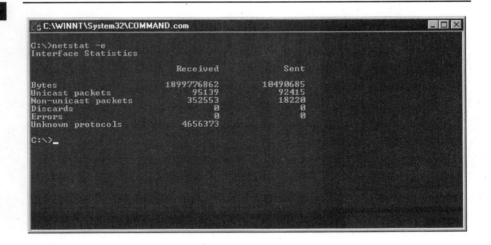

```
C:\WINNT\System32\COMMAND.com                                    _ □ ×

C:\>netstat -e
Interface Statistics

                              Received               Sent

Bytes                       1899776862           10490685
Unicast packets                  95139              92415
Non-unicast packets             352553              18220
Discards                             0                  0
Errors                               0                  0
Unknown protocols              4656373

C:\>_
```

Using NETSTAT to Troubleshoot

NETSTAT is useful in troubleshooting protocol-related issues. A prime
example is a situation where you suspect a problem with TCP connectivity.
You use the netstat -a command to verify that the TCP status of a desired
connection is not returning an *established* status message. Other messages tend
to indicate a problem with the connection or with the queue. To retrieve and
verify routing information, use netstat -r.

NBTSTAT

The NBTSTAT utility is useful for relating protocol statistics and current
active NBT connections describe NetBIOS over TCP/IP. Essentially,
NBTSTAT describes the computer names cache of a computer. For example,
my computer's NetBIOS name is Ducati, my neighbor's computer NetBIOS
name is Honda. My computer is aware of Ducati as its computer name but
uses an LMHOSTS file, WINS, or a broadcast to populate its NBT computer
names cache. In order to view your computer's NetBIOS cache type **nbtstat
-n**, as shown in Figure 13-7.

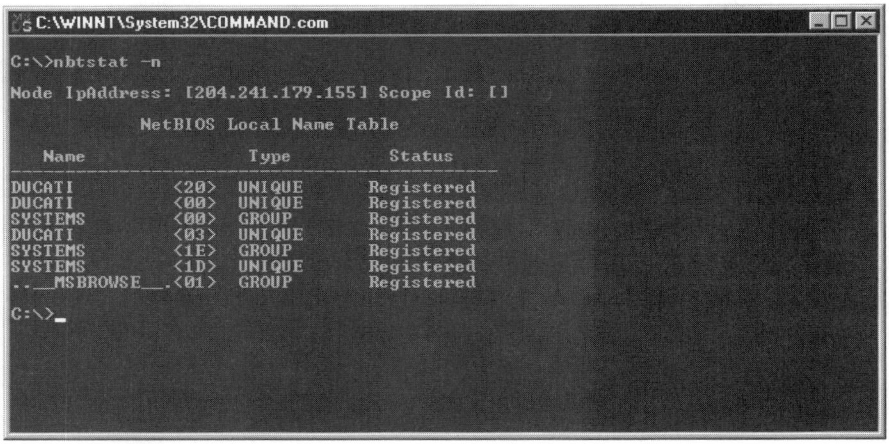

FIGURE 13-7

An example of a
computer's NetBIOS cache

```
C:\WINNT\System32\COMMAND.com                                    _ □ X

C:\>nbtstat -n

Node IpAddress: [204.241.179.155] Scope Id: []

            NetBIOS Local Name Table

    Name              Type       Status
DUCATI        <20>   UNIQUE     Registered
DUCATI        <00>   UNIQUE     Registered
SYSTEMS       <00>   GROUP      Registered
DUCATI        <03>   UNIQUE     Registered
SYSTEMS       <1E>   GROUP      Registered
SYSTEMS       <1D>   UNIQUE     Registered
..__MSBROWSE__.<01>  GROUP      Registered

C:\>_
```

NBTSTAT also has command-line options such as [-a remotename], which lists the remote computer's name cache. Type **nbtstat ?** to view other NBTSTAT options.

Using NBTSTAT to Troubleshoot

Using NBTSTAT to troubleshoot is limited to NetBIOS-related issues. A common problem that can be resolved using NBTSTAT is one in which the local LMHOSTS file contains errors. This situation demands that you correct the LMHOSTS file. Once the file has been replaced, simply type **nbtstat -R**. This switch removes all the entries in the NBT name cache and reloads the information from the corrected LMHOSTS file. You might also use nbtstat to investigate an error message such as Event 4320, NetBt Error. This error tells you that another computer on your network has the same IP address. You can't have more than one NetBIOS name per IP address; therefore, you must troubleshoot the issue using nbtstat -n. The result is the name of the machine with the same IP address.

IPCONFIG

The IPCONFIG utility is extremely useful, as it relates the entire TCP/IP configuration present in your machine. In addition to the configuration information the utility provides, it has the added capability of interfacing with DHCP services to renew or release a leased DHCP TCP/IP address. Using IPCONFIG will return the computer's TCP/IP address, its subnet mask, and default gateway.

Figure 13-8 shows the results of typing ipconfig.

IPCONFIG has several command-line options. The most widely used is the [/all] parameter. The ipconfig /all command will issue an abundance of information, including the computer's host name, DNS servers, node type, physical address (MAC address), DHCP status, IP address, subnet mask, and default gateway. Computers that derive their IP addresses from a DHCP server can use additional command-line options of ipconfig [/renew [adapter]] and [/release [adapter]], which enable you to renew your DHCP IP address lease or release your DHCP lease on specific or all network adapters using DHCP.

Figure 13-9 shows an example of using command-line options to view all TCP/IP configuration information available on a Windows NT workstation.

Using IPCONFIG to Troubleshoot

IPCONFIG is one of the first tools to turn to in your troubleshooting efforts. Engineers use it regularly since it provides such detailed and useful information regarding a computer's complete TCP/IP configuration. Typing ipconfig is a

FIGURE 13-8

Sample IPCONFIG output

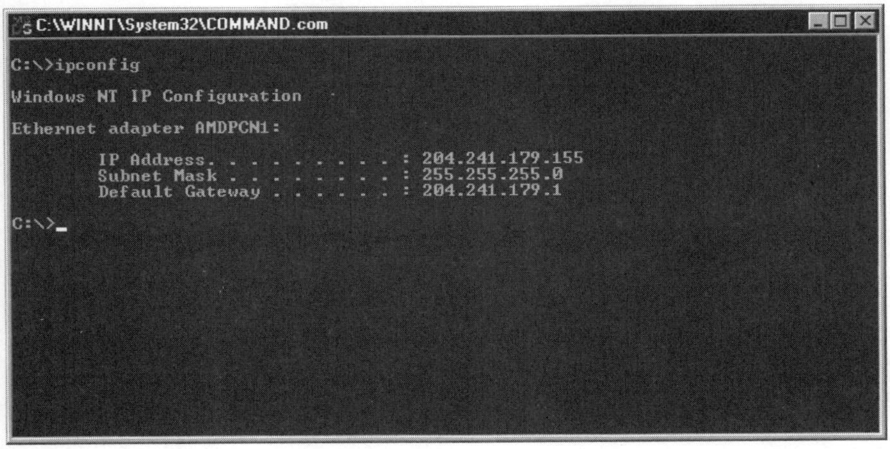

```
C:\WINNT\System32\COMMAND.com

C:\>ipconfig

Windows NT IP Configuration

Ethernet adapter AMDPCN1:

        IP Address. . . . . . . . . : 204.241.179.155
        Subnet Mask . . . . . . . . : 255.255.255.0
        Default Gateway . . . . . . : 204.241.179.1

C:\>_
```

FIGURE 13-9

Sample IPCONFIG output
using the /all parameter

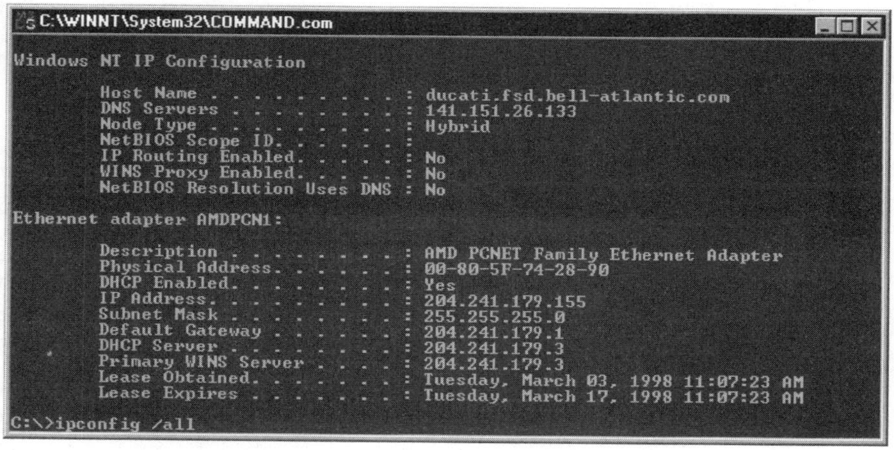

```
C:\WINNT\System32\COMMAND.com                                        _□×

Windows NT IP Configuration

        Host Name . . . . . . . . . : ducati.fsd.bell-atlantic.com
        DNS Servers . . . . . . . . : 141.151.26.133
        Node Type . . . . . . . . . : Hybrid
        NetBIOS Scope ID. . . . . . :
        IP Routing Enabled. . . . . : No
        WINS Proxy Enabled. . . . . : No
        NetBIOS Resolution Uses DNS : No

Ethernet adapter AMDPCN1:

        Description . . . . . . . . : AMD PCNET Family Ethernet Adapter
        Physical Address. . . . . . : 00-80-5F-74-28-90
        DHCP Enabled. . . . . . . . : Yes
        IP Address. . . . . . . . . : 204.241.179.155
        Subnet Mask . . . . . . . . : 255.255.255.0
        Default Gateway . . . . . . : 204.241.179.1
        DHCP Server . . . . . . . . : 204.241.179.3
        Primary WINS Server . . . . : 204.241.179.3
        Lease Obtained. . . . . . . : Tuesday, March 03, 1998 11:07:23 AM
        Lease Expires . . . . . . . : Tuesday, March 17, 1998 11:07:23 AM

C:\>ipconfig /all
```

quick way to determine if an IP address, subnet mask, or default gateway is valid for your network. Imagine administrating two subnets. Tom is the only user having problems accessing an IP host on another subnet. The subnet mask of Tom's network is 255.255.255.192 and the results of typing ipconfig on Tom's machine are:

```
IP address          : 204.241.155.70

Subnet mask         : 255.255.255.192

Default gateway     : 204.241.155.130
```

With a subnet mask of 255.255.255.192 on a Class C network, there can be two subnets with a block size of 64. Therefore, Tom's IP address is not on the same subnet as the default gateway. You have determined that other users on Tom's subnet have no problems connecting to the remote subnet and their IP addresses are within the same block with the default gateway. The conclusion is that Tom's IP address is incorrect.

EXERCISE 13-2

Troubleshooting Scenario Using IPCONFIG

1. Log on as Administrator to a system that has TCP/IP installed.
2. Click the Start button and select Programs | Command Prompt.

3. At the prompt type **ipconfig**.

4. Examine the output and verify it relates valid subnet mask, default gateway, and IP address configurations for your network.

exam ⓦ**atch** *Make sure you understand how to utilize ipconfig output to diagnose potential connectivity problems such as the example presented in the previous section.*

FROM THE CLASSROOM

A Troubleshooting Scenario

Let's troubleshoot a scenario that could occur many times within any given day. A user calls and tells you they cannot log on to the Windows NT domain in a TCP/IP network.

It is best to start analyzing the problem at the bottom layer of the TCP/IP network architecture.

1. Can you PING the user's workstation using the IP address?

    If the answer is yes, then IP between the Network layer and the Internet layer is working fine.

    IP is resolving the IP address to hardware address. The lower layers are working great.

    If the answer is no, then check the workstation's IP configuration information. Use IPCONFIG to view the IP parameters. Look at the values of the IP address, subnet mask, and default gateway. Usually the problem will be in one of these settings.

2. Can you PING the user's workstation using the host name?

    If the answer is yes, then things are working fine between the Network all the way up through the Application layer.

    If the answer is no, then the problem is within resolving the name to the IP address. Check the various methods that your network may be using to resolve names to IP addresses. An incorrect entry in any of these will prevent name resolution (WINS, DNS, LMHOSTS file, or HOSTS file).

3. Go and watch the user. This is not a TCP/IP problem preventing a login to the domain. The user could be using the wrong username, password, or domain.

—By D. Lynn White, MCT, MCSE

```
C:\WINNT\System32\COMMAND.com                                          _ □ ×

C:\>tracert www.whitehouse.gov

Tracing route to www.whitehouse.gov [198.137.240.91]
over a maximum of 30 hops:

  1    <10 ms    <10 ms    <10 ms   tempo-new.fsd.bell-atlantic.com [204.241.179.1]
  2    <10 ms    <10 ms     10 ms   inet-gw.fsd.bell-atlantic.com [199.100.163.33]
  3     31 ms     40 ms     30 ms   38.1.1.1
  4    180 ms    200 ms    200 ms   38.146.180.1
  5    691 ms    290 ms    120 ms   rc5.southeast.us.psi.net [38.1.25.5]
  6    180 ms     60 ms     80 ms   ip2.ci3.herndon.va.us.psi.net [38.25.11.2]
  7     70 ms     40 ms     50 ms   198.137.240.33
  8    210 ms    381 ms    380 ms   www1.whitehouse.gov [198.137.240.91]

Trace complete.

C:\>_
```

TRACERT

The TRACERT utility is commonly used to locate failures along a TCP/IP
communications path. It is similar to PING in that it makes use of ICMP

```
C:\WINNT\System32\COMMAND.com                                          _ □ ×

C:\>tracert -d www.whitehouse.gov

Tracing route to www.whitehouse.gov [198.137.240.91]
over a maximum of 30 hops:

  1    <10 ms    <10 ms    <10 ms   204.241.179.1
  2    <10 ms    <10 ms     10 ms   199.100.163.33
  3     30 ms     40 ms     30 ms   38.1.1.1
  4     70 ms     40 ms     30 ms   38.146.180.1
  5     50 ms     50 ms     41 ms   38.1.25.5
  6     90 ms    401 ms    350 ms   38.25.11.2
  7    441 ms    140 ms     80 ms   198.137.240.33
  8     60 ms     61 ms     80 ms   198.137.240.91

Trace complete.

C:\>_
```

echo request packets to follow the route the packet takes to a specific destination. A benefit that TRACERT provides over PING is its implementation of Time-to-Live (TTL) values which effectively relate a route metric (hop count). Routers along the communications path of an ICMP echo request packet must reduce the packets TTL by at least one before forwarding it to the next router, and continuing in this fashion until the destination address is reached or the maximum TTL is reached. In order to determine the number of hops to the White House's WWW server, you simply type **tracert www.whitehouse.gov**, as shown in Figure 13-10.

TRACERT offers several command-line options. A common parameter, the [-w] option, enables you to specify the time-out in milliseconds for each hop. To see the host name associated with each of the hops during a TRACERT, use the [-d] parameter. To specify the maximum number of hops, use [-h]. The [-j] option tells TRACERT to lose the source route along a host list.

Figure 13-11 shows an example of using the **tracert -d** command.

Using TRACERT to Troubleshoot

TRACERT is helpful when attempting to troubleshoot the point at which an ICMP packet fails to be forwarded in a route. This information is useful for following the connection path of packets on your local network as well as an accepted method for testing Internet connections. A common situation in which to use TRACERT is when a user is accessing your network via a PPTP connection using their Internet Service Provider (ISP). For example, Sue is at home and wants to telecommute. She has dialed into her ISP and is attempting to establish a connection to you network but is unsuccessful. The first step in supporting Sue is instructing her to use TRACERT. If she receives the message "destination host unreachable," you know that TRACERT lost its route at that point. Sue may also find that TRACERT times out or enters a loop state where a problem exists.

EXERCISE 13-3

Troubleshooting Scenario Using TRACERT

    1. Log on as Administrator to a system that has TCP/IP installed.

2. Click the Start button and select Programs | Command Prompt.

3. At the prompt type **tracert 200.200.200.5**, where the IP address is a host on one of your company's subnets.

4. Examining the output of the TRACERT you realize that the packets are being routed over the Internet to reach a host within your own network. You decide that your router is not aware of the subnet at which the host resides and correct its configuration.

5. Running tracert 200.200.200.5 again shows that the echo requests are routed appropriately within your network.

ROUTE

The ROUTE utility is used to configure network routing tables. This is the tool used to add, delete, change, or print entries in your routing tables. Manually entering routes may be tedious but necessary in some cases to ensure connectivity. For example, to add and delete a route:

```
ROUTE ADD 200.200.210.0 MASK 255.255.255.0 200.200.210.1

ROUTE DELETE 200.200.210.0 MASK 255.255.255.0
```

Additional features help make using the ROUTE command more bearable. The command-line option [-f] in addition to a command cleans the routing table prior to making a change. This is a useful feature that allows you to make changes to your routing tables, while at the same time ensuring they will be refreshed and updated with your change. Imagine having to retype routes every time the router is recycled or restarted. Another parameter ensures that routes added will remain static and persistent. This is the option [-p], which is used with the ADD command.

Using ROUTE to Troubleshoot

The ROUTE utility is used mainly as a result of troubleshooting. The following scenario depicts a situation in which you would use the ROUTE add command as the last phase of troubleshooting. The IS department decides to update the company's intranet. During their upgrade they plan to change the IP address associated with the home page URL. The weekend comes and goes, and IS has successfully updated the intranet. Tom shows up the next morning and is the first end user who decides to surf the corporate Web site. Tom enters the URL and the usual page does not appear. Tom notifies you that he is not able to access the intranet home page. You immediately remember that without an interior routing protocol such as RIP, you must manually update the routing table of your router using the ROUTE add utility. Once the routes are updated reflecting the new subnets, TCP/IP traffic can flow to the new subnets on which the intranet Web pages now reside.

NSLOOKUP

NSLOOKUP is used to examine information from DNS servers. It is helpful to have an understanding of how DNS servers provide IP address to host name resolution services. NSLOOKUP consists of both interactive and noninteractive modes based on the original UNIX tool. Tasks requiring one bit of information should be derived in noninteractive mode. Tasks that require more information require the use of interactive mode.

Here is an example of using noninteractive mode:

```
NSLOOKUP WWW.WHITEHOUSE.GOV DNSSERVER1
```

and an example of using interactive mode:

```
NSLOOKUP -
```

Using NSLOOKUP to Troubleshoot

The NSLOOKUP utility is used only for troubleshooting DNS issues. For example, nslookup would be useful if you find that IP address to host name translation is not working as expected. Using NSLOOKUP you can review information contained in the reverse lookup file or other DNS zone files of your DNS server.

Event Viewer and Network Monitor

Event Viewer and Network Monitor are tools that analyze and identify TCP/IP connectivity issues.

Event Viewer is a valuable tool for front-line recognition of a problem that may be hardware, software, network, security, or system related. It has a user-friendly interface with icons that run blue in color if acceptable, yellow for a potential problem, and red for an event that should be researched immediately. A description of the event noted will be included with logged events.

Figure 13-12 shows the details of an Event Viewer.

Network Monitor is capable of a high degree of complexity in diagnosing network traffic. It is capable of using both capture and display filters to aid in your evaluation of network packets. Network Monitor utilizes the NDIS 4.0 driver, which enables a particular network interface card (NIC) to capture outbound or inbound packets of the associated computer. Therefore, NDIS

FIGURE 13-12

Example of an event detail

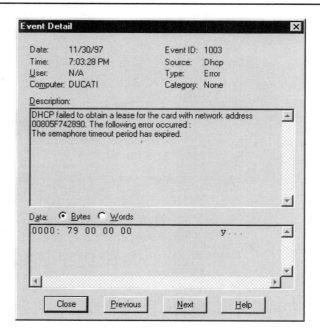

4.0 enables Network Monitor to consume much less of a processor's resources than a NIC card set to operate in promiscuous mode. In essence, Network Monitor can function as a protocol analyzer or as an NIC specific trap filter.

Using Event Viewer and Network Monitor to Troubleshoot TCP/IP Protocol Statistics

Event Viewer offers a quick and simple method for identifying a problem. Simply open the Event Viewer and you see current status information that is potentially relevant to an issue you are attempting to resolve.

Network Monitor enables you to collect protocol statistics. In order to view TCP/IP protocol statistics, you should enable a capture filter. This filter should be configured to capture TCP/IP statistics and log them to a file. This is a nice feature, allowing you to go back and review the files at your leisure. In addition, you can set up a display filter to diagnose the captured TCP/IP statistics based on properties such as source and destination address of the packets.

EXERCISE 13-4	**Using Event Viewer to View TCP/IP Messages**

1. Log on as Administrator to a system that has TCP/IP installed.
2. Click the Start button and select Programs | Administrative Tools | Event Viewer.
3. Double-click an event with a TCP/IP-related source description.
4. Examine the description in the Event Detail window.

CERTIFICATION OBJECTIVE 13.03

Troubleshooting Process

Troubleshooting processes vary based on the administrator's experience in dealing with and resolving TCP/IP connectivity issues. For example, you cannot just turn to page 69 in a manual and find out why your network just lost TCP/IP connectivity with your home office in Montana. A manual certainly will not provide instructions on dealing with your end users, all of whom have urgent deadlines, need connectivity with that office, and will soon be haunting your every move. Remember to approach your dilemma logically and methodically. It is often best to start locally and progress more toward the WAN in your network diagnosis. In addition, attempt to re-create the problem, draw the problem representation on paper, and verify the extent to which your network is being affected. Finally, narrow down the possible problem areas by successively testing different network areas using the troubleshooting utilities discussed here.

CERTIFICATION SUMMARY

The troubleshooting section on the Microsoft exam are heavily rooted in your ability to evaluate results from the utilities discussed in this chapter and apply them to a TCP/IP connectivity issue. The most commonly used utilities that deal with most TCP/IP network problems are PING, IPCONFIG, and TRACERT. The other utilities are definitely important but are specialized for specific issues.

It is essential that you understand the concepts of IP addressing, subnetting, network classes, and basic network connectivity. Reviewing how each utility assists in determining the nature of a problem also plays a big role in how effectively you can tie the TCP/IP ideas together. You should know the results of an incorrectly configured subnet mask, default gateway, and IP address. You must also understand how to troubleshoot from your desktop to the remote networks in your system.

 # TWO-MINUTE DRILL

- ❑ There are some fundamental troubleshooting procedures that allow you to move up the learning curve to quickly identify and resolve your TCP/IP connectivity issues.
- ❑ The first step in troubleshooting is recognizing that a problem exists.
- ❑ A network TCP/IP problem occurs when data is not being passed between networks.

❏ A subnet TCP/IP problem occurs when data is not being passed between hosts on the same subnet.

❏ A host TCP/IP problem occurs when a host computer/printer is configured incorrectly, preventing other hosts from communicating with it.

❏ A service TCP/IP problem occurs when a service such as Telnet, FTP, or DNS is not functioning properly.

❏ There are several TCP/IP utilities that can assist you in your investigation and troubleshooting of TCP/IP network issues.

❏ The PING utility is a fast method to test TCP/IP connectivity and verify that a TCP/IP address is reachable.

❏ When attempting to troubleshoot a connectivity issue, ping in successive order: the loopback address, a local host, the default gateway, the far-side of the router, and finish by pinging the remote host.

❏ The ARP utility is used to view and make changes to IP address to MAC address translation tables.

❏ The NETSTAT utility is useful for relating protocol statistics and current active connections utilizing TCP/IP. Local addresses are shown as IP address and port number of the connection.

❏ The NBTSTAT utility is useful for relating protocol statistics and current active NBT connections describe NetBIOS over TCP/IP.

❏ The IPCONFIG utility is extremely useful, as it relates the entire TCP/IP configuration present in your machine.

❏ Make sure you understand how to utilize ipconfig output to diagnose potential connectivity problems.

❏ The TRACERT utility is commonly used to locate failures along a TCP/IP communications path.

❏ The ROUTE utility is used to configure network routing tables.

❏ NSLOOKUP is used to examine information from DNS servers.

❏ Event Viewer and Network Monitor are tools that analyze and identify TCP/IP connectivity issues.

❑ Troubleshooting processes vary based on the administrator's experience in dealing with and resolving TCP/IP connectivity issues.

❑ Remember to approach your dilemma logically and methodically. It is often best to start locally and progress more toward the WAN in your network diagnosis.

SELF TEST

The Self Test questions will help you measure your understanding of the material presented in this chapter. Read all the choices carefully, as there may be more than one correct answer. Choose all correct answers for each question.

1. Which utility is used to send a ICMP packet to test whether a remote host is reachable?

   A. Event Viewer

   B. NBTSTAT

   C. NETSTAT

   D. Ping

2. Which utility is used in order to make changes to IP address to media access card address translation tables?

   A. TRACERT

   B. Event Viewer

   C. ARP

   D. Ping

3. It is important that you quickly identify current active and established TCP connections by your computer. Which of the following utilities is most useful?

   A. Ping

   B. Tcpstat

   C. TRACERT

   D. NETSTAT

4. You want to determine if a computer acquires its IP address from the DHCP server. Which utility will return the desired information?

   A. ARP

   B. Ipconfig /all

   C. Ipconfig /lease

   D. Ping /services

5. Point-to-point tunneling protocol is used to connect remote users via their ISPs. Your director is correctly configured to use PPTP communication but is unable to reach your network. Which utility could identify the location of the problem?

   A. Ping

   B. Network Monitor

   C. TRACERT

   D. Telnet

6. It is urgent that users on a specific subnet not be allowed to access a subnet which now contains secure data. Which utility could you use to remove connectivity between these networks?

   A. ARP

   B. ROUTE delete

   C. Filternet

   D. Prevent /securenet

7. Which utility allows for researching DNS files for specific IP address to host name assignments?

   A. ARP

B. NBTSTAT

C. NETSTAT

D. NSLOOKUP

8. Which of the following utilities is used to relate NetBIOS over TCP/IP statistics?

A. NBTSTAT

B. NetBEUI /all

C. NETSTAT

D. Netsho /nbt

9. What address should you PING to verify that TCP/IP is correctly installed and configured on a computer?

A. the default gateway

B. a remote host

C. the loopback address

D. a network printer

10. Typing ipconfig at a prompt does not produce which of the following information?

A. the default gateway

B. the MAC address

C. the subnet mask

D. the IP address

11. Name the utility which provides metrics in its output.

A. TRACERT

B. PING

C. netstat -M

D. NSLOOKUP

12. In order to send a specific amount of echo_requests when using ping you must specify which of the following command line options?

A. Ping -a

B. Ping -#

C. Ping -n

D. Ping -r

13. You would use the following command to view Ethernet network statistics:

A. ether /stat

B. TRACERT

C. Event Viewer

D. netstat -e

14. What is the best method for verifying network connectivity between different networks which do not use routers or level three communication devices?

A. Ping

B. TRACERT

C. NSLOOKUP

D. none of the above

15. Your first step in identifying general TCP/IP connectivity should be to use which utility?

A. ARP

B. Ping

C. Event Viewer

D. TRACERT

A

Self Test Answers

Answers to Chapter 1 Self Test

1. TCP/IP software is available on which of the following?
   D. TCP/IP is not tied to one operating system; rather it is the standard from which operating systems will implement network components.

2. (True/False) The Internet is a collection of networks that communicate using the UDP/ARP protocol.
   False. The Internet is a collection of networks that communicate using TCP/IP protocol.

3. Internet protocol software is designed in:
   B. TCP/IP protocol stack software is developed and designed in layers.

4. An IP address is:
   C. IP addresses are 32-bit numbers separated into 4 equal octets and represented decimally.

5. A Windows NT machine with two network cards is known as a:
   A. It is also known as a multi-homed system, but in this case we were asking about routers.

6. The transmission of a message from one network to another through a router is known as:

7. Which one of the following is not a valid TCP/IP network class?
   C. Class F is not currently a valid address level. The four types of address classes are discussed in Chapter 3.

8. A private or internal TCP/IP is known as:
   D. A TCP/IP Network that is not directly connected to the Internet through a firewall or at all is known as an Intranet.

9. Which type of machine can a Windows NT Server 4.0 communicate with?
   D. TCP/IP is found in multiple operating systems and on multiple hardware platforms. TCP/IP is a model that is implemented by the vendor.

10. RFC is an acronym for:
    D. RFC is a Request for Comments.

11. The management service that automatically assigns IP parameters to clients is called:
    C. Automatic assignment of IP parameters as well as WINS, DNS, and gateway information is done by DHCP.

12. The new 32-bit TCP/IP protocol stack is available on which platforms?
    A, B, D. Windows 3.1 used the older more restricted TCP/IP protocol stack, whereas the redesigned, rewritten 32-bit TCP/IP protocol stack is used in the other platforms.

    C. Forwarding of messages between subnets is known as routing.

Answers to Chapter 2 Self Test

1. What layer of the OSI model does an electronic mail program use?
   D. An electronic mail program uses the Application layer.

2. How many layers are in the TCP/IP model?
   B. The TCP/IP model consists of 4 layers.

3. What layer of the TCP/IP model does the User Datagram Protocol operate from?
   A. The User Datagram Protocol operates from the Transport layer of the TCP/IP model.

4. From the sending computer, what does each layer of the TCP/IP model add to the data when it receives it?
   C. Each layer adds its own header to the data when it receives it.

5. The Application layer of the TCP/IP model equates to what layer(s) of the OSI model?
   A, C, D. The Application layer of the TCP/IP model equates to the top three layers of the OSI model: Application, Presentation, and Session.

6. What protocol provides a reliable, connection-based delivery service?
   A. TCP provides a reliable, connection-based delivery service.

7. How many layers are in the OSI model?
   C. The OSI model contains 7 layers.

8. What protocol(s) is available at the Internet layer of the TCP/IP model?
   B,D. The Internet layer of the TCP/IP model consists of IP and ICMP.

9. What protocol(s) provide(s) a connectionless datagram service that is an unreliable "best effort" delivery?
   C. UDP provides a connectionless datagram service that is an unreliable "best effort" delivery. While IP also makes an unreliable "best effort" delivery, it is not a datagram service.

10. What is the IP checksum used for?
    A. The IP checksum checks the integrity of only the IP header.

11. What layer of the TCP/IP model does the HyperText Transfer Protocol operate from?
    C. The HyperText Transfer Protocol operates from the Application layer of the TCP/IP model.

12. What is the most common usage(s) of ICMP messages?
    B, D. The most common usages of ICMP messages are PING and TRACERT.

13. What layer of the OSI model performs data encryption?
    A. The Presentation layer of the OSI model performs data encryption.

14. What makes up a TCP header?
    A. The TCP header is made up of 6 words of 32 bits each.

15. What protocol provides IP address-to-physical address resolution for IP packets?
    D. ARP provides IP address-to-physical address resolution for IP packets.

16. What layer of the OSI model is responsible for providing error-free transfer of frames from one computer to another computer using the Physical layer?
    C. The Data Link layer of the OSI model is responsible for providing error free transfer of frames from one computer to another computer using the Physical layer.

17. What is layer 4 of the TCP/IP model?
    B. Layer 4 of the TCP/IP model is the Application layer.

18. What is layer 5 of the OSI model?
    A. Layer 5 of the OSI model is the Session layer.

Answers to Chapter 3 Self Test

1. Which address is valid for Class C?
   C. 202.67.13.87 is the only valid choice. Choice B is wrong because the third octet is not valid.

2. What is the binary representation for 124.58.76.6?
   D. By converting the decimal to binary you would end up with 01111100 00111010 01001100 00000110.

3. What utility would you use to verify the internetwork connectivity of a system located in another state?
   B. PING would allow you to instantly find out if the host in the other state had internetwork connectivity.

4. The IP address consists of _____ octets.
   B. There are 4 octets in the IP address.

5. The purpose of using #PRE in the LMHOSTS file is _____
   A. #PRE will preload a name into the name cache when used correctly in the LMHOSTS file.

6. What is the default subnet mask for a Class C address?
   C. The default subnet mask for a Class C address is 255.255.255.0.

7. How many hosts can a Class B network have if the default subnet mask is used?
   D. A Class B can have 65,534 hosts when it uses the default subnet mask.

8. A system has an IP address of 172.24.10.62. What is allowed to be done with this system?
   B. The system can be used on an Intranet as that is one of the addresses allowed by RFC 1597 to be issued by a Network Manager.

9. What Class of addresses has a 0 as the Most Significant Bit in the first octet?
   A. Class A addresses have a 0 as the MSB in the first octet.

10. How do you add additional gateways to a Windows NT Server that is configured with TCP/IP?
B. Additional gateway can be added by selecting the Advanced button on the IP Address tab of TCP/IP Properties.

11. What would you type at the command prompt to receive detailed IP information for a machine?
C. IPCONFIG /ALL would give you *detailed* IP information for the machine. Typing IPCONFIG would only give *summary* information.

12. What file can be used as a replacement for local DNS?
D. The HOSTS file can act as a replacement for local DNS.

13. What Class of addresses has 110 as the three Most Significant Bits in the first octet?
C. Class C addresses have 110 as the three MSBs in the first octet.

14. What is the purpose of the Class E addresses?
B. Class E addresses are reserved for future use.

15. What is the network ID for the IP address 148.34.18.42 that has a subnet mask of 255.255.255.0?
C. 148.34.18 is the network ID for the IP address 148.34.18.42. Remember to convert to binary format and use the

Boolean AND function to separate the network ID from the host ID by adding the IP address and the subnet mask.

Answers to Chapter 4 Self Test

1. Given Figure 4-4, answer the following scenario:
The following network uses static IP addresses. The computer with IP address 210.116.204.12 on Subnet B is trying to communicate with a computer on Subnet A with IP address 210.116.135.17. The machines are having trouble communicating. The computer on Subnet C with IP address 210.116.157.110 is able to communicate with the computer on Subnet B with no problems. Analyzing the information given, what is the problem?
D. The IP address for the workstation on Subnet A is for a workstation on Subnet C. This causes a routing problem and this is why the workstations cannot communicate.

2. Given Figure 4-5, answer the following: Considering the layout of IP addresses and subnet addresses, what would the value of the ? be in Figure 4-5?
A. The subnet address of Subnet B would be 210.116.24.0. Following the multiple rule starting with Subnet C and the first subnet address being 8, the second would be 16 and the third would be 24.

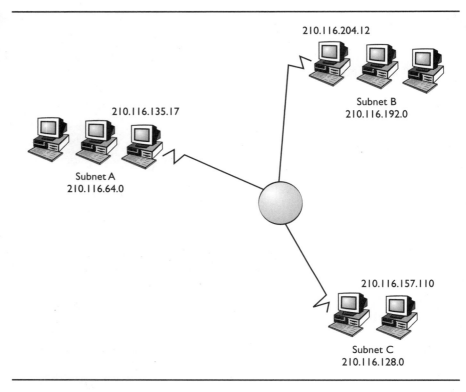

FIGURE 4-4

Review Question 1

3. What is the following decimal value in 8-bit binary form: 179?
   B. Converting the value comes up with 10110011 or 128+32+16+2+1=179.

4. What is the following 8 binary value in decimal form: 01111010?
   D. Converting the value comes up with 122 or 64+32+16+8+2=122.

5. Refer to the Figure 4-6 for the following scenario:
   You have a network with 6 subnets. You know the following:

   ■ You will never have more than 20 subnets.

   ■ You will never need more than 2,048 hosts per subnet.

   ■ You are running Windows 95 on your workstations.

   ■ You use DHCP on your network.

   ■ TCP/IP is your major protocol.

   ■ Each subnet is a separate site connected via a router.

   All links are T1 connections between sites.

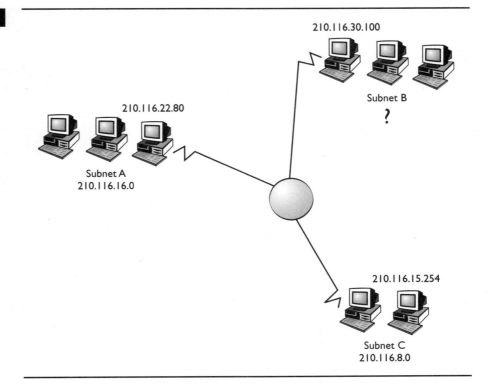

Review Question 2

With a Class B network ID of 172.42.0.0 what would your subnet mask be?
B. The subnet mask would have to be 255.255.224.0 to allow for 6 subnets. This does allow for over 8,000 hosts, but if we try to come closer and match up the 2,048 hosts, we would have room for only 14 subnets.

6. Refer to Figure 4-7 for the following scenario:
You have a large network divided up into subnets. You know the following:

- You use TCP/IP and IPX/SPX as your protocols.
- Each subnet is in a different city.
- You will never have more than 15 subnets.
- Your workstations are a mix of Windows NT Workstation and Windows 95.
- You will never need more than 2,000 hosts per subnet.
- You PDC is in your office with BDCs in each remote office.

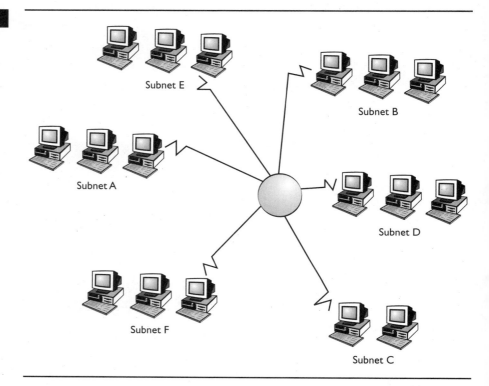

FIGURE 4-6

Review Question 5

- You also have 3 BDCs at your location. Considering the list of known facts as well as Figure 4-7, which subnet mask would you use in this circumstance? You have a choice between a Class A, B, or C network. What do you choose and what subnet mask within the class do you use?

  B. This is the best answer to meet both the host and subnet requirements. Answer A would work but B is a better choice so there is not a waste of IP addresses. Answers C and E allow for only 14 subnets and we need 15. Answer D allows for only 6 hosts.

7. Refer to Figure 4-8 for the following scenario:

   Using the box in Figure 4-8, convert the following decimal numbers to binary:

   - 145
   - 37
   - 254
   - 128
   - 195

   E. 145=10010001   37=00100101
   254=11111110   128=10000000
   195=11000011

FIGURE 4-7

Review Question 6

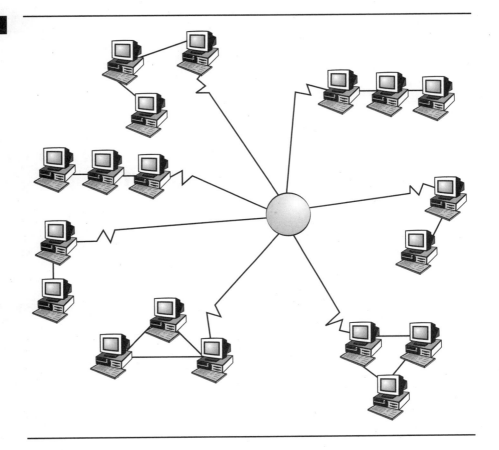

8. Refer to Figure 4-9 for the following scenario:
Figure 4-9 is missing some numbers.

First fill in the missing decimal values for each bit.
Next fill in either 0 or 1 to complete the binary equivalent of 166.

FIGURE 4-8

Review Question 7

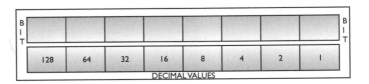

BIT							BIT
128	64	32	16	8	4	2	1

DECIMAL VALUES

FIGURE 4-9

FIGURE 4-9

Review Question 8

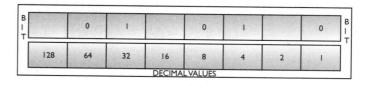

Take the following subnet mask and determine which of the following choices are valid subnet addresses for this mask: 255.240.0.0 (Choose all that apply.)
A, C, D. These subnet addresses fall into some of the acceptable values. The multiplier in this case is 16. A,C, & D are all multiples of 16. This is another way of checking it.(See Figure 4-10.)

9. You have a network with 4 subnets. The network addresses for your subnets are Network A: 192.1.16.0, Network B: 192.1.32.0, Network C: 192.1.48.0, and Network D: 192.1.64.0. With a subnet mask of 255.255.248.0 what will your ranges or addresses be?
B. This subnet mask allow for 30 subnets and each network increment is by only 8.

Answers to Chapter 5 Self Test

1. What are the two characteristics of a gateway?
A,D. Protocol Translation and IP Forwarding. There is no security or scheduling with a basic Gateway.

2. How do you print the current routing table?
D. ROUTE PRINT. The -P option makes a route persistent / permanent.

3. How do you add a route to 221.2.3.0 via port 221.2.2.20 requiring two hops to the routing table?
C. route Add 221.2.3.0 MASK 255.255.255.0 222.2.2.20 metric 2

FIGURE 4-10

Answer to Question 8

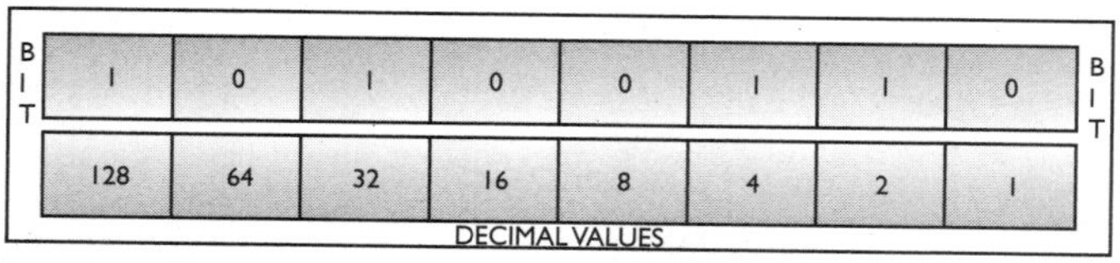

4. What must you configure for static routing?
   B. Enable IP Forwarding

5. What does OSPF stand for?
   C. Open Shortest Path First

6. How do you delete the 221.2.3.0 route from the current routing table?
   D. route delete 221.2.3.0 - No other parameters needed.

7. What does RIP provide?
   B. Dynamic Routing - use the ROUTE command to display route information.

8. What utility will display the gateways between two hosts?
   D. TRACERT - Trace Route

9. How many IP addresses can be maintained for one network interface?
   C. 5 IP addresses per network interface

10. How would you add additional gateway IP addresses to any client ?
    A. TCP/IP Properties - IP Address | Advanced option

11. What is the default Network Mask for a Class B network?
    C. 255.255.0.0

12. What is the default Network Mask for six subnets in a Class B network? (Hint: Subnets is 2**n-2 where n is the number of bits.)
    C. 255.255.224.0 - requires 3 bits for 6 (formula is 2**n-2: 2**3 -2=6)

Answers to Chapter 6 Self Test

1. What type of option is used in a scope if you want it to affect all DHCP clients?
   D. A global option is used if you want it to apply to all the DHCP clients.

2. What is required if you are using a single DHCP server to support DHCP clients on remote subnets?
   B, D. You must use either a router that conforms to RFC 1542 or a DHCP Relay Agent so that the clients can communicate with the DHCP server.

3. What message is sent from the DHCP server during the *requesting* state?
   D. The DHCP server does not send any message during the requesting state. The DHCP client sends the DHCPREQUEST message during the requesting state.

4. Your network uses multiple DHCP servers located on separate subnets. What is a benefit that can be realized from this configuration?
   A. Multiple DHCP servers on separate subnets creates a high degree of fault tolerance for your network.

5. When does a DHCP client first attempt to renew its lease?
   B. A DHCP client will first attempt to renew its lease after 50% of the lease time has expired.

6. What command do you use to return an IP address to the DHCP server?
   C. IPCONFIG /release returns the IP address to the DHCP server.

7. What is the purpose of the JETPACK utility?
   D. JETPACK is used to compact the DHCP database.

8. What option would you use if you wanted to set the default gateway for a subnet?
   B. A scope option would be used to set the default gateway for a subnet.

9. During what state is the DHCPACK message sent from the DHCP server?
   D. The DHCPACK message is sent during the bound state by the DHCP server. It sends the lease for the IP address as well as any other configuration information that is required for the DHCP client.

10. A DHCP client tried to renew its lease with the DHCP server that originally issued the IP address. What happens when 87.5% of the lease time has expired?
    D. After 87.5% of the lease time has expired, the DHCP client will attempt to contact any DHCP server. It uses a DHCPREQUEST message, not a DHCPDISCOVER message.

11. What information is required in the Unique Identifier dialog box when adding a reservation for a client?

B. The MAC address for the client system is required in the Unique Identifier dialog box.

12. What file is used if DHCP needs to recover the database from a failure?
    C. The J50.log is used to recover the dhcb.mdb in case of a failure.

13. What can be configured to be a DHCP Relay Agent?
    B,D. Both Windows NT Server and Windows NT Workstation can be used as a DHCP Relay Agent.

14. What information is contained in the DHCPOFFER message?
    A. The DHCPOFFER message contains the DHCP client's MAC address, an offered IP address, the correct subnet mask, the IP address of the DHCP server, and the length of the lease.

15. Which default gateway is used if one is not specified?
    C. If a default gateway is not specified, then 0.0.0.0 is used.

Answers to Chapter 7 Self Test

1. NetBIOS is a(n) _____.
   C. API or Application Programming Interface. It is the interface that

programmers use to connect computers on a network.

2. NetBIOS uses _____ to connect remote computers.
B. Names. All NetBIOS needs to connect two computers is a name. Depending upon the transport protocol, an IP address or MAC address may be used by lower protocols like TCP/IP, IPX/SPX, or NetBEUI.

3. NBT provides which of the following services?
D. All the above. The NetBIOS Name Service runs at UDP port 137, the Datagram service runs at UDP port 138, and the Session Service runs at TCP port 139.

4. How many bytes are used in a NetBIOS Host Name?
C. 16 bytes. There are 15 characters used for the text portion of the name and a 16th hex control character that identifies the service associated with the name.

5. An example of an NT command that uses NetBIOS is _____.

C. net use. Net use maps drives and printers to remote computer shares using NetBIOS names for connections.

6. One of the three NetBIOS Functional Processes is _____.
A. Name Release. The other NetBIOS Functional Processes are Name Registration and Name Discovery.

7. Which of the following methods are used in Windows NT by default?
D. h-node. The other method used by default in Microsoft networking is called Enhanced b-node.

8. Which name resolution source does NT use just before looking in the LMHOSTS file when configured to use the h-node method?
A. Broadcasts. When configured to use a WINS server NBT checks the Name Cache, WINS, broadcasts, lmhosts, hosts, and DNS in that order.

9. On NT the default location for the LMHOSTS file is _____.
C. C:\WINNT\system32\drivers\etc. The hosts, lmhosts, networks, protocol, and services files are all stored in this directory.

10. The command to list the NetBIOS Name Cache is _____.
D. NBTSTAT -c. NBTSTAT -a lists remote NetBIOS names and NBTSTAT -n lists local NetBIOS names.

Answers to Chapter 8 Self Test

1. What is the first step in the name resolution process?
C. NetBIOS Cache. The Cache is always checked first, followed by WINS, a Broadcast, LMHOSTS, HOSTS, and finally DNS.

2. What is not a disadvantage of the LMHOSTS file?
D. Preloads the cache. The LMHOSTS file is Static, and therefore requires Manual Updates. It is not Dynamic, but it can Preload the cache using the #PRE keyword.

3. What is not a characteristic of a broadcast for name resolution?
D. Sent directly to WINS Server. A Broadcast is heard and processed by all computers on the subnet. It cannot cross a router. A WINS Proxy will hear one, and forward the request to a WINS Server on a different subnet. A WINS Server doesn't answer broadcasts for resolution.

4. Which is not a benefit of WINS?
A. Needs more administration. WINS makes maintenance and administration easier on a network. It provides automatic name registration, and internetwork and interdomain browsing. The manually updated LMHOSTS is not needed.

5. (True/False) Only DHCP can configure a WINS Client.
False. It can be done manually through TCP/IP Properties.

6. How many WINS Servers are required for a network with 15 subnets and 1000 users?
A. 1, plus one additional for a backup. One WINS Server is required for every 10,000 users. The number of subnets does not matter. It always a good idea to have a secondary as a backup.

7. Which methods can a non-WINS Client use to resolve names?
A, B, C. WINS Proxy, LMHOSTS, and Broadcast. A non-WINS Client cannot use the WINS Server for resolution. It can use WINS via a WINS Proxy.

8. (True/False) Every subnet on a network, that does not have a WINS Server, must have a WINS Proxy.
False. A Proxy is only required on subnets with non-WINS Clients. WINS Clients know the IP Address of the WINS Server, and can reach it regardless of subnets.

9. WINS network traffic usually accounts for __ % of total network traffic.
A. 1. WINS usually accounts for less than 1% of all network traffic.

10. The first step in the WINS process is.
B. Name Request. Before anything else can occur, a name must be requested. After the request it will be registered. A Query, or Lookup, occurs after the registration is successful.

11. The default TTL for a registered name is
A. 6 days. This is the default TTL of a registered name. Renewal occurs at ½ TTL, or 3 days by default. Turning a computer off does not affect registration. At reboot, a renewal will occur.

12. How many attempts to a Primary WINS Server will a Client make, before using the Secondary, for Name Resolution?

B. 3. A Client will attempt to contact the Primary WINS Server 3 times before contacting the Secondary.

13. How often, after a default installation, does WINS back up the database?
D. Never. The database is not backed up until a backup directory is specified.

14. How many pairs of WINS Servers and Backups are needed for a network with 150 subnets, each subnet having over 100 Clients?
B. 2. This network has 15,000 Clients. Since WINS can handle only 10,000, two pairs are needed.

15. (True/False) WINS is installed through Add/Remove Programs in Control Panel.
False. WINS is a network service and is installed through the Network icon in Control Panel.

16. (True/False) WINS Manager can manage any number of WINS Servers.
True. The WINS Manager can manage any number of WINS Servers, provided they are all configured in the Manager.

17. Which of the following would need a permanent, static, IP address?
A, B. DHCP Server, WINS Server. DHCP because it hands out all other IP addresses. WINS because DHCP must have the WINS address configured to hand out to DHCP Clients. This is what allows WINS to work. File and print servers, and application servers do not require static

addresses. It may be better for them, but it is not required.

18. (True/False) A WINS Proxy Server cannot be a WINS Client.
False. A Proxy must be a WINS Client.

19. Which of the following operating systems cannot use WINS?
B. UNIX. A UNIX machine cannot be a WINS Client. It must use a Proxy to resolve names via a WINS Server.

20. A WINS Client should use which node type for name resolution?
B. H Node. H Node provides for a WINS query followed by a broadcast. This is the optimum setting. B Node is broadcast only. M Node uses broadcast, then WINS. This increases network traffic. P Node uses WINS only, there is no backup.

21. (True/False) Replication can be initialized only by a push partner.
False. Replication can be initialized by either partner. The particular configurations and actual usage patterns determine which one will actually start the process.

22. (True/False) Once a computer is turned off, its registered names are not immediately available to other computers.
True. Names are not released immediately for reuse. This allows machines to be off for several days without causing unneeded registrations later.

23. To start automatic, daily backups of the WINS Database, you must

D. Specify a location for the backup. WINS will not back up until this directory is specified. NT Backup will back up the machine, but not create a separate back up for the database.

24. Jetpack should be run when the WINS Database reaches what size?
    C. 30 MB. Jetpack should be run whenever the database size approaches 30MB. A larger database can become corrupted easily, and also causes delays in resolution.

25. All of the following will speed up WINS, except:
    C. Reduce the default registration TTL from 6 days to 3 days. Reducing the TTL will cause more renewals and registrations, having the opposite effect. A second processor can speed WINS by 25%. Increasing the priority is only effective if other services are running on the machine. Logging uses computer resources that can be used by WINS.

Answers to Chapter 9 Self Test

1. By which methods can TCP/IP host names be resolved to IP addresses?
   B, D. The LMHOSTS file and WINS resolve NetBIOS names to IP addresses. TCP/IP will resolve host names with entries in the local HOSTS file, and can also use DNS, a distributed database of host name to IP address mappings.

2. Which method is the most recommended way to enable internetwork browsing?
   D. WINS is the best way to make internetwork browsing work because it is dynamic and does not require manual configuration once it is operational. WINS will allow browsers to easily find other browsers on the internetwork to send and request resource lists.

3. Which type of browser services client requests for resource lists?
   C. Clients will contact the master browser to get a list of backup browsers. After a client has this list, it will request resource lists from the backup browsers.

4. Which of the following statements are true?
   A, D. The domain master browser will always be a PDC, and provides resource lists to master browsers. The domain master browser can also be a master browser.

5. Which events will cause a browser election to occur?
   A, B, D. Browser elections will be forced if a computer cannot find a master browser, a domain controller is started, or a preferred master browser is started. The master browser will simply designate a new backup browser when an existing backup browser is shut down.

6. Which of the following occur when routers forward UDP port 137?
   B, C, D. Configuring routers to forward UDP port 137 traffic will eliminate the need to configure LMHOSTS files or set up

WINS servers, but it will also increase the amount of browser traffic seen on each segment. Since timing is important in browser elections, slow links are likely to cause problems with elections.

7. Which of the following are valid TCP/IP host names?
A, B, D. TCP/IP host names can consist of alphanumeric characters and the dash (-). The underscore character was allowed in older versions of BIND but is not commonly used or accepted.

8. Which entries must be made in LMHOSTS files for internetwork browsing to function without WINS or UDP port 137 forwarding?
A, C, D. The LMHOSTS files on browsers must be configured according to choices A, C, and D, but client computers do not need to have any entries in their LMHOSTS files since they will find the master browser on their subnet by broadcasting.

9. Which entity regulates Internet domain names?
D. TCP/IP domain names used on the Internet must be approved by the InterNIC, ensuring that duplicate domain names do not occur.

10. Which of the following is a fully qualified domain name?
C. A fully qualified domain name consists of a TCP/IP host name and domain name. Network administrators assign

host names while the InterNIC regulates domain names.

11. Which of the following statements are correct?
B, D. TCP/IP host names can be the same as or different from the NetBIOS computer name. WINS is a method of resolving NetBIOS computer names to IP addresses, and entries can be made in the HOSTS file on a computer so that those names can be resolved to IP addresses.

12. Comments in the HOSTS file can be added after what symbol?
A. The # sign is used to designate comments in the HOSTS file.

13. Which TCP/IP protocol is used to find the hardware address of host or router after the host name has been resolved to an IP address?
C. ARP (Address Resolution Protocol) will find the hardware address of a TCP/IP network device. If the IP address is on the same subnet, ARP will return the hardware address of the host with that IP address. If the IP address is on a remote network, ARP will return the hardware address of the default gateway.

14. Which of the following choices will cause host name resolution to fail using the HOSTS file?
A, B, C, D. More than one entry for the same host can cause host name resolution to fail. Moving the HOSTS file without

changing a registry entry will result in the computer not being able to find the HOSTS file at all. Host names are case sensitive, so a capitalization error will result in a failed resolution attempt. Since NetBIOS names and TCP/IP host names are not necessarily the same, they cannot be interchanged in the HOSTS file.

15. A network segment with 120 computers will have how many backup browsers?
C. A network segment with 120 computers will have four backup browsers unless more are manually configured as backup browsers or there are more than four backup domain controllers.

Answers to Chapter 10 Self Test

1. From where is the DNS Service installed?
D. Network Applet in Control Panel. The Network Applet is where all network services are added. Click the Services Panel and then click Add. The Microsoft DNS Service option appears. Click it and then click OK. Exit out of the Network Applet, and reboot your system.

2. In what order is a basic DNS record entry?
B. Host Name, Record Type, IP Address. This is important since there is a reverse record entry that matches the response in A.

3. What is a PTR record?
B. Reverse Pointer Record. Only found in the Reverse Lookup Zone.

4. What is the default data file name for the zone urcorp.net?
C. urcorp.net.dns. The data file can actually be anything, but the default supplied would be the domain name plus the .dns extension.

5. How do you configure a DNS domain to use WINS?
C. Click the domain object, click the DNS menu, select Properties. You can also right-click the object and select the Properties option.

6. What is the name of the general (default) Reverse Lookup zone as displayed in the DNS Manager?
A. in-addr.arpa. Alternatively, the reverse lookup may have the network number in reverse order appended to the front of this name. For example, if your network were dd.ff.gg.0, then the reverse lookup name could be gg.ff.dd.in-addr.arpa.

7. What is the name of the specific Reverse Lookup zone for the domain place.dom representing the network 219.145.86.0 when displayed in the DNS Manager?
B. 86.145.219.in-addr.arpa.

8. What is the information needed by a client to use DNS? Select all that apply.
B, C, D. The domain name and its IP address as well as any optional subdomain names to be used if the host is not defined in the main domain data records.

Answers to Chapter 11 Self Test

1. Network Monitor is capable of monitoring traffic _____
   E. Network monitor is available in two different versions. The version that ships with Windows NT Server 4.0 is capable of monitoring only traffic that is to and from the server it is installed on. The version that ships with SMS is capable of monitoring the traffic of any machine on the network.

2. RAS servers can be configured to assign IP addresses to the RAS clients using any of the following except:
   B. RAS servers are capable of being configured to assign IP addresses to the RAS clients using DHCP, manual assignment, or a hybrid of DHCP and manual assignment. WINS is not involved in the assignment of IP addresses.

3. Reading a co-worker's e-mail using Network Monitor is _____
   D. Using Network Monitor to read anyone's e-mail is at a minimum unethical, and in many situations considered to be illegal.

4. What port does the FTP protocol use as its control port?
   B. The FTP protocol that can be used to transfer files between a workstation and an FTP server uses port 21 for its transfers.

5. Which port does the HTTP protocol use?
   D. The HTTP protocol, which is used for WWW access, uses port 80 for its transfers. Port 23 is used for Telnet, port 21 for FTP, port 119 for NNTP, and port 110 for POP3.

6. What is the address called that is assigned to hardware that can be determined by using Network Monitor to capture packets from the network?
   C. The MAC address is an address assigned to a hardware device. In most cases MAC addresses are pre-defined by the manufacturer of the network interface card, and are not changeable by the user.

7. Network Monitor is capable of viewing _____ packets.
   B. Network Monitor is capable of viewing all packets that are transmitted onto the network. It is considered to be unethical to use Network Monitor to view user-generated packets.

8. RAS. . .
   D. RAS provides the ability to connect a remote workstation to a RAS server using a non-Ethernet connection. RAS is most commonly used with modems or ISDN adapters. RAS clients can connect to services provided by the RAS server and, if the RAS server is configured to allow it, any resources that the RAS server is capable of accessing.

9. RAS is most commonly configured to use a combination of both DHCP and manual assignment . . .

A. RAS is most commonly configured to use a combination of both DHCP and manual assignment when a permanent link to the outside world is being established. A good example of this is when a RAS connection is used as a permanent link to the Internet, in which case it would be desirable for the IP address not to change.

10. Which of the following are considered user-generated packets?
    E. FTP, HTTP, POP3, and SMB among many other types of packets are considered to be user-generated.

11. What of the following are not types of WINS messages?
    B. There are primarily three different types of WINS messages: broadcast, announce, and request.

12. PPP is an acronym that stands for
    _____.
    D. Point-to-Point Protocol is a cross-platform protocol that can be used to connect to both NT and UNIX systems.

13. The acronym SLIP stands for _____.
    B. Serial Line Internet Protocol is a protocol that can be used by RAS to connect a RAS client and a dialup server.

14. The IP section of a packet can contain information such as . . .
    E. The IP section gives information such as the source and destination addresses, the version of IP that was used to create the packet, a packet identification number, a

Time to Live for the packet, along with some other information that is less important.

15. The Hardware Ethernet Frame contains information such as . . .
    D. The Hardware Ethernet Frame gives information such as the source and destination MAC addresses. This information can be used to pinpoint exactly where packets are coming from and going to, since in general MAC addresses are unchangeable.

Answers to Chapter 12 Self Test

1. What command is not available to an SNMP management system?
   C. Trap. Only an SNMP agent can issue a trap. The trap command allows an agent to alert management systems to extraordinary events, such as program errors.

2. The Windows NT SNMP service must be loaded in which situation?
   A. Monitoring TCP/IP statistics with Performance Monitor. Performance Monitor relies on the SNMP service to provide TCP/IP performance statistics. If SNMP is not loaded, all values will be null.

3. What kind of name tree does SNMP use to define manageable objects?
   D. Hierarchical. The SNMP system uses a hierarchical name tree to define manageable objects. The hierarchy makes it easier for

companies to manage their own objects
for MIBs.

4. Which two components make up an SNMP
managed network?
B. SNMP management system and SNMP
agent. An SNMP management system sends
requests to SNMP agents, which return
performance, software, and hardware
statistics. Agents can also issue traps to alert
management systems.

5. SNMP agents can initiate which command?
C. Trap. An SNMP agent can issue a trap
to alert management systems to
extraordinary events, such as program
errors. SNMP management systems cannot
issue the trap command.

6. Which one of the following is not a tab
from the SNMP service properties sheet?
B. Management. Agent, Traps, and Security
are used to configure the Windows NT
SNMP service. They allow the network
manager to determine what the service
should report, as well as whom it can report
it to.

7. What SNMP service setting allows the
maximum security from unauthorized
access?
A. Only Accept SNMP Packets from These
Hosts. This SNMP service Security setting
allows the most security when configuring
the windows NT SNMP agent. Accepted
Community Names cuts down the potential
for unauthorized access, but specifying the

individual hosts provides the maximum
security. Send Authentication Trap and
Trap Destinations help only in telling the
SNMP service where to send notification
when unauthorized access is attempted.

8. Which MIB is defined by the SNMP RFC?
D. Internet MIB II. This MIB is defined in
RFS 1213, which defines the SNMP
standard. Internet MIB II defines common
objects necessary for network management
and configuration. DHCP, LAN Manager,
and Internet Information Server MIBs
define objects for Microsoft products.

9. When setting up an SNMP agent to report
traps, what information must be supplied?
B. Community name and IPX address of
the management system.

10. Performance Monitor requires which service
in order to monitor TCP/IP statistics?
D. SNMP. The SNMP service provides
TCP/IP statistics to Performance Monitor.
DHCP and WINs are TCP/IP services and
can be monitored by Performance Monitor
for their own performance, but they do not
provide general TCP/IP statistics.

Answers to Chapter 13 Self Test

1. Which utility is used to send a ICMP
packet to test whether a remote host is
reachable?
D. Ping. Ping is the only utility mentioned

which sends an ICMP echo_request packet to a remote host.

2. Which utility is used in order to make changes to IP address to media access card address translation tables?
    C. ARP. The ARP utility is used to make changes to a computer's IP address to MAC address translation table. Arp -s adds an entry to the table.

3. It is important that you quickly identify current active and established TCP connections by your computer. Which of the following utilities is most useful?
    D. NETSTAT. The netstat -a command can be used to quickly identify current active and established TCP connections. The utility tcpstat does not exist.

4. You want to determine if a computer acquires its IP address from the DHCP server. Which utility will return the desired information?
    B. Ipconfig /all. The ipconfig /all switch will identify whether or not a computer uses DHCP.

5. Point-to-point tunneling protocol is used to connect remote users via their ISPs. Your director is correctly configured to use PPTP communication but is unable to reach your network. Which utility could identify the location of the problem?
    C. TRACERT. Using the TRACERT utility, the director should be able to

pinpoint the metric at which his communication drops via message destination host unreachable.

6. It is urgent that users on a specific subnet not be allowed to access a subnet which now contains secure data. Which utility could you use to remove connectivity between these networks?
    B. ROUTE delete. Using route delete with the -f option, end users will be prevented from accessing the subnet which the router was previously aware of. Filternet and Prevent /securenet are not valid utilities.

7. Which utility allows for researching DNS files for specific IP address to host name assignments?
    D. NSLOOKUP. NSLOOKUP with the hostname and DNS server information could easily parse the DNS reverse lookup file for translation verification.

8. Which of the following utilities is used to relate NetBIOS over TCP/IP statistics?
    A. Nbtstat. Nbtstat is used to relate NetBIOS over TCP/IP statistics. Netbeui /all and Netsho /nbt are not valid utilities.

9. What address should you PING to verify that TCP/IP is correctly installed and configured on a computer?
    C. The loopback address. A reply when pinging the loopback address 127.0.0.1 will verify that TCP/IP has been correctly installed and configured on a machine.

10. Typing ipconfig at a prompt does not produce which of the following information.
    B. The MAC address. Typing ipconfig at a prompt will result in the default gateway, the subnet mask, and the IP address of a computer.

11. Name the utility which provides metrics in its output.
    A. TRACERT. TRACERT provides the capablity of deriving metric (hop count) information from the utility's output.

12. In order to send a specific number of echo_requests when using PING you must specify which of the following command-line options.
    C. Ping -n. Ping -n allows you to specify the amount of echo_requests sent to a destination.

13. You would use the following command to view Ethernet network statistics:
    D. netstat -e. Typing netstat -e displays current Ethernet statistics of your computer.

14. What is the best method for verifying network connectivity between different networks which do not use routers or level three communication devices?
    D. None of the above. Without routers, no cross network communication will happen.

15. Your first step in identifying general TCP/IP connectivity should be to use which utility?
    B. PING. The PING utility is the first and most commonly used diagnostic utility

B

About the CD

CD-ROM Instructions

This CD-ROM contains a full web site accessible to you via your web browser. Browse to or double-click **index.htm** at the root of the CD-ROM and you will find instructions for navigating the web site and for installing the various software components.

Electronic Book

An electronic version of the entire book in HTML format.

Interactive Self-Study Module

An electronic self-study test bank linked to the electronic book to help you instantly review key exam topics that may still be unclear. This module contains over 300 review questions, the same questions that appear at the end of each chapter. If you answer a multiple choice question correctly by clicking on the right answer, you will automatically link to the next question. If you answer incorrectly, you will be linked to the appropriate section in the electronic book for further study.

Sample Exams

Demos from market-leading certification tools vendors, including Self-Test Software's PEP, Transcender's CERT, VFX Technologies' Endeavor, BeachFront Quizzer's BFQuizzer, and Microhard Technologies' MCSEQuest. These exams may be installed either from the "Exams and Simulations" web page or from Windows Explorer. See the following for instructions on either type of installation.

From the Web Page

Internet Explorer users will be prompted to either "open the file" or "save it to disk." Select "open the file" and the installation program will automatically be launched, installing the software to your hard disk. Follow the vendor's instructions. The software will be installed to the hard disk. Once installed, you should run the programs via the Start Programs taskbar on your desktop.

Netscape Navigator users will be asked to "save as..." the setup file. You should save it to a folder on your hard drive, then click on it in Windows Explorer to launch the installation. Follow the vendor's instructions. The software will be installed to the hard disk. Once installed, you should run the programs via the Start Programs taskbar on your desktop.

Note regarding VFX Technologies' exam demo: Internet Explorer users should select the "Open File" box, not "Save it to Disk."

From Windows Explorer

You can also launch the installation of any of these programs from Windows Explorer by opening the "Demo Exams" folder on the CD. Each vendor's installation program is inside the designated folder. Click on the appropriate SETUP.EXE file and then follow the vendor's instructions. The software will be installed to the hard disk. Once installed, you should run the programs via the Start Programs taskbar on your desktop.

Note regarding VFX Technologies' exam demo: Netscape Navigator users should install from Windows Explorer by clicking on the Setup.exe file.

MICROSOFT CERTIFIED SYSTEMS ENGINEER

C

About the
Web Site

Access Global Knowledge Network

As you know by now, Global Knowledge Network is the largest independent IT training company in the world. Just by purchasing this book, you have also secured a free subscription to the Access Global web site and its many resources. You can find it at:

http://access.globalknowledge.com

To acquire an ID to use the Access Global web site, send e-mail to access@globalknowledge.com and type **Access ID Request** in the subject field. In the body of the message, include your full name, mailing address, e-mail address, and phone number. Within two business days you will receive your Access Global web site ID. The first time you visit the site and log on, you will be able to choose your own password.

What You'll Find There. . .

You will find a lot of information at the Global Knowledge site, most of which can be broken down into three categories:

Skills Gap Analysis

Global Knowledge offers several ways for you to analyze your networking skills and discover where they may be lacking. Using Global Knowledge Network's trademarked Competence Key Tool, you can do a skills gap analysis and get recommendations for where you may need to do some more studying (sorry, it just may not end with this book!).

Networking

You'll also gain valuable access to another asset: people. At the Access Global site, you'll find threaded discussions as well as live discussions. Talk to other MCSE candidates, get advice from folks who have already taken exams, and get access to instructors and MCTs.

Product Offerings

Of course, Global Knowledge also offers its products here—and you may find some valuable items for purchase: CBTs, books, courses. Browse freely and see if there's something that could help you.

INDEX

Page numbers in *italics* refer to illustrations or charts.

D

E

F

M

N

U

Z

Custom Corporate Network Training

Train on Cutting-Edge Technology   We can bring the best in skill-based training to your facility to create a real-world, hands-on training experience. Global Knowledge Network has invested millions of dollars in network hardware and software to train our students on the same equipment they will work with on the job. Our relationships with vendors allow us to incorporate the latest equipment and platforms into your on-site labs.

Maximize Your Training Budget   Global Knowledge Network provides experienced instructors, comprehensive course materials, and all the networking equipment needed to deliver high quality training. You provide the students; we provide the knowledge.

Avoid Travel Expenses   On-site courses allow you to schedule technical training at your convenience, saving time, expense, and the opportunity cost of travel away from the workplace.

Discuss Confidential Topics   Private on-site training permits the open discussion of sensitive issues such as security, access, and network design. We can work with your existing network's proprietary files while demonstrating the latest technologies.

Customize Course Content   Global Knowledge Network can tailor your courses to include the technologies and the topics that have the greatest impact on your business. We can complement your internal training efforts or provide a total solution to your training needs.

Corporate Pass   The Corporate Pass Discount Program rewards our best network training customers with preferred pricing on public courses, discounts on multimedia training packages, and an array of career planning services.

Global Knowledge Network Training Lifecycle: Supporting the Dynamic and Specialized Training Requirements of Information Technology Professionals

- Define Profile
- Assess Skills
- Design Training
- Deliver Training
- Test Knowledge
- Update Profile
- Use New Skills

College Credit Recommendation Program   The American Council on Education's CREDIT program recommends 34 Global Knowledge Network courses for college credit. Now our network training can help you earn your college degree while you learn the technical skills needed for your job. When you attend an ACE-certified Global Knowledge Network course and pass the associated exam, you earn college credit recommendations for that course. Global Knowledge Network can establish a transcript record for you with ACE that you can use to gain credit at a college or as a written record of your professional training that you can attach to your resume.

Registration Information:

COURSE FEE: The fee covers course tuition, refreshments, and all course materials. Any parking expenses that may be incurred are not included. Payment or government training form must be received six business days prior to the course date. We will also accept Visa/MasterCard and American Express. For non-U.S. credit card users, charges will be in U.S. funds and will be converted by your credit card company. Checks drawn on Canadian banks in Canadian funds are acceptable.

COURSE SCHEDULE: Registration is at 8:00 a.m. on the first day. The program begins at 8:30 a.m. and concludes at 4:30 p.m. each day.

CANCELLATION POLICY: Cancellation and full refund will be allowed if written cancellation is received in our office at least six business days prior to the course start date. Registrants who do not attend the course or do not cancel more than six business days in advance are responsible for the full registration fee; you may transfer to a later date provided the course fee has been paid in full. Substitutions may be made at any time. If Global Knowledge Network must cancel a course for any reason, liability is limited to the registration fee only.

GLOBAL KNOWLEDGE NETWORK: Global Knowledge Network programs are developed and presented by industry professionals with "real-world" experience. Designed to help professionals meet today's interconnectivity and interoperability challenges, most of our programs feature hands-on labs that incorporate state-of-the-art communication components and equipment.

ON-SITE TEAM TRAINING: Bring Global Knowledge Network's powerful training programs to your company. At Global Knowledge Network, we will custom design courses to meet your specific network requirements. Call (919)-461-8686 for more information.

YOUR GUARANTEE: Global Knowledge Network believes its courses offer the best possible training in this field. If during the first day you are not satisfied and with to withdraw from the course, simply notify the instructor, return all course materials and receive a 100 percent refund.

US:
1 888 762 4442
Canada:
1 800 465 2226
US:
www.globalknowledge.com
Canada:
www.global-knowledge.com.ca
CALL
1 888 762 4442 US
1 800 465 2226 Canada
FAX
1 919 469 7070 US
1 613 567 3899 Canada
MAIL
Check and this form to:
US
Global Knowledge Network
114 Edinburgh South,
Suite 200
P.O. Box 1187
Cary, NC 27512
Canada
393 University Ave.,
Suite 1601
Toronto, ON M5G 1E6

REGISTRATION INFORMATION

Course title _____

Course location _____ Course date _____

Name/title _____ Company _____

Name/title _____ Company _____

Name/title _____ Company _____

Address _____ Telephone _____ Fax _____

City _____ State/Province _____ Zip/Postal Code _____

Credit card _____ Card # _____ Expiration date _____

Signature _____